The CHEFS of THE TIMES

MORE THAN 200 RECIPES AND REFLECTIONS FROM
SOME OF AMERICA'S MOST CREATIVE CHEFS,
BASED ON THE POPULAR COLUMN IN

The New York Times

The CHEFS *of* THE TIMES

EDITED BY

MICHALENE BUSICO

CHEF PORTRAITS BY VINCENT LAFORET
FOOD PHOTOGRAPHS BY TONY CENICOLA

ST. MARTIN'S PRESS
NEW YORK

www.stmartins.com

BOOK DESIGN BY MICHELLE McMILLIAN

Chef photographs copyright © 2001 by Vincent Laforet, except as follows: Photograph of Deborah Madison © 2001 by Peter Da Silva. Photograph of Thomas Keller © 2001 by Monica Almeida. Photograph of Michel Richard © 2001 by Susana Raab. Photograph of Philippe Conticini © 2001 by Owen Franken. All rights reserved. Reprinted with permission.

Food photographs copyright © 2001 by Tony Cenicola, except as follows: Photograph of Summer Soups © 2001 by Deborah Jones. Photograph of White Chocolate Pudding © 2001 by Tim Turner. All rights reserved. Reprinted with permission.

Library of Congress Cataloging-in-Publication Data

The chefs of the times: More than 200 recipes and reflections from some of America's most creative chefs, based on the popular column in *The New York Times* / Michalene Busico, editor.—1st ed.

   p. cm.

ISBN 0-312-28447-0

  1. Cookery. 2. Cooks—United States. I. Busico, Michalene. II. New York Times Company.

TX714. C46665 2001

641.5

2001041951

First Edition: November 2001

10 9 8 7 6 5 4 3 2 1

CONTENTS

RECIPE LIST BY COURSE

APPETIZERS AND FIRST COURSES

SOUPS

SALADS

MEAT DISHES

Roasted Triple Lamb Chops with Olives and Lemon (Malouf)   176

Filets Mignons on Charred Onions and Zucchini with
 Balsamic Vinegar Sauce (O'Connell)   207

Crispy Pork Cutlets with Spicy Tomato Sauce (Ono)   215

Beef with Miso-Chile Sauce (Ono)   218

Grilled Loin of Lamb with Fava and Fruit Dressing (Dufresne)   246

Lamb Loin with Basil Crust and Fennel (Richard)   256

Grilled Hanger Steak with Lemongrass-Caramel Glaze (Yeo)   275

Apple-Brined Pork Chops with Prunes Marinated in Armagnac and Tea (Yeo)   282

Braised Lamb Shanks with Apricot-Curry Sauce (Trotter)   313

POULTRY DISHES

Roasted Wild Turkey with Apple-Sausage Stuffing (Romano)   9

Roast Chicken with Spiced Apples and Onions, and Yogurt Rice (Samuelsson)   29

Salt-Cured Duck with Root Vegetable Risotto (Samuelsson)   36

Chicken Stuffed with Toasted Sesame-Millet Mousse in Zaatar Broth (Forley)   52

Fairchild-Blass Spring Collection Chicken (Boulud)   60

Marinated Chicken with Braised Red Cabbage (Portale)   121

Pan-Roasted Duck Breasts with Creamed White Corn and Morels (Keller)   167

Ten-Herb Roasted Chicken with Herbed Bread and Mushroom Salad (Malouf)   173

Brined Chicken (O'Connell)   206

Asian Duck Confit with Roasted Duck Breast and Wasabi Sauce (Ono)   214

Sage Chicken in a Fried Potato Crust (Richard)   258

FISH DISHES

Red Snapper with Tomato-Onion Compote and Tomato Nage (Romano)   5

Cod in Zucchini Broth (Vongerichten)   17

Gently Cooked Salmon with Mashed Potatoes (Vongerichten)   18

Oven-Steamed Black Sea Bass with Warm Citrus-Beet Juice (Samuelsson)   37

Sautéed Skate with Lemon Risotto (Forley)   44

Whole Roasted Salmon with Root Vegetables (Palmer)   83

Roast Cod with Ragout of Savoy Cabbage, Cannellini Beans,
 and Black Truffles (Portale)   114

Seared Striped Bass on Whipped Chive Potatoes with Truffle Vinaigrette (Moonen)   127

COOKIES

ACKNOWLEDGMENTS

I'd like to acknowledge, beyond the chefs and the food writers who worked with them, some of the many people at *The New York Times* whose individual contributions were invaluable.

Closest to me are Regina Schrambling and Pat Gurosky, fellow editors on the Dining desk and collaborators on every level of the Chef column, two wonderful editors and terrific people to work with. The Style Department copy desk—Shelly Belzer, Steve Coates, Susan Guerrero, Charles Klaveness, Bernie Kirsch, Alison MacFarlane, Roland Miller, William Niederkorn, Christopher Phillips, and Roberta Zeff—for taking our work and refining it until it became the final product you now have in your hands.

Always there have been our art directors, Nicki Kalish and Richard Aloisio before her, who made the column look so good on the page.

In bringing the newspaper columns to book form, there is Vincent Laforet, whose funny, surprising, and reflective portraits gave us a glimpse of the inner lives of these chefs; and Tony Cenicola, whose beautiful, sensual food photography brought the dishes to life in a way that words never could. And of course, there is Mike Levitas, who had the idea for this book and shepherded it into publication, along with Marian Lizzi at St. Martin's Press.

I would also like to thank Richard Flaste, the Dining section's first editor and the creative mind behind the concept for the Chef column.

And finally, I want to thank my former boss, John Montorio, and my present boss, Barbara Graustark, for their great support and guidance.

INTRODUCTION

A recipe is a stark piece of work: a list of ingredients and a series of precise, almost militaristic, directions. But cooking, when it's executed at the highest level, is a true art form. There's nothing stark about it, or about the thinking behind the recipe. A dish can begin with the slightest impulse, some fragile recollection, a triumphant accident, or just a vaguely understood objective. The transformation takes the supple mind of a painter, the lyricism of a composer.

The idea behind the column called simply "The Chef"—which first appeared when *The New York Times* inaugurated its new Dining section in 1997—is to reveal something of that creative process, of how a thought becomes a dish, along with the insights into a great chef's thinking that are rarely explored in cookbooks, or anywhere else for that matter.

In launching the column, we might have chosen a single, wonderful chef as its voice and followed his thinking wherever it led. But in a city filled with great chefs—in a country filled with great chefs—it seemed almost a waste to explore just a single mind. So we reached out to the best chefs, in New York and beyond, and asked them to try their hands as guest columnists, each for an eight-week stint.

The result, when we assembled the first group of twenty-three in this book, is a gathering of superstars. It includes men and women as inventive as Thomas Keller of Napa Valley, as inspiring as Jean-Georges Vongerichten of New York, and Chicago's legendary Charlie Trotter.

At the same time, our choices were not bound by celebrity. The selections here sometimes catch a superstar mind in early formation. Which is to say: You may not instantly recognize every name in the book, but trust me, you will find that each chef has something distinct and engaging to say about cooking and will very likely affect the way you think about food and cooking.

As the editor of the Dining section, I found that as a group famous for eccentricity and stubbornness, sometimes even given to tantrums in the kitchen, these men and women were a revelation: models of collegiality. They all worked hard to fulfill the assignment, exploring their minds to reveal thought processes often hidden even to them. And they were spectacularly cooperative in searching out dishes that the reader would find interesting and instructive.

They suppressed an almost overwhelming need for perfection and complexity to create dishes that could be made in the home kitchen, far from the Vulcan stoves, line cooks, and other minions that most big-time executive chefs have at their command.

The recipes in this collection are both sophisticated and doable. Take a look at Daniel Boulud's milk chocolate tart, studded with cherries steeped in port—a four-star dessert that sprang from the memory of a favorite childhood candy. Or Wylie Dufresne's sea bass in a crust of edamame and rye bread—a simple, delicious homage to the many cuisines of Manhattan's Lower East Side. Or Christian Delouvrier's luxurious risottos, lessons in professional pragmatism that require absolutely no stirring.

Even when they are adapted for the home, these dishes are very much like the ones that wow the clientele in the restaurant (and sometimes, on the dinner tab, too). But making them at home isn't just a bargain, it's a genuine pleasure. They'll be impressive when you entertain and satisfying when you're simply serving the family.

Of course, the aim of this book isn't merely to put good recipes in your hands. In the end, we hope you will enjoy discovering how those recipes came to be, and how the creative mind produced a culinary work of art. And how, emboldened with a peek behind the swinging kitchen doors, you can, too.

—MICHALENE BUSICO

The CHEFS of THE TIMES

MICHAEL ROMANO

Michael Romano is the chef at the Union Square Cafe in Manhattan. He was photographed outside Conrad's Bike Shop in the city. These columns were written with Amanda Hesser.

INSPIRATION FOR A SOUP, FROM FAR AND NEAR

The idea for this corn bisque began with the beautiful corn available at the Union Square farmers' market, just down the street from my restaurant. I'd been thinking about combining a traditional bisque with the vivid flavors I'd just brought back from a trip to India. As I admired the corn, I recalled the time a friend had served popcorn flavored with toasted and ground cumin. It was a wonderful marriage, and the memory of it was all the reassurance I needed to forge on.

As the dish developed in my mind, I knew I wanted a rich texture to go with the intense flavor. A technique I remembered from a cookbook of the American South seemed right: pureeing part of the corn into the bisque to provide much of the desired richness, allowing me to cut down on the cream.

As for the other ingredients, I chopped the onion and leek as small as the corn kernels so they wouldn't assume an inappropriately important role, and I sliced tiny fingerling potatoes into delicate rounds to preserve the beauty of their natural shape.

Here are some spice tips: Buy whole cumin seeds (they're usually fresher in Middle Eastern or Indian markets) and grind them yourself in a coffee grinder reserved for spices. When you add the cumin (or any raw spice) to the pot, be sure it gets a chance to cook for at least five minutes to take away the raw edge and to allow the flavor to bloom.

This corn bisque can stand alone, but all that abundance in the market just begs for a whole menu. So what follows are two menus that reflect the passing of summer to fall.

SPICED CORN AND POTATO BISQUE

4 cups raw corn scraped from cobs
    (4 to 6 ears of corn)
1 cup heavy cream
2 cups milk
2 tablespoons butter
1 cup chopped onion
1 cup chopped leeks
2 teaspoons minced ginger
1 tablespoon minced jalapeño pepper with
    seeds
⅛ teaspoon turmeric
1½ tablespoons freshly ground cumin seeds
Kosher salt to taste
1 cup sliced fingerling potatoes
1 cup vegetable or chicken stock
Freshly ground black pepper to taste

1. In a large saucepan, combine 2 cups raw corn, heavy cream, and milk, and simmer for 5 minutes. Transfer mixture to a food processor and pulse until almost pureed. Pass through a large-mesh sieve and set aside.

2. In a large, heavy saucepan, heat butter over medium-high heat until foaming. Add onion and leeks. Sauté until soft, stirring 3 minutes.

3. Add ginger and jalapeño pepper, lower heat to medium-low, and simmer 2 minutes. Stir in turmeric and cumin, and simmer an additional 8 minutes. Season lightly with salt.

4. Add remaining 2 cups raw corn and fingerling potatoes, and heat through, about 2 minutes. Add stock and cream-corn mixture, and simmer over medium-low heat until potatoes are tender and flavors are blended, about 20 minutes. Season with salt and ground pepper.

Yield: 6 servings
Time: 1 hour

RISOTTO, IN A LIGHT MOMENT

With the ever-growing popularity of risotto in New York restaurants, many chefs—myself included—have put on their thinking toques to come up with new flavor combinations and twists on the old classics. Something I'd had in mind was a purely vegetarian risotto. So, just add vegetables, right? Well, with risotto there's a bit more to it than that.

A risotto's character and quality rely on the choice of stock or cooking liquid absorbed by the rice. In this case the typical chicken or veal stock was obviously out of the question. Of course, there was always the option of vegetable stock, but its diffused, nonspecific flavor was not what I was after.

An experience with pumpkin risotto was instructive. I found that the pumpkin flavor truly permeated the risotto only if I also flavored the stock I was using—chicken in this case—by cooking pumpkin in it. With the vegetarian risotto I took it a step further: Why not sharpen the focus by using pure vegetable juice in place of stock?

Of the many variations that ensued, cucumbers became a favorite choice because of their bright, refreshing flavor and for the ease with which their juice can be extracted. I'm really impressed with how strongly the cucumber flavor comes through in the finished dish, imparting a clean, zesty taste to the risotto.

Given the stick-to-your-ribs reputation of most risotto, this one surprises the palate with its lightness. You do want a risotto to be creamy and smooth, but it does not have to be heavy. I add the traditional butter at the end of cooking, but not the cheese, which I found dulls the sparkle of the cucumber flavor. The jalapeño, yellow peppers, and cilantro add perky yet harmonious notes that increase the depth and interest of the cucumber rice.

Risotto challenges you every time you make it. It is the constant stirring action that draws out the creaminess and texture of the rice, and it is vigilance and testing that allow the cook to identify the precise al dente *point, signaling the dish's perfection.*

CUCUMBER RISOTTO WITH YELLOW PEPPERS AND CILANTRO

3 yellow bell peppers
10 large cucumbers, peeled and cut in 1-inch chunks
4 to 6 jalapeño peppers
2 tablespoons extra-virgin olive oil
1 tablespoon minced shallots
1 teaspoon kosher salt
$\frac{1}{8}$ teaspoon freshly ground black pepper
1$\frac{3}{4}$ cups Arborio rice
1 cup white wine
2 tablespoons unsalted butter
$\frac{3}{4}$ cup chopped cilantro
1 tablespoon lime juice

1. Preheat broiler. Place bell peppers on a broiler rack 2 to 3 inches from heating element. Roast, turning occasionally, until skins bubble and blacken. Let cool, then peel and seed peppers. Cut into $\frac{1}{2}$-inch dice and reserve.

2. Using a food processor or blender, process cucumbers until reduced to a smooth puree, about 3 minutes. Strain puree through a fine-mesh strainer into a large bowl, stirring and pressing to extract as much juice as possible. Do this in batches if necessary. Measure 6 cups cucumber juice; add water if there is less. Place juice in a medium saucepan and bring to a boil, then remove from heat and reserve until needed.

3. Using care not to come into contact with seeds or juice (wear rubber or latex gloves if possible), halve and seed jalapeños. Mince by hand. In a 3-quart saucepan over medium-high heat, heat olive oil. Add jalapeño peppers and sauté for 2 minutes. Remove peppers with a slotted spoon and reserve. Add shallots, salt, and black pepper to saucepan. Sauté 2 minutes, until shallots are soft. Add rice and stir about 2 minutes.

4. Lower heat to medium and add wine. Stir until wine is absorbed. Begin adding cucumber juice, $\frac{1}{2}$ cup at a time, stirring constantly. Allow each addition of juice to be absorbed before adding more. Continue until risotto is creamy and rice grains are *al dente,* 25 to 30 minutes.

5. Stir in jalapeño and bell peppers and butter. Season to taste with salt and pepper. Stir in cilantro and lime juice, and serve immediately.

Yield: 6 servings
Time: 1$\frac{1}{2}$ hours

A SNAPSHOT OF THE SEASON

*In the farmers' markets the vivid colors of summer's pro-
duce are giving way to the burnished hues of the autumn harvest. This main course—red snapper fillet
with a simple tomato-onion compote and a flavorful tomato nage—suggests the softer colors of the new season.*

*Traditionally, a nage begins as a broth flavored
with white wine, vegetables, and herbs. Fish or shellfish
are poached in the broth, which is then reduced and
heavily enriched with butter and cream to serve as the
accompanying sauce. It was one of the first things I
learned as an apprentice in the kitchens of the Hotel
Bristol in Paris. Years later, in Italy, I watched as
Italian chefs in peak tomato season prepared minimally
cooked sauces that delivered maximum flavor. Combining these two concepts gave me what I wanted: a nage
that would capture, as in a snapshot, the flavor and
freshness of ripe tomatoes. To accomplish this I would
minimally cook really ripe tomatoes and lightly enhance the resulting broth with herbs and a touch of butter and cream. For the compote, the tomatoes are roasted,
then chopped into large chunks so they remain distinct
when eaten. Simmering the compote just before serving
cooks off the excess water, concentrating the flavors.*

*This dish is typical of restaurant food in that it is
not really one recipe but several, arranged so that the
flavors and textures layer and complement one
another—acidic and sweet, crisp and pulpy. I know it
sounds complex, but it can be accomplished at home with
ease: The trick is doing ahead as much as you can. Both
the tomato nage and the tomato-onion compote can be
made two to three days in advance, then warmed while
the fish is cooking. But if you make the nage ahead, do
not add the butter and cream until you're ready to serve.*

RED SNAPPER WITH TOMATO-ONION COMPOTE AND TOMATO NAGE

15 very ripe medium tomatoes, stems
   removed
5 tablespoons extra-virgin olive oil
1 cup thinly sliced onions
Kosher salt
1 tablespoon balsamic vinegar
4 tablespoons thinly sliced fresh basil leaves
3 tablespoons cold unsalted butter
2 shallots, sliced
1 clove garlic, peeled and sliced
2 sprigs fresh parsley
2 sprigs fresh basil
2 tablespoons heavy cream
6 7- to 8-ounce red snapper fillets, with skin,
   scaled
Freshly ground black pepper to taste

1. To prepare tomato compote: Position an
oven rack one-third from top and preheat oven to
400 degrees. Cut 9 tomatoes in half horizontally
and place, cut side down, on a cooling rack posi-
tioned over a baking sheet. Roast until skins blister and begin to peel away, about 40 minutes.
While tomatoes are roasting, warm 2 tablespoons
olive oil in a large sauté pan over medium-low
heat. Add onions and sauté until tender and
lightly caramelized, about 30 minutes. Remove
from heat, season with salt to taste, and reserve
until needed.

2. When tomatoes are cool enough to handle,
gently remove skins and squeeze out seeds. Cut or
break into 1-inch chunks. Reserve in a small
bowl.

3. In a medium saucepan over medium-high
heat, heat 1 tablespoon oil. Add roasted tomatoes
and onions, and sauté until liquid is reduced and

texture is pulpy, about 5 minutes. Add balsamic vinegar and 2 tablespoons thinly sliced basil. Cook for 3 to 4 minutes. Remove from heat, salt to taste, and reserve compote until needed.

4. To prepare tomato nage: Cut remaining 6 tomatoes into chunks and puree in a food processor until liquefied. Press through a sieve into a bowl, discarding pulp. In a medium saucepan over medium-low heat, melt 1 tablespoon butter. Add shallots and garlic, and cook until softened, about 5 minutes. Add parsley and basil sprigs, and cook for 1 minute. Add tomato puree and bring to a boil. Reduce heat and simmer for 10 minutes.

5. Whisk cream into tomato mixture. Whisk in remaining butter, 1 tablespoon at a time. Nage should be slightly thickened, like an enriched broth. Remove from heat and add remaining 2 tablespoons sliced basil. Stir well and set aside for 10 minutes to infuse basil flavor. Gently press through a sieve, discarding pulp. Season to taste with salt and reserve until needed.

6. Season both sides of red snapper fillets with salt and pepper. Heat remaining 2 tablespoons oil in a well-seasoned iron skillet or nonstick sauté pan over medium heat. Sauté snapper, skin side down, for 4 to 5 minutes. Don't overcrowd pan; sauté in 2 batches if necessary. Turn fish with a spatula and cook 1 or 2 minutes more.

7. To serve, warm compote and nage over medium-low heat. Spoon a bed of compote on each plate. Place a snapper fillet, skin side up, on top of compote. Pour nage around compote. Serve immediately.

Yield: 6 servings
Time: 2 hours

GOOD OLD APPLE PIE: HOW TO GET THE CRUST AND FILLING JUST RIGHT

Our pastry chef, Stacie Pierce, taught me a terrific variation on the familiar apple pie. I'm fond of it because it takes the homespun taste of the classic deep-dish pie and adds a twist—a crisp crumb topping—and it also avoids one of the major pitfalls of apple pie. The usual approach, placing raw apples in a raw pie shell and baking them together, often results in runny pie filling and a gummy, undercooked inside crust.

To prevent that, we prebake the crust and separately precook the apples. Once assembled, the apples are covered with the crisp topping, which I find much more interesting than just another layer of crust, and the baking is completed. Another advantage of this method is that it enables the home cook to prepare the three elements of the pie—crust, filling, and topping—in advance and then assemble the pie for the final baking close to the time when it will be served.

We like using Macintosh apples because of their wonderful balance of sweetness and acidity. The raw Macintosh is relatively soft, and when it is cooked once and then cooked some more in the oven, it is transformed into something like applesauce—just waiting for the counterpoint of that crisp topping.

The pie dough is made in the usual way, though you might want to try the neat trick of chilling not only the butter but the flour as well. This helps prevent the butter from melting into the flour as it is cut in. The crust will be flakier (as the butter melts during baking, it percolates in the dough, creating the tiny air pockets that we perceive as flakiness).

To vary the texture and flavor of the crisp topping still more, the adventurous baker may want to substitute one-third cup of rolled oats for the equivalent amount of flour, or add two tablespoons of raisins, dried fruits, or chopped nuts.

Be sure to serve the pie warm. And, of course, a scoop of ice cream can't hurt.

APPLE CRUMB PIE

For the crust:
    1 cup unbleached all-purpose flour
    Pinch of kosher or sea salt
    8 tablespoons (1 stick) cold unsalted butter
    2 to 2½ tablespoons ice water

For the topping:
    1 cup unbleached all-purpose flour
    ½ cup packed dark brown sugar
    2 teaspoons ground cinnamon
    8 tablespoons (1 stick) cold unsalted butter

For the filling:
    1 cup granulated sugar
    2 teaspoons cinnamon
    5 tablespoons unsalted butter
    3 pounds Macintosh apples, peeled and cut
        into 1-inch dice (8 to 9 cups)
    1 vanilla bean, cut in half lengthwise
    ¼ cup unbleached all-purpose flour
    Squeeze of fresh lemon juice

1. To make piecrust: In a medium bowl, combine flour and salt. Cut butter into small cubes and add to flour mixture. Using a pastry blender or fingertips, cut or blend butter into flour until pea-size pieces are formed. Add just enough ice water so mixture can be formed into a ball. Do not overwork dough or crust will be tough. Wrap dough in plastic wrap and chill for at least 1 hour.

2. Meanwhile, make crumb topping: In a medium bowl, combine flour, brown sugar, and cinnamon. Cut butter into small pieces. Add to flour mixture and with your hands or a pastry blender work into flour mixture until crumbs are formed (lumps will be about size of hazelnuts). Refrigerate until needed.

3. Preheat oven to 350 degrees. Place oven rack in lower third of oven. On a lightly floured surface, roll out dough ⅛ inch thick. Press into a 9-inch pie pan and trim excess dough; flute or fold, and press edges to make a border. Prick bottom of pie shell with tines of a fork and refrigerate or freeze briefly to set crust. When crust has set, line dough with foil and fill with pie weights or dried beans. Bake for 15 minutes. Remove weights and foil, and continue baking about 15 minutes, or until crust just begins to brown. Remove from oven and let cool.

4. To make filling: Combine sugar and cinnamon. In a large skillet or sauté pan, melt butter over medium heat. Add diced apples and sugar mixture. With a small knife, scrape seeds from vanilla bean into apple mixture, then discard bean. Cook apples, stirring, about 5 minutes, or until edges just begin to soften. Add flour and continue to cook, stirring, until flour is completely absorbed, about 2 to 3 minutes. Remove from heat and add lemon juice to taste.

5. Preheat oven to 350 degrees.

6. To assemble pie: Add cooked apple mixture to pie shell, mounding it high in center. Cover with crumb topping. Bake until filling bubbles and crumbs are lightly browned, about 30 to 40 minutes. Serve warm, cut in wedges.

Yield: 6 to 8 servings
Time: 2½ hours, plus chilling time

THE BETTER POTATO

My friend and paesano *the late Vince D'Attolico was proud of the organic produce he sold at the Union Square Greenmarket, and he introduced me to things like salsify, burdock, and his beautiful Jerusalem artichokes. He explained that the name of this misunderstood tuber had nothing to do with geography but rather was derived from the Italian word* girasole, *meaning sunflower, since the plant is a member of that genus.*

A few years ago I was looking for something that would go well with venison and game birds, a root vegetable that would be lighter than potatoes and yet dynamic in flavor. We were having great success with the parsnip pancakes on our menu, so I thought I would give Jerusalem artichokes a try in the same context. Although artichokes have a wetter texture than parsnips, there is still enough starch to bind into a patty.

The nut oil is a key ingredient in these pancakes. It intensifies the nuttiness of the artichokes themselves and helps their subtle flavor stand out over the necessary binding ingredients, eggs and flour. The inherent sweetness of the pancakes invites accompaniments like applesauce and fruit chutneys, but sour cream and caviar are right at home here as well.

JERUSALEM ARTICHOKE PANCAKES

2 pounds Jerusalem artichokes, scrubbed clean
1 medium onion
1 large egg, plus 1 egg yolk, lightly beaten
$1/8$ teaspoon cayenne pepper
$1/8$ teaspoon freshly grated nutmeg
$3/4$ teaspoon kosher salt
Freshly ground black pepper to taste
$1\frac{1}{2}$ teaspoons hazelnut or walnut oil
$1/3$ cup all-purpose flour
$1/4$ cup peanut or vegetable oil
1 tablespoon unsalted butter

1. Preheat oven to 200 degrees. Using a food processor fitted with a coarse shredding blade or the coarse side of a hand grater, shred artichokes. Place in colander to drain. Shred onion and add to colander. Drain about 10 minutes.

2. Pat shredded mixture with paper towels, squeezing gently to extract as much moisture as possible. Place mixture in a large mixing bowl and add beaten egg and yolk, cayenne, nutmeg, salt, black pepper, hazelnut oil, and flour. Mix together lightly by hand.

3. Line a baking sheet with paper towels. Form mixture into pancakes 3 inches in diameter and $1/2$ inch thick. In a large iron skillet over medium heat, heat peanut oil and butter. Place pancakes in pan; do not overlap. Cook until well browned on both sides, about 5 minutes a side. Place cooked pancakes on paper towels on a baking sheet and keep warm in oven. Repeat with remaining pancakes, adding more oil and butter to pan if necessary.

Yield: 6 servings
Time: 45 minutes

APPLES SWEETEN A WILD TURKEY

When I set out to roast a turkey in the fall, especially at Thanksgiving, I'll often choose a wild turkey. It's actually a separate species from the domestic bird we know, and it is not terribly wild: The birds available to us are free-range and farm-raised, not hunted. Wild turkeys are smaller and leaner, with denser flesh and an enticingly sweet gaminess. The leanness means they cook faster and can be dry if overdone. I like to rub a great deal of butter on the bird before roasting and baste it often during cooking to keep it moist and tender. A trick I use with wild turkey and other poultry at the restaurant is to season it with salt the day before roasting. This gives the salt a chance to be drawn into the flesh to season it thoroughly.

I know some people like to use flat or V-shaped roasting racks for their birds, but I prefer cooking a fairly small turkey on a bed of chopped vegetables and spices. In addition to protecting the bottom of the bird from burning, this mirepoix then browns and softens, absorbing the juices from the turkey as it cooks; it later plays a major role in layering the gravy with robust flavors. To expand on the classic mirepoix—carrot, celery, and onion—I added parsnips and juniper berries, flavors that enhance the gaminess of the turkey. I also wanted the gravy made from the pan drippings to have a fruitiness that would tie in with the flavors of the apple-sausage stuffing, so I deglazed the roasting pan with apple cider.

To balance the wild turkey's leaner meat, I prepare a stuffing that's extra moist, with more of a soft pudding texture than the standard chunky stuffing. Since it is so moist, it has to be cooked outside the bird, which means it's not, strictly speaking, a stuffing but a dressing. The bread and apples break down with slow simmering in the oven, and the apple cider provides a sweet backdrop for the flavors of fennel sausage, celery, and sage.

ROASTED WILD TURKEY

1 6- to 8-pound wild turkey
Kosher salt to taste
Freshly ground black pepper to taste
1 medium onion, sliced
2 carrots, peeled and sliced
2 stalks celery, sliced
1 small parsnip, peeled and chopped
1 bay leaf
6 cloves garlic
1 teaspoon whole black peppercorns
3 whole juniper berries
3½ tablespoons unsalted butter at room temperature
2 cups sweet apple cider
2 tablespoons flour
2 cups chicken stock or canned chicken broth

1. The day before roasting, season turkey inside and out with salt and pepper. Truss turkey with kitchen twine and refrigerate overnight.

2. When ready to cook, preheat oven to 500 degrees. In a heavy roasting pan large enough to hold turkey, place onion, carrots, celery, parsnip, bay leaf, garlic, peppercorns, and juniper berries. Rub turkey all over with 1½ tablespoons butter and place on top of vegetables.

3. Place turkey in oven and lower heat to 325 degrees. Roast, uncovered, for 45 minutes, basting frequently with remaining 2 tablespoons butter. Add apple cider to pan and cover turkey loosely with aluminum foil. Continue roasting for 45 minutes more, basting every 15 minutes.

4. Uncover turkey and roast 10 to 15 minutes to brown further. The drumsticks should move easily in the sockets, and the meat should be 180 to 185 degrees; do not overcook. Transfer turkey to a serving platter and cover with foil.

5. Pour off excess fat from roasting pan, leaving cider and pan drippings. Place pan over medium heat and stir in flour. Cook flour for 3 to 4 minutes, stirring constantly. Add stock and bring to a boil. Lower heat and simmer until gravy is thickened, about 10 to 15 minutes. Season with salt and pepper. Strain into a serving dish. Serve carved turkey with gravy and apple-sausage stuffing.

Yield: 6 servings
Time: 2¹/₂ hours, plus refrigeration

APPLE-SAUSAGE STUFFING

¾ cup raisins
3 cups sweet apple cider
1 tablespoon unsalted butter
1 cup sliced celery
1 cup diced onion
1 pound fennel pork sausage
2 apples, peeled and diced
4 leaves fresh sage, finely chopped
4 cups cubed day-old sourdough bread
½ teaspoon kosher salt
¼ teaspoon freshly ground black pepper

1. Preheat oven to 325 degrees. In a small saucepan, combine raisins and apple cider, and bring to a boil. Remove from heat and set aside for raisins to plump.

2. In a large saucepan or Dutch oven over medium heat, melt butter. Add celery and onion, and cook until vegetables have softened, about 5 to 7 minutes.

3. Add sausage to vegetables. Use a wooden spoon to break up meat into small pieces and sauté until meat is well browned, about 5 minutes. Stir in apples and sage. Sauté for 5 minutes.

4. Stir in bread cubes. Season with salt and pepper, and add cider and raisins. Bring to a boil, cover, and transfer pan to oven. Bake for 25 minutes, stirring once halfway through. Remove cover, stir, and bake, uncovered, 10 minutes more. The liquid should be absorbed and the stuffing moist.

Yield: 6 servings
Time: 1¹/₄ hours

THE PEAR GETS A STRONG SUPPORTING CAST

The pear is a very modest fruit—usually firm-textured with a gentle, understated sweetness. It's best either propped up with neutral flavors that yield to its subtlety or framed by bold tastes that allow its purity to shine. This pear tart takes the latter approach. It was inspired in part by an experience during my training in France. After finishing my very first apprenticeship in Paris twenty-three years ago, I decided to prepare something truly American for my newfound French colleagues. I scoured the city's specialty food shops for the ingredients and, with more enthusiasm than expertise, turned out a passable example of pecan pie. Years later I met the master pâtissier Gaston Lenôtre. One of my favorite desserts from his repertory was a pear tart in almond cream.

My recipe today is a blending of those experiences: an American taste with the sophistication of French pastry. Pecan pie meets tarte aux poires. In place of the almond cream I have devised a variation on pecan pie filling. Replacing the corn syrup or molasses with brown sugar makes it less gooey, and chopping the pecans allows the texture to approach the fineness of a French des-

sert. *Grated coconut gives body and nicely bridges the richness of the filling and the simplicity of the pears.*

And you don't have to be Gaston Lenôtre to succeed with this piecrust. It isn't a fragile thing. Almost like a cookie dough, it can be easily pressed into the pie shell.

For an added touch of sophistication you may want to brush the tart with a glaze. Melt some quince jelly or a mixture of equal parts molasses and maple syrup in a small pan and brush lightly over the cooled tart. I like serving this pear-pecan tart topped with maple ice cream as the finale to Thanksgiving dinner or any festive event.

PEAR-PECAN TART

2 Anjou or Comice pears
2 cups white sugar
2 teaspoons vanilla extract
6 tablespoons butter at room temperature
1¾ cups plus 2 tablespoons brown sugar
¾ cup plus 2 tablespoons flour
Pinch of salt
3 large eggs
1½ cups coarsely chopped pecans
⅓ cup packaged grated coconut

1. Peel pears and halve lengthwise. In a medium saucepan (3 to 4 quarts), combine white sugar, 2 cups water, and 1 teaspoon vanilla. Bring to a boil, reduce heat to low, and simmer, stirring, until sugar dissolves. Add pears to pan and simmer until tender, about 15 minutes. Remove with a slotted spoon and allow to cool.

2. Using an electric mixer fitted with a whisk, cream butter with ⅓ cup brown sugar. Add ¾ cup flour, salt, and remaining 1 teaspoon vanilla. Knead briefly to form a smooth dough. Press into a ball, wrap in plastic wrap, and refrigerate for 15 minutes.

3. Preheat oven to 350 degrees. On a lightly floured surface, roll dough into a 10-inch circle. Transfer to a 9-inch pie pan; trim edges if necessary. Bake crust until it begins to color, about 5 minutes. Remove from oven and set aside.

4. In a medium bowl, combine eggs, pecans, coconut, 2 tablespoons flour, and remaining brown sugar. Whisk until blended. Remove cores from pear halves with a melon baller or knife. Slice each half into thin wedges while leaving attached at narrow end of pear.

5. Pour pecan mixture into tart shell. Place pears on top, with narrow ends in center of tart. Fan slices so they lie nearly flat, covering surface of tart. Bake until tart is set and golden brown, about 35 minutes. Remove to a cooling rack and allow to rest for 20 minutes before slicing.

Yield: 9-inch tart (8 servings)
Time: 1¾ hours

JEAN-GEORGES VONGERICHTEN

Jean-Georges Vongerichten is the executive chef and a co-owner of the Manhattan restaurants Jean Georges, Jo Jo, and Vong. He was photographed at Jean Georges. The columns were written with Mark Bittman.

SHRIMP BY WAY OF BANGKOK

Bangkok changed my life. When I arrived to work there for two years in a hotel kitchen, I was a classically trained French chef who knew little else. By the time I was ready to move on, my repertory included lemon grass and cilantro, coconut milk and ginger—and, in fact, all the sharp, sour, salty, and spicy flavors of the East.

I start this assignment with Bangkok on my mind, but being French to the core, I'm not going to abandon all that early training, either, as you'll see. The dish I offer here is a variation on shrimp satay, skewered shrimp, a relatively ordinary dish in Thailand. Like cooks in many other cultures, the Thai like to puree their seafood, particularly for fish cakes. It struck me that I could coat whole shrimp with pureed shrimp and something completely novel would result. The coating would keep the interior shrimp moist, the flavor would intensify, and the textures—moving from the soft and

yielding exterior into the denser interior—promised to be an adventure.

As soon as I tried the combination, I knew I was on to something good but not yet perfect. The outside of the mixture absorbed too much oil, and although the Thai spices I'd added gave it a bright flavor, it seemed to lack something important: crunch. So the Frenchman in me didn't hesitate to dredge the shrimp in bread crumbs before cooking.

I was tremendously pleased with the result, and I've been serving this dish for some time now. Inventing it took work, but the cooking takes very little. The only trick in the preparation of this dish is that you must allow plenty of time for the soft shrimp mousse to chill in the refrigerator at different stages (about one hour of the total cooking time noted in the recipe). The chilling firms what would otherwise be a very fragile assembly.

A simple and satisfying way to serve these shrimp is with a wedge of lemon or lime and a sprinkling of minced cilantro, or just offer a small bowl of soy sauce for dipping. But I wanted to go one step further and add a sauce made especially for this dish. Thinking about the sort of creamy acidic sauces that go so well with oysters, I did something similar for my shrimp-on-shrimp skewers, but with a Thai accent. The buttery sweet-and-sour sauce is an excellent counterpoint to the crunchy, slightly hot shrimp.

SHRIMP SATAY

24 medium to large shrimp (about 1 pound)
1 teaspoon vindaloo curry paste or curry
    powder
2 teaspoons nam pla or nuoc mam (Asian fish
    sauce)
Salt and cayenne pepper to taste
Freshly toasted coarse bread crumbs
3 tablespoons canola, corn, or other neutral-
    flavored oil
Oyster Sauce (see recipe below) or lemon or
    lime wedges, or soy sauce and minced
    cilantro

1. Combine half of shrimp, curry paste or pow-der, and nam pla in a food processor or blender. Process until mixture is pureed, stopping machine and scraping down sides as necessary. Mixture will be thick and pasty. Refrigerate, covered, until stiff, at least 30 minutes or as long as overnight.

2. Place remaining shrimp on 4 skewers; make sure skillet is large enough to hold skewers. Season with salt and cayenne. Spread 1 side of shrimp with chilled puree, then dip into bread crumbs. Repeat on other side and place on waxed paper; chill at least 30 minutes to firm up.

3. Preheat oven to 500 degrees. Place oil in a flat-bottomed ovenproof skillet (preferably non-stick) and turn heat to high. When oil begins to smoke, add shrimp skewers and cook about 2 minutes, or until shrimp are nicely browned on bottom. Turn, then place skillet in oven for 3 minutes, or until shrimp are nicely browned all over. Remove and serve with oyster sauce or other accompaniment.

Yield: 4 appetizers or 2 main courses
Time: about 1¼ hours, largely unattended

OYSTER SAUCE

1 tablespoon butter
1 large shallot, minced
Salt
1 stalk lemongrass, trimmed and slapped in
    several places with back of a knife
1 small chili pepper, slashed once or twice
    with a paring knife
1 cup dry white wine
6 oysters
1 cup heavy cream
Cayenne pepper to taste

1. In a small saucepan, combine butter and shallot, and turn heat to medium. Add about ¼ teaspoon salt and cook about 5 minutes, until shallot softens.

2. Add lemongrass (cut into several pieces if necessary to fit into pan) and chili pepper, and cook 1 minute more. Add wine and turn heat to high. Cook, stirring occasionally, about 5 min-utes, or until approximately 2 tablespoons liquid remain.

3. Shuck oysters over a bowl to catch liquid. Chop fine and return to bowl with liquid.

4. When wine has reduced sufficiently, add cream, bring to a boil, and turn heat to low. Taste and add salt or cayenne if necessary. Stir in

oysters and their liquid, and simmer for 10 seconds. Remove lemongrass and chili, and serve immediately.

Yield: 4 servings
Time: about 30 minutes

VEGETABLE BROTHS TRANSFORMED INTO FRESH, SIMPLE SAUCES

Two of the dishes I've been refining over the years strike me as especially festive and suited to the holidays; one has a brilliant orange-colored sauce and the other has a shimmering green one.

I started developing these dishes in the 1980s when I was the chef at Lafayette and determined to create vividly gorgeous sauces that were unlike anything else. It was a time when many of my customers seemed sauce-phobic. They believed sauces were heavy and unhealthy. Not necessarily so, of course, but that's what they thought. They demanded their sauces served on the side or requested that they be left in the kitchen. What a waste.

So I moved away from the customary stocks for sauces and turned to vegetable juices, which I was sure would result in sauces that were more inviting. Chefs were already producing vegetable-based sauces, but these were mostly cooked purees. I wanted something nearly raw, and simple and fresh.

My first objective was to devise a sauce for shrimp or scallops. I thought of carrots; they are in almost every traditional stock, so there is something comfortingly familiar about them. And I was using a juicer to make carrot juice each morning, so the notion of a carrot sauce was almost inescapable. By simmering carrot juice with spices—I began with the kind of dry spices used in car-

rot cake, like cinnamon, nutmeg, and cloves—and finishing the sauce with butter, I developed a fine brothlike sauce that complemented shellfish perfectly. Over the years I have changed it, cutting back on the butter (it's now about one-half tablespoon a serving) and seasoning the sauce with lemongrass and chili, which complement the sweetness of the carrot.

My next experiment was with zucchini juice. Since I consider this a classically Provençal vegetable, I stuck with typical seasonings: olive oil, garlic, and thyme. I think you'll find that zucchini juice, briefly heated with these simple ingredients, gives you one of the purest, freshest sauces you've ever tasted.

These creations are easy if you have a juicer, but you can make them even if you don't. Carrot juice can be bought in any health-food store and many supermarkets, and you can make zucchini juice by pureeing the vegetable in a food processor and squeezing it through a towel or cheesecloth.

Either sauce can be made an hour or two in advance, but make sure never to bring them to a boil or they will break. Serve them with any simply cooked fish; my preferences are steamed scallops or shrimp with the carrot broth, and sautéed cod or other plain white fillets with the zucchini juice.

And please eat these dishes with a spoon. It makes me crazy when people use a fork, because these sauces are not thick enough to adhere to the fish, and you must get both fish and sauce in each mouthful or the dish simply does not work. The line between sauce and soup is always blurry. That's especially true of this carrot sauce. Triple its ingredients and leave out the fish, and if you've been searching for a terrific soup, you've just found it.

SCALLOPS IN CARROT BROTH

1½ pounds carrots, peeled, or 1½ cups carrot juice
2 stalks lemongrass
2 tablespoons butter
Juice of 1½ limes
1 small (1-inch) chili, minced
1½ pounds sea scallops
Butter or oil if sautéing
10 mint leaves, coarsely chopped
10 cilantro leaves, coarsely chopped

1. Juice carrots and measure 1½ cups juice. Trim lemongrass stalks to expose their tender inner core and finely mince 3 teaspoons. Combine carrot juice, lemongrass, butter, lime juice, and chili, and bring to a simmer over low heat, stirring frequently. Do not boil.

2. Meanwhile, steam scallops over boiling water until just done, about 4 minutes (you may also grill or sauté scallops). Place 6 scallops in each of 4 bowls, then garnish with broth and chopped herbs. Eat with a spoon.

Yield: 4 servings
Time: 40 minutes

COD IN ZUCCHINI BROTH

1½ pounds zucchini, washed and trimmed
6 tablespoons extra-virgin olive oil
1 tablespoon minced garlic
1 teaspoon thyme leaves
4 pieces cod fillet (about 1½ pounds total)
Salt to taste
Pinch of cayenne pepper

1. Preheat oven to 500 degrees. Juice the zucchini.

2. In a saucepan, combine 2 tablespoons oil with garlic and thyme, and turn heat to medium. Cook just long enough to color the garlic slightly, then turn heat to low and add zucchini juice. Bring to a simmer, stirring frequently. Do not boil.

3. Place 2 tablespoons oil in a large ovenproof skillet and turn heat to high. When oil smokes, add cod and transfer pan to oven. Cook fish about 3 minutes; turn and cook until done, about 8 minutes total.

4. Whisk remaining 2 tablespoons oil into zucchini broth. Taste and add salt and cayenne. Place a cod fillet in each of 4 bowls and garnish with broth. Eat with a spoon.

Yield: 4 servings
Time: 40 minutes

THE SECRET TO PURE, FLAKY SALMON: LOW HEAT

The demand for salmon, both in restaurants and at home, has been climbing steadily for years now. I concede that anyone can cook it more or less decently, but to cook it truly well—so that the rich, natural butteriness is not only preserved but also enhanced—is not as easy as it might seem.

Whenever the fish hits a hot surface—a grill, a skillet, or a roasting pan in a hot oven—it starts to dry out. Keeping the interior rare helps but isn't a total answer. High heat makes the exterior unpleasantly chalky and drives out some of the fatty oils in the flesh, a disintegration of the fish you can actually see as that white, oily substance that oozes into the pan and is sadly lost.

A little more than a year ago one of my chefs, Didier Virot, and I set about trying to find a better method than any we'd known so far. After some experimentation we hit on a stunningly simple technique that stands the usual approach on its head: baking at a temperature so low that the oven is barely hot. At first we feared the cooking time would have to be long, an hour or so, and long cooking dries the fish out as surely as high heat does. We kept cutting back until we were baking our 1¼-inch fillets for just 10 minutes at 200 degrees. That's in a professional convection oven. (A good home convection oven should work as well.) The ordinary oven will need to be set for 250 degrees, about 200 degrees less than is typical these days.

The cooking is so gentle that the fish looks almost raw—it doesn't get that opaque look you're used to—but it doesn't have a raw taste. It even flakes. It is simply pure, intense salmon.

Once we had mastered the salmon, we had an easy time figuring out how to serve it. I've always loved fish with mashed potatoes; I like the combination of sea and earth, and I think the textures, rather than offering the

sharp contrast you might look for in other dishes, actually harmonize beautifully. I chose Yukon Golds because they're so creamy when mashed, even without a lot of butter.

We finish the dish with a simple chive oil, which is no more than chives (or you can use parsley or chervil) and oil pureed in a blender. There was a time when I made chive oil by combining chive juice and oil, a more elaborate preparation, but this method results in better, purer flavor because you lose nothing to the juicer. Don't expect a real emulsion to form, though; this is more like a broken oil, which is actually gorgeous on the plate.

GENTLY COOKED SALMON WITH
MASHED POTATOES

> 2 pounds Yukon Gold or other baking
>   potatoes (about 5 or 6), peeled and cut
>   into quarters
> Salt
> 3 tablespoons plus ¼ teaspoon butter
> 4 6-ounce center-cut salmon fillets, about
>   1¼ inches thick at thickest point, skin
>   on and scaled
> ½ ounce chives (about 40 to 60 chives,
>   a small handful)
> 4 tablespoons neutral-flavored oil, such as
>   grapeseed or canola
> ¾ cup milk, gently warmed
> Freshly ground pepper
> Coarse salt and cracked black pepper to taste

1. Boil potatoes in salted water to cover until soft, about 30 minutes.

2. Meanwhile, smear a baking dish with ¼ teaspoon butter and place salmon, skin side up, on butter. Let sit while you preheat oven to 250 degrees.

3. Mince a tablespoon or so of chives for garnish. Tear remaining chives into 2-inch lengths and place in container of a blender with oil and a little salt. Blend until oil has a creamlike consistency, stopping machine to push mixture down once or twice.

4. When potatoes are done, put salmon in oven and set timer for 10 minutes.

5. Drain potatoes, then mash well or put through a food mill. Return potatoes to pot over very low heat and stir in 3 tablespoons butter. Gradually add milk, beating with a wooden spoon until smooth and creamy. Season with salt and pepper to taste. Keep warm.

6. Check salmon after 10 minutes; skin should peel off easily, meat should flake, and an instant-read thermometer should display about 120 degrees. It may look undercooked, but if it meets these criteria, it is done. (If it is not finished or you prefer it better done, return it to oven for 3 minutes.) If you like, scrape off the gray fatty matter on the skin side (or just turn the fish over). Sprinkle with some coarse salt and cracked black pepper.

7. To serve, place one-fourth of mashed potatoes on a plate and top with a piece of salmon. Drizzle chive oil all around plate and garnish with minced chives.

Yield: 4 servings
Time: 45 minutes

MAKING THE BEST OF A SOUR FRUIT

The tamarind tree produces a gnarled pod that hides within it a marvelous pulp with a taste reminiscent of sour plums. In various tropical places it is commonly used in soups or on fish or meat. The rich sourness is so appealing that I wanted to devise my own uses for tamarind pulp, which is readily found in Asian and Hispanic stores and in many produce markets.

I tried incorporating it into a vinaigrette and other French-style sauces, but the tamarind had too much character and had to be paired with other strong-willed ingredients. Chilies came to mind, and so did nam pla, the Asian fish sauce, and garlic, vinegar, and sugar. The sourness came through, enhanced and mellowed, in a kind of ketchup that was begging for a simple use to show it off.

One was obvious: I'd come up with some kind of spring roll to dip into this startling sauce. I drew on the technique for a traditional spring roll, which usually contains ground meat or shrimp and ground pork. But it was crab that I had in mind, and I created a fundamental spring roll with not much more than crab meat, mayonnaise as a binder, and some chili for bite. The wrapper is a plain wonton shell, and it offers an almost foolproof way to produce a crisp, nongreasy crust.

With a cool lettuce wrap around the roll and the tamarind ketchup for dipping, you have an appetizer that will set people talking for some time to come.

I had to keep thinking of other ways to use this sauce, of course, so I thinned it with warm water and a little more vinegar and used it as a salad dressing with crab, bean sprouts, and avocado. I have also used it as a barbecue sauce for basting ribs. As a simple condiment it does wonders for steamed lobster, grilled shrimp or swordfish, chicken breasts or steak. I also like to dip raw or lightly steamed vegetables into it. Or stir it into soups.

But thanks to its wonderful acidity and texture, I think that tamarind ketchup may be at its best acting as a binder for many pan juices, much as you use the combination of butter and lemon. You might bake a piece of cod with white wine and butter and finish the pan sauce with a couple of spoonfuls of tamarind ketchup. The same principle will work with poultry pan juices. I've used it with duck, and it's perfect with chicken.

CRAB SPRING ROLLS

8 ounces picked crab, such as lump or
    peekytoe
2 tablespoons mayonnaise
½ small chili, finely minced
Salt to taste
2 egg yolks
8 8-inch-square wonton wrappers
Oil for frying
8 leaves Boston lettuce
16 cilantro leaves
16 mint leaves

1. Combine crab, mayonnaise, chili, and salt. Stir gently, letting some crab lumps remain.

2. Beat egg yolks in a small bowl. Place a 3-inch portion of crab across center of each wonton wrapper. Fold over 2 sides of wrapper so they meet in middle, then brush with a little beaten yolk. Roll tightly and set aside, uncovered (rolls can be refrigerated for as long as a day before frying).

3. Place at least 1 inch of oil in a saucepan or deep fryer and heat to about 365 degrees. Fry spring rolls in 2 batches, until lightly browned, just 1 or 2 minutes.

4. To serve, wrap each roll in a lettuce leaf with some cilantro and mint, and accompany with tamarind ketchup.

Yield: 8 spring rolls
Time: 20 minutes

TAMARIND KETCHUP

8 ounces tamarind (see Note)
2 small chilies, stems removed
2 large cloves garlic, peeled
½ cup rice wine vinegar
¼ cup nam pla (Asian fish sauce)
2 tablespoons sugar
4 tablespoons grapeseed, canola, or other
    neutral-flavored oil

1. In a small saucepan, place tamarind with about ½ cup water. Turn heat to medium and cook, stirring and mashing, until water is absorbed. Continue to add water as necessary, to a total of about 1 cup, until you have a smooth, thick paste. Cool slightly, then put through a food mill or coarse strainer for a coarse puree.

2. Measure 1 cup of puree and place in a blender with remaining ingredients. Puree and then let rest for a while (up to 1 hour) before tasting and adjusting seasoning. The ketchup keeps well for weeks if refrigerated.

Yield: 1 cup
Time: 20 minutes

NOTE: Tamarind is sold as a small brick, with seeds but also as a seedless pulp. If you can find the seedless pulp, skip Step 1.

MAKING THE DISH: BEETS DO IT, CARROTS DO IT

Sometimes it is the condiment that makes the dish. I have developed a number that actually began as vegetable side dishes but whose strong personalities begged to play a more central role. Two of my favorites—carrot confit and beet tartare—are made with winter vegetables, and both are best served with simply steamed or broiled fish.

My carrot confit resembles a carrot dish that I learned in Morocco. The cooking liquid is a blend of olive oil (in Morocco it was camel butter), orange juice, and seasonings, especially cumin, which is always wonderful with carrots. It's made extraordinary by the melding of the flavors in slow cooking. During the nearly two-hour braising time, the carrots become incomparably tender. (I call it a confit because its texture reminds me of the classic preserved duck.) Yet, thanks to the gentle heat, they do not fall apart.

When you make this dish, stay away from big, thick carrots. In fact, I recently tried it with a one-pound bag of pre-peeled baby carrots, and the results were perfect. To serve it, just spoon some of the carrots and their juices over lightly steamed white fish, such as black sea bass, red snapper, or halibut. Don't season the fish until after it is cooked or the salt will leach out some of the moisture.

Beet tartare is far more than a play on words. I developed it when I wanted to keep the traditional seasonings used in beef tartare but to get away from serving raw beef. To me the combination of cornichons, capers, vinegar, Worcestershire, and so on, works just as well with beets as it does with beef. And the result is really much like beef tartare in color, but the sweetness of the beets makes the flavor even more intense. This dish can be made well in advance, and its color makes any white-fleshed fish shine. Serve it with bay scallops when they are in season. I place a mound of beets in the center of a plate surrounded by scallops.

By the way, if you have never tried baking beets, you should; there is nothing easier.

BEET TARTARE

6 medium beets (about 1¼ pounds)
1 shallot, peeled and roughly chopped
1 teaspoon Worcestershire sauce
Few drops Tabasco or other bottled hot sauce
1 teaspoon sherry vinegar
6 cornichons, roughly chopped
⅓ cup capers, drained
1 tablespoon mayonnaise
2 tablespoons chopped parsley, plus more for garnish
Salt and freshly ground black pepper

1. To bake beets: Preheat oven to 350 degrees. Wash beets, leaving them wet, and wrap individually in aluminum foil. Place in a roasting pan or on a baking sheet and bake about 90 minutes, or until tender. (To test, poke a thin-bladed knife through foil.) Let cool in foil. (To cook in water, drop beets into salted water to cover, bring to a boil, and cook over medium heat until tender, 45 minutes to 1 hour.)

2. When beets are cool enough to handle, peel and cut into eighths.

3. Place beets in container of a food processor with all ingredients except mayonnaise, parsley, salt, and pepper. Pulse until mixture is minced but not pureed. You may have to scrape mixture down between pulses.

4. Spoon mixture into a bowl and stir in mayonnaise and parsley. Taste and adjust seasonings; you may need to add salt and pepper and more vinegar, Worcestershire, or Tabasco. (This dish keeps well up to 2 days. Refrigerate, keeping it

well wrapped or in a covered container, and bring to room temperature before serving.) Garnish and serve with steamed fish.

Yield: 4 servings

Time: 1½ to 2 hours (10 minutes with precooked beets)

CARROT CONFIT

1 pound fresh carrots, preferably ¾ inch at their thickest part and 6 to 8 inches long
1 teaspoon cumin seed
1 teaspoon grated or minced orange zest
1 teaspoon minced garlic
¼ cup extra-virgin olive oil
Pinch of salt
⅛ teaspoon sugar
1 cup freshly squeezed orange juice
1 teaspoon lemon juice
2 tablespoons chopped cilantro

1. Trim and peel carrots. Leave whole if they are the size recommended; if they are bigger, cut into chunks or in half lengthwise. Set aside. In a saucepan large enough to hold carrots, place cumin, orange zest, garlic, oil, salt, sugar, and orange juice. Turn heat to medium and bring to a boil, stirring.

2. Add carrots, cover, and turn heat to low. Mixture should be bubbling gently, not vigorously, whenever you remove cover. Cook virtually undisturbed (check progress if you like) about 1½ hours, or until carrots are very tender but not yet falling apart.

3. Gently stir lemon juice into carrots. Sprinkle with cilantro, stir once, serve with steamed fish.

Yield: 4 servings

Time: 1½ to 2 hours

ROAST LAMB GETS A CRUNCHY, COLORFUL MAKEOVER

In the late 1980s when I was the chef at Lafayette, the cost of food was no object; we simply tried to make the most luxurious creations possible. One such dish that I came up with and that was especially popular was a boneless loin of lamb rolled in a combination of chopped black truffles and a little parsley. Needless to say it was outrageously expensive, and we charged accordingly. But that black exterior against the red, rare-cooked lamb medallions made for a stunning contrast of color; and, of course, the dish was delicious.

When I opened Jo Jo in 1991, I couldn't afford to have truffles as a part of my daily menu, and my customers did not seem to want them as a steady diet. So, I began to think about how to make the dish equally flavorful and even more beautiful. If the original dish lacked anything, it was crunch. There was no way to add enough truffles to the outside of the lamb to form a crust; they were for flavor only. So I began to dredge the dish in a coarse powder made from dried black trumpet mushrooms.

Even then the crust was not as thick as I would have liked. The answer was to treat the mushroom powder like bread crumbs: I dredged the lamb loin lightly in flour, then in egg, and finally in as much of the mushroom powder as would adhere. After the lamb was seared and roasted, it was perfect: deep black and crunchy on the outside, reddish pink and tender inside. Served on a bed of pureed leeks and garnished with a few sautéed mushrooms, it was (and is) among the most colorful and delicious dishes I know, and better than the original.

There are several keys to making this deceptively simple dish successfully. Although black trumpet mushrooms are my first choice, you can use any dried mushrooms you like. For appearance' sake, though, the darker the better; you can consider Chinese black mush-rooms (which are very inexpensive), dried porcini, or black chanterelles.

Although the preparation takes almost no active working time at all, it's best to allow the lamb to rest for several hours after it is coated in order for the mushrooms to rehydrate, which they do by absorbing moisture from both the egg and the lamb itself. For best flavor make the leek puree almost at the last minute; cook the leeks, drain them, and puree them just before cooking the lamb.

I always make this dish with lamb, but you can try it with beef tenderloin (filet mignon) or loin of venison. Both have sufficiently strong flavor to stand up to the mushrooms and will give you the lovely color combination that makes the dish so distinctive. But whatever meat you use, remember that the crust keeps the heat inside the meat, so it continues to cook after you remove it from the oven. Be careful not to overcook.

BONELESS LAMB WITH MUSHROOM CRUST AND LEEK PUREE

2 ounces dried black trumpet or other dried mushrooms
1 egg
Salt and freshly ground black pepper to taste
Flour for dredging
2 racks of lamb, boned
2 large or 4 medium leeks, trimmed of hard green parts, split in half, well washed, and roughly chopped
1 tablespoon butter
4 tablespoons extra-virgin olive oil
4 ounces fresh mushrooms, such as shiitake, trimmed and cut into chunks
2 cloves garlic, lightly smashed
2 sprigs thyme

1. Put dried mushrooms in a spice or coffee grinder, grind to consistency of coffee, and place on a plate. Beat egg in a bowl with a little salt and pepper. Place flour on a plate. Dip lamb very lightly into the flour and shake off excess. Dip into egg and then into mushrooms, coating heavily. Pat mushrooms to adhere. Refrigerate on a sheet of waxed paper about 4 hours.

2. When ready to cook, preheat oven to 500 degrees. Cook leeks in boiling salted water until tender, 5 to 10 minutes. Drain, reserving a little cooking liquid, and transfer leeks to blender. Puree with butter, adding a little cooking liquid if necessary to help the machine do its work. Add salt and pepper, and place in a saucepan over very low heat to keep warm.

3. Heat 2 tablespoons oil in a 10-inch skillet. Add fresh mushrooms, garlic, and thyme. Cook, stirring occasionally, until mushrooms are tender, about 10 minutes.

4. Meanwhile, place remaining 2 tablespoons oil in an ovenproof skillet and turn heat to medium-high. One minute later add lamb and cook for 2 minutes on one side. Turn lamb and place skillet in oven for 5 to 6 minutes for medium-rare or a little longer if you like lamb done more. (Medium-rare lamb will measure about 125 degrees when you remove it from oven; meat will keep cooking, and internal temperature will quickly rise to 130 degrees.)

5. Let lamb rest for 1 or 2 minutes, then cut into ¾-inch-thick slices. Place a dollop of leek puree on each plate and top with a portion of mushrooms. Place lamb on top and serve.

Yield: 4 servings
Time: About 5 hours, largely unattended

~⌒~

MY GREATEST MISTAKE

The most popular dessert I have ever created started out as a mistake. About fourteen years ago I regularly served a small rich chocolate cupcake as part of a petits fours platter. It was a ridiculously simple recipe but easy to overcook. One day I overcompensated and removed the cakes from the oven far too early. I would have realized that in a second but got distracted before I had a chance to check them. By the time I turned around, someone else had cut into one, and the hot, undercooked interior had spilled out onto the plate. After I was done screaming, I realized that the effect was beautiful.

Since then, my warm soft chocolate cake has been on all my menus without exception, and more than half our customers order it. They are easy to bake at home. The only trick lies in the timing. When I baked them in a home oven last week, they were done in exactly 12 minutes; but since the timing is precise and all ovens are different, I suggest that you practice on a batch before preparing them for guests. All you have to learn is the look the cakes have when they are done: The outer rim is thoroughly cooked, like a brownie, but the center remains jiggly and quite runny, like a properly cooked custard. Since you serve them immediately, they have no time to firm up.

We often serve these cakes with coconut sorbet, but a good vanilla ice cream is wonderful, too.

WARM SOFT CHOCOLATE CAKE

8 tablespoons (1 stick) butter, plus a little for
    molds
2 teaspoons flour, plus a little for dusting
4 squares (4 ounces) bittersweet chocolate
2 eggs, plus 2 egg yolks
¼ cup sugar

1. Preheat oven to 450 degrees. Butter and
lightly flour four 4-ounce molds, custard cups,
ramekins, or similar containers. Tap out excess
flour. Either in a double boiler or small saucepan,
gently heat butter and chocolate together until
chocolate is almost completely melted. In the
meantime, beat eggs, yolks, and sugar together
with a whisk or electric beater until light and
thick.

2. Beat melted chocolate and butter together.
While still warm, pour into egg mixture, then
quickly beat in flour until combined.

3. Divide batter among molds. (At this point
you can refrigerate desserts for several hours, until ready to eat. Bring to room temperature before
cooking.)

4. Bake molds on a baking sheet for 12 minutes; the center will still be quite soft, but the
sides will be set.

5. Invert each mold onto a plate and let sit
about 10 seconds. Unmold by lifting up one corner of mold; cake will fall out onto plate. Serve
immediately.

Yield: 4 servings
Time: 30 minutes

MARCUS SAMUELSSON

Marcus Samuelsson is the executive chef and a co-owner of the
Manhattan restaurant Aquavit. He was photographed outside the restaurant.
These columns were written with Amanda Hesser.

ROAST CHICKEN, SAVORY AND PERFUMED

*It is cold for so much of the year in Sweden, where I grew
up, that fresh herbs are like the tourists: They arrive for
a brief period in summer when the weather is congenial
and the days are long, and then they slip away before
dark. Even so, the herbs that do manage to flourish in
Sweden are the cold-resistant ones like parsley, chives,
and, of course, dill. I must have been thirteen before I saw
fresh basil for the first time.*

*Of necessity, spices move to the foreground: star anise,
cardamom, cinnamon, nutmeg, and clove, all of which
made their way into the Swedish culinary stream centuries ago when the East India Company brought them
from Asia and India.*

*Although I've worked in restaurants in Europe and
America, I learned cooking from my grandmother, and
with this dish I want to pay homage to her. This is her
robust roast chicken, relying on root vegetables and typical Swedish spices. Our family lived in Göteborg, but she
came from Hälsingborg. Sweet potatoes are common there,
and they were always part of her stuffing. She crushed the
spices for the stuffing and also rubbed them on the outside
of the chicken. Then she roasted it at a relatively low temperature, 350 degrees, so that flavors infused it from both
inside and outside. There is no need to rush this process.*

*The stuffing has no bread in it and, in fact, is not a
conventional stuffing but rather a vegetable side dish
meant to harmonize with the highly spiced chicken; the
vegetables happen to be cooked inside the bird. After the
vegetables are cooked, they are mixed with rice. The mixture is moistened by juices from the roasting pan, and the
spices are softened by a little yogurt. Be prepared for a
sensory experience: Almost as soon as the chicken begins to
roast, the kitchen is perfumed by the spices. If eating it
weren't so enjoyable, you might be tempted just to keep on
roasting.*

ROAST CHICKEN WITH SPICED APPLES AND ONIONS

1 3½-pound free-range chicken
1 medium sweet potato, cut into ½-inch cubes
1 onion, cut into ½-inch cubes
2 Granny Smith apples, peeled, cored, and cut into ½-inch cubes
2 shallots, cut into ½-inch pieces
1 clove garlic, chopped
Leaves from 2 sprigs fresh thyme
Leaves from 2 sprigs fresh mint, chopped
1 tablespoon olive oil
½ teaspoon ground cinnamon
2 cardamom pods or ¼ teaspoon ground cardamom
2 whole star anise
2 whole cloves or ⅛ teaspoon ground cloves
4 white peppercorns
2 black peppercorns
Kosher salt
Yogurt Rice (see recipe below)

1. Preheat oven to 350 degrees. Rinse chicken with cool water and pat dry with paper towels. Fill a medium saucepan halfway with water and bring to a boil. Add cubed sweet potato and blanch for 2 minutes. Drain, rinse with cold water, and drain again. In a mixing bowl, combine blanched sweet potato, onion, apples, shallots, and garlic. Add thyme and chopped mint leaves. In a small bowl, combine oil with 2 tablespoons water and add to vegetable mixture.

2. Using a mortar and pestle, or with the base of a heavy pot on a cutting board, lightly crush together cinnamon, cardamom, star anise, cloves, white peppercorns, and black peppercorns, along with salt to taste. Add half of spice mixture to vegetables and reserve rest.

3. Place chicken on a rack in a medium roasting pan. Lightly stuff cavity with about half of vegetable mixture. Place remaining vegetables around bird in bottom of pan. Truss bird with kitchen string and rub with remaining spice mixture.

4. Place pan in oven and roast about 1½ hours, or until internal temperature reaches 160 degrees. Check pan occasionally and add a little water if it becomes completely dry. When vegetables in base of pan are tender, remove and reserve.

5. When chicken is cooked, remove vegetables from cavity and add to reserved pan vegetables. Carve chicken, cover securely, and keep warm. Add enough water to pan juices to make 1 cup, stirring well to deglaze pan. Use vegetables and pan juices to make yogurt rice. Serve carved chicken with yogurt rice.

Yield: 4 servings
Time: 2¼ hours

1 cup basmati rice
1 cup cooking liquid from roast chicken
Roasted vegetables from roast chicken
½ cup plain yogurt
Kosher salt
1 tablespoon sliced chives

1. In a medium saucepan, combine rice with 1 cup water. Bring to a boil, then reduce heat and simmer, covered, until rice is almost tender and liquid is almost gone, about 10 minutes.

2. Add cooking liquid from roasted chicken and the roasted vegetables, and toss gently. Cover pan and continue cooking until rice is tender, 5 to 10 minutes. Fold in yogurt, add salt to taste, and stir in chives. Serve with carved chicken.

Yield: 4 servings
Time: 30 minutes

PICKLED HERRING GETS A PASSPORT

For a chef, New York is the land of the free. It's not that you can do anything at all, but this city is so ready to embrace innovation that the problem is how to show a certain restraint in the face of liberation, to stay within what you know. My objective as the chef (French- and Swiss-trained) at a Swedish restaurant is to take the ingredients and proclivities of Sweden and marry them to the international ferment of New York.

Nothing, for instance, is more Swedish than pickled herring. And I start off the way I would if I were still in my grandmother's kitchen in Sweden. To pickle the salted fish I use the traditional "1-2-3 method": one part vinegar, two parts sugar, three parts water. The three ingredients are brought to a boil, and then aromatics like leeks, white peppercorns, onion, and bay leaf are added. Simple as it is, the preparation is delicious just that way, and perfect as part of a smorgasbord. But I want to add some excitement, so depending on my inclination, I reach for accents that are distinctly non-Swedish, like ginger or lemongrass, and add them to the 1-2-3 base.

The pickled herring is not served on its own but as a base for any number of salads. Because it is so sweet, I usually cut it into thin slices or cubes and fold into it tangy, acidic dressings to balance the flavors. At the restaurant I often make a tomato dressing or one with Swedish mustard, which is sharp but sweeter than Dijon. This beet salad is a beautiful use for the herring—pink from the beets and sweet with small pieces of apple.

HERRING SALAD WITH BEETS AND APPLES

2 large beets
Pickled Herring (see recipe below)
2 large Granny Smith apples, peeled, cored,
    and cut into $\frac{1}{4}$-inch dice
1 yellow onion, cut into $\frac{1}{4}$-inch dice
2 tablespoons mayonnaise
2 tablespoons sour cream
1 tablespoon chopped parsley

1. Preheat oven to 350 degrees. Place beets in a small roasting pan and bake until tender when pierced with a fork, about $1\frac{1}{2}$ hours. Cool, peel, and cut into $\frac{1}{4}$-inch dice.

2. Select 4 pickled herring fillets and reserve rest for another use. Cut fillets into $\frac{1}{4}$-inch dice and place in a medium bowl. Add beets, apples, onion, mayonnaise, sour cream, and parsley. Mix gently. Chill thoroughly, 4 hours to overnight, before serving.

Yield: 4 servings
Time: 2 hours, plus refrigeration

PICKLED HERRING

12 herring fillets in brine
2 cups sugar
1 cup Swedish vinegar or white wine vinegar
1 carrot, thinly sliced
1 red onion, chopped
$\frac{1}{2}$ leek, white part only, chopped
1 bay leaf
4 black peppercorns
4 white peppercorns

1. In a medium mixing bowl, combine herring with enough water to cover. Refrigerate overnight.

2. Drain herring and pat dry with paper towels. Arrange fillets in a shallow pan and set aside.

3. In a medium saucepan, combine 3 cups water, sugar, and vinegar. Bring to a boil, stirring to dissolve sugar. Remove from heat and add carrot, onion, leek, bay leaf, and peppercorns. Allow pickling brine to cool completely and then pour over herring. Refrigerate overnight.

Yield: 12 fillets
Time: 45 minutes, plus two nights of refrigeration

A LITTLE OF THIS, A PINCH OF THAT
Here are several options to enhance the basic pickled herring recipe.

Add 5 tablespoons chopped cilantro and 2 lightly crushed dried chilies to the pickling liquid. Or add 2 tablespoons chopped ginger, 5 tablespoons chopped mint, or 2 chopped lemongrass stalks.

Once you have pickled the herring, you can use them in salads or as an hors d'oeuvre, or you can fold them into a dressing: Combine 2 tablespoons freshly squeezed lime juice, grated zest of $\frac{1}{2}$ lime, $\frac{1}{4}$ cup mayonnaise, $\frac{1}{2}$ cup sour cream, 1 tablespoon finely chopped cilantro, and kosher salt and freshly ground white pepper to taste. Blend until smooth, refrigerate overnight, and then fold in 4 sliced herring.

A SPICY BITE OF LAMB
FROM ETHIOPIA

I have no memories of Ethiopia, where I was born. The marvelous Swedish family that adopted me when I was three is the only one I know. But when I found myself working as a chef in New York, I gravitated toward Ethiopians here.

Wandering around the midtown area, not far from my own restaurant, I came on a place called Meskerem Ethiopian Restaurant on Forty-seventh Street. There I fell into conversation with the owner, Philipos Megistu. Soon we were friends, and he and his cook, Zewiditu Tadesse, who knows everything there is to know about Ethiopian cooking, were teaching me about my forgotten past. She is expert in the mildly spiced stewed lentils called miser alecha, the raw beef salads, and, perhaps preeminently, the sautéed lamb called tibs.

Tibs is a stimulatingly spicy but fairly simple peasant dish. Small cubes of lamb are marinated in red wine with jalapeño peppers and then seared in butter flavored with turmeric, garlic, and cardamom. It's generally served with a flat bread called injera, which is moist, spongy, and as big around as a pizza. To eat tibs, a piece of the bread is cupped in the hand and used to pick up the meat. Injera is made from a fermented Ethiopian grain called tef, prepared like a pancake batter and ladled onto a hot iron griddle. Its natural sourness marries beautifully with the spiciness of the tibs. The usual approach in Ethiopia, as it has been taught to me by my friends at Meskerem, is for the host to prepare the first serving, tearing off a piece of the bread, scooping up some tibs, dipping the tibs and bread into an accompanying chili sauce, and then handing the combination to a guest.

It is marvelous food with intense character, but of course it has no place in my fundamentally Swedish restaurant. Nevertheless, I keep thinking about it. Maybe I'll open another restaurant one of these days. Who knows?

TIBS

2 pounds boneless lamb loin, cut into ½-inch cubes
1 red onion, minced
1 jalapeño pepper, seeded and minced
1¼ cups dry red wine
12 ounces (3 sticks) butter, to be seasoned and clarified (3 tablespoons used for recipe)
½ tablespoon turmeric
1 clove garlic, crushed
2 cardamom pods, crushed
2 tablespoons mild chili powder
Kosher salt and freshly ground black pepper to taste
1 tablespoon chopped fresh rosemary

1. In a medium mixing bowl, combine lamb, onion, and jalapeño. Add ¾ cup red wine and mix well. Cover and refrigerate 1 to 2 hours.

2. In a small saucepan, combine butter, turmeric, garlic, and cardamom. Bring to a boil. Using a skimmer or large spoon, remove any impurities that rise to surface. Carefully pour only clarified butter into a clean container, discarding rest.

3. In a small saucepan over low heat, combine 1 tablespoon clarified butter with chili powder. Stir about 1 minute to toast powder; do not allow to burn. Add remaining ½ cup wine. Remove chili sauce to a serving bowl and reserve.

4. Using a slotted spoon, remove meat from marinade and drain on paper towels; reserve marinade. Place a large iron skillet over medium-high heat until very hot. Add 2 tablespoons clarified butter; reserve remaining butter for another use. Add lamb and sauté until seared on all sides. Add marinade to pan and continue stirring until

lamb is cooked through, 2 to 3 minutes. Season with salt, pepper, and rosemary. Allow liquid in pan to reduce until slightly thickened. Serve lamb and pan juices in individual bowls, accompanied by bowls of chili dipping sauce and injera, pita bread, or tortillas with which to scoop up meat.

Yield: 4 servings

Time: 45 minutes plus 1 to 2 hours of refrigeration

THE SECRET TO NOT OVERCOOKING VENISON

A trick in cooking venison is to think of fish. Like most fish, venison has a low fat content and needs to be seared quickly in a hot pan; you must be especially vigilant because it crosses the boundary into an overcooked state about as easily as a Swede slips into Norway. For me, the similarity of cooking venison and fish is a relief. I grew up eating very little meat (later, in fact, preparing it made me anxious, until I finally reached some level of mastery), and it's fish I always think of first—a handicap when you're trying to run a well-rounded kitchen.

When venison is overcooked, the meat turns bone dry, and there is no way to bring it back. So you want to undercook it slightly, then let the meat rest away from direct heat for a few minutes. This gives the venison a chance to finish cooking in the gentle residual heat and makes it less likely to skip into that overcooked zone. I generally buy farm-raised venison chops, which are tender and full of flavor, though not as intense as wild venison.

Venison has such a distinct flavor that it needs sharp, deep-flavored accompaniments. For this dish I chose a berry chutney layered with spices like cinnamon and star anise. And because so many foods in Sweden are preserved to last through the winter, chutney is a common accompaniment for meats. The chutney can be made with any mixture of berries and can be doubled or tripled if you want to store it in the refrigerator for a few weeks. I like to match it with both lavish and simple foods, with sautéed foie gras or with toasts spread with cheese and walnuts. I might even add the chutney to a spring roll made with duck and fresh greens.

The venison and chutney together, though, demand a lot of your palate, and you don't want too many superstars on one plate. Serve them with something mild but hearty on the side, like garlic mashed potatoes or an apple-parsnip puree.

SAUTÉED VENISON CHOP WITH BERRY CHUTNEY

4 venison rib chops or veal chops
2 tablespoons canola oil
2 tablespoons gin or aquavit
2 tablespoons extra-virgin olive oil
¼ cup brown sugar
1 shallot, minced
1 clove garlic, minced
1 tablespoon chopped fresh ginger
1 cinnamon stick
2 star anise, left whole
4 dried apricots (preferably California),
    chopped
4 prunes, chopped
2 dates, pitted and chopped
½ cup mixed fresh berries (blueberries,
    blackberries, raspberries)
¼ cup cranberries or lingonberries
½ teaspoon minced lime zest
3 sprigs fresh thyme
Juice of ½ orange
2 tablespoons sherry vinegar
1 tablespoon Dijon or other spicy mustard
Kosher salt and freshly ground black pepper

1. Place venison chops in a mixing bowl or a large zippered plastic bag. Add canola oil and gin, and mix to coat chops well. Cover bowl or seal bag and refrigerate for 24 hours. Remove from refrigerator 15 minutes before cooking.

2. In a large sauté pan over medium heat, combine olive oil and brown sugar. Stir to dissolve sugar slightly. Add shallot, garlic, ginger, cinnamon stick, and star anise. Sauté until shallot softens, about 2 minutes. Add apricots, prunes, and dates. Sauté for 1 minute. Add fresh berries, cranberries, lime zest, and thyme. Mix well. Add orange juice and vinegar. Lower heat and simmer until liquid is almost absorbed, about 5 minutes. Stir in mustard and season with salt and pepper to taste. Keep warm over very low heat.

3. Heat oven to 400 degrees. Heat a large iron skillet until very hot. Season venison chops with salt and pepper, then sear quickly in skillet, about 1 minute per side. Place skillet in oven and roast, about 3 or 4 minutes for rare, 5 or 6 minutes for medium-rare. Remove chops to a cutting board, cover with aluminum foil, and let rest for 5 minutes.

4. To serve, spoon chutney onto each of 4 plates. Thinly slice venison chops parallel to bone and place, fanned out, over chutney. Serve immediately.

Yield: 4 servings
Time: 40 minutes, plus 24 hours of refrigeration

BRINE DOES THE TRICK FOR SWEDISH DUCK CONFIT

So many of the curing and preserving techniques persist today less for their original purposes than because we've come to admire the flavors these processes impart. That's particularly true of preserved duck, which gains a delicate complexity during the process. Most people know cured duck as duck confit, which is accomplished in the traditional French way by rubbing dry salt on the duck. I prefer the quick Swedish method of curing duck in brine. You combine water with enough salt so that an egg will float in the water, add the duck, and in a few hours the meat is cured.

For this dish, salt-cured duck, I've done just the tender duck breasts. After the breasts are brined, I sauté them to brown the skin and warm the meat through. This is probably the trickiest part of the whole recipe. The duck is placed skin side down in an iron skillet and cooked over very gentle heat so that the fat renders out while the skin crisps, but not one before the other. The secret is to finish the duck in the oven so that it heats through without the edges drying out or the skin burning.

Once sautéed, cured duck breasts can be treated just like fresh duck breasts. Slice them and lay them over a warm salad, serve them with sautéed potatoes or a vegetable puree, or as my grandmother would have served them: with pickled beets or pickled mushrooms.

During the winter, cured duck breast is delicious when paired with root vegetables because saltiness and sweetness go so well together. Here I've stretched the definition of a risotto to apply the term to root vegetables rather than rice. By finely dicing any combination of celery root, carrots, parsnips, rutabagas, yams, sweet potatoes, and turnips, and cooking them so that they are very tender, you get a confetti of vegetables that look much like risotto on the plate. In the restaurant we puree some of the vegetables and mix the puree into the cooked diced vegetables to bind them and also to play up the illusion of creaminess. It's extra work but worth trying if you have time. The vegetables should be served like risotto: mounded into small hills as a prop for the fanned slices of duck.

The salinity and the richness of the duck against the sourness of the balsamic reduction, moderated by the sweetness from the vegetables and apple, makes for a careful, delicate balance—Swedish food in a nutshell.

SALT-CURED DUCK

1½ cups kosher salt
2 whole boneless duck breasts with skin
Root Vegetable Risotto (see recipe below)

1. In a deep mixing bowl, combine 2 quarts water with salt. An egg should be able to float in water. If not, add more salt until it does. Immerse duck breasts in solution. Place a piece of plastic wrap over bowl and a small plate over wrap to weight duck so it is completely submerged. Refrigerate for 6 hours to cure duck.

2. Preheat oven to 400 degrees. Remove duck breasts from solution and pat dry with paper towels. Place an iron skillet over medium-low heat. Lay duck breasts skin side down and cook until skin is crisp and browned, about 12 to 15 minutes. Transfer to a baking sheet, skin side down, and bake for 3 to 4 minutes. Reserve fat in skillet for preparing root vegetable risotto. Remove duck from oven, slice thinly on diagonal, and keep warm until ready to serve. Prepare root vegetable risotto.

3. Place vegetables in center of a serving plate. Drizzle reduced vinegar from risotto recipe around vegetables. Arrange sliced salt-cured duck in a fan over vegetables and serve.

Yield: 4 servings
Time: 6½ hours, including 6 hours of refrigeration

ROOT VEGETABLE RISOTTO

¼ cup extra-virgin olive oil
½ cup canola oil
2 carrots, peeled and cut into ¼-inch dice
1 small beet, peeled and cut into ¼-inch dice
1 small rutabaga, peeled and cut into ¼-inch dice
1 parsnip, peeled and cut into ¼-inch dice
2 small potatoes (such as red waxy), peeled and cut into ¼-inch dice
5 cloves garlic, peeled
2 shallots, minced
1 apple, peeled and cut into ¼-inch dice
Kosher salt and freshly ground black pepper
2 tablespoons port wine
¼ cup chicken broth
1 tablespoon butter
2 tablespoons grated Parmesan cheese
½ cup balsamic vinegar

1. Heat oils in a large, well-seasoned cast-iron or nonstick sauté pan over medium-high heat until a bread cube added to oil browns in 30 seconds. Add carrots, beet, rutabaga, parsnip, potatoes, and garlic. Fry until barely tender, 3 to 4 minutes. Remove to a plate lined with paper towels.

2. Place iron skillet with duck fat over medium-high heat. Add vegetables, shallots, and apple. Season with salt and pepper to taste. Sauté, stirring, for 2 minutes. Add wine and broth. Reduce until liquid has evaporated. When vegetables are browned and tender, remove from heat. Stir in butter and cheese. Cover and keep warm.

3. In a small saucepan over medium-low heat, simmer vinegar for 2 or 3 minutes, until syrupy and reduced to about 2 tablespoons.

Yield: 4 to 6 servings
Time: 30 minutes

STEAMING, THE PERFECT METHOD FOR SEA BASS

For some fish, steaming is just about always the perfect choice. I'm thinking especially of fillets of fish with particularly clean flavors like black sea bass and halibut. You want to treat them delicately, condense their natural flavor, keep them pure. But I do want to add some flavoring to my steamed fish, of course—flavoring of the gentle, aromatic sort.

Frequently, I'll use a bamboo steamer. But if I'm going to steam black sea bass fillets in a skillet, as is the case with this recipe, I usually use a layer of seasonings, like shallots, garlic, ginger, and herbs, in the bottom of the pan to enhance the fish and to serve as a bed to keep it out of the liquid, where it would begin to poach rather than steam. Whole fish can be steamed or poached, of course, but fillets tend to lose their firmness when they are immersed in liquid.

In this recipe I've used white wine as the steaming liquid, an aromatic touch that complements the sweetness of the fish. But you could also turn to fish stock, vermouth, or just water. I bring the liquid to a boil on the range to give the steaming process a jump-start, then transfer the skillet to a hot oven to finish the steaming.

The sauce for the sea bass is a very simple warmed juice. It starts with the beets of my Scandinavian background. But their natural sugar is a bit too strong, so I cut it with the acid of orange and lime. I soften and thicken the juice slightly by whisking in some butter. The sauce is subtle and remains in the background, as it should.

Then, to provide some contrast to the bright red juice and white fish, I sauté fresh greens, like Swiss chard, and stir in cubes of beet. Each fish fillet is laid atop a bed of greens surrounded with the sauce. The vivid colors and precise, elegant presentation suggest a Japanese approach. It resonates with Japanese cooking on another level, too: All the flavors are completely dependent on the quality of the raw ingredients. Inferior ingredients have nowhere to hide.

OVEN-STEAMED BLACK SEA BASS WITH WARM CITRUS-BEET JUICE

3 shallots
2 tablespoons extra-virgin olive oil
2 medium red beets, peeled and cut into $\frac{1}{4}$-inch dice
Juice of 2 oranges
Juice of 1 lime
Kosher salt and freshly ground black pepper
2 sprigs fresh thyme
5 white peppercorns
4 5-ounce fillets black sea bass or Chilean sea bass
$\frac{1}{4}$ cup white wine
2 cloves garlic, chopped
12 ounces fresh Swiss chard
1 sprig fresh mint
4 tablespoons butter

1. Preheat oven to 400 degrees. Finely chop 1 shallot. In a small saucepan over medium heat, combine 1 tablespoon oil with chopped shallot and beets. Cover pan and simmer until beets begin to soften at edges, 2 to 3 minutes. Add orange and lime juices, and salt and pepper to taste. Simmer until beets are soft, about 6 to 8 minutes. Using a slotted spoon, remove beet-shallot mixture to a small bowl, reserving cooking liquid in pan.

2. Roughly chop remaining shallots and spread over bottom of a large cast-iron skillet, along with thyme and peppercorns. Season fish fillets with salt and pepper to taste, and place, flesh side down, over shallots. Sprinkle wine over

fish and cover pan loosely with aluminum foil. Place skillet over high heat and cook until wine begins to boil.

3. Transfer skillet, still covered with foil, to oven. Steam fish until flesh is opaque and flakes when pressed with a fork, about 5 to 7 minutes.

4. While fish is steaming, place a large sauté pan over medium-high heat. Heat remaining 1 tablespoon oil and add garlic. Sauté until lightly browned, about 1 minute. Add Swiss chard, mint, and 3 tablespoons beet cooking liquid. Toss until chard is wilted, about 1 minute. Add reserved beet-shallots mixture to chard and toss to mix. Season with salt and pepper to taste.

5. Warm remaining beet cooking liquid over medium heat. Whisk in butter 1 tablespoon at a time. Sauce should thicken slightly. Season to taste with salt.

6. To serve, make a bed of chard on each of 4 plates. Place a fillet on top and pour sauce around chard. Serve immediately.

Yield: 4 servings
Time: 35 minutes

SWEDISH MEATBALLS TEAR OFF THEIR GLASSES AND BURST INTO SONG

Nearly every cuisine has a traditional dish involving cooked ground meat. There are French pâté, American meat loaf, Chinese dumplings, and, of course, Italian meatballs in red sauce. They are loved, even revered. Sweden's meatballs in gravy have become, it seems to me, the only example that is actually reviled—the dreaded dish of wedding buffets around the world. I find this disrepute rankling, and I've tried, with my own approach to the sauce, to give this maligned meatball enough of a twist to restore its charms.

The Swedish meatball is always distinguished by a touch of sweetness. In Sweden we add beet syrup to the meat mixture of ground beef, veal, and pork, but here in New York I use honey or corn syrup, which are more readily available. The meatball is held together by a bit of egg and bread crumbs.

Most Swedish meatballs are so basic that they vary little from cook to cook. If they are too dense, the cook may have added too many bread crumbs. A heavy-handed cook might make them too salty or too sweet, of course, but that's about all that can go wrong. Traditionally, the sauce leans on veal stock and cream.

But here's my rescue attempt. In an adventurous mood I prepared a novel sauce of red peppers, pickled plums, and plum sauce—spicy and tart, very far from bland. And to my mind it turns those weary Swedish meatballs into an exciting dish. The red peppers must be cooked to mellow their bitter aftertaste. Shallots and chopped pickled plums simmer with the peppers, and then chicken broth and some cream are added. Plum sauce, to taste, finishes the dish. The more plum sauce you add, the more tart the sauce will be. Don't be afraid to edge the sauce toward the high-flavor end of the spectrum as a counterpoint to the understated meatballs.

For dinner serve the meatballs with bread-and-

butter pickles and mashed potatoes, followed by a salad. It won't seem stodgy, I promise. It will warm your heart.

SWEDISH MEATBALLS WITH SPICY
PLUM SAUCE

½ cup fine dry bread crumbs
¾ cup heavy cream
1½ tablespoons olive oil
1 medium yellow onion, minced
⅔ cup ground beef
⅔ cup ground veal
⅔ cup ground pork
2 tablespoons honey
1 large egg
Kosher salt and freshly ground black pepper
3 tablespoons butter
1 large shallot, minced
½ red bell pepper, minced
6 pickled plums, pitted and minced
2 cups chicken broth
¼ cup plus 2 tablespoons plum sauce

1. In a small bowl, combine bread crumbs and ½ cup cream. Stir with fork until smooth. Set aside. Heat oil in a small sauté pan over medium heat. Add onion and sauté until softened but not browned, about 5 minutes.

2. In a large bowl, combine beef, veal, pork, honey, cooked onion, and egg. Season with salt and pepper to taste. Add bread crumb–cream mixture to meat and mix well. With wet hands (to keep meat from sticking) shape a meatball the size of a golf ball. If meat is too soft to shape, more bread crumbs may be added to mixture. Make about 24 meatballs and place on a plate brushed with water.

3. In a large skillet over medium-high heat, melt butter and add meatballs. Sauté, browning on all sides, until cooked through, about 7 minutes. Remove to a plate and discard fat from skillet.

4. Return skillet to heat and add shallot, bell pepper, and plums. Sauté until softened and lightly browned. Add broth and remaining ¼ cup cream. Stir in plum sauce and season to taste with salt and pepper. Add meatballs to sauce and simmer over medium heat until sauce thickens slightly and meatballs are heated through, about 5 minutes. Serve.

Yield: 4 to 6 servings
Time: 45 minutes

DIANE FORLEY

Diane Farley is the chef and owner of the Manhattan restaurant Verbena, where she was photographed. These columns were written with William Grimes.

A SINGLE VEGETABLE, A CASCADE OF ASSOCIATIONS

This dish got its start when my eye fell on some particularly fine-looking zucchini (that's how a lot of my dishes begin, with a single vegetable prompting a cascade of associations). That beautiful zucchini pointed me in the direction of the Mediterranean—and couscous.

The classic couscous of North Africa, the south of France, or the Middle East revolves around zucchini and also carrots or string beans. These are soup vegetables, too, of course, and in reaching for a twist of my own, I decided to invert the idea of couscous, making it a garnish for a vegetable soup rather than the base for other ingredients, which it usually is. To one experienced in Mediterranean cuisines, all the flavors of this soup would be familiar and in harmony and yet also entertaining in a somewhat surprising reformulation.

For this dish Israeli couscous is the key. Couscous is pasta—semolina—although because of its tiny shape, it doesn't usually look like it. Its pastalike characteristics are most apparent in Israeli couscous, which is atypically large, almost the size of a BB pellet, and works much better here than finer varieties, which are apt to turn mushy in soup.

Now here's the key: Toasting the couscous, which seals in the starch and reinforces the exterior, allowing it to absorb liquid without falling apart. Toasting also caramelizes the starch for a sweeter, nuttier flavor. This is actually a second toasting because Israeli couscous is lightly oven-dried and is usually sold as "toasted." If you can't find Israeli couscous, you can substitute angel-hair pasta, cut into half-inch lengths.

Turmeric is sweet and spicy, with an almost mustardlike bite, and really brings out the sweetness of the zucchini. It can be overpowering, so it has to be used carefully. Rosemary, also a traditional Mediterranean flavor, is zucchini's frequent companion, and I rely on it here.

ZUCCHINI SOUP

2 allspice berries
8 coriander seeds
10 black peppercorns
1 sprig rosemary
2 tablespoons olive oil
1 large onion, coarsely chopped
(about 1½ cups)
4 medium zucchini, cut into 1-inch dice
(about 6 cups)
5 cups chicken or vegetable stock
Toasted Israeli Couscous (see recipe below)
⅛ teaspoon nutmeg
Salt and pepper to taste

1. Make a sachet: Place allspice, coriander, peppercorns, and rosemary in center of 6-inch-square cheesecloth. Fold to make a triangle, roll folded side, and tie ends together. Set aside.

2. Heat oil in a 4-quart saucepan. Add onion and sauté over medium heat until translucent, about 8 minutes. Add zucchini and cook until softened, about 10 minutes. Add sachet to saucepan and cover with 4 cups stock. Simmer until vegetables are quite soft, about 15 minutes. Let cool slightly. As soon as stock starts to simmer, begin making Israeli couscous.

3. Remove sachet. Puree stock and vegetables in a blender in batches. Season with nutmeg, salt, and pepper. If soup is too thick (like potato soup as opposed to tomato soup), dilute with remaining stock. Add couscous, stir, and serve immediately.

Yield: 4 to 6 servings
Time: 1 hour

TOASTED ISRAELI COUSCOUS

1 tablespoon butter
1 tablespoon finely chopped shallot
½ cup Israeli toasted pasta (couscous)
1 teaspoon turmeric
1 cup chicken stock or water

1. Melt butter in a 2-quart saucepan. Add shallot and stir to coat with butter. Cook over low heat until softened, about 5 minutes.

2. Add couscous and brown lightly, stirring with a wooden spoon to keep from burning, about 5 to 7 minutes. Add turmeric, cook for 1 minute, and then add stock or water. Bring liquid to a boil, lower heat, and cover. Cook for 15 to 20 minutes. Remove from heat and let sit for 10 minutes.

Yield: 4 to 6 servings
Time: 30 minutes

LEMONY RICE, WITH BODY

I wanted to make a different kind of risotto to serve with fish, one that wasn't weighed down with a lot of eggs, butter, and cream. I wanted a lemony rice with a little bit of body. Instead of merely flavoring it with lemon, I aimed for a saucelike base to hold the rice together.

In a moment of free association, I thought of avgolemono, the traditional Greek soup that's thickened with lemon and eggs. It turned out to be the perfect solution. The egg yolk binds the rice, and the lemon complements the fish. What's important is that you add egg and lemon off the heat; otherwise the egg will curdle. This is an excellent rice dish with all kinds of fish—salmon and halibut come immediately to mind—but it is perfect with skate, a sweet fish that matches up well with sharp, briny flavors like lemon or capers.

My version has a more porridgelike consistency than traditional risotto, so you can afford to overcook it by a few minutes. It can also be prepared ahead of time: Remove it from the stove after two cups of the chicken stock have been absorbed and resume the cooking later.

The texture of skate is unique. It shreds like crabmeat and has the sweetness of crabmeat, but it's definitely a fish in flavor. It's the first fish I ever caught, when I was eight, fishing on Long Island Sound. When it came out of the water, wings flapping and tail twitching, I thought it was some kind of monster. These days I buy it, of course, already filleted and skinless. Be sure to get a relatively thick wing so the fish holds together well in the pan.

To sear skate properly, be sure the pan is quite hot; the skate should slip back and forth on the oil when you give the pan a shake. If it does stick, don't touch it until it is seared. Then use a flexible slotted spatula to loosen the fish gently and flip it.

LEMON RISOTTO

2 tablespoons olive oil
1¼ cups coarsely chopped onion
2 cups Arborio rice
6 cups chicken stock
1 tablespoon salt
½ teaspoon freshly ground black pepper
Finely grated zest of 2 lemons
Juice of 2 lemons
3 eggs
2 tablespoons chilled unsalted butter, cut in small pieces, optional

1. Heat oil in a 2½- to 3-quart heavy-bottomed saucepan over medium heat. Add onion and cook until translucent, about 8 minutes. With a wooden spoon, stir in rice, taking care that grains are coated.

2. Stir in 2 cups stock. Increase heat slightly, bring to a boil, and simmer until rice has absorbed most of stock, 7 to 8 minutes. Stir occasionally to prevent rice from sticking. Add salt and pepper and 2 more cups stock. Stir until liquid is once again nearly absorbed, 7 to 8 minutes longer. Add remaining 2 cups stock and lemon zest, and cook about 3 minutes. (Once rice has been added, risotto should cook about 20 minutes total. The third and final addition of stock should not be fully absorbed, and mixture should be soupy rather than thick and creamy.) Remove from heat.

3. In a small bowl, whisk together lemon juice, eggs, and chilled butter pieces. Whisk a small amount (about ½ cup) of hot rice mixture into egg mixture. Pour egg mixture into rice, stirring constantly, and return pan to low heat. Cook, stirring constantly to prevent curdling,

until rice takes on a thick, creamy consistency, just a minute or so. Serve immediately with sautéed skate.

Yield: 4 servings
Time: 40 minutes

SAUTÉED SKATE

2 skate wings, about 10 ounces each, skin
    and bone removed
Salt and freshly ground black pepper to taste
2 tablespoons olive oil
1 tablespoon unsalted butter
Lemon risotto (see recipe above)

1. While lemon risotto is cooking, wash skate wings, cut in half, and pat dry. Season on both sides with salt and pepper.

2. When risotto is moments from being done, heat oil and butter over medium-high heat in a 12-inch skillet. When foam subsides, add skate, top side down (top side has no membrane), and sauté about 3 minutes. Turn and sauté a minute or so longer.

3. To serve, place a serving of lemon risotto in middle of plate and a portion of sautéed skate on top of it.

Yield: 4 servings
Time: 10 minutes

UPDATING MOTHER'S ROLLED SOUFFLÉ

This is a dish from my childhood, one of those home-entertaining concoctions from the 1960s, but I tweaked it. When my mother served a rolled soufflé—a rectangle of airy baked egg formed into the shape of a jelly roll—it was filled with chopped spinach and ricotta cheese. I wanted to re-create it in a more refined way, with the spinach smooth rather than chopped, and flavored with tarragon and fresh pot herbs, or soft herbs, that work well as vegetables or cooked greens.

Spinach is the binder, the neutral ingredient that stretches the herbs. This puree is sweet and sharp. You get sweetness and a mintlike quality from the tarragon, and an oniony counterpoint from the chives. The smoothness of the puree allows the herbs to infuse the soufflé. Since the puree is intensely flavored, you get only a little of it.

The roll is almost like a soufflé omelet, and it goes really well with greens, allowing them to be the primary actors. I also wanted a soufflé with some longevity; a real soufflé has to be served right away. This has more staying power. It won't fall, and you can keep it overnight and reheat it, either by steaming or baking. It won't settle, and it retains its lightness.

Semolina will add a little flavor and texture. I used it originally because I also made this as a corn soufflé, with fresh corn in the mix. You can serve it with sautéed baby vegetables. In spring I sauté English peas, Bibb lettuce, and leeks in butter, chicken stock, and herbs. In summer I serve it with corn succotash: lima beans, corn, yellow and green squash, and pearl onions. Another idea: Make a sauce by adding butter and chicken stock to some of the filling. It's a great light dish for lunch.

There are a couple of things to remember: Be sure to add the herbs in the blender; otherwise they turn black.

Rolling is the tricky part. You cannot let the soufflé cool, and once you begin rolling, you cannot stop. No hesitation!

ROLLED SOUFFLÉ

Nonstick baking spray
8 tablespoons (1 stick) butter
¾ cup all-purpose flour
⅓ cup semolina (also sold as pasta flour)
2½ cups milk
1 cup heavy cream
10 large eggs, separated
⅛ teaspoon cayenne pepper
Salt and freshly ground black pepper
½ cup grated Parmesan cheese
¼ teaspoon cream of tartar
1 tablespoon sugar, optional
Spinach Filling (see recipe below)

1. Preheat oven to 375 degrees. Line a half-sheet (17 by 12-inch) jelly roll pan with parchment paper and coat with nonstick baking spray. In a large (4-quart) saucepan over medium heat, melt butter. Using a wooden spoon, mix in flour and semolina, stirring constantly for 3 minutes. Stir in a small amount of milk to thin and smooth mixture. Add remaining milk and cream, beating with a whisk until smooth. Remove pan from heat and slowly pour in egg yolks while whisking vigorously. Whisk for 2 minutes. Season with cayenne, salt, and pepper to taste. Stir in cheese and set aside.

2. Using an electric mixer on low speed, beat egg whites until frothy. Add cream of tartar and sugar, increase speed to medium-high, and continue to beat just until very soft peaks form when beater is lifted. Gently but thoroughly fold whites into batter, one-third at a time. Pour onto parchment-lined sheet, filling pan three-quarters full. Bake for 15 minutes, turn pan, and bake 5 minutes more, or until surface is golden brown.

3. Run a knife around inside edge of baking pan to free soufflé. Place a sheet of waxed paper or cotton cloth over baking sheet and invert onto a counter. Remove pan and parchment paper. Spread spinach filling to within 1 inch of edges; lift the short end of waxed paper or cloth until end curves, then roll soufflé into a log shape. Transfer, seam side down, to a plate, cut into 8 slices, and serve.

Yield: 4 main-course servings
Time: 1 hour

SPINACH FILLING

8 ounces fresh spinach
1 tablespoon butter
Salt
2 tablespoons chopped fresh tarragon
4 tablespoons chopped fresh chives
4 tablespoons chopped fresh flat-leaf parsley
Freshly ground black pepper

1. Wash spinach and drain but do not dry. In a large (4-quart) saucepan over low heat, melt butter and add spinach and ½ teaspoon salt. Cover and steam until wilted, 3 to 5 minutes.

2. Transfer spinach and its liquid to a blender or food processor while hot. Add tarragon, chives, and parsley. Puree until smooth and season with salt and pepper to taste.

Yield: About 1½ cups
Time: 15 minutes

FROM STEM TO TIP, COAXING OUT THE FLAVOR OF ASPARAGUS

Asparagus is the sort of ingredient that really should be eaten in its prime—from late April through May. This dish is a good example of how to use all the parts of a vegetable, something that home cooks do not always do. Most people cut off the bottom ends of the asparagus and throw them away. They also discard the peelings. But there's a lot of flavor in there, or in any stem you can think of, for that matter. The stem of an artichoke, for example, is fibrous but very flavorful and can be used in soups, sauces, and vinaigrettes.

This dish layers asparagus flavors, using the pureed ends in the vinaigrette for an intensifying effect, while at the same time imparting a mild character to the dressing. I used grapeseed oil because it has a neutral taste, much more so than peanut oil or soy oil, and I don't want the oil to compete with the other flavors in a dish. It's important to strain the vinaigrette, to remove the fibers from the woody part of the asparagus. A crumble of egg yolk makes a bright garnish. Traditionally, egg sauces like hollandaise have been paired with asparagus because it's a watery vegetable that can take a rich sauce.

I use a lot of salt when cooking the asparagus because it doesn't get seasoned again. I want to get the salt into the asparagus to give it a little zing. When it's tender, it's plunged into ice water to arrest the cooking; I put a tablespoon of salt in the ice water, too, because when you shock a vegetable in ice water and it sits there, some of the flavor leaches out, so you want to compensate with a little seasoning.

ASPARAGUS VINAIGRETTE

2 teaspoons minced shallots
½ cup sherry vinegar
1 pound jumbo asparagus
Salt
1 large bunch basil, leaves only
1 tablespoon Dijon mustard
1 cup grapeseed oil
Freshly ground black pepper
2 hard-boiled eggs
1 head frisee lettuce
1 bunch chervil, leaves only
4 ounces prosciutto or serrano ham

1. In a small saucepan over medium heat, combine shallots and vinegar. Bring to a boil and reduce liquid by half. Remove from heat and reserve.

2. Peel bottom 2 inches of asparagus stalks, reserving peelings. Fill a medium saucepan with water, add 2 tablespoons salt, and bring to a boil. Fill a large bowl with ice water and 1 tablespoon salt, and place near stove. Add asparagus peelings to boiling water and blanch for 3 minutes, then transfer to ice water. Add basil to boiling water and blanch until green color brightens, about 45 seconds, then transfer to ice water. Cook asparagus in boiling water until quite tender when squeezed at the ends, about 5 minutes. Transfer to ice water.

3. Remove asparagus stalks from water and drain well. Cut off bottom 2 inches of stalks and place in a food processor or blender. Reserve asparagus stalks. Remove peelings and basil from water, drain, and add to food processor. Add mustard and vinegar-shallot mixture. With processor running, pour in oil in a thin stream. Season mixture with salt and pepper to taste, and strain

through a fine sieve or chinois, discarding solids.

4. To assemble salad: Remove yolks from hard-boiled eggs, press through a sieve, and set aside. In a large mixing bowl, combine lettuce, chervil, and vinaigrette. Cut ¼-inch rounds from bottom 4 inches of asparagus stalks and add to mixing bowl. Arrange asparagus spears on a serving plate or individual plates. Place mixed greens on top of asparagus. Arrange prosciutto slices around greens and sprinkle sieved egg yolks on top.

Yield: 6 servings
Time: 40 minutes

A LIGHTER VARIATION ON A RICH FRENCH THEME

Spring begs for light fruit desserts. This variation on a traditional dacquoise, which usually has layers of buttercream, is much lighter, using no flour. It's very efficient, too: The egg yolks that are separated and set aside while making the baked meringue disks are used in the sabayon, and so is the poaching liquid for the pears. There's no waste.

In a twist, I've added almond paste to the poaching liquid, which flavors and perfumes the pears. There's a fine play of textures, with the meringue giving the dessert a nice crunch, and the sabayon adding a wonderful creaminess.

There are a few little tricks to this recipe. Many sabayon recipes call for adding wine directly to the egg yolks, which is easier. But my way, heating the eggs in a double boiler, or bain-marie, lightens the yolks and also cooks them, an important point for people worried about the health risks of raw eggs.

Remove the meringue from the oven while it still rebounds slightly when you poke it softly, because it will still dry out a bit while cooling. If the parchment paper sticks to it, rub a damp napkin or paper towel back and forth over the stuck part until it loosens. Cut out the meringue rounds before the meringue cools completely, because the meringue can crack.

Adding sugar to the almonds when you grind them is also a bit of a trick. When the almonds warm up, they start to release their oils, and if the sugar isn't there to absorb them, the almonds tend to clump.

This is a versatile dessert. You can make the meringue ahead of time and store it in a tightly sealed container. You can also substitute peaches for the pears, or add a small handful of seasonal berries to the plate. Hazelnuts—almost any nut, in fact—can be used instead of almonds.

DACQUOISE WITH POACHED PEARS AND SABAYON

2 cups whole almonds

1¾ cups sugar

8 large eggs

4 cups white wine

¼ cup almond paste

1 vanilla bean, sliced in half lengthwise and seeds removed

1 orange, peeled and cut into 4 round slices

Juice of 1 lemon

1 cinnamon stick

2 pieces star anise

5 cloves

2 tablespoons grenadine, optional

3 Bartlett pears

1 cup heavy cream, whipped until stiff

1. To make dacquoise disks: Preheat oven to 250 degrees. Line a half-sheet (13 by 17-inch) baking pan with parchment paper.

2. Using a food processor, chop almonds with ⅓ cup sugar until finely ground. Separate eggs and place 8 whites in bowl of an electric mixer and 5 yolks in a small covered container. Refrigerate yolks until needed. Whip whites until soft peaks form, then gradually add ⅔ cup sugar. Continue to whip until whites are barely stiff. Fold in almond mixture. Pour into baking pan and bake until meringue is dry on surface but still slightly springy to touch, about 1 hour and 20 minutes. When meringue is baked, turn onto sheets of aluminum foil or waxed paper and remove parchment paper. Using a cookie cutter or glass, cut into twelve 4-inch rounds.

3. While meringue is baking, prepare poached pears: In a wide nonreactive saucepan (6 quarts or larger), combine wine and almond paste. With a wooden spoon, break paste into pieces. Add ½ cup sugar, vanilla bean, orange slices, lemon juice, cinnamon stick, star anise, cloves, and grenadine. Peel pears, cut in half, and remove cores with a melon-baller. Place in saucepan, cut side down, and put a clean cotton napkin over them to keep them submerged. Place pan over medium heat and bring to a simmer. Reduce heat to low and simmer until pears are cooked through, about 25 minutes. Remove cloth and place pears in a bowl until needed. Strain poaching liquid, retaining ½ cup for sabayon.

4. To make sabayon: Reheat poaching liquid if it has cooled. In a metal bowl, briefly beat egg yolks and remaining ¼ cup sugar. Fit bowl over a saucepan with about 1 inch boiling water. Continue to beat egg mixture by hand until it thickens. Transfer to an electric mixer and beat at medium speed while adding ½ cup poaching liquid in a thin stream. Beat until mixture has cooled, about 5 to 7 minutes. Fold in whipped cream.

5. To assemble: Place a dacquoise disk on each of 6 serving plates. Place a small amount of sabayon on each disk, top with a pear half, and add more sabayon. Lean a second disk against pear. Serve immediately.

Yield: 6 servings

Time: 2 hours

A VEGETARIAN VERSION OF STUFFED CABBAGE

Stuffed cabbage is a dish you encounter all over the world in different forms. It doesn't have any one ethnic origin or base; every country or region adds its own spices and somehow makes the dish its own. In the Middle East you find cabbage stuffed with rice and lamb, and seasoned with cumin and coriander. In Hungary it's spiced with paprika and dill. It's a humble dish, but satisfying.

Almost always, meat is used to hold the stuffing together, but I wanted to make a vegetarian version. The trick was to come up with a meatlike consistency. I hit on the idea of using ground barley as a paste to hold together a filling made of barley grains and sautéed cabbage. The filling is substantial. Barley is a full-flavored, highly nutritious grain with a chewy texture. Toasting gives it a very nutty flavor, but the dish requires a piquant sauce to bring it to life.

There are a few things that can make cabbage taste good. One is a nice caramelization, which we have in this dish. The sliced cabbage filling is sautéed with onions until it browns well and brings out the natural sweetness in the vegetable. You can also use condiments, like onion, caraway seed, mustard, or spices. Anything pickled works well, too, which is why I decided on a tangy sweet-and-sour sauce of tomatoes, orange, honey, and vinegar.

When you make the filling, you can play around, adding mushrooms, carrots, celery, squash, or chopped green beans. This dish can be served as an entree or in smaller portions as a side dish with chicken or fish.

BARLEY-FILLED CABBAGE IN PICKLED TOMATO SAUCE

7 tablespoons olive oil
1 large onion, diced
42 ounces canned crushed tomatoes
1 orange, peeled and chopped
1 cup honey
½ cup apple cider
½ cup cider vinegar
1½ cups raw barley
Salt and freshly ground black pepper
1 extra-large cabbage head
1 onion, thinly sliced
1½ teaspoons mustard seeds
2 teaspoons Dijon mustard
¼ cup champagne vinegar or cider vinegar
2 cups chicken or vegetable stock

1. Prepare pickled tomato sauce: In a medium saucepan, heat 2 tablespoons oil over low heat. Add diced onion and cook until translucent. Add tomatoes, orange, honey, apple cider, and cider vinegar. Simmer until thickened, about 40 minutes.

2. While sauce is simmering, prepare barley: In a medium skillet, heat 2 tablespoons oil over low heat. Add raw barley and toast, stirring constantly, until it is lightly browned and has a nutty aroma, about 5 minutes. Cool in pan. Remove ½ cup barley and grind in a spice grinder until powdery. Place ground barley in a small saucepan and add 1½ cups water. Place over medium-low heat and cook, stirring constantly, until mixture has consistency of porridge, about 7 minutes. Season with salt and pepper to taste, and set aside.

3. Add 3 cups water to barley in skillet and bring to a boil over high heat. Reduce heat to low and simmer, uncovered, until barley is tender and

water has evaporated, about 20 minutes. Remove from heat and set aside.

4. Remove 12 outer leaves from cabbage, being careful not to tear them. Set aside. Thinly slice remaining cabbage to make about 2 quarts. In a large (14-inch or larger) sauté pan, heat 3 tablespoons oil over medium-high heat. Add sliced cabbage and sliced onion, and sauté until well browned, about 15 minutes. Stir in mustard seeds and mustard. Add champagne vinegar and stock, and stir well to deglaze. Cook until cabbage is soft and liquid has evaporated, about 15 minutes. Add both barley mixtures to cabbage and toss to blend thoroughly.

5. Bring a large pot of salted water to a boil and set aside a bowl of ice water and a 9- by 12-inch baking pan. Blanch whole cabbage leaves in boiling water until tender, 3 to 4 minutes, then transfer to ice water. Preheat oven to 375 degrees.

6. To assemble cabbage rolls: Spread half of tomato mixture in baking pan. Place a single leaf on a work surface and trim off thick stem. Place about ⅓ cup cabbage-barley filling in center, fold sides over, and roll up leaf. Place, seam side down, in baking pan. Repeat to make 8 rolls, using extra leaves to patch tears or to extend leaves that are too small. Top rolls with remaining tomato sauce and cover pan with aluminum foil. Bake until rolls are tender, about 50 minutes.

Yield: 4 servings
Time: 2 hours

MILLET-STUFFED CHICKEN, MIDDLE EASTERN SPICES

Even though people are trying to bring more grain into their diets, few of us actually cook with millet. It's still a grain that most people encounter as birdseed. But millet has a lot going for it. Millet has a mild, cornlike flavor, and it's packed with nutrients—the only grain that has more protein is quinoa. Millet also soaks up the flavor of a broth, which makes it ideal for this dish.

The other unfamiliar actor here is zaatar (pronounced ZAT-are), a mixture of powdered spices used widely in the Middle East to season grain salads, rub on fish, or sprinkle over flat breads with drizzlings of olive oil. Its formulation varies but usually includes thyme, hyssop, sesame seed, oregano, and sumac, with the sumac lending a distinct lemony tang. Here I use the zaatar in an unusual way, as the flavoring for a poaching broth, which turns a light olive green from the spices. I wanted to use it a little more subtly than rubbing it directly on the meat.

This is very light entree, almost a spa dish, with practically no fat at all. The poaching performs two functions: It imparts flavor and it helps keep the chicken moist. To reduce the fat even further, chicken stock can be substituted for the cream.

The main thing to remember in working with the mousse is to keep all the ingredients chilled; otherwise, the fat and the protein can separate, and the mousse can take on a grainy consistency. The same thing can happen if the poaching liquid is allowed to boil.

You can prepare the mousse up to a day in advance, and assemble and cook the dish at the last minute. Leftover mousse can be formed into a patty and sautéed in olive oil, or dropped into a broth to make soup dumplings.

CHICKEN STUFFED WITH TOASTED SESAME-MILLET MOUSSE IN ZAATAR BROTH

1 cup dried millet

8 ounces ground chicken

2¼ cups chicken stock or canned broth

¼ cup heavy cream

1 egg

2 tablespoons finely chopped chives

1 cup finely chopped parsley leaves

Pinch of ground cloves

Pinch of nutmeg

Salt and freshly ground black pepper

2 tablespoons toasted sesame seeds

4 whole boneless chicken breasts

¼ cup zaatar spice

Juice of 2 lemons

3 tablespoons butter, optional

1 pound fresh spinach, washed and trimmed
  of thick stems

1. In a small saucepan, combine millet and 3 cups water. Place over high heat and bring to a boil, then reduce heat to low. Simmer, partially covered, until millet is tender and water is absorbed, about 25 minutes. Set aside.

2. While millet is cooking, prepare mousse: Place ground chicken in a food processor and process until smooth, about 1 minute. While machine is running, add ¼ cup stock, cream, and egg. Transfer mousse to a bowl and add chives, parsley, cloves, and nutmeg, and salt and pepper to taste. Add millet and sesame seeds, and mix well. Refrigerate until chilled, 15 to 30 minutes.

3. Lay a chicken breast on a cutting board, cover with plastic wrap, and pound with a mallet until ¼ inch thick. Repeat with remaining breasts. Place ½ cup chilled filling toward one end of each breast and roll until closed. Tie with string at 1-inch intervals to create a sausage shape.

4. Preheat oven to 350 degrees. In a large (6-quart) casserole, combine remaining stock, zaatar spice, and 2 cups water. Bring to a boil over high heat. Remove from heat, place chicken rolls in casserole, and cover. Place casserole in oven and bake until a meat thermometer placed in center of a chicken roll reads 160 degrees, about 12 to 15 minutes.

5. Remove chicken to a platter, remove strings, and keep warm. Add lemon juice to broth in casserole and mix in butter, if desired. Season with salt and pepper to taste. Strain broth through a chinois or fine sieve and keep warm.

6. In a large pot over medium heat, combine spinach with ¼ cup water. Steam just until wilted, 5 to 7 minutes, then drain well. To serve, slice chicken into rounds, set on top of a bed of steamed spinach, and spoon broth over top.

Yield: 4 servings
Time: 1¼ hours

DANIEL BOULUD

Daniel Boulud is the chef and owner of the restaurant Daniel in Manhattan. He was photographed on Park Avenue, near the restaurant. These columns were written with Dorie Greenspan.

A LESSON IN BALANCE

This dish is a play on one I learned as an apprentice at Nandron, a two-star restaurant in Lyons, France, where it was a house specialty. It's a favorite of mine not just because it brings back memories of my hometown, but because it accomplishes what we so often strive for in cooking: a sense of counterpoint, striking just the right balance between mild and pungent. The mild part is the liver, rich and silky and luxurious in texture, and so subtle in flavor it is almost tasteless.

Calf's liver always needs a pick-me-up, and here it is brightened by the mustard in the crust. (Be sure to use a mustard so strong it makes your eyes water; it will lose some of its punch as it cooks.) There's additional pungency in the vinegar-glazed sweet-and-sour onions, and then just as the critical balance is about to go awry, it is restored by the bit of cream in the sauce that smooths, soothes, and pulls the dish together.

Beyond the choice of ingredients, the cut of the liver and the triple-cooking method of searing, roasting, and broiling elevate this recipe to the extraordinary. In order to sear the liver well and to give it a good crust, you need one large, thick block of meat. You may have to order this in advance from your butcher, but it's crucial because thin slices overcook before they are properly seared. The pan-searing followed by oven-roasting keeps the outside crusted and the inside juicy, giving the liver the feel of foie gras. The finishing touch is the quickly broiled mustard crust.

Since I'm always looking to build flavor in a dish, and this is especially true with liver, I stud the meat with sage; it is a way to infuse flavor in such a large cut. (You can use garlic or even truffles if you're feeling flush.) Then I add garlic and more sage to the roasting pan for another layer of flavor and serve the meat with garlic-scented spinach and thick wedges of red onions slowly braised in a mixture of sherry vinegar (for acidity) and aged balsamic vinegar (for spicy sweetness).

It may seem odd, but I use an electric knife in the

preparation of this dish, and so does every cook in my kitchen. It is great for anything delicate, anything with a crust, and anything as tender as this calf's liver.

MUSTARD-CRUSTED CALF'S LIVER WITH SWEET-AND-SOUR ONIONS

3 large red onions, peeled but with root end
   intact
3 tablespoons olive oil
⅓ cup sherry vinegar
2 tablespoons aged balsamic vinegar
8 large fresh sage leaves
Salt and freshly ground white pepper
3 tablespoons unsalted butter
1 shallot, peeled and finely diced
⅓ cup heavy cream
2 tablespoons Dijon mustard
1¾ pounds calf's liver, in one piece,
   skin removed
½ cup milk
Flour for dredging
5 cloves garlic, peeled and crushed
1½ pounds spinach, stemmed, center veins
   removed, well washed and dried
1½ teaspoons finely grated Parmesan cheese
1½ teaspoons fine bread crumbs

1. Preheat oven to 400 degrees. Cut each onion, from top to root, into 6 wedges. In a large (12-inch) ovenproof skillet over medium heat, heat 1 tablespoon oil. Add onions and sauté, turning as needed, until lightly browned, about 10 minutes. Reduce heat to low and cook 3 minutes more. Add 3 tablespoons sherry vinegar, balsamic vinegar, 1 sage leaf (chopped), and salt and pepper to taste. Transfer to oven and braise for 20 to 30 minutes, turning onions once or twice, until very tender.

2. In a small saucepan over medium heat, melt 1½ tablespoons butter. Pour 1 tablespoon into a small heatproof bowl and reserve. Add shallot to pan and sauté until translucent. Add remaining sherry vinegar and allow to evaporate. Add cream, boil for 2 minutes, and stir in 1 tablespoon mustard and salt and pepper to taste. Strain through a fine-mesh sieve into a serving bowl. Set aside and keep warm, or reheat gently before serving.

3. Cut 3 sage leaves into quarters. Make a small slit in liver and immediately insert a piece of sage with tip of knife. Continue to cut and fill a total of 12 slits, 3 slits each on the top, bottom, and 2 sides. Season liver with salt and pepper to taste, dip in milk, and dredge in flour, shaking off excess. Place a large ovenproof skillet over medium heat, add remaining 2 tablespoons oil, and sauté liver until evenly browned, about 3 minutes a side. Remove from heat and add 1 tablespoon butter, 4 whole sage leaves, and 3 cloves garlic. Remove onions from oven and set aside. Roast liver for 6 minutes, turning once.

4. While liver roasts, prepare spinach. Place a large sauté pan or deep pot over medium-high heat. Melt remaining ½ tablespoon butter and add remaining 2 cloves garlic, spinach, and salt and pepper to taste. Toss until spinach is wilted, about 5 minutes. Discard garlic and any liquid. Spoon spinach into center of a warm platter, surround with onions, and keep warm while you finish liver.

5. Preheat a broiler. Coat top of liver with remaining 1 tablespoon mustard. In a small bowl, combine cheese and bread crumbs, and pat onto mustard. Drizzle with reserved tablespoon of melted butter. Broil liver 6 inches from heat until crust is lightly browned, about 3 minutes. Remove from pan and, using an electric knife or

thin, sharp knife, cut crosswise on bias into 8 slices, each ½ inch thick. Place on bed of spinach, pour sauce over meat, and serve immediately.

Yield: 4 servings
Time: 1½ hours

~

MORELS AS GIVERS AND TAKERS

This is a dish that sings out "spring," marrying the mysterious, woodsy flavor of morels with the fresh, sweet flavors of the garden's early harvest. I'm partial to morels, and I put them on my menu the instant they're available. They have a very distinctive look—conical, bulbous, and honeycombed—and their spongy texture makes them perfect for anything with broth.

In fact, I think of morels as generous givers and takers: They take on some of the flavor of whatever they are cooked with while giving their own intriguing, musky flavor to the mix. These days I use morels from Oregon and always look for the largest ones, not because they are most flavorful (size and flavor are unrelated) but because they present possibilities. For instance, really large morels can be poached solo, then stuffed with the gnocchi mixture in this recipe and gently poached again.

Look for firm morels that have a faint, foresty aroma and a touch of natural moisture; too much moisture and they'll have an unpleasant damp-wood smell. And avoid any with dry stems and tips, a sign of age. If you can't find just-right morels, choose chanterelles or even oyster mushrooms for this preparation.

I use gnocchi for this dish because it shares so many taste and texture characteristics with morels: Both are tender, soft and spongy, mild and sweet. I flavor the gnocchi with pea shoot leaves because their light, rather refined taste keeps the dish's delicate balance.

Here the shoots are used two ways: pureed and mixed into the feather-light ricotta gnocchi, where they provide a subtle back flavor, and then added to the broth to tie up loose flavor ends. The base of the broth is vegetable or chicken stock. It is first used as the poaching liquid for the morels, then for a variety of spring vegetables, and finally for the gnocchi.

With the addition of each ingredient the broth gets richer, deeper, and more complex. I debated turning this dish into a soup—the broth is that good—but decided to keep the liquid to a minimum and give the spring vegetables the starring role. While you can tinker with the selection of vegetables, I think the dish should retain the root flavors and crunch of carrots and radishes, and the sweetness of fresh peas. But if you find ramps at the market, you can mince a small amount of them to stand in for the garlic. And if you find zucchini blossoms, they will make your entire trip worthwhile. I love this dish with a few petals added to the broth along with the gnocchi.

OREGON MORELS AND PEA-SHOOT GNOCCHI IN A LIGHT BROTH

3½ ounces pea shoot leaves, also called snow
    pea sprouts (from about 6 ounces shoots
    or sprouts)
¾ cup ricotta cheese, squeezed dry of excess
    moisture in a tea towel
⅓ cup (approximately) olive oil
2 tablespoons plus 1 teaspoon all-purpose
    flour
Salt and freshly ground white pepper
1 tablespoon unsalted butter
1 large shallot, peeled and finely diced
4 scallions, white and light green parts only,
    trimmed and cut on the bias into 1-inch
    pieces
1 sprig rosemary
2 long, thin carrots, peeled, trimmed, and
    cut on the bias into very thin slices
2 cloves garlic, peeled and thinly sliced
1½ cups (approximately) vegetable stock,
    chicken stock, or water
1 pound morels, ends trimmed, washed, and
    dried
1 cup fresh peas (from about 1½ pounds in
    the shell)
4 small pink French radishes, trimmed and
    cut into very thin rounds
1 tablespoon finely minced chives

1. Bring a medium-size pot of salted water to a boil and add 3 ounces pea shoot leaves. Cook until tender, 2 to 3 minutes, drain, and cool under cold running water. Press leaves between your palms to remove excess water, then thoroughly dry between paper towels. Put leaves, ricotta, and 3 tablespoons oil in a small food processor or blender and process until smooth. Add flour, salt, and pepper, and pulse just to blend. Taste and correct seasonings. Press this gnocchi dough through a sieve into a bowl.

2. Bring 1 quart water to a simmer, then add 1½ teaspoons salt. Using 2 teaspoons, make 1-inch-diameter gnocchi dumplings by picking up some dough on one spoon and, with the other, scraping it off and into the gently simmering water. Poach gnocchi in 3 batches, cooking each batch for 4 to 5 minutes. Carefully transfer gnocchi with a slotted spoon to a bowl of ice water; gnocchi are delicate and mousselike. When cold, use a slotted spoon to transfer gnocchi to a plate. Drizzle with a little oil, cover with plastic, and refrigerate until needed, or up to 4 hours.

3. In a medium sauté pan, melt butter over medium heat. Add shallot, scallions, and rosemary, and sauté until vegetables are translucent, 3 to 4 minutes. Add carrots, garlic, and 1½ cups stock, and simmer for 3 minutes. Add morels, salt, and pepper, and cook, covered, for 5 minutes. Uncover, add peas, and cook another 4 to 5 minutes. Stir in 1 tablespoon oil and salt and pepper. Check that liquid is at a very gentle simmer and add gnocchi. Heat gently for 3 minutes without stirring, then add radishes and remaining pea shoot leaves.

4. To serve, use a slotted spoon to transfer gnocchi and vegetables to shallow bowls. Taste broth and add more salt, pepper, stock, or oil if needed. Pour at least 1 tablespoon broth over each portion and sprinkle with chives.

Yield: 4 servings
Time: 1 hour

A TASTE OF SUMMER:
CORN AND LOBSTER

When the lobster season is upon us, I am powerfully drawn to the classic combination of sweet corn and the tenderest briny lobster. It is a pairing that I begin to work with in late spring and one that just gets better and better as the summer arrives and progresses into early fall. There is a problem early on, of course: the sweet corn part of the equation.

The way around this, oddly enough, is to use pallid polenta and boost its flavor with fresh corn until it is everything the dish calls for.

But first, there is the lobster. When I want to keep the purest, briniest lobster flavor, I boil it in nothing more than salt water, as I do in this essentially simple preparation: a bowl of polenta topped with warm lobster.

Because I'm going to reheat the lobster after boiling, I undercook it slightly in the first place. The lobster flavor I want here is going to come less from the prized meat than from the shells that usually get tossed into the trash. The shells are what will carry the lobster's flavor deep into the dish. I wipe them clean and add them to the seasoned stock in which the polenta cooks.

In this dish, it's the polenta that needs the biggest boost. To reinvigorate the dried ground corn, I give it a double dose of fresh corn: First, I scrape the juicy pulp from the cobs and save it to stir into the polenta, and then I boil the cobs in the liquid I use to cook the polenta, thereby transferring every bit of the fresh corn's flavor to the dried.

While traditionalists will insist on using long-cooking polenta, I use the instant variety because it produces a softer polenta, which is just what I'm after. No matter what kind you use, it is important to understand that you may have to adjust the amount of liquid. Keep the polenta at a gentle simmer and add more liquid (there is extra in this recipe) if it is thickening too much. You will definitely have to add more liquid

and maybe a tad more butter if, for convenience, you make the polenta ahead, cover it with plastic, and keep it warm over a pan of simmering water.

If you end up with leftovers, you're in for a treat. Mix the cooked lobster, scallions, and polenta together, line a baking dish with plastic wrap, pack the mixture into the dish, cover it with plastic, and chill overnight. The next day unmold the polenta (the plastic wrap makes this easy), dust it with some Parmesan cheese, and reheat it in a nonstick pan with a little olive oil. The outside will turn brown and crusty, but the inside will stay soft and moist. It is a dish that turns ritzy lobster into comfort food.

Salt

2 2-pound live hard-shelled lobsters

8 large ears of corn, shucked

4 cups whole milk

5 cloves garlic, peeled and crushed

2 shallots, peeled and thinly sliced

2 sprigs fresh rosemary

Freshly ground white pepper

3 tablespoons unsalted butter

Pinch of freshly grated nutmeg

1 cup instant polenta

1 tablespoon finely grated Parmesan cheese

6 scallions, trimmed and cut into 1½-inch
   lengths

1 tablespoon snipped chives

4 slices prosciutto, dried in a 250-degree
   oven for about 1 hour, or 4 slices well-
   cooked bacon, optional

1. Fill a large (10-quart or larger) pot three-quarters full of water. Add 1 tablespoon salt, place over high heat, cover, and bring to a boil. Add lobsters and boil for 7 minutes. Drain and cool lobsters under running water. Pull head shell from each and split it. Break remaining shell and pull out tail and claw meat, reserving shells. Devein and cut each tail into 5 medallions. Set lobster meat aside. Wipe shells, discarding any soft parts. Cut or break shells into small pieces and place in pot that held lobsters; set aside.

2. Run point of a chef's knife down center of each row of corn kernels. Working over a deep, wide bowl, use back of knife (or a small knife if you wish) to press down firmly on kernels to release as much pulp and liquid as possible. There should be about 1½ cups. Set aside. Add corn cobs to pot with lobster shells. Add milk, 2 cups water, 3 cloves garlic, shallots, and 1 sprig rosemary. Bring to a boil, lower heat, and simmer for 10 minutes. Season with salt and pepper to taste. Strain and reserve liquid; discard solids.

3. Pour 4 cups reserved liquid into a large (4- to 6-quart) saucepan. Add 2 tablespoons butter and nutmeg. Bring to a boil, then reduce heat to low. Add polenta in a fine, steady stream, whisking constantly. Simmer gently, stirring, for 5 minutes. Add reserved corn pulp and cook until polenta has consistency of loose mashed potatoes, about 5 minutes. If polenta is too dry or thick, add more liquid or butter as necessary. Stir in cheese and add salt and pepper to taste. Remove from heat and keep warm.

4. While polenta is cooking, place a medium skillet over medium heat and add remaining 1 tablespoon butter. Add scallions and remaining 2 cloves garlic and 1 sprig rosemary. Cover and cook until softened, 3 to 5 minutes. Add lobster, replace cover, and heat until lobster is hot, about 1 minute. Discard garlic and rosemary. Add chives and season to taste with salt and pepper.

5. To serve, spoon polenta into a large, warm serving bowl. Make an indentation in polenta and spoon in lobster. If using dried prosciutto or bacon, drape it over lobster. Serve immediately.

Yield: 4 servings
Time: 1¼ hours

CHICKEN THAT TAKES CODDLING

This recipe has never appeared on any of my menus. I created it on the spur of the moment thirteen years ago when John Fairchild, the publisher of Women's Wear Daily, *and Bill Blass, the clothing designer, came for lunch at Le Cirque. They asked for a simple chicken with robust flavor, and I've been making this dish for them each spring ever since, with a few changes here and there.*

When the order came into the kitchen, I decided to keep the chicken whole to show off its lustrous skin, but I also wanted to give it the depth of flavor I would get if I cut it up and cooked it on top of the stove, like a fricassee. I dug into the day's produce and came up with the perfect spring vegetables to go with the chicken: porcini mushrooms, tiny fingerling potatoes, artichokes, a head of garlic, and bulbs of Texas spring onions.

Although the dish is simple, it requires patience; each step must unfold at the right time and temperature. And it has to be babied.

I start with the chicken alone in the pan. (It should take up only a quarter of the pan. If you crowd the pan, the ingredients won't cook evenly.) I baste it often and listen to it pop, sputter, and splat, telling me it's browning and roasting. Then I add the vegetables in batches, stirring and basting and coaxing everything to brown, all the time keeping a close eye on the temperature. If the cooking is going too quickly and the ingredients are in danger of burning, I lower the oven 50 degrees, to 375.

The real babying comes when I add the second batch of vegetables. Because I don't want to lower the temperature of the ingredients that are already in the oven, I sauté the incoming vegetables to "preheat" them. Then, well, maybe this is the real babying step: I mist the chicken with water during the last twenty minutes of roasting to keep the skin crisp and the meat and vegetables as moist as a fricassee.

I have also pushed the flavors even further by mashing the chicken liver (which had roasted inside the chicken) with pan juices and some of the cooked garlic to make a dressing for a watercress salad. The peppery cress was a good contrast to the sweet roasted vegetables, and I loved using the delicious but usually discarded liver.

FAIRCHILD-BLASS SPRING COLLECTION CHICKEN

3 tablespoons extra-virgin olive oil

1 3½-pound organic, free-range chicken, neck halved and liver reserved

Salt and freshly ground white pepper

3 sprigs fresh thyme

2 sprigs fresh sage

2 tablespoons butter (1 tablespoon melted)

2 large fresh artichokes

1 teaspoon lemon juice

12 ounces whole small fingerling potatoes, or small Yukon Gold potatoes, quartered

1 head garlic, broken into cloves, unpeeled

2 medium Texas onions, bulbs and some green, peeled and quartered

8 ounces fresh porcini or other spring mushrooms, trimmed (if large, cut in half or quarter)

2 bunches watercress, leaves only, washed and dried well

White wine vinegar, optional

1. Preheat oven to 425 degrees. Place a large roasting pan in oven and heat for 5 minutes. Add 1 tablespoon oil, tilting pan to coat bottom.

2. While pan is heating, clip chicken wings at second joint; reserve with neck. Season chicken inside and out with salt and pepper. Place liver in cavity with 1 sprig thyme and 1 sprig sage. Truss

chicken and brush with 1 tablespoon melted butter. Put wing and neck pieces in center of pan and place chicken on top of them. Roast chicken for 20 minutes, brushing with a little oil every 5 or 10 minutes.

3. While chicken is roasting, prepare artichokes: Bring a small pan of water to a simmer. Cut off stems, top 2 inches, tough outer leaves, and dark green portion of base. Quarter artichokes and simmer for 4 minutes, until just tender when pierced. Drain well and let cool. Using a small spoon, remove prickly choke from center of each quarter. Set quarters aside in a small bowl of water and add lemon juice.

4. Add potatoes, garlic, remaining 1 tablespoon butter, and remaining thyme and sage to roasting pan. Stir well to coat all with fat in pan. Roast 20 minutes more. If chicken or vegetables seem to be browning too fast, lower heat to 375 degrees. After about 10 minutes (or 30 minutes of roasting chicken), warm a large skillet over high heat. Add 1 tablespoon oil, onions, drained artichoke hearts, mushrooms, salt, and pepper. Sauté until vegetables are very hot, about 8 to 10 minutes. Add vegetables to roasting pan and stir well.

5. Roast chicken an additional 20 to 30 minutes. Stir vegetables but do not baste chicken. Instead, fill a plant mister with water and mist chicken and vegetables every 10 minutes.

6. Remove pan from oven and keep warm. Remove chicken liver from cavity and pick out 5 to 8 large cloves garlic from pan. Push garlic out of its skin into a mixing bowl and add liver and a spoonful of cooking fat. With back of a fork, lightly mash ingredients. Place watercress in a serving bowl and add mashed liver and garlic. Toss lightly, adding more cooking fat, salt, and pepper to taste, and a splash of vinegar if desired.

Present and carve chicken in its roasting pan or on a platter, accompanied by roasted vegetables and watercress salad.

Yield: 4 servings
Time: 1½ hours

⌒

COGNAC LENDS A KICK TO CRAYFISH

As an eighteen-year-old assistant cook at La Mère Blanc, I was surrounded by grand cuisine, none of which my fellow cooks and I could afford. On our days off we headed to the area we thought of as the bayou of Lyons, Les Dombes, and ate local crayfish in cheap bars and truck-stop cafés. I date my love for these freshwater creatures from that time.

But the flavors in this dish take me back to many periods in my life. I first made the cocktail sauce when I was an apprentice at Nandron, a two-star restaurant in Lyons. The crawfish remind me of my time at La Mère Blanc. And the salad's tart Florida grapefruit and buttery avocado are flavors I came to love during more than twenty years in America.

I probably wouldn't have made this sauce again if I were not haunted by the gloppy dressings I see at salad bars (and at my golf club). Thousand Island or Russian dressing doesn't stand up to seafood as well as this complex sauce. Surprisingly, its typically American ingredients—ketchup and Worcestershire sauce—are original to the recipe, as is the very French touch of adding a drop of cognac to elevate the flavors.

In France I would have used lemon juice in the mayonnaise base, but once I added grapefruit segments to the salad, I wanted to keep its flavor going, so I reduced the grapefruit juice to concentrate its taste and used that instead. In fact, none of the grapefruit goes to waste, nor do the stems from the salad's tarragon: They're all tossed into the court bouillon, the crayfish cooking stock. Because crayfish come from fresh water, they are mild and need a flavor boost at every stage. The almost briny bouillon gives them a kick-start, and the lightly spiked cocktail sauce is a nice finish.

A note about crayfish: They are good in spring and summer and best bought from a reliable supplier and, ideally, purchased live. If you can't find them live, opt for freshly cooked and peeled ones (skip the boiling step). Try to buy crayfish from Louisiana or Texas. They'll be hard-shelled, and their meat will be plump, rich, and really flavorful.

And don't give up on this sauce if you can't find crayfish. The sauce—indeed, the entire salad—is equally good with lobster, shrimp, or jumbo lump crabmeat.

CRAYFISH SALAD WITH FRENCH COCKTAIL SAUCE

1 large bunch fresh tarragon

Salt

1 teaspoon cracked peppercorns

Ground cayenne pepper

1 large pink grapefruit, peeled and rind reserved

3 pounds live crayfish, rinsed under cold running water

1 head Boston lettuce, cut into thin strips

4 plum tomatoes, peeled, seeded, and finely chopped

2 avocados, pitted, peeled, and cut into 6 wedges

1 raw egg yolk (see Note)

1 tablespoon Dijon mustard

Freshly ground white pepper

$\frac{1}{4}$ cup vegetable oil, preferably grapeseed or safflower

$2\frac{1}{2}$ tablespoons ketchup

1 teaspoon white wine vinegar

1 teaspoon Worcestershire sauce

4 drops Tabasco sauce

$\frac{1}{2}$ teaspoon cognac or Armagnac

2 tablespoons toasted sliced almonds

1. In a large pot over high heat, bring 1 gallon water to a boil. Set aside 12 large tarragon leaves and add rest to pot along with $\frac{1}{4}$ cup salt, peppercorns, a pinch of cayenne, reserved grapefruit rind, and crayfish. Return water to a boil and simmer for 2 minutes. Remove pan from heat and set aside for 10 minutes. Drain crayfish and let cool. To peel, twist head and tail, and pull to separate; discard head. Peel off upper sections of shell and pull out meat while squeezing tip of tail. If vein that runs up center of tail remains, re-

move it and rub off any yellow coral clinging to meat. Set crayfish aside.

2. Using a sharp knife, cut grapefruit into its natural segments, slicing next to membranes that separate sections. Work over a bowl to save juice and membranes. Set grapefruit slices aside. Squeeze out as much juice as possible from membranes; discard membranes and reserve juice.

3. In a large, shallow serving bowl, arrange lettuce in an even layer. Place an even layer of tomatoes in center of bowl. Surround tomatoes with alternating slices of grapefruit and avocado. Cut reserved tarragon leaves into thin strips and sprinkle evenly over tomatoes.

4. Place grapefruit juice in a small saucepan over high heat. Boil until reduced to 2 teaspoons; set aside. In a medium mixing bowl, whisk together yolk and mustard, and add salt, pepper, and cayenne to taste. Whisking constantly, slowly add oil in a thin stream until it reaches consistency of mayonnaise. Whisk in the grapefruit juice, ketchup, vinegar, Worcestershire sauce, Tabasco, and cognac. Taste and correct seasoning if necessary.

5. To serve, arrange crayfish in a crown over tomatoes in a serving bowl. Sprinkle with toasted almonds and serve with cocktail sauce.

Yield: 4 servings
Time: 1 hour

NOTE: You may substitute 4 tablespoons bottled mayonnaise for egg yolk and oil.

A HUMBLE CUT OF LAMB THAT'S LONG BEEN THE COOK'S SECRET

When I was a young cook in France, it was common for the butcher to give the kitchen staff the lamb neck. We would take the cut, considered too humble to serve to the restaurant's guests, and slice it so that each piece had some of the firm, chewy meat and the flavor-giving bones. We would roast the lamb with garlic, dried fennel, and herbs and, to a cook, the crew would love it. These days when lusty flavor is so much in demand, the neck of the lamb is as welcome in the dining room as it was in the kitchen.

At my restaurant I serve the neck as part of "an epigram of lamb," a dish that uses many parts: The neck and shoulder are boned, stuffed, and braised; the rack and saddle are marinated and roasted; and the leg is studded with garlic and herbs, and given a long, juicy roast. This time I decided to create a special dish for this underappreciated cut.

In the best of all possible worlds you would have your butcher reserve a whole neck, which is about a foot long and looks a little like an oxtail. He would bone and butterfly it so that you could stuff it with savory ground pork, roll and tie it, and then braise it. But necks can be hard to come by. If you can't get one, use a boned and butterflied shoulder. (You can also skip the stuffing and just braise lamb shanks.)

To get the most from the neck, which is a relatively tough cut, I brown the meat first and then braise it slowly in white wine with a lot of carrots, Texas onions, and fresh fennel. By the time the lamb emerges from the oven, the vegetables, nourished by the cooking juices, have softened and sweetened, in the style of the classic beef dish boeuf aux carottes.

And like so many rustic dishes, this one proves what good cooks have always known: The poorest cuts can produce the richest flavors. You just have to treat them right.

BRAISED LAMB NECK WITH SPRING CARROTS, ONIONS, AND FENNEL

¼ cup olive oil

1 medium onion, finely diced

3 large white mushrooms, cut into ¼-inch dice

Salt and freshly ground black pepper

6 cloves garlic, peeled

2 teaspoons finely chopped fresh thyme leaves

1 slice stale or oven-dried crustless white bread, cut into ¼-inch dice

1 tablespoon finely chopped fresh parsley leaves

2 tablespoons finely chopped fresh basil leaves

8 ounces ground pork

1 whole lamb neck, about 10 to 12 inches long, bone removed lengthwise, meat deveined and butterflied so that it lies flat and is ½ inch thick (or 1 lamb shoulder cut in the same manner)

4 tablespoons unsalted butter

12 medium carrots (preferably California), peeled and cut diagonally into ½-inch slices

6 Texas or Vidalia onions, trimmed and cut in half from root to top

1 fennel bulb, trimmed and cut into ½-inch wedges

1 bottle dry white wine, preferably chardonnay

1. In a medium sauté pan over medium heat, heat 2 tablespoons oil. Add onion and cook, stirring, until translucent, about 4 minutes. Add mushrooms and salt and pepper to taste. Sauté until mushrooms are just tender. Finely chop 1 clove garlic. Add to pan with half of thyme and sauté for 2 minutes. Stir in bread cubes and parsley, and sauté for 1 minute. Remove pan from heat and allow to cool. Add basil, pork, and salt and pepper to taste. Knead mixture by hand to blend well and set aside in a cool place.

2. Preheat oven to 375 degrees. Place lamb on a work surface and season with salt and pepper. Spoon stuffing down center of meat, forming a cylinder. Roll meat firmly around stuffing, shaping it into a roast. Tie roast with kitchen string at 1-inch intervals to secure stuffing.

3. Place a large, deep roasting pan over medium-high heat and add remaining oil. Slip lamb into pan and sear it, turning frequently, until well browned all over. Add 2 tablespoons butter and baste lamb with combined pan fats. Roast lamb in oven for 15 minutes, basting regularly. Give lamb a quarter turn and roast 15 minutes more. Remove pan from oven and carefully pour off accumulated fat. Slice remaining 5 cloves garlic and add to pan with remaining thyme, 2 tablespoons butter, carrots, onions, fennel, and salt and pepper to taste. Continue roasting for 20 minutes, turning and basting meat and stirring vegetables twice during this time, and add wine. If vegetables brown too quickly, lower oven temperature to 350 degrees. Braise meat and vegetables for an additional 1½ hours, turning and basting every 15 minutes.

4. Transfer roast to a cutting board. Remove strings, cut roast into 8 pieces, and arrange on a warm serving platter. Top with vegetables and keep warm. Pour pan juices into a saucepan and boil until reduced to 1 cup. Pour juices over lamb and vegetables, and serve immediately.

Yield: 4 to 6 servings
Time: about 3 hours

A TART THAT GIVES CHOCOLATE AND BOOZY CHERRIES EQUAL BILLING

When I was a kid, I was forbidden to drink alcohol but was allowed to eat Mon Cheri, a chocolate-cherry candy that tasted boozy and made me feel like a grown-up. This cherry-chocolate tart, with its cherries poached in port, is definitely not kid stuff, but it was inspired by those foil-wrapped candies of childhood.

The tart has three elements: a cocoa crust, cherries, and a soft, sensuous milk chocolate filling. The challenge was to keep the chocolate intense without letting it overwhelm the cherries.

The crust was easy. I wanted it to have a full flavor (that is why I based it on bitter cocoa powder), a crisp texture, and a quiet personality. The crust had to be a supporting player in every sense of the word, and because it is not too sweet, it is.

But chocolate is a notorious scene stealer. So I gave the cherries the extra complexity they needed by poaching them in a citrus-infused port. Cherries have a resilient firmness and their own sweet, ever-so-slightly acidic taste. Poaching softened their texture, using port gave them a deeper flavor, and tossing in an orange added zing.

Thus fortified, these cherries might have been a match for many chocolates, but I chose companionable milk chocolate. When you taste this tart, half the experience is cherries, half chocolate. And to make certain the textures are equally harmonious, I decided on a satiny filling, a cross between a custard and a flan. It is made with a runny ganache: a mixture of cream and chocolate that's bound with eggs. Baked slowly in a moderately low oven, it retains a silkiness that's the right counterpoint to the crisp crust and semisoft cherries.

I make miniature versions of this dessert at the restaurant, but at home I serve a family-size tart. If you want, you can boil down the leftover poaching mixture until it is thick enough to be poured as a sauce (it's too good to waste) and serve it alongside the tart.

MILK CHOCOLATE AND CHERRY TART

3 large eggs
8 tablespoons (1 stick) unsalted butter at room temperature, cut into 8 pieces
1 cup confectioners' sugar
1½ cups all-purpose flour
⅓ cup cocoa powder
1 cup ruby port
4½ tablespoons sugar
½ vanilla bean, split lengthwise and scraped
1 thin strip orange zest (all pith removed)
Juice of 1 orange
8 ounces cherries, halved and pitted
4½ ounces high-quality milk chocolate, finely chopped
1 cup heavy cream
Pinch of finely grated orange zest
Unsweetened whipped cream for garnish

1. In a small bowl, lightly beat 1 egg and set aside. In bowl of an electric mixer with a paddle attachment, combine butter pieces, confectioners' sugar, flour, and cocoa. Mix on low speed until crumbly. Add beaten egg and mix until dough comes together in a ball.

2. Divide dough in half and shape into disks. Wrap in plastic and refrigerate 1 disk for at least 1 hour or overnight. (Freeze other disk for another tart; it is necessary to make the full quantity of dough to achieve the proper consistency.)

3. While dough is chilling, prepare filling: In a small saucepan, combine ruby port, 1 tablespoon sugar, vanilla bean, strip of orange zest,

and orange juice. Bring to a boil, lower heat, and simmer for 10 minutes. Add cherries, bring back to a boil, then reduce heat and simmer for 2 minutes. Remove pan from heat and let cool to room temperature. Drain cherries, reserving port mixture, and pat dry between paper towels. To make a sauce, strain mixture into a small pan and boil down to a glaze; set aside.

4. Preheat oven to 350 degrees. Butter an 8-inch-round, 1¼-inch-deep fluted tart pan with a removable bottom. On a lightly floured surface, roll dough to a thickness of ⅛ inch. Fit dough into pan and trim excess even with rim. Cover dough with parchment paper or aluminum foil and fill with dry beans or rice. Bake until firm but not fully baked, 13 to 15 minutes. Remove paper and beans, and let cool to room temperature.

5. Lower oven temperature to 300 degrees. Place chocolate in a large heatproof mixing bowl. In a small saucepan, combine cream and remaining 3½ tablespoons sugar. Bring to a boil and immediately add to bowl of chocolate. Whisk until smooth. Add remaining 2 eggs, one at a time, whisking until smooth. Stir in grated orange zest.

6. To assemble, place crust on a baking sheet. Arrange cherries, cut side down, in crust. Pour chocolate filling over; it will come nearly to top. Bake until center of tart is gently set, 35 to 40 minutes. Cool to room temperature. Serve drizzled with port glaze and garnished with whipped cream.

Yield: 8-inch tart (8 servings)
Time: 3 hours

DEBORAH MADISON

Deborah Madison is the former chef of Greens in San Francisco and the author of *Vegetarian Cooking for Everyone*. She was photographed in the desert on the outskirts of her home in Santa Fe, New Mexico, by Peter Da Silva. These columns were written with Mark Bittman.

THE TART IN A STARRING ROLE

A chef working in a vegetarian restaurant, as I did in my days at Greens in San Francisco, is always searching for a centerpiece for the plate, something with enough substance—visually and in actual heft—to pull the dish together. For me, vegetable tarts were often the answer. A wedge of tart surrounded by a multicolored salad, for instance, looks dazzling and is filling, too. Sometime in 1980 I started refining the tarts I served.

Usually a tart dough, like pie dough, is dense and brittle. But I began to use yeast. It was my way of lightening the crust. It requires much less fat than other crusts do and is naturally airier. And it turned out to be a better complement for the filling: A yeasted crust is crisp on the outside but tender on the inside, a subtle transition to the delicate interior mixture. It's also a lot easier to work with, more supple, and less likely to tear.

Over the years I've reached far beyond the lovely, creamy Roquefort filling that I used at first.

In early summer I like to rely on our first local crop of green leafy vegetables. The bulk of the mixture here is spinach and chard, complemented by an assortment of unexpected greens—herbs like cilantro, parsley, and dill are perfect and can result in a wild and fresh, unforgettable combination.

But really the choice is yours. When I was in northern Italy last spring, I saw vegetable pies made with spinach, asparagus, leeks, and even wild greens like borage and chicories. (I cover my tarts with dough lids, so many people are going to argue that I should be calling them pies, too.)

The only trick to it is to remember that this dough must be rolled thin, to a thickness of about an eighth of an inch, or else it will become too bready. The tart should be served just slightly warm or at room temperature. It needs resting time to set up well; in fact, it stores beautifully overnight, and there's nothing better for a picnic.

GREEN HERB TART WITH YEAST CRUST

2 teaspoons active dry yeast

½ teaspoon sugar

1 cup warm milk or water

Salt

3 eggs

8 tablespoons (1 stick) butter at room temperature or olive oil, or a combination

3 cups flour

1 cup minced scallions, the whites plus about 1 inch of green

1 cup chopped parsley leaves

½ cup chopped cilantro leaves

⅓ cup chopped fresh dill leaves

8 cups trimmed and roughly chopped spinach, thickest stems discarded

4 cups trimmed chard, the stems chopped finely, the leaves coarsely

1 cup ricotta cheese

3 ounces feta cheese, optional

Zest of 1 lemon, minced

Freshly ground black pepper

1. Dissolve yeast and sugar in milk or water. In a large bowl, combine liquid with a hefty pinch of salt, 1 egg, and 6 tablespoons butter. Add flour gradually, beating with a wooden spoon. When dough is too stiff to work with a spoon, knead by hand until smooth, adding small amounts of flour as needed. (To make dough in a food processor, place flour, a hefty pinch of salt, 1 egg, and 6 tablespoons cold butter in a work bowl fitted with the steel blade. Let machine run for 10 seconds, then add liquid-yeast mixture. Process until a dough ball forms.) Place dough in a lightly buttered or oiled bowl, cover, and let rest for about 1 hour.

2. Place remaining 2 tablespoons butter in a large skillet over medium heat. When heated, add scallions, parsley, cilantro, and dill. Cook, stirring, for 5 to 10 minutes, until soft. Remove and set aside.

3. Add spinach to skillet with ¼ cup water. Cook, stirring, until spinach wilts, then remove to a colander. Repeat process with chard. When spinach and chard have cooled slightly, press them gently to remove moisture; do not squeeze.

4. Combine greens and herbs with ricotta, feta if using, lemon zest, salt, and pepper. Beat remaining eggs lightly and stir all but 2 tablespoons into greens mixture.

5. Preheat oven to 375 degrees. When dough is ready, cut off a piece a little larger than a third of total. On a lightly floured surface, roll larger piece of dough to a thickness of about ⅛ inch and 14 inches in diameter. Lightly butter or oil an 11- or 12-inch tart pan with a removable rim. Place dough in pan and trim so that an inch hangs over rim all around. Roll out remaining dough to a diameter just under 12 inches. (It should fit inside rim of pan.)

6. Pile greens mixture into tart, then top with dough lid. Fold excess dough from bottom piece onto top piece, pleating or rolling as you like. Brush lightly with reserved beaten egg.

7. Put tart on baking sheet and bake for 35 minutes. Remove rim from tart pan (it is best to wear long sleeves when doing this in case the hot pan touches your arm) and bake 10 minutes more to brown sides. Serve hot, at room temperature, or cold.

Yield: at least 10 servings
Time: 2 hours

BUILDING A STEW FROM CORN

Many years ago while traveling in Mexico, I was served a stew made with an unusually fragrant, chewy corn. It was unlike anything I had ever had before. The complex flavors of the stew—nutty, bright, and most of all big—came from something that appeared utterly simple. I soon learned that posole is the name for corn kernels that are dried and then boiled, and are the soul of the stew. The dish, naturally enough, is also called posole. In Mexico it is often the center of a large communal dish surrounded by an array of garnishes like avocado for creaminess, onions for crunch, and oregano for aromatic flavor. And then there are grated cheese and tortilla chips.

In New Mexico where I now live, posole is more likely to be a side dish in place of beans. It sometimes serves as a simple main course, containing pork, onion, oregano, and garlic. The pork makes a kind of broth as it simmers with the corn, rendering the meat tender and integrating it beautifully into the stew. But I have become more inclined to make a vegetarian version of the dish and to look for other ways to enliven it. My variation begins with roasted fresh, mild green chilies. (If you can't get these, substitute long-frying peppers and add fresh jalapeño or another hot chili.) I add zucchini near the very end; I want it to become soft but not mushy. Then, in the Mexican fashion, I serve my posole with a few condiments, including a fresh cilantro salsa, avocado, and chopped cabbage.

Like beans, posole takes longer to cook as it ages, so cooking times are approximate. But this dish can be prepared in advance; it gets better as it sits. You can double or triple the amounts and add chunks of pork at the beginning of the cooking time. But practicalities aside, the result is a beguiling, hearty stew of bursting corn kernels.

SUMMER POSOLE

1½ cups dried posole, available at health-food stores or stores selling Mexican or Southwest ingredients
2 or 3 dried red chili peppers
2 teaspoons dried Mexican oregano, plus more for garnish
1 large onion, minced
2 tablespoons minced garlic
4 fresh, mild green chili peppers, such as Anaheims
1 big bunch cilantro, well washed, large stems removed, minced (about ⅔ cup finely minced cilantro)
1 jalapeño pepper, stem and seeds removed, very finely minced
⅓ cup minced scallions or shallots
⅓ cup plus 1 tablespoon canola oil
2 avocados, peeled and minced
Salt and freshly ground pepper to taste
2 medium zucchini, cut lengthwise into quarters, then into chunks
Lime wedges
2 cups fresh shredded and chopped cabbage

1. If time allows, soak posole overnight in water to cover. Drain and place in a pot with 8 cups water, red chilies, 2 teaspoons oregano, onion, and all but 1 teaspoon garlic. Bring to a boil, lower heat so that mixture bubbles gently, and cover.

2. Roast green chilies over an open flame on either a grill or a gas stove (just let them sit on a burner; they won't make much of a mess). Turn frequently until blackened and blistered all over. Remove to a bowl, cover, and let sit while you prepare salsa.

3. Combine cilantro with remaining 1 teaspoon garlic, jalapeño, scallions, oil, and 1 avocado. Add salt and pepper, then taste and adjust seasoning as necessary.

4. When roasted peppers have sat for at least 30 minutes, uncover and remove skins, stems, and seeds. Chop flesh roughly and add to stew. When posole kernels begin to pop (not audibly but visibly), add salt and pepper to taste.

5. The stew is done when posole is tender but not mushy; many kernels will have popped. Add zucchini and cook a few minutes more, until it becomes tender. Taste and adjust seasoning.

6. Serve with salsa, remaining avocado, lime, a small bowl of oregano, and cabbage. Each should be added by individual diners, to taste.

Yield: 4 servings

Time: at least 2 hours, plus optional soaking time

GIVING RAGOUT A LITTLE FORM AND TEXTURE

There is nothing more satisfying than a warm stew or ragout, but they are difficult to serve at a serious restaurant. The very qualities that make them so pleasing—a comforting formlessness and simplicity—also make them less than elegant on the plate.

All of this explains why I was so taken by the noodle cakes I saw in a Chinese restaurant years ago. The cakes were large, soft pillows waiting to be served as beds for stir-fries. These panfried cakes, I thought, could have a role in my own cooking, but I would top them with a vegetable stew instead. What I like so much about the noodle cakes is that they do indeed have a form, something for the eye to settle on. And since I make mine with a crisp exterior, there's also something for the knife and fork. In these two important ways— form and texture—noodle cakes seemed the perfect complement to tender braised vegetables.

At first I modified the noodles only slightly, substituting olive oil for the peanut oil used in Chinese cooking. Then I discovered the cakes worked whether I used fresh noodles or dry, Chinese or Italian, fat or thin— although I do especially like the look of the fine threads formed by capellini. It wasn't long before I began to enliven their flavor with herbs. Then I had the idea of laying half the noodles in the pan, followed by some cheese and the remaining noodles. The result is a crisp cake with a luxuriously creamy center. You can vary the cheese—and the herb, of course—according to the vegetable accompaniment.

CRISP NOODLE CAKE WITH VEGETABLE RAGOUT

8 ounces capellini or other thin pasta
Salt to taste
8 tablespoons olive oil
¾ cup minced parsley
4 to 6 small eggplants (about 2 pounds),
    cut lengthwise into quarters
1 large red onion, roughly chopped
2 large bell peppers (preferably 1 red and
    1 orange or yellow), cut into strips
3 cloves garlic, thinly sliced
2 teaspoons paprika
2 tablespoons tomato paste
5 plum tomatoes, peeled, seeded, drained,
    and chopped
Freshly ground black pepper to taste
1½ cups chicken stock or water
1 cup or more freshly grated mozzarella,
    Gruyère, or other semisoft cheese, or a
    combination

1. Bring a large pot of salted water to a boil. Cook pasta until tender but firm. Drain, rinse in cold water, and drain again. Toss with 1 tablespoon oil and ½ cup parsley. Set aside.

2. Put 3 tablespoons oil in a large skillet over medium-high heat. Add eggplants and brown on all sides, turning frequently, until tender, 10 to 15 minutes.

3. Put 2 tablespoons oil in a large Dutch oven or saucepan over medium heat. Add onion, bell peppers, and garlic. Cook, stirring occasionally, until they soften. Add paprika, tomato paste, eggplants, tomatoes, remaining ¼ cup parsley, and salt and pepper to taste. Add liquid gradually, scraping pan to loosen any browned bits. Cover and turn heat to low. Cook, stirring occa-

sionally, until mixture is quite thick and soft, about 30 minutes.

4. Put 1 tablespoon oil in a 10- or 12-inch nonstick skillet over medium-high heat. After a minute, add half of pasta, spreading noodles out with a spatula. Top with cheese and remaining noodles, again spreading them out evenly. Lower heat to medium (the cake must not brown too fast) and cook, shaking pan occasionally, until cake is lightly browned on bottom, 5 to 10 minutes. Slide onto a plate, top with another plate, and invert.

5. Add remaining 1 tablespoon oil to skillet and slide cake back in, cooked side up. Brown second side, then remove to a platter. To serve, place a wedge of noodle cake on a plate with some ragout alongside.

Yield: 4 servings
Time: 1 to 1½ hours

IMPROVISING A SALAD
FROM THE GARDEN

When I was the chef at Greens, the vegetarian restaurant in San Francisco, we were affiliated with Green Gulch Farm, which was just across the Golden Gate Bridge, in Marin County. I lived at the farm and worked closely with the head gardener, and together we found and grew unusual seeds. After driving the crates of produce across the bridge to the restaurant, more often than not I found that I had nothing in enough quantity to feature by itself. So one of my menu standards was what we called Farm Salad—a composed salad of raw, steamed, pickled, and grilled vegetables with a few sauces, usually accompanied by a wedge of frittata or some hard-cooked eggs, also from the farm. By necessity these salads were ever-changing, but all presented a variety of tastes and textures.

Now I choose vegetables from the farmer's market and my small garden, and I've vastly simplified the number of ingredients and the method, using just one dressing for everything. This dish allows you to improvise based on what's around and how much you want to do.

Lately I've been making a pesto-like dressing based on fresh, fragrant marjoram. Like basil, marjoram is widely used in Liguria, the region around the Italian Riviera. Marjoram has a wonderful, powerful flavor, and it's tied together here with other typical ingredients, like capers, pine nuts, and olives, in a sauce akin to one used in the Ligurian salad called cappon magro, *which is usually composed of a variety of fish and vegetables. (If you want to add cold steamed or grilled fish to the farm salad, it's perfectly appropriate.) I find it difficult to avoid eating this delicious sauce with a spoon or spreading it on bread.*

FARM SALAD WITH MARJORAM SAUCE

4 medium beets, or more small ones
12 small new potatoes
1 pound green beans, trimmed
4 to 8 small carrots, peeled
2 red onions, peeled and cut into $\frac{1}{2}$-inch rounds
2 small zucchini, cut in half lengthwise
$\frac{1}{2}$ cup plus 2 tablespoons extra-virgin olive oil
$1\frac{1}{2}$-inch-thick slice good white bread, crusts trimmed
2 tablespoons red wine vinegar
1 teaspoon minced garlic
2 tablespoons marjoram leaves
3 tablespoons drained capers
$\frac{1}{2}$ cup pine nuts
1 cup finely minced parsley leaves
2 tablespoons pitted olives, such as Niçoise
Salt and freshly ground black pepper to taste
12 radishes, trimmed
4 to 8 pickled artichoke hearts (canned are fine)
1 medium cucumber, trimmed and cut into eighths
4 hard-boiled eggs, cut in half

1. In separate batches, steam or parboil beets, potatoes, green beans, and carrots until each is tender. Plunge into ice water to cool. Peel beets and potatoes if you like; cut into wedges if large. Cut green beans and carrots into 2-inch lengths if large. Refrigerate until ready to serve.

2. Grill or broil onions and zucchini, brushing occasionally with 2 tablespoons oil, until tender. Refrigerate until ready to serve.

3. Soak bread in vinegar. In a mortar and pestle or small food processor, combine garlic,

marjoram, capers, pine nuts, parsley, and olives. Grind until coarse but not pureed. Add bread and ½ cup oil, and grind some more; again, the texture should be coarse. (If you are using a food processor, pulse on and off to maintain control over texture.) Season with salt and pepper, and add a little more oil and/or vinegar if necessary to thin. The sauce should be pasty rather than creamy. Refrigerate until ready to serve, up to 1 day.

4. To serve, bring ingredients to room temperature. Decorate a platter with vegetables and eggs, and place sauce in a bowl in the middle. Serve, using marjoram sauce as a dip for other ingredients.

Yield: 4 servings
Time: about 1 hour

LEEK AND POTATO: A TENDER CRUNCH

Leeks and potatoes are a natural, classic, and delicious combination. So maybe it isn't too surprising that when I was looking for an alternative to a traditional wheat crust for a leek pie, I thought of making one from thinly sliced potatoes. I loved the idea of buttery, slightly crisp potatoes cradling soft, delicate leeks. But I didn't love the preparation: I had to cook individual slices of potatoes carefully to make them soft enough to form a crust, and then painstakingly layer them along the edge of a large springform pan.

Eventually I discovered an easier way: Quickly baking the potatoes with a little butter gives them the right consistency, and lining little ramekins is a bit easier than lining a larger form. The individual pies are quite charming, especially if they are inverted onto their serving plates, much like a pastry or timbale.

Unlike the heavy, custardy centers of most quiches, the filling is made mostly from leeks and is only lightly bound with cream and eggs. Because leeks contain a natural gelatin-like substance, the filling holds together beautifully, whether served hot, warm, or at room temperature. The other major flavor in this filling is cheese, and here you have many choices. Strong cheeses, such as Taleggio or Gorgonzola, work beautifully, but so do milder, distinctively flavored goat cheeses. A combination is nice, too.

LEEK TART WITH CRISP POTATO CRUST

2 tablespoons butter, plus more for baking sheet and ramekins
8 cups thinly sliced leeks (about 10 medium leeks), white and light green parts only
2 teaspoons chopped fresh thyme
½ cup dry white wine
½ cup heavy cream
Salt and freshly ground black pepper
2 large baking potatoes, peeled
2 large eggs, lightly beaten
4 ounces Taleggio, Gorgonzola, or goat cheese, grated or crumbled

1. Place 2 large skillets over medium-high heat and add 1 tablespoon butter to each pan. When butter has melted, add half of leeks to each pan. Cook, stirring, until leeks just begin to brown, about 10 minutes. Add ¼ cup water to each pan and stir well until leeks have softened, about 10 minutes more. Remove from heat.

2. Preheat oven to 400 degrees. Combine contents of both skillets in a large saucepan and add thyme. Sauté over medium-low heat until leeks are very tender, about 10 minutes. Add wine and sauté until almost completely evaporated. Remove pan from heat and add cream and salt and pepper to taste. Set aside and let cool.

3. Using a mandoline or a sharp knife to make thinnest slices possible, slice 1 potato lengthwise and the other crosswise. Brush a baking sheet (or 2 if necessary) with butter and lay potato slices in a single layer. Bake potatoes until they just begin to brown, no longer, and remove from oven.

4. Lower oven temperature to 375 degrees. Using a wooden spoon, beat eggs and cheese into leek mixture. Butter six 1-cup ramekins. Line with a single layer of potato slices, allowing them to overlap slightly. Use round slices for bottom and oval slices for sides. Divide leek mixture among ramekins. Bake just until filling sets, about 20 to 30 minutes. Let cool for 5 minutes, then run a sharp knife around edge, invert onto individual plates, and serve.

Yield: 6 servings
Time: 1¼ hours

WHEN THE CREPE MEETS THE ENCHILADA

A blessing for the cook is that a crepe, unlike a tortilla, is easily made from scratch. Tortillas involve rolling or pressing, the kinds of activity that benefit from years of practice. Crepes are quicker to make and more forgiving; most troubles can be fixed by adjusting the amount of batter in the pan or thinning it with a little water.

This dish was inspired by one of my favorite enchiladas. The wrap is a corn-flavored crepe. The filling is nothing more than fresh corn, stripped from the cob and sautéed with onion, zucchini, and seasonings. But the true star of this dish is mole, a dazzling nuanced Mexican sauce that contains ground red chili, spices, Mexican chocolate, and a bit of vinegar (you'll find the chili and the chocolate in stores selling Mexican or Southwest ingredients).

Ground chili is a natural thickener, so it binds the sauce and gives it body. If you use a mild chili powder, which I call for, you'll find the sauce hot but not at all fiery. The chocolate further mellows the mole while adding complexity. Don't expect to taste the chocolate, though; it disappears as it harmonizes with the other ingredients.

CORN CREPES WITH RED CHILI MOLE

⅔ cup all-purpose flour
⅓ cup cornmeal
1¼ cups milk
Salt
2 large or extra-large eggs, lightly beaten
2 tablespoons melted and cooled butter, plus extra for cooking crepes
¼ cup roughly chopped raisins
⅓ cup pignoli nuts
1 cup grated goat cheddar or other cheddar cheese (about 2 ounces)
⅓ cup chopped cilantro
1½ teaspoons coriander seed
1 teaspoon anise seed
1 teaspoon cumin seed
1 teaspoon dried Mexican oregano
5 tablespoons canola or sunflower oil
1½ cups minced onion
2 teaspoons minced garlic
⅓ cup mild ground chili
1 ounce Mexican chocolate, chopped
½ teaspoon sherry vinegar, or to taste
1 cup diced zucchini
2 cups fresh corn kernels
½ cup crème fraîche or very lightly beaten heavy cream

1. In a medium bowl, place flour, cornmeal, milk, and ½ teaspoon salt, and blend well. Add eggs and melted butter, and mix until smooth. Place a 6- to 8-inch nonstick skillet over medium heat. When hot enough for a drop of water to skitter over surface, add about ½ teaspoon butter. Ladle a scant ¼ cup batter into skillet and swirl to form a thin layer; pour any excess back into bowl. When top of crepe is dry, after about 1

minute, turn and cook other side for 15 to 30 seconds. The crepe should brown only slightly; it should not be crisp. Put it on a plate and repeat process, adding butter as needed. The cooked crepes should make a stack of 12.

2. Cover raisins with warm water and set aside. Place a dry skillet over medium heat. Put in pignoli nuts and stir or shake pan until they begin to brown; transfer immediately to a small bowl. Drain raisins and squeeze gently to remove excess liquid. Add raisins to pignoli nuts along with cheese and cilantro; set aside. In a dry skillet, combine coriander, anise, cumin, and oregano. Cook over medium heat, stirring, until fragrant, about 2 minutes. Transfer to a spice grinder and grind to a powder; set aside.

3. To prepare mole, place a medium saucepan over medium-high heat and add 3 tablespoons oil. When oil is hot, add ½ cup onion and sauté, stirring, until it just begins to brown. Add 1 teaspoon garlic and stir for 1 minute. Stir in reserved spice mix and remove from heat. Add ground chili and 1½ cups water. Return pan to medium heat and slowly bring to a boil, stirring frequently. Add chocolate and 1 teaspoon salt. Lower heat and simmer, stirring, about 5 minutes. Add vinegar, adjust seasonings, and keep warm until ready to serve.

4. Place a skillet over medium heat and add remaining 2 tablespoons oil. When oil is hot, add remaining 1 cup onion and sauté until translucent. Add remaining 1 teaspoon garlic, zucchini, and 1 tablespoon water. Sauté until zucchini is tender, about 5 minutes. Add corn and cook, stirring, about 5 minutes. Remove from heat and stir in raisin-pignoli mixture.

5. Heat oven to 400 degrees. To assemble, place about 2 tablespoons filling on 1 quadrant of a crepe. Flatten filling slightly, fold crepe over, and place 1 tablespoon filling on crepe covering original portion of filling. Fold again and tuck a tablespoon of filling into fold that was just made. The finished crepe will be folded into quarters and have 3 pockets of filling. Place crepes on a baking sheet and bake until heated through, about 10 minutes. To serve, place 2 or 3 crepes on each plate and top with a spoonful of mole and a little crème fraîche.

Yield: 4 to 6 servings
Time: 1¼ hours

AN EGGPLANT VARIATION THAT MAKES THE MOST OF SUMMER

An eggplant gratin—typically a dish with a layer of toasted bread crumbs topping softened eggplant—is a fine enough thing. But a variation I've always preferred is one devised by Richard Olney, which features a blanket of custard in place of the bread crumbs. Now I've developed my own version: layers of roasted eggplant that sandwich a rustic tomato and pepper confit, all covered by a saffron-scented custard.

In the summer when all the ingredients are at their peak, the combination of succulent eggplant, delicate custard, and flavorful confit is just irresistible. This dish cannot be rushed. The confit needs gentle heat to reach its ideal state—a thick, luscious jam bound with the sweet juices of the vegetables.

The custard is distinguished by the saffron, which gives it a deep yellow color and a hint of bitterness. (It is really not replaceable, but you can omit it entirely if you have none.) You can use the custard just as a topping, but I make extra so that it drips down into the eggplant and the vegetables. The very top, exposed directly to the oven's heat, puffs and browns; the portion that seeps into the vegetables remains creamy.

Although off-season eggplant must be salted to reduce its bitterness, the local varieties available in season are quite sweet and can be cooked right after slicing. This is a wonderful summer side dish, warm or at room temperature; it will remain in perfect condition for a couple of hours after cooking. It is especially nice served with grilled lamb chops or tuna steaks, but it looks and tastes so great on its own that you can easily offer it as a main course. To make it a more elegant entree, serve it in individual gratin dishes or ramekins and reduce the baking time to twenty minutes or so.

EGGPLANT GRATIN WITH SAFFRON CUSTARD

About ½ cup olive oil
3 cups diced onions
Salt
2 large bell peppers (preferably 1 yellow and 1 red), stemmed, seeded, and chopped
1 tablespoon minced garlic
½ teaspoon anise seeds, crushed with a knife
3 large tomatoes, peeled, seeded, and diced
2 tablespoons tomato paste
Freshly ground pepper (preferably white)
3 to 4 pounds eggplant, cut into slices just under ½ inch thick
⅛ to ¼ teaspoon saffron
1½ cups ricotta cheese
3 eggs
¾ cup freshly grated Parmesan cheese
1 cup plus 2 tablespoons milk or heavy cream
½ cup torn-up basil leaves

1. Preheat oven to 425 degrees. Place 3 tablespoons oil in a large, deep skillet or saucepan over medium heat. Add onions and a healthy pinch of salt, and cook, stirring, until translucent, 10 minutes or longer. Add bell peppers, garlic, and anise, and cook, stirring occasionally, until peppers are very tender, about 15 minutes. Add tomatoes and tomato paste. Adjust heat so mixture simmers steadily. Stirring occasionally, cook until mixture is thick and jammy, about 30 minutes. Taste and add salt and pepper as needed.

2. Lightly brush each slice of eggplant with oil. Place slices in 1 layer on 1 or more baking sheets. Bake, turning after about 20 minutes, until eggplant is lightly brown and slightly shriveled, a total of 30 to 40 minutes.

3. Dissolve saffron in ¼ cup hot water. Mix together ricotta, eggs, Parmesan, milk, and salt and pepper to taste. Add saffron and its liquid. Stir basil into tomato sauce.

4. Turn heat to 375 degrees. Brush inside of a large gratin dish or baking pan with oil. Make a layer of eggplant, then a layer of tomato sauce; repeat. Top with custard and bake about 45 minutes, or until nicely browned. Serve hot, warm, or at room temperature.

Yield: 4 main-course or 8 side-dish servings
Time: 1½ to 2 hours

CHARLIE PALMER

Charlie Palmer is the chef and owner of Aureole in Manhattan.
He was photographed in the sommelier's area of the restaurant.
These columns were written with Judith Choate.

ROASTING SALMON, WITH
A TASTE OF THE WILD

A few years ago, needing some days of fishing to clear my head, I took my wife, Lisa, and our eldest son, Court, to the San Juan Islands off the coast of Washington. This part of America has some of the world's most spectacular natural scenery, with a series of pristine, forested islands dotting the tranquil waters of Puget Sound. We stayed in a small cabin on Orcas Island, where I'd heard that the salmon fishing would be stupendous. It was.

In fact, one day I caught nine silver salmon weighing three to seven pounds each, which were perfect for cooking whole. Good fishing always gets my creative juices flowing. Right up from the dock I would head to the garden next door to the cabin. It was overflowing with ripe vegetables, which made it easy to put together a feast.

Silver salmon is quite fatty, so it didn't seem suited to the pungent dill and rich sauces that frequently accompany salmon. I thought the scent of an aromatic herb like rosemary, with its lemony pine flavor, and a simple roasting over some garden-fresh vegetables would better highlight my catch. I wrapped it in very thin slices of lean home-cured bacon, which added a wonderful smoky flavor. Served with bottles of the local Riesling, perfectly chilled, this was great American food at its best.

WHOLE ROASTED SALMON WITH ROOT VEGETABLES

1½ pounds whole baby turnips, well washed
    and trimmed
1½ pounds fingerling potatoes, well washed
1 6-pound whole salmon, cleaned, head and
    tail on
3 5-inch sprigs fresh rosemary
1 whole lemon, well washed and sliced
    crosswise
Coarse salt and freshly ground pepper
12 ounces very thinly sliced premium-quality
    bacon
6 leeks, white part with a trace of green,
    well washed and split lengthwise
1 teaspoon fresh rosemary needles
Cracked black pepper to taste
2 bunches arugula, well washed and
    trimmed, optional
6 fresh lemon slices, optional

1. Place turnips in boiling salted water to cover and simmer for 2 minutes. Add potatoes and simmer 5 minutes more. Drain and pat dry. Set aside.

2. Preheat oven to 375 degrees. Rinse salmon and pat dry. Place rosemary sprigs into cavity. Cover rosemary with lemon slices. Season to taste with salt and pepper, noting that the bacon will add saltiness. Carefully wrap salmon in bacon strips, completely covering top side.

3. Place leeks, along with reserved turnips and potatoes, in a shallow roasting pan large enough to hold salmon. Sprinkle vegetables with rosemary needles and season to taste with salt and pepper, again noting that bacon will add saltiness. Lay bacon-wrapped salmon on top of vegetables. Season top with cracked black pepper.

4. Place pan in oven and roast about 15 minutes per inch of thickness of fish, or until fish is just opaque by backbone. (An instant-read thermometer inserted into center of fish will register 135 degrees.)

5. Remove fish from oven and allow to rest about 30 minutes, or until fish and vegetables have come to room temperature.

6. Place fish on a serving platter and surround with vegetables. If desired, garnish platter with bunches of arugula or any other bitter green and a few lemon slices. Serve at room temperature.

Yield: 6 servings
Time: 1½ hours

FROM SCRATCH—ALMOST

When I was just learning about fine cooking as a four-teen-year-old apprentice at an inn in upstate New York, I was fascinated by the dessert cart, as any kid would be. I was particularly taken with the elaborate pastry cream creations like the napoleon. And as I learned by the time I got to culinary school, the ability to create those creamy classics was a hallmark of the professional.

Later, as rich desserts fell out of favor, I began experimenting, like many of my contemporaries, with savory alternatives: doing crisp potato or vegetable napoleons as side dishes to accompany meat or game. All of them were fine, as far as they went, but I missed the old ways.

And more recently, I had the urge to revisit the tantalizing traditional French dessert cart. But this time I could see no reason at all to make the napoleon some kind of test of chefhood. Experience brings with it the confidence to take it easy every now and then. So I made a few changes, the most significant being the replacement of the time-consuming, delicate puff pastry with easy-to-use frozen strudel dough, a more than adequate commercial product.

Beyond the most obvious benefit—avoiding the make-it-from-scratch madness of puff pastry—frozen strudel dough adds character to the dessert. It is, for instance, a bit richer in taste than frozen phyllo dough, although both serve well. Once baked, the strudel dough has a nutty taste that I like a lot. And when working with the frozen dough, you don't have to make a sheet pan full of desserts, as I was trained to do; it is much easier to make individual napoleons.

Then for the cream: I added a bit of gelatin, which gives extra body. The touch of gelatin ensures that the cream will stay set and not ooze out the edges of the napoleon. It is more attractive that way, I think.

Finally, instead of the traditional fondant glaze, I use a dusting of confectioners' sugar and a refreshing raspberry-citrus sauce.

I know it sounds as if I've done a lot of cheating here, but I really haven't, if the test is in the results. This is a terrific dessert. It is a direct descendant of the classic napoleon, if somewhat lighter. If you try it, just don't let on how easy it is. It still looks difficult.

RED RASPBERRY NAPOLEON

$\frac{1}{2}$ teaspoon gelatin
3 large egg yolks
1 large egg
Salt
$\frac{1}{2}$ cup sugar
$\frac{1}{4}$ cup Wondra flour
2 cups half-and-half or whole milk
1 vanilla bean
2 tablespoons chilled unsalted butter
1 package frozen strudel dough, thawed
    according to directions (see headnote)
1 cup melted unsalted butter
1 cup (approximately) superfine sugar
3 cups fresh raspberries
3 tablespoons confectioners' sugar
Raspberry-Citrus Sauce (see recipe below)
4 sprigs fresh mint for garnish

1. In a small saucepan, combine gelatin with $\frac{1}{4}$ cup cold water. Place over low heat and stir until gelatin has softened, about 1 minute. Remove from heat and set aside.

2. In a medium mixing bowl, combine egg yolks, egg, salt, and $\frac{1}{4}$ cup sugar. Whisk to blend. Add flour and whisk until smooth.

3. In a large saucepan over medium heat,

combine half-and-half and remaining ¼ cup sugar. Split vanilla bean lengthwise, scrape pulp into pan, then add bean. Stir to dissolve sugar, bring to a boil, and immediately remove from heat. Whisk about 1 cup hot half-and-half into egg mixture, then immediately pour mixture back into saucepan. Return pan to medium heat and whisk constantly until thickened, about 2 to 3 minutes. Add reserved gelatin, reduce heat to low, and whisk 2 minutes more. Remove from heat and whisk in chilled butter. Pour mixture into a shallow container and place a piece of plastic film over surface. Refrigerate until well chilled, about 4 hours.

4. Preheat oven to 375 degrees. Cut a 2 by 4-inch rectangle of cardboard. Line 2 baking sheets with parchment paper.

5. Spread dough on a dry counter covered by a slightly dampened kitchen towel. Remove 1 sheet, brush lightly with melted butter, and sprinkle with superfine sugar. Repeat with 3 more sheets and stack them one on top of the other. Repeat with 4 more sheets to make another stack. Cut eight 2 by 4-inch rectangles from each stack by placing cardboard rectangle on top sheet and cutting around it all the way through. (Twelve pieces are needed; extra allowed for breakage.) Place rectangles on baking sheets and cover with parchment paper and another baking sheet. Bake until lightly golden, about 5 minutes. Remove from oven, uncover, and allow to cool. Place rectangles on wire racks and reserve.

6. Remove vanilla bean from pastry cream. Set aside 20 raspberries. Place 4 rectangles on each of 4 plates. Spoon a heaping tablespoon of cream on pastry and top with a few raspberries. Add a small spoonful of cream and top with another rectangle of pastry. Repeat to make another

layer, topped by pastry. Lightly sift confectioners' sugar over top. Serve in a pool of raspberry-citrus sauce, garnished with 5 raspberries and a sprig of mint.

Yield: 4 servings
Time: 1 hour, plus 4 hours of chilling

RASPBERRY-CITRUS SAUCE

2½ cups fresh raspberries
¼ cup fresh orange juice
1 teaspoon grated orange zest
3 tablespoons sugar

1. In a medium saucepan over low heat, combine raspberries, orange juice, zest, and sugar. Cook, stirring, until raspberries are soft, about 5 minutes. Remove from heat and transfer to a blender. Process until smooth.

2. Pour raspberry sauce through a very fine sieve, pressing to extract all puree. Discard seeds. Pour sauce into a nonreactive container and refrigerate until needed.

Yield: 1 cup
Time: 15 minutes

FOR AN EMBARRASSMENT
OF SWEET CORN

It happens every September, if you're lucky enough to have a garden. The irrational exuberance of spring—marked by serious overplanting of fruits and vegetables—inevitably ends in the glut of late summer. For some people it's tomatoes or zucchini. For me it's corn.

My mother never found that daunting. I grew up in the farm country of central New York, and my mother had a well-honed skill for turning the burden of excess into the joy of variety. I try to do that, too. With more determination than ever, I've been combining corn with other vegetables in breads, salads, relishes, and savory stuffings.

But it's when I turn back to an old and very traditional American recipe, one for corn pudding, that I think I've found my greatest success. I've devised all sorts of flavorings and additions, but this combination of musty chanterelles and sharp Parmesan is, I think, the best. Although I originally created this pudding as a side dish for pheasant, it can also make a generous appetizer or a light entree, served with a crisp salad of bitter greens.

WARM SWEET CORN PUDDING WITH CHANTERELLES AND SHAVED PARMESAN

4 tablespoons plus 2 teaspoons butter
1 pound fresh chanterelles
1½ teaspoons fresh thyme leaves
8 ears of corn
2 large eggs, separated
½ cup half-and-half
⅓ cup Wondra flour
¼ teaspoon freshly grated nutmeg
Cayenne pepper
Salt and freshly ground white pepper
2 shallots, minced
¾ cup rich chicken stock
6 sprigs fresh thyme for garnish
8 ounces Parmigiano-Reggiano cheese, in one piece

1. Preheat oven to 400 degrees. Using about 1 tablespoon butter, lightly butter six 6-ounce ramekins and set aside.

2. Mince 4 ounces of chanterelles to make about ½ cup. In a medium sauté pan over medium heat, melt 2 teaspoons butter and add minced chanterelles and ½ teaspoon thyme leaves. Sauté until mushrooms are soft and have released most of their liquid, about 4 minutes. Remove from heat and set aside.

3. Shuck corn and remove silk. Remove kernels by setting corn upright on a cutting board and slicing downward with a sharp knife. Set cobs aside on a plate. Over a shallow bowl, scrape each cob with a small spoon to remove any remaining corn. Place these scrapings in container of a blender or food processor and add 3 cups corn kernels, reserving remainder. Puree until smooth.

4. Melt 2 tablespoons butter and place in a medium mixing bowl. Add corn puree, egg

yolks, half-and-half, remaining corn kernels, and reserved sautéed chanterelles. Whisk in flour, nutmeg, cayenne, and salt and pepper to taste.

5. Bring a kettle of water to a boil. Using an electric mixer, beat egg whites until soft peaks form. Gently fold into corn mixture. Spoon mixture into ramekins and place in a baking dish large enough to allow about 1 inch around each ramekin. Pour in enough boiling water to come halfway up sides of ramekins. Bake until puddings are golden brown, about 35 minutes.

6. While puddings are baking, prepare remaining chanterelles. If large, slice in half lengthwise. In a large sauté pan over medium heat, melt remaining tablespoon butter and add shallots and remaining 1 teaspoon thyme leaves. Sauté until shallots are translucent, about 2 minutes. Add chanterelles and sauté until tender, about 3 minutes. Add stock and season with salt and pepper to taste. Reduce heat to low and sauté until mushrooms are well cooked and silky, about 5 minutes.

7. To serve, spoon equal portions of sautéed chanterelles onto each of 6 warm plates, reserving a small quantity for garnish. Run a small, sharp knife around inside edge of each ramekin and unmold into center of each plate. Garnish with a sprig of fresh thyme inserted in center and a couple of chanterelles. Using a cheese shaver or slicer on a box grater, shave 2 or 3 very thin slices of Parmigiano-Reggiano over plate. Serve immediately.

Yield: 6 servings
Time: 1 1/2 hours

LETTING FRUITS LAZE AROUND IN A WARM OVEN HAS AMBROSIAL RESULTS

For some years now I have been using low, dry heat to add intense flavor to tomatoes or to make sweet root vegetable chips. I simply put the vegetables in a very low oven and let them laze away as the moisture is slowly drawn out and the sugars become caramelized and profoundly sweet. Recently I began experimenting with this oven-drying technique to bring out the inherent syrupy goodness in fruits I use for desserts and condiments.

At the restaurant we have turned out ambrosial, lightly dried peaches, plums, and nectarines as they hit the height of their ripeness in the summer. As fall approaches we begin drying heirloom apples and pears. Drying fruit (or vegetables) at home is just as easy. Any type of oven will do: gas, electric, or convection.

If you are in no hurry and if you have an oven setting of less than 200 degrees, which is usually marked "warm," use that setting and let the fruit dry for up to twelve hours. If 200 degrees is your lowest setting, dry the fruit for no longer than six hours. The larger the pieces, the moister the fruit (or vegetable) will remain.

For this fall salad, the pears are only lightly dried. They retain a great deal of their moisture, and their sugar takes on just a hint of caramel. To add an even greater depth of flavor, I marinate them in port and ginger before sending them off for a long bask.

COMPOSED SALAD WITH FENNEL, OVEN-DRIED PEARS, WALNUTS, AND MAYTAG BLUE CHEESE

6 Comice pears
1 cup port wine
3 tablespoons light brown sugar
1 teaspoon grated fresh ginger
½ cup extra-virgin olive oil
3 tablespoons fine-quality, well-aged
    balsamic vinegar
Coarse salt and freshly cracked black pepper
    to taste
2 medium fennel bulbs
2 heads red oak leaf lettuce, well washed,
    dried, and pulled apart
½ cup toasted walnut pieces (if available,
    black walnuts add an interesting note)
4 ounces Maytag blue cheese

1. Peel pears, cut in half lengthwise, and carefully remove core and stem.

2. Combine port, brown sugar, and ginger in a shallow baking dish. Add pear halves, cut side down, and spoon port mixture over them. Cover with plastic film and marinate for 1 hour, turning from time to time.

3. Preheat oven to 200 degrees. Place marinated pears on a parchment paper–lined baking sheet in oven and dry about 1 hour, or until pears are just beginning to firm but remain moist in center.

4. Whisk together oil and vinegar. Season with salt and pepper. Wash and trim fennel bulbs, cut in half lengthwise, and then cut into very thin slices.

5. Beginning at wide end, cut each pear half lengthwise, down to but not through stem end.

6. Toss fennel and lettuce together. Add a small amount of dressing and toss to combine. Place equal portions of dressed mixture on each of 6 luncheon plates. Fan 2 pear halves across greens, overlapping stem ends. Sprinkle a few walnut pieces around edge of plate. Crumble an equal portion of cheese over each plate. Drizzle a bit of remaining dressing on top and serve.

Yield: 6 servings
Time: 2 ¼ hours, including 2 hours of marinating and drying

A FARM SUPPER WITH A TOUCH OF EXTRAVAGANCE

My mom had a stick-to-your-ribs approach to cooking —which was fine by me and my six brothers and sisters—and her braised pork chops with mashed potatoes and cream gravy was one of our favorite fall meals. In those days pork was a different meat. Rich and fatty, it was the sort of everyday food that rarely appeared on the menus of fine restaurants. Today, hogs are being raised for more flavor and less fat. And along with many other chefs, I now use pork in both hearty and light dishes. Its tender texture lends the meat to a quick roast or braise, and its mild flavor makes a good match for most vegetables and a great variety of herbs and spices.

In this dish I moved only a little bit away from family tradition by combining a simply roasted pork tenderloin with a creamy French gratin. The leanness of this cut allowed me a bit of extravagance with heavy cream and cheese. To liven things up I added turnips to the gratin for a contrast in taste and texture. Cooked, the turnips become lighter and add a sweet, astringent counterpoint to the soft butteriness of the potatoes. As a final bit of tinkering, I infused the cream with roasted garlic for sweetness and depth.

On the plate, the dish cries out for the color and balance of fresh greens; try some sautéed kale or spinach.

ROAST TENDERLOIN OF PORK WITH POTATO-TURNIP GRATIN

Butter for greasing dish
4 cloves garlic, roasted (see Note)
1 cup heavy cream
1 pound potatoes, peeled and cut into ⅛-inch slices
1 pound turnips, peeled and cut into ⅛-inch slices
4 tablespoons butter at room temperature, cut into small pieces
½ cup grated Emmenthal cheese
Freshly ground nutmeg
¼ cup fresh bread crumbs
3 pork tenderloins, 10 to 12 ounces each, well trimmed of all fat and silver skin
Kosher salt and freshly ground black pepper
2 tablespoons canola oil
1½ cups chicken stock or low-sodium canned broth
¾ cup dry white wine
2 teaspoons minced fresh thyme
2 teaspoons minced fresh sage
1 teaspoon minced fresh flat-leaf parsley
6 sprigs fresh thyme for garnish

1. Preheat oven to 425 degrees. Lightly butter a round gratin dish, 10 by 2 inches. Whisk roasted garlic into cream until very well blended; set aside.

2. In a large mixing bowl, toss potato and turnip slices until well combined. Using a clean kitchen towel, pat slices until very dry. Spread half of slices evenly across bottom of gratin dish. Sprinkle with 2 tablespoons butter, ¼ cup cheese, and nutmeg to taste. Repeat with remaining potato and turnip slices, butter, cheese, and nutmeg. Pour garlic-flavored cream on top. Sprinkle with

bread crumbs. Bake until vegetables are tender and top is golden, about 30 minutes.

3. While gratin is baking, prepare pork tenderloins: Season pork with salt and pepper to taste. In a large nonstick ovenproof sauté pan, heat oil over medium-high heat. Add tenderloins to pan and sear, turning frequently, until well browned on all sides, about 6 minutes. Transfer tenderloins to a plate and drain excess oil from pan.

4. Return tenderloins to pan and add stock, ½ cup wine, 1 teaspoon thyme, and 1 teaspoon sage. Stir to blend. Place sauté pan in oven with gratin. Roast until an instant-read thermometer inserted into thickest part of meat registers 150 degrees, about 15 minutes; the pork should be slightly pink in the center. Remove pan from oven and let pork rest for 5 minutes. Transfer to a platter and carve crosswise into ¼-inch-thick slices. Cover loosely with aluminum foil and keep warm.

5. Strain pan juices into a small saucepan and skim off excess grease; set aside. Place sauté pan over high heat and add remaining ¼ cup wine. Cook, stirring constantly, until pan is deglazed, about 1 minute. Pour deglazing juices into pan juices. Place saucepan over high heat and bring to a boil. Lower heat and simmer about 3 minutes. Add remaining 1 teaspoon thyme, remaining 1 teaspoon sage, and parsley. Adjust salt and pepper to taste.

6. Cut 6 equal wedges of potato-turnip gratin and place 1 in center of each of 6 warm dinner plates. Place 3 to 4 slices of pork tenderloin around 1 side of wedge on each plate. Drizzle pan juices around plate. Garnish with a thyme sprig and serve.

Yield: 6 servings
Time: 1 hour

NOTE: To roast garlic, trim top third from a large head of garlic. Rub head with olive oil, wrap in aluminum foil, and bake at 325 degrees until cloves are soft, about 45 minutes.

———

SIMPLY THE FLAVOR OF APPLES, BUT MORE SO

My sister and her husband run an old-fashioned cider mill in Fly Creek, New York, just outside Cooperstown. The mill's 1889 press, powered by a thumping water wheel, makes a rich and delicious apple cider that has become a fixture on our fall table. After a day at the mill, it always seems natural to use the cider or just-picked apples in some part of the evening meal. Frequently, it is a main course of apples with pork or game. But if a vote were taken, an apple dessert would be my family's choice—and this one would be the favorite.

It is a simple tart made of razor-thin slices of apple and a flat disk of traditional American pastry. No frangipane. No pastry cream. No dense apple filling. Just a thin pastry paved with a layer of tart apples.

All this simplicity is a little deceptive. There are several reasons the tart tastes so intensely—almost overpoweringly—of apple. First, the thin slices dry a little as they brown, becoming chewy and more concentrated in flavor. I spike them with another layer of apple flavor—the cider—and balance it with a bit of cinnamon. The crust has just the right crunchy resistance. And I like to give it yet another zap of apple with a scoop of cider sorbet. Because the sorbet is made with a puree of cooked apple rather than apple juice, it is creamy, not icy, and has a more substantial texture.

But I'm sure a scoop of premium vanilla ice cream would bring no complaints.

RUSTIC APPLE TART WITH CIDER SORBET

3 medium Granny Smith apples, peeled and
    cored
Juice of 1 lemon
3 tablespoons apple cider
1/2 cup sugar
3 tablespoons Wondra flour
1 tablespoon ground cinnamon
3 tablespoons unsalted butter, melted
Flaky Pastry Dough, chilled (see recipe
    below)
2 tablespoons cinnamon sugar
Cider Sorbet (see recipe below)

1. Halve apples lengthwise and cut each half into almost paper-thin slices. Place slices in a mixing bowl and sprinkle with lemon juice. Add cider and toss to combine. Add sugar, flour, and cinnamon, and toss to coat well. Drizzle butter over top and toss again to combine.

2. Preheat oven to 375 degrees. Place dough on a lightly floured surface and roll it from center out into a circle about 9 inches in diameter and 1/4 inch thick. Carefully lift dough onto an 8-inch pizza pan or a pizza stone. There will be about 1 inch of overhang. Fold overhang under to give pastry circle a double thickness along edge. Using fingertips, crimp a neat, fluted rim on edge.

3. Working from edge toward center, make concentric circles of slightly overlapping apple slices, keeping outside edge of slices facing crimped edge of dough. At center of tart use a few apple slices to make a slightly raised rosette shape. Sprinkle top of apples with cinnamon sugar.

4. Place tart in oven and bake until crust is golden and apples are barely tender, caramelized, and beginning to brown on edges, about 40 min-

utes. Remove from oven and allow to rest for 15 minutes. Cut into wedges and serve with cider sorbet.

Yield: 8-inch tart (8 to 10 servings)
Time: 1 1/2 hours

FLAKY PASTRY DOUGH

1 1/4 cups all-purpose flour
1 1/2 teaspoons sugar
1/2 teaspoon salt, or to taste
1/2 cup vegetable shortening, chilled and cut
    into small pieces
3 tablespoons (approximately) ice water

1. Sift flour, sugar, and salt into a medium mixing bowl. Add shortening and, using a fork, toss to coat well. Use a pastry blender or 2 knives to cut shortening into flour mixture until it resembles a rather lumpy, coarse meal.

2. Add ice water, 1 tablespoon at a time, around edge of bowl. Using a fork, mix dough together as water is added; all the water may not be needed. Dough will begin to form solid lumps. When there are more lumps than there is loose flour and dough holds together when pressed against side of bowl, quickly form dough into a ball with floured hands. Flatten ball into a large disk and cover with plastic wrap. Refrigerate at least 30 minutes or up to 3 days.

Yield: 9-inch single crust
Time: 20 minutes plus chilling time

APPRECIATING A ROYAL BIRD

2 pounds (about 4) Granny Smith apples,
    peeled, cored, and finely chopped
1 cup fresh apple cider or hard cider
1 cup sugar
1 3-inch cinnamon stick
1 teaspoon fresh orange zest
⅓ cup fresh lemon juice

1. In a medium saucepan, combine apples and ⅓ cup apple cider. Bring to a boil, then reduce heat to low. Simmer, stirring frequently, until apples have softened, about 15 minutes. Remove from heat and allow to cool. Stir to blend into a smooth puree, or puree in a blender or food processor.

2. In a medium saucepan, combine sugar, 1 cup cold water, cinnamon stick, and orange zest. Bring to a boil over high heat and boil for 1 minute. Remove from heat and add lemon juice. Allow to cool (for faster cooling, place bowl over ice water). Strain through a very fine sieve, discarding solids.

3. Measure 2½ cups apple puree and combine in a bowl with strained sugar syrup and remaining ⅔ cup cider. Stir to blend well. Pour mixture into an ice cream maker and freeze according to manufacturer's instructions.

Yield: about 5 cups
Time: 45 minutes plus freezing time

Unlike most of today's outdoorsmen, my dad hunted and fished for sustenance rather than sport. As soon as we were old enough, my brothers and I joined him in the fields and forests of upstate New York, bringing home deer, rabbit, pheasant, partridge, and a host of other game birds. Years later, while training to become a chef, I learned truly to appreciate the complex flavor of game. And as it becomes more widely available in the market, game is becoming more popular among home cooks who aren't living as close to the land as I once did.

Today, most game animals are raised on farms or in game preserves. It's true: farm-raised game birds do not have the subtlety of flavor of those taken in the wild. But they do have some advantages: They have a more assertive flavor than more familiar poultry, they are lean, and they allow the cook to prepare game throughout the year.

At the table, pheasant has a long history as the king of game birds, notably in classic French preparations. Like all royalty, though, it requires careful handling. Pheasant, particularly the breast, quickly loses moisture when it is roasted. Instead, I give it a quick searing at high heat, which seals in the juices and creates a crisp crust. Kale and cabbage make a fine complement in flavor and texture. I finish the dish with a subtle pan sauce of sweet sherry and pungent shallots infused with thyme, citrus, and mint.

In the end, the dish is a balance of the straightforward and the sophisticated, delicate and hearty: humble greens and royal bird.

PHEASANT BREAST WITH HARDY GREENS

¼ cup plus 3 tablespoons shelled pistachios
8 ounces fresh kale
6 boneless pheasant breasts, with skin
Kosher salt and freshly ground black pepper
3 tablespoons corn oil
5 tablespoons minced shallots
2 teaspoons minced fresh thyme
⅓ cup sherry
1 cup rich chicken stock or low-sodium canned broth
6 tablespoons butter
1 pound savoy cabbage, roughly chopped
6 sprigs fresh thyme for garnish

1. Preheat oven to 350 degrees. Spread pistachios on a baking sheet and bake until slightly crisp and brown, about 5 minutes. Set aside. Bring a large pot of water to a boil. Add kale and blanch for 10 seconds. Drain immediately, rinse with cold water, and drain again. Set aside.

2. Season pheasant breasts with salt and pepper to taste. In a large sauté pan over medium heat, heat oil and add breasts, skin side down. Sear until a crisp, golden crust forms, 6 to 7 minutes. Turn and sear other side for 4 to 5 minutes. Remove breasts to a warm platter and cover lightly with aluminum foil to keep warm.

3. Return sauté pan to medium heat. Add 3 tablespoons shallots and thyme. Sauté until shallots are softened, about 2 minutes. Add sherry and stir to deglaze pan. Raise heat to medium-high and simmer until sherry is slightly reduced, about 3 minutes. Stir in stock, reduce heat to low, and simmer for 4 minutes. Whisk in 4 tablespoons butter, 1 tablespoon at a time, until a smooth sauce forms. Adjust salt and pepper to taste, and keep warm.

4. In a large sauté pan over medium heat, melt remaining 2 tablespoons butter. Add remaining 2 tablespoons shallots and sauté until softened, about 2 minutes. Add cabbage, kale, and salt and pepper to taste. Reduce heat to low and sauté greens until wilted and well coated with butter. Add ¼ cup pistachios and toss to mix. Remove from heat.

5. To serve, place an equal amount of greens in center of each of 6 warm dinner plates. Place a pheasant breast on top of each plate of greens. Drizzle pan sauce over pheasant and around edge of plate. Sprinkle each plate with some of remaining pistachios. Place thyme sprig in each pheasant breast and serve immediately.

Yield: 6 servings
Time: 1 hour

FRANÇOIS PAYARD

François Payard is the chef and owner of Payard Patisserie and Bistro in Manhattan. He was photographed in front of the restaurant. These columns were written with Dorie Greenspan.

DESSERTS ANYONE CAN DO AT HOME

When I opened my own pastry shop, I wanted the selection of pastries, cakes, and chocolates to be so dazzling that people would not only have trouble deciding what to taste first, but also wonder how everything was made. Most of what we do at the shop is pretty complicated, and after all, if everyone could make these sweets at home, who'd need us?

But I also have a large repertory of desserts that anyone can do at home. They're the desserts I prepare on my day off and the ones that my wife, Alexandra, makes for friends. These are the desserts I'm going to share with you, starting with a pain d'épices from my childhood. All through my school years, my four o'clock snack was always the same: Van Damme's pain d'épices—literally, spice bread; in reality, a cross between a honey cake and a spice loaf. Even though my

father and my grandfather were pastry chefs, I got the same straight-from-the-grocery cake everyone else did.

Years later, still in love with the memory of Van Damme's, I decided to do my own version, one with deeper flavor and lots more add-ins. My pain d'épices is three-quarters nuts and dried fruits. When you cut a slice, you see a mosaic of ingredients that are held together by the batter, which is nothing more than honey, water, sugar, flour, and fragrant spices. There are no eggs and no butter in the cake, a rarity in the annals of pastry.

This recipe makes four small loaves. There's no reason to cut the recipe down, because this cake is an excellent keeper. In fact, it should not really be eaten until three days after it's made: Its flavors need time to ripen. In addition, this cake is great toasted for breakfast and superb with savory foods.

Butter for greasing pans

Flour for dusting pans

2 cups nuts, preferably a mix of sliced almonds, slivered almonds, skinned pistachios, skinned hazelnuts, walnut halves, and pine nuts

1 cup dried fruit cut in ¼-inch dice, preferably equal amounts of apricots, figs, prunes, and dates

¼ cup dark raisins

¼ cup golden raisins

Zest of 1 lemon, finely grated

Zest of 1 orange, finely grated

4 teaspoons baking soda

1 teaspoon pastis or other anise-flavored liqueur

¼ teaspoon ground cinnamon

¼ teaspoon freshly grated nutmeg

¼ teaspoon ground cloves, optional

Pinch of salt

1 cup pine honey or other strongly flavored honey

¾ cup sugar

2 tablespoons dark rum

2 pieces star anise, tied in cheesecloth

3 cups all-purpose flour, sifted

1. Preheat oven to 350 degrees. Butter 4 aluminum foil baby loaf pans, each 5¾ by 3¼ by 2 inches. Dust insides with flour and tap out excess. Place pans on baking sheet and set aside.

2. In a large mixing bowl, combine nuts, diced fruit, dark raisins, golden raisins, lemon zest, and orange zest. Mix well. Add baking soda, pastis, cinnamon, nutmeg, cloves, and salt. Stir to mix.

3. In a medium saucepan over medium heat, combine 1¾ cups water with honey, sugar, rum, and star anise. Bring to a boil and immediately take off heat. Remove and discard star anise. Pour liquid into bowl of fruit and nuts, and stir gently. Let mixture rest for 5 minutes, stirring occasionally. Add flour, stir well, and let rest for 2 or 3 minutes.

4. Divide batter among pans; they will be about three-quarters full. Place baking sheet in oven. Bake until knife inserted in center of cakes comes out with a tiny bit of moist batter at the tip, 45 to 50 minutes. (Check cakes after 20 minutes of baking; if at any time the cakes appear to be browning too quickly, cover them loosely with a tent of aluminum foil.)

5. Transfer cakes to a rack and let cool to room temperature. Unmold and wrap in plastic film. To serve, cut into thin slices. The cakes are best after ripening for three days at room temperature. They may be frozen for a month if sealed in airtight wrap.

Yield: 4 small loaves

Time: 1¼ hours, plus cooling

A SWEET LESSON FROM MY GRANDFATHER

At my grandfather's pastry shop in Nice there was always a large selection of sweets that were called "mamie cakes" because they were the favorites of that French city's grandmothers, the "mamies" who took up teatime as a daily treat. Any cake that didn't have cream, custard, or mousse was a mamie cake (it's pronounced ma-MEE, with the "a" as in mat).

It wasn't until I was older that I learned that these mamie cakes have a real name. Pastry chefs call them gateaux secs, or dry cakes, and the category includes anything from a cookie to a kugelhopf. And as you'll see from this recipe, the word "dry" has nothing to do with consistency or texture.

This particular mamie cake—it's really a tart, but my grandfather always called it a cake—is filled with sweet fresh pineapple and is topped with a macaroon-like layer of coconut. It was one of the first cakes I learned to make when I was thirteen, and it is one I continue to make, delighted to find it has fans of every age.

The coco-mamie is made in a pâte sucrée, or sweet tart crust. The crust, mixed in the food processor, is soft and crumbly, and is itself the stuff of great cookies. It's easiest to work after it's been chilled. If crusts have frightened you in the past, try this one; perfection is not required. In fact, unlike most crusts, this one should be rolled fairly thick. And because the cake's topping is spread all the way to the edge of the crust and even beyond, there's no need to worry about the edges being exactly even.

The sweetness comes from the pineapple. If your pineapple is great, your coco-mamie will be great. That is the key to success. My first choice is pineapples from Costa Rica. They're supersweet, and since I use the fruit in its natural state, sweetness counts. If you can't get a soft, golden pineapple with that wonderful ripe perfume, you can try doctoring the best pineapple you can find by sautéeing it in butter, a little sugar, and the scraped-out pulp of a fresh vanilla bean. Or in a pinch you can use well-drained canned pineapple.

COCO-MAMIE CAKE

For the crust:
   9 tablespoons unsalted butter at room temperature
   1 cup all-purpose flour
   ½ cup confectioners' sugar
   ½ teaspoon salt
   1 large egg, lightly beaten

For the filling:
   ½ small pineapple, cut into tiny dice (about 2 cups)
   3½ tablespoons unsalted butter, softened
   ½ cup sugar
   1½ cups finely shredded unsweetened coconut (available in health-food stores)
   1 large egg, lightly beaten

1. To make crust: Put butter, flour, sugar, and salt in bowl of a food processor and process until ingredients are well blended. Scrape down sides of bowl and add egg. Process just until egg is completely incorporated; you will have a very soft, creamy dough. Remove dough, flatten it out into a disk shape, wrap in plastic film, and freeze for 1 hour.

2. Butter an 8-inch-round fluted metal tart pan, 1¼ inches high, with a removable bottom, and place on a baking sheet. On a lightly floured work surface, roll dough into a circle about ⅛ inch thick. Fit dough into pan and trim off excess so dough is level with top of pan.

3. To make filling: Spread pineapple evenly along bottom of crust and return crust to freezer for about 1 hour. At end of that time, preheat oven to 350 degrees.

4. Blend butter and sugar together, working with a rubber spatula. Stir in coconut, and when it is well blended, incorporate egg. Still using spatula, spread filling evenly over frozen pineapple, pressing down lightly on fruit to get filling into crevices. Spread filling all the way to edge of crust. Slide cake into oven and bake for 50 to 55 minutes, or until crust is baked through and filling is golden brown and firmly set on top. Transfer cake to a rack and let cool.

Yield: 6 to 8 servings
Time: 1 hour, plus 2 hours of freezing

WHY THE BEACH TASTES OF A FRENCH CHILDHOOD

"Chi-chi, beignets, glace, et boissons fraiches," the French vendors would call out along the beach in Nice: "Crullers, beignets, ice cream, and cold drinks." The sing-song phrase is engraved in my memory from summer days playing along the Mediterranean. I can't recall how we managed to eat those beignets—thin slices of apple dipped in batter and fried—with sandy, salty fingers, but I know we did because each time I make one I can see the beach.

Most cultures have some form of beignet; I'm thinking of American fritters, Japanese tempura, or the fried puffs of dough dipped in honey that my wife's Italian family serves after every holiday meal. In France, beignets are considered a classic dessert, but they can be savory, too—what you dip in a beignet batter is up to you.

In the fall I make beignets with quinces. Quinces are a lot like apples, but the texture is firmer, so I poach them for a few minutes in a citrus-infused sugar syrup to soften their bite and add some extra flavor. When quinces are no longer at the market, you can use apples or pears or even bananas, which don't need to be poached. And while some beignet batters are nothing more than flour, water, and salt, and others use both beer and yeast to leaven them, I make a batter with beer as the leavening and an egg for richness, flavor, and more puff.

It's your choice whether to serve the beignets hot enough to burn a few fingers or to stack them up and enjoy them at room temperature. But hot or cold, they should be dusted with confectioners' sugar. You can stop there, or you can make a wonderful crème anglaise, a pouring custard that I think is the best beignet dip. Too bad the beach vendors didn't have this; it would have made a great thing even greater.

QUINCE BEIGNETS

1 cup plus 3 tablespoons sugar
2 broad strips orange zest
1 broad strip lemon zest
1 vanilla bean, split lengthwise
4 medium quinces, peeled
1 cup all-purpose flour
Salt
1 large egg
1 cup beer
4 cups oil for deep frying
Confectioners' sugar for dusting
Orange Flower Crème Anglaise (see recipe
  below)

1. In a medium saucepan, combine 4 cups water, 1 cup sugar, orange zest, lemon zest, and vanilla bean. Place over high heat and bring to a boil. In the meantime, cut each quince crosswise into 4 slices. Using a thin, sharp knife, cut core from each slice.

2. Add quince slices to boiling syrup and reduce heat to low. Poach slices until they can be pierced easily with a knife, about 8 to 10 minutes. Drain on a cooling rack.

3. In a medium mixing bowl, combine flour, remaining 3 tablespoons sugar, a pinch of salt, and egg. Whisk together to blend thoroughly. Very gradually add beer, whisking until batter is smooth and consistency of heavy cream.

4. In a medium saucepan over medium heat, heat oil until a bit of batter tossed in sinks and then pops up quickly. Working with 4 at a time, dip slices into batter to coat evenly, then drop into oil. Fry until golden on both sides, about 3 minutes. Drain on paper towels and continue with remaining quince slices. Dust beignets with confectioners'

sugar. Serve hot or at room temperature, accompanied by orange flower crème anglaise for dipping.

Yield: 16 beignets
Time: 45 minutes

ORANGE FLOWER CRÈME ANGLAISE

6 large egg yolks
1 cup sugar
1 teaspoon flour
2 cups half-and-half
2 broad strips orange zest
2 tablespoons orange flower water

1. In a medium mixing bowl, combine egg yolks, sugar, and flour. Whisk together until thick and pale.

2. In a small saucepan, combine half-and-half and orange zest. Place over medium heat and bring to a boil. While whisking egg mixture, very slowly pour about half of hot cream over yolks. Pour yolk mixture back into pot.

3. Stirring constantly with a wooden spoon, heat until crème anglaise is thick enough to coat back of a spoon, about 5 minutes. If you run your finger down back of spoon, mixture should not run into track that is made. Remove from heat immediately and strain into a bowl.

4. Press a piece of plastic wrap against surface. Refrigerate until cool, about 30 minutes, then stir in orange flower water. Serve chilled with quince beignets.

Yield: 3 cups
*Time: 25 minutes, plus about 30 minutes for
  cooling*

A BUTTERY APPLE CAKE,
JUST LIKE PAPA MAKES

This simple apple loaf cake, made from a buttery bat-
ter and filled and topped with chunky apple wedges, is
exactly the same cake my father created for his pastry
shop in Nice twenty years ago. I wouldn't think of
changing it, and the truth is, my father would never
let me. To his way of thinking, a recipe should be
changed only if customers don't like it. And his cus-
tomers liked his apple cake so much that, the first day
he made it, he had to rush out and buy extra cake pans
to bake more. Today he still sells one hundred of these
small cakes a day.

In France, Papa would use only one kind of apple,
la reine des reinettes, a juicy apple that retains its
moistness no matter how long it is baked. My father
used it in his loaf cakes until June when the apples from
the fall harvest were no longer firm and fine, and then
he stopped making the cake.

Or at least he tried to stop. His customers, used to
their daily dose, didn't care that apples weren't avail-
able; they wanted their cake. And so my father made
the only change to the recipe he ever considered accept-
able: He made the cake with fresh—only fresh, never
canned—apricots. Fortunately, by the time the supply
of apricots was depleted, it was apple season again.

In New York I use Fuji apples. They have a good
sweet-tart balance and, like la reine des reinettes, they
keep their juiciness and their shape under heat. To make
the cake really taste like an apple cake, cut the apples
into hefty, broad wedges. To make it look like an apple
cake, I set two decorative rows along the top of the loaf.
I use an apple slicer, one of those contraptions that cores
the apple and cuts it into a dozen perfectly even wedges
at the same time.

Papa soaked the raisins that dot this cake in rum,
and so do I. But if rum is not to your liking, you can
omit this step. I promise I won't tell Papa, if you prom-
ise not to tell him that I once served slices of this cake
with piña colada crème anglaise. He'd never approve.

PAPA'S APPLE POUND CAKE

Butter and flour for baking pan
1⅓ cup raisins
1 tablespoon plus 2½ teaspoons dark rum
2 Fuji apples, peeled and cored
1 cup plus 3 tablespoons all-purpose flour
¼ teaspoon baking powder
8½ tablespoons unsalted butter at room
   temperature
1⅓ cups confectioners' sugar
3 large eggs at room temperature
4 tablespoons apricot jam, melted and still
   warm

1. Place rack in center of oven and heat oven
to 350 degrees. Butter and flour an 8 by 4 by 2½-
inch loaf pan. Line pan with parchment paper, allowing an extra 1 or 2 inches to drape over
opposite ends. This will allow finished cake to be
lifted from pan before serving.

2. Bring a small pan of water to a boil, add
raisins, and boil for 1 minute. Drain and repeat
process. Drain raisins well a second time and
place in a small bowl with 1 tablespoon rum; stir
and set aside. Cut 1 apple into 12 wedges and set
aside. Cut other apple into 8 wedges and then cut
each wedge in half crosswise; set aside. In a medium mixing bowl, sift flour and baking powder
together; set aside.

3. In a mixer with a paddle attachment or by
hand with a rubber spatula, beat butter until
smooth. Slowly add 1 cup confectioners' sugar

and beat until creamy. Add eggs, 1 at a time, beating until mixture is well blended.

4. Fold sifted flour mixture into egg mixture just until blended. Fold raisins into batter. Spoon half of batter into prepared pan and smooth top. Lay 12 apple wedges down center of pan so their sides touch and domed side of each wedge is on top. There will be a thin strip of exposed batter on either side of row. Spoon remaining batter over and around apples, and again smooth top. Arrange halved apple slices in a single row along each long side of pan, pressing center-cut sides of apples against sides of pan. There will be 2 rows of apple slices, with their points toward center of pan, and exposed batter in center. Gently push apples into batter, leaving top of apples exposed. Mixture in center of pan will be slightly shallower than sides. Let rest for 10 minutes.

5. Place pan in oven and bake for 10 minutes. Using a sharp knife, cut a slit down center of batter to help it rise evenly. Continue to bake until a knife inserted into cake comes out clean, another 40 to 50 minutes. Remove pan from oven and turn off heat. Gently brush warm apricot jam over hot cake; allow glaze to dry for 5 minutes.

6. Meanwhile, in a small pan, combine remaining 2½ teaspoons rum and ⅓ cup confectioners' sugar. Stir well and warm icing over low heat for a minute. Brush over dried apricot glaze and return pan to turned-off oven just until rum icing is dry, about 2 minutes. Place cake on a rack and cool to room temperature. To keep cake moist, leave it in its pan until serving time. To remove cake from pan, lift it by edges of parchment paper, carefully remove paper, and transfer to a platter. Cut into slices and serve.

Yield: 6 to 8 servings
Time: 1¾ hours, plus cooling

AFTER THE FEAST, AN INNOVATIVE ENDING

It wasn't until I came to America twelve years ago that I learned a real Thanksgiving feast required more than a turkey—it had to be accompanied by stuffing (preferably with chestnuts), sweet potatoes (with or without marshmallows), cranberry sauce, and pumpkin pie. Of course, we have all those things on our Thanksgiving table, but I've also added a newcomer: my squash and fennel tartlets.

I've been playing around with the idea for years. My original thought was to have rounds of puff pastry spread with star anise pastry cream and some candied fennel, topped with lemon sorbet and a few pistachio nuts. I occasionally mentioned the idea to other French pastry chefs, and the response was always the same: "It's too crazy. Forget it." But I couldn't get the idea out of my head.

So I thought I'd try out my dessert on an American audience. Unfortunately, test one was a flop—the anise pastry cream was too strong for the fennel, but without it the puff pastry and fennel were too dry. Three tests later I thought of pumpkin pie and got the idea to use a butternut squash puree in place of the pastry cream. Since I didn't want the usual spices that go into pumpkin pie— they, too, would overwhelm the fennel—I selected squash puree au naturel, mild, smooth, and almost as rich and buttery as the pastry cream it replaced.

The squash was the right choice, but the tartlets lacked acidity, a problem solved with the lemon sorbet and a splash of lime juice in the puree. Then, just when I thought I was done, I realized that the pistachio nuts were too bland. First, I toasted them; their flavor was better, but their color was lost. Then I omitted them, but the tart needed crunch. Finally, I tossed them in egg white and sugar and baked them until they were bumpy, crackly, and lightly caramelized. Voila! Nuts with looks, taste, and enough crunch for the tart.

¼ cup confectioners' sugar

1 egg white

⅓ cup shelled and skinned pistachio nuts

8 ounces packaged puff pastry

2 cups sugar

Zest of 1 lemon, cut in broad strips

Zest of 1 orange, cut in broad strips

1 clove

1 star anise

2 small bulbs fennel, trimmed and cut into thin slices

2 tablespoons unsalted butter

1 butternut squash (about 1½ pounds), peeled, seeded, and cut into ¾-inch dice

¼ cup apple cider

Juice of 1 lime

2 cups lemon sorbet

1. Preheat oven to 300 degrees. Line a baking sheet with parchment. Place confectioners' sugar in a small bowl. Spoon half of egg white onto a plate (discard other half). Toss pistachios in egg white to coat them, then toss in confectioners' sugar until they are lightly coated and do not stick together. Place nuts on baking sheet and bake until brown and starting to crack. Remove from oven and set aside to cool.

2. Increase oven temperature to 400 degrees. On a lightly floured work surface roll out puff pastry to ⅛-inch thickness and cut into eight 4-inch circles. Place on a parchment-lined baking sheet and put a lightweight wire cooling rack on top pastry to keep it from puffing too much. Bake until golden, 5 to 6 minutes. Cool on a rack to room temperature.

3. In a large saucepan, combine sugar, lemon zest, orange zest, clove, and star anise with 1 cup water. Place over high heat and bring to a boil. Turn off heat, cover, and allow mixture to rest 5 minutes. Using a slotted spoon, remove zest and spices, and return mixture to a boil. Add fennel and reduce heat to medium-low. Poach fennel until translucent, about 15 minutes. Cool fennel in liquid.

4. While fennel is poaching, place a large skillet over medium heat. Melt butter and add squash. Sauté until squash is very tender, about 15 minutes. Add cider and continue stirring until it evaporates. Transfer squash and pan juices to container of a blender. Add lime juice and process until mixture is smooth.

5. With a small spoon, hollow out center of each pastry round, leaving some pastry for a base. Fill each hollow with about 2 tablespoons squash puree. Top with poached fennel, place some around edge of tartlet, and mound some in center. Scatter pistachio nuts on top of tartlet and around plate, and top each tartlet with a small scoop of lemon sorbet.

Yield: 8 servings
Time: 1 hour

A TOUCH OF CINNAMON IN PUFF-PASTRY COOKIES

I heard a story that may or may not be true, but it certainly makes a point. After World War II, inspectors were going through the food depots somewhere in France and discovered that most of the supplies had been ravaged by rats. One observant inspector was supposed to have said, "We can be sure of only one thing—the rats were French. The cinnamon is untouched."

As much as Americans love cinnamon, that's about how much we French don't. Vanilla is the typical Frenchman's favorite flavor, so you can imagine the adjustment I had to make when I came to work in America. Fortunately for me, I've come to like cinnamon—as long as it's not overpowering. These puff-pastry cookies are perfect for my taste: They sandwich just a dollop of cinnamon-scented pastry cream.

The inspiration for these festive cookies, great for the holidays, came from a classic French petit four: the allumette, or match, a thin rectangle of puff pastry topped with a baked-on glaze. For my cookies, made with store-bought puff pastry, the pastry is rolled paper-thin and spread with royal icing, a blend of confectioners' sugar and egg white. Then—and here's a feature that makes them right for the holidays—the pastry can be frozen for a month. When you want cookies, all you have to do is defrost, cut out (I make these star-shaped), and bake in a double process: First, you put the cookies into a hot oven to set the icing, which pulls away from the pastry so that you can lift it off and keep it aside; next, you bake the bottoms until they're puffed and perfectly caramelized, a trick to avoid the common problem of soggy half-done puff pastry. Give the cookies their pastry cream filling, and you're set.

You can add ground cinnamon to the icing if you want more of that spice, or sprinkle the icing with colored sugar or even sprinkles. You can vary the pastry cream, too. Make a plain pastry cream and flavor it with orange zest, instant coffee, or cocoa powder; or, if you're French, go for vanilla.

CINNAMON STARS

8 ounces packaged all-butter puff pastry
2 cups whole milk
3 cinnamon sticks
½ cup sugar
3 tablespoons all-purpose flour
3 tablespoons cornstarch
4 large eggs
4 large egg whites
5½ cups confectioners' sugar

1. On a sheet of parchment paper, roll out puff pastry into a paper-thin rectangle. Prick deeply all over with tines of a fork. Slide paper and pastry onto a baking sheet. Cover with plastic wrap and chill for at least 2 hours.

2. Prepare pastry cream: In a medium saucepan, combine milk and cinnamon sticks. Place over high heat and bring to a boil, then immediately remove from heat. Cover and allow to sit for 5 minutes. Strain, and discard cinnamon sticks. In a medium bowl, combine sugar, flour, and cornstarch; whisk to blend. In another bowl, whisk eggs until frothy, then add to dry ingredients. Whisk mixture vigorously, and while whisking, pour hot milk into bowl. Return mixture to saucepan and place over medium heat. Whisk without stopping until pastry cream comes to a boil; cook 1 minute more. Pour cream onto a piece of plastic wrap laid on a baking sheet. Cover with plastic wrap and refrigerate at least 1 hour.

3. Prepare royal icing: In a mixer with a paddle attachment or by hand with a whisk, beat egg whites on low speed until foamy. Gradually add confectioners' sugar and beat until icing is shiny and as thick as taffy. Keep at room temperature until needed.

4. Remove puff pastry from refrigerator. Using an offset spatula, spread royal icing evenly over pastry. Set aside at room temperature until icing dries, 1 to 2 hours.

5. To bake cookies, preheat oven to 400 degrees. Use a star-shaped (or any other shape) cookie cutter to cut out cookies. Release cookies from cutter by blowing into cutter. Put cookies on a baking sheet lined with parchment paper and place in oven. Immediately turn oven off and bake until icing tops separate from puff pastry bottoms. Remove from oven and return oven to 400 degrees. Carefully pull icing tops off pastry bottoms and place on a large plate; set aside. Return bottoms to oven and bake until pastry is golden and caramelized, about 10 to 15 minutes. Cool cookies on a rack.

6. To serve, whisk chilled pastry cream to loosen it and put in a pastry bag with a star tip. Pipe a little pastry cream onto each pastry bottom (or put on a small dollop with a spoon). Cap with a royal icing top.

Yield: about 60 cookies

Time: 30 minutes, plus 4 hours of chilling and drying

AN ORANGE-CHOCOLATE CANDY BECOMES A CAKE

In France the muscadine is a candy, always chocolate and orange, always about the size of a Tootsie Roll, and always as popular as a truffle. This confection is meltingly smooth on the inside and ever so slightly crackly on the outside, the result of its being brushed with chocolate, which hardens into a shell. The outer chocolate is kept rough and craggy so that when it is rolled in powdered sugar, it looks like the bark of a snow-dusted tree. Enlarged from candy to cake, it makes an untraditional but ideal bûche de Noël.

In my rendition I play with the chocolate and orange base in several ways. The heart of my muscadine, which is essentially a jelly roll, is a feather-light rectangle of ladyfinger cake whose crumb is designed to sop up liquids and creams. Here it soaks up a Grand Marnier sugar syrup and is rolled up with a bitter chocolate ganache studded with store-bought candied orange zest. Then it is finished in the same way the candy is—with chocolate and sugar.

If you want to give it a straight-from-the-patisserie look, decorate it with caramel spikes or buy (or make) meringue mushrooms. This cake is great whether you make it the day you serve it or whether you prepare it— up to the chocolate coating—a month in advance and keep it in the freezer.

10 ounces bittersweet chocolate

1 cup heavy cream

2 tablespoons finely chopped candied orange
    zest (at specialty food stores)

5 tablespoons sugar

3 tablespoons Grand Marnier

4 large eggs, separated

¾ cup confectioners' sugar, plus extra for
    sprinkling and dredging

1 teaspoon vanilla extract

¼ cup plus 3 tablespoons cake flour

Caramel Spikes, optional (see recipe below)

1. To prepare chocolate ganache: Finely chop 6 ounces of chocolate and place in a mixing bowl. In a small saucepan, bring cream to a boil. Whisk hot cream into chocolate until smooth, then add orange zest and stir to mix well. Set aside to cool and thicken, or chill 40 minutes, stirring occasionally.

2. To prepare Grand Marnier syrup: In a small saucepan, combine sugar with ¼ cup water. Bring to a boil, then remove from heat. Stir in Grand Marnier, then set aside to cool to room temperature.

3. Preheat oven to 350 degrees. Line a 15 by 10-inch jelly roll pan with parchment paper, allowing paper to overlap slightly at ends.

4. Using a mixer, whisk egg whites until foamy. Gradually add ½ cup confectioners' sugar and beat until whites form firm, glossy peaks. In a large bowl, whisk egg yolks by hand with ¼ cup confectioners' sugar. Add vanilla and whisk to blend. Turn mixer to lowest speed and add yolk mixture to whites, mixing only to combine; do not overmix. Place flour in a sifter and sift over mixture. Using a rubber spatula, gently fold in flour. Scrape mixture into jelly roll pan and smooth top. Sprinkle cake lightly with 2 tablespoons confectioners' sugar. Let sit 5 minutes, then sprinkle with 2 more tablespoons confectioners' sugar.

5. Bake cake until lightly golden and springy to the touch, about 10 minutes. Slide it on parchment paper onto a rack and cool to room temperature. Place a piece of parchment paper on counter and invert cake on paper. Peel away baking paper. Brush Grand Marnier syrup over surface of cake. Using an offset spatula, spread chocolate ganache evenly over syrup. Starting from one of shorter ends of cake, using paper for assistance, roll up cake. Cover with plastic wrap and refrigerate for 1 hour. (The cake can be chilled and, when set, wrapped airtight and frozen for 1 month.)

6. Just before serving, spread a generous amount of confectioners' sugar on a baking sheet. Chop and melt remaining 4 ounces of chocolate. Unwrap cold cake and brush it with a coating of melted chocolate, then roll it in confectioners' sugar. Return cake to refrigerator for 5 minutes to set chocolate, then transfer to a serving platter. If desired, decorate with caramel spikes.

Yield: 8 servings

*Time: 1 hour, plus 1 hour 40 minutes of
    refrigeration*

1 cup sugar
2 tablespoons corn syrup

1. In a small saucepan, combine sugar, corn syrup, and $\frac{1}{4}$ cup water. Place over medium heat and bring to a boil. Boil until syrup is a light caramel color, about 5 minutes. Remove from heat and let cool for 5 minutes.

2. Line a baking sheet with parchment paper. Drop a small spoonful of syrup on paper to make a dot $\frac{1}{2}$ inch in diameter. Using a small icing spatula or knife, and starting at center of dot, draw caramel out to shape a spike or plume. Continue to shape about 7 spikes. Refrigerate until firm, about 15 minutes. Stand spikes up in cake and serve.

Time: 15 minutes, plus cooling

ALFRED PORTALE

Alfred Portale is the executive chef and owner of Gotham Bar and Grill in Manhattan. He was photographed in his living room at home in Manhattan. These columns were written with Dorie Greenspan.

ENNOBLING CAULIFLOWER FOR A HOLIDAY SOUP

While I know that there are just four seasons, I cook as though there were twelve. For me, each month has a certain feel to it, and it's the feel as much as the foods that are available in the market that inspire me to create new dishes. On my culinary calendar, December is luxury season, a time to drink champagne and eat oysters, foie gras, and cauliflower soup—at least this cauliflower soup, lavished with sea scallops and osetra caviar.

Cauliflower, a stalwart in make-do cooking, might not leap to mind as the stuff of luxe holiday fare. But when I saw it in the Greenmarket, I remembered its virtues, which I learned working with Michel Guerard at his spa in France. There we used pureed cauliflower to thicken soups and sauces that would normally take cream. Pureed, cauliflower's mild flavor and voluptuous texture make it ideal for this sleight of hand. But cau-

liflower is a chameleon; left whole, its flavor is stronger, its texture firm. I knew that using it both ways in one dish, as I do in this soup, would be exciting.

I took hot vichyssoise as my reference and replaced the starchy potatoes with the cauliflower but kept the leeks for sweetness. To build in more flavor and texture, I decided to caramelize a few florets so that the soup would taste of cauliflower both subtle and strong. Then, looking for something that would make the dish not just delicious but also celebratory, I hit upon diver scallops. Their clean, sweet taste and silky texture made them cauliflower-friendly, but their hint of brininess was a tease that left you wanting more. So, in the spirit of the season, I added caviar. The combination is perfect—if served right.

First, construct a minitower in the center of the bowl. Start with the sliced leeks, proceed to the caramelized florets, then the scallops, and, finally, top it all with the caviar. At the table, ladle soup around the towers, keeping the caviar cool and dry on its scallop cushion. Of course, everyone—including me—is tempted to eat the caviar solo. But show restraint. If you break down the tower and swirl the caviar into the soup, you'll be rewarded with a little of every luxurious flavor in every spoonful.

CAULIFLOWER AND LEEK SOUP WITH SEA SCALLOPS AND OSETRA CAVIAR

1 tablespoon plus 1 teaspoon canola oil

1 medium onion, peeled and finely diced

2 medium leeks, white and light green parts only, cut into rounds, washed, and dried

1 large head cauliflower, cored and cut into florets

4 cups chicken stock

Salt and freshly ground white pepper

4 large sea scallops, preferably diver-harvested

2 tablespoons unsalted butter

1 ounce osetra caviar

1. In a stockpot over medium-high heat, heat 1 tablespoon oil. Add onion and leeks, and sauté until vegetables soften but do not color, 3 to 4 minutes. Add cauliflower and stock, and bring to a boil. Reduce heat to low and simmer for 3 minutes, then spoon out 12 rounds of leek and 3 large cauliflower florets. Set leeks aside. Slice cauliflower into ⅛-inch-thick slices and set aside.

2. Simmer soup until cauliflower is tender, about 18 minutes. Season to taste with salt and pepper. Working in batches, puree soup in a blender or food processor; set aside and keep warm.

3. In a small nonstick skillet over medium-high heat, heat remaining 1 teaspoon oil. Season reserved cauliflower slices with salt and pepper to taste. Sauté until lightly browned on both sides, then set aside and keep warm. Season scallops with salt and pepper, and add to pan. Sauté until golden brown on outside and medium-rare inside, about 2 minutes a side.

4. Reheat soup if necessary and swirl in butter. Divide leek rounds and cauliflower slices among 4 warm soup bowls, mounding vegetables in center of each bowl. Top each mound with a scallop and a spoonful of caviar. Ladle soup around vegetables. Serve immediately.

Yield: 4 servings
Time: 45 minutes

A SICILIAN CHRISTMAS EVE FEAST

During most of December, my childhood home in Buffalo, New York, could have been beamed to Sicily without a single Sicilian noticing anything peculiar about it.

The preparations for our Christmas Eve feast—the ravioli my mother would make and stash in the freezer right after Thanksgiving, the dandelion greens that my grandfather had harvested from roadside patches in the fall, and the fig-stuffed cookies that were stored in tins in the cool hallway—would be as familiar to my Sicilian relatives as the crèche, wreaths, and bottomless bowls of nuts and tangerines that were arranged around our house. Certainly, they would recognize the fish dishes on our Christmas Eve menu. Ours was a celebration bound by Old World traditions.

It was the observance of the Cena della Vigilia, the wait for the miraculous birth of Christ. In the early Christian centuries, Catholics waited on an empty stomach: Christmas Eve was a day of fasting, and nothing but water was permitted before holy communion at midnight Mass. Later it became a penitential day, meaning that all foods except meat were allowed, and that is probably when the fast became a feast of fishes.

By today's standards and certainly by those I grew up with, every Christmas Eve dinner of my childhood was indeed a feast. Everyone in my family remembers special dishes from those meals, but no one can remember whether there was a set number of dishes, even though one of the rituals is to eat by number. The number of dishes is significant, although it can range from three, representing each of the Wise Men or the Trinity, to as many as thirteen, one for each of the Apostles plus one for Jesus. In any event, the number of dishes at our house was always many.

There was always a shrimp cocktail with a spicy red sauce, mostly because everyone loved it, and always a dish of cod, the most traditional of the Christmas fishes. Cod is an ancient animal, so ancient that I can imag-

ine its being served at the first Cena della Vigilia. Often there was salt cod, or baccala, *an Italian staple, soaked for a day or two before Christmas and served with potatoes or with lots of onions and a very thin tomato sauce—tomato sauce being the litmus test of a good cook in our family.*

A fried dish was always part of the dinner, usually fresh cod, although sometimes it was a large, whole breaded fish. And there was always eel, usually smoked (I'm not sure you could find fresh eel in Buffalo then) and served as a salad.

It wasn't until I was older that I learned that eel, an element of pre-Christian cult rituals, was essential to the Italian Christmas Eve tradition. I don't know how essential the clams that my father baked with pancetta and bread crumbs were, but I still make them for Christmas.

There were so many other dishes, too, like shrimp and clams and calamari and octopus with tentacles that terrified me. But if I got through the tentacles, I could have dessert: the coveted Christmas cookies.

Each of my aunts had her specialty—crisp anise pizzelle, biscotti, sesame seed cookies—and each of us had a favorite. I could never get enough of my mother's soft, spicy, crumple-in-your-mouth cocoa balls, rich with raisins and walnuts and glazed with a thin icing.

My mother never parted with her copy of the recipe, handwritten, as most of her recipes were, on a dog-eared index card, but I was her kitchen helper for so many years that I can now bake them from memory. And a few years ago I made a discovery: If you use fine cocoa, like Valrhona or Callebaut, they turn out even richer and more chocolaty.

Today, no one in my family celebrates Christmas Eve as extravagantly as we did when I was young. Even my parents have streamlined their menu, cutting it down to champagne, shrimp cocktail, and one fish dish. But because the memories of those childhood celebrations are such an important and wonderful part of my life, I try to keep the rituals alive and to pass them on to my children by making an all-fish meal with dishes inspired by those my family cherished.

Every year, my wife, Helen, and our daughters, Olympia, ten, and Victoria, seven, have Christmas Eve dinner together, and it is always just us around the table. This year's dinner will begin, as all our Christmas Eve dinners have, with champagne. (For almost twenty years Helen and I have had champagne on Christmas Eve, dated and decorated each of the Christmas corks, and turned them into ornaments that hang on our tree.) And then we'll have shrimp cocktail, but I'll make a lemony aioli with capers as the dipping sauce. (I guess I can admit this now: I never really liked the red cocktail sauce.) We always have a clam dish, of course—sometimes linguine with clams and sometimes steamed clams on thick slices of bread, but usually it's my father's baked clams, as it will be this year.

And there will be eel. I'll make a salad, as my mother did, but this year it will be warm and reminiscent of both the fresh and salted cod dishes of my childhood. I'll use smoked eel and serve it with fingerling potatoes—the salt cod was often served with potatoes —and I'll use my mother's favorite seasonings for fresh cod: lots and lots of minced garlic and parsley and really good extra-virgin olive oil.

My cod will be quickly seared and set on a ragout of garlicky cannellini beans and creamy savory cabbage, humble ingredients from my childhood that are also foods I serve regularly at the restaurant. But because it is Christmas, I'll dress up the dish with a generous helping of luxurious black truffles.

Finally, there will be a risotto with seafood, a rice version of my family's pasta dish, but this year, along with the clams, mussels, shrimp, and squid, I'll toss in some lobster. I'll use the shells to make a broth; cooking the rice in a rich seafood broth really intensifies the flavor of the risotto. And I'll stir the tender chunks of lobster into the saucepan at the last minute.

As always, there will be cookies for dessert: the gingerbread cookies we make with our daughters, the pizzelle Helen makes in such outrageous numbers that we give plates of them away to our neighbors, and the irresistible cocoa cookies of my childhood. We'll make a pot of hot chocolate, leave a cup out for Santa along with a plate of cookies that would make my mother proud, tuck the girls into bed, and do what the grownups in my family used to do: crack walnuts, eat tangerines, and wait for St. Nick.

ROAST COD WITH RAGOUT OF SAVOY CABBAGE, CANNELLINI BEANS, AND BLACK TRUFFLES

⅔ cup dried cannellini beans, soaked
    overnight and drained
1 small onion, peeled, trimmed, and
    quartered
3 cloves garlic, peeled and crushed
2 sprigs fresh thyme
Salt and freshly ground white pepper
1 small carrot, peeled, trimmed, and cut into
    ¼-inch dice
1 small (1 pound) savoy cabbage, outer leaves
    discarded, cored, and cut into ½-inch-
    thick slices
¼ cup heavy cream
4 tablespoons unsalted butter
1 ounce black truffle, sliced as thinly as
    possible
2 tablespoons canola oil
6 cod fillets, 6 to 7 ounces each
2 tablespoons finely minced chives

1. In a large saucepan, combine beans, onion, garlic, and thyme. Add enough water to cover beans by 2 inches. Bring to a boil and then reduce heat to medium-low. Simmer beans for 30 minutes. Add salt and pepper to taste, and continue to simmer until beans are tender, about 15 minutes more. Set aside 1 cup of cooking liquid and drain beans. Remove and discard onion, garlic, and thyme. Cover beans and set aside.

2. Place a large pot of lightly salted water over high heat and bring to a boil. Place a bowl of ice water close to stove. Add carrot to pot and boil for 2 minutes; remove with a slotted spoon and set aside. Add cabbage to pot and boil until barely tender, 3 to 4 minutes. Drain and immedi-ately plunge cabbage into ice water. When cabbage is cool, drain well and gently squeeze cabbage to remove excess water.

3. In a large saucepan over high heat, bring reserved cooking liquid to a boil. Reduce heat to medium, add cream, and bring mixture to a simmer. Reduce heat to its lowest setting and add butter in 4 or 5 additions, whisking until emulsified. Season mixture with salt and pepper to taste, and stir in beans, carrot, cabbage, and black truffle. Keep pan over very low heat for 5 minutes to warm ragout and allow truffle flavor to infuse mixture.

4. While ragout is warming, prepare cod fillets: Place a large nonstick or well-seasoned sauté pan over medium-high heat and add oil. Season cod fillets on both sides with salt and pepper to taste. Add to sauté pan and cook until outsides are golden and centers are opaque, 3 to 4 minutes a side.

5. To serve, use a slotted spoon to transfer some ragout to a warm platter or individual serving plates. Arrange cod fillets on top of ragout and spoon over remaining ragout and sauce. Top with minced chives and serve immediately.

Yield: 6 servings
Time: 1¼ hours, plus overnight soaking for beans

SMOKED EEL AND WARM POTATO SALAD

Kosher salt

2 pounds fingerling or baby white potatoes,
    scrubbed

2 pounds smoked eel

6 tablespoons extra-virgin olive oil

2 tablespoons finely chopped parsley leaves

2 cloves garlic, peeled and minced to a paste

1 shallot, peeled and finely chopped

Freshly ground white pepper to taste

1. Fill a medium saucepan halfway with water, add salt to taste, and bring to a boil. Add potatoes and boil until tender enough to be pierced easily with a knife, about 15 minutes.

2. While potatoes are cooking, prepare eel. Starting at center of one side, peel skin up and off in one piece; the skin is thick and will remove easily. Scrape off any fat and gray flesh. Slice eel in half lengthwise, separating the 2 fillets from the backbone. Pull out any small pin bones. Cut fillets crosswise into pieces 1/2 inch thick; set aside.

3. When potatoes are tender, drain and slice into rounds 1/2 inch thick. In a large bowl, combine oil, parsley, garlic, and shallot. Mix well. Add potatoes and eel, and toss gently to combine. Season generously with white pepper and toss again. Serve warm.

Yield: 6 servings
Time: 30 minutes

SHELLFISH RISOTTO

1/2 teaspoon salt, plus more to taste

2 lobsters, 1 1/4 to 1 1/2 pounds each

1 pound jumbo shrimp, preferably with
    heads

4 tablespoons extra-virgin olive oil

2 1/2 cups thinly sliced onions

1 small head garlic, cut in half crosswise,
    plus 3 cloves garlic, peeled and smashed

5 whole sprigs fresh thyme, plus 1 teaspoon
    fresh thyme leaves

1 bay leaf

8 cups chicken stock, plus additional if
    desired

28 ounces canned pureed Italian plum
    tomatoes

1 teaspoon black peppercorns

1/2 teaspoon red pepper flakes

10 sprigs parsley, plus 3 tablespoons chopped
    parsley leaves

3 cups dry white wine

1 pound littleneck clams, well scrubbed

2 pounds cultivated black mussels,
    well scrubbed

7 tablespoons unsalted butter

2 large shallots, peeled and minced

2 pounds Arborio rice

10 ounces squid, cleaned and cut into rings

Freshly ground white pepper

1. Place 4 cups water in a large stockpot and add 1/2 teaspoon salt. Bring to a boil and add lobsters. Cover and cook over high heat for 4 minutes. Add shrimp, cover, and cook 2 minutes more; shellfish will be partly cooked.

2. Remove lobsters and shrimp from pot. When cool enough to handle, remove tail, claw, and knuckle meat from lobsters; reserve shells.

Remove heads from shrimp and peel them; reserve heads and shells. Cut shrimp in half crosswise. Cut lobster meat into 1-inch chunks. Cover both and refrigerate.

3. In a 6- to 8-quart pot over medium heat, warm 1 tablespoon oil. Add 1½ cups onions and split head of garlic. Sauté until softened but not colored, about 3 minutes. Add 2 sprigs thyme and bay leaf, and cook for 1 minute. Add reserved shellfish shells and heads. Sauté, stirring, until shells turn bright red, about 10 minutes. Add stock, tomatoes, peppercorns, pepper flakes, and parsley sprigs. Raise heat to high, bring broth to a boil, and then reduce heat to low. Simmer for 40 minutes. Strain through a colander into a heat-proof bowl and discard solids. Pour broth through a fine strainer into a saucepan. Place over very low heat.

4. In a 6- to 8-quart saucepan, combine 2 cups wine, remaining 1 cup onion, smashed garlic, and remaining 3 sprigs thyme. Cover, place over high heat to bring to a boil, and then reduce heat to low. Uncover and simmer until reduced by half. Add clams, cover, raise heat to high, and cook for 2 minutes. Add mussels, cover, and cook, stirring occasionally, until mussels and clams open, about 5 minutes more. Spread mussels and clams out to cool (discard any that did not open), then transfer them to a bowl and cover. Pour cooking liquid through a strainer lined with a double layer of cheesecloth. Add 1½ cups to shellfish broth and reserve remainder.

5. Bring shellfish broth to a boil, then reduce to a simmer. In a 6- to 8-quart pot over medium heat, combine 3 tablespoons butter and remaining 3 tablespoons oil. Add shallots and sauté for 1 minute. Add rice, stirring frequently, until grains are opaque and glisten, about 7 minutes. Add remaining 1 cup wine, which will be absorbed quickly. While stirring constantly, add shellfish broth 1 cup at a time, allowing each cup to be absorbed before adding next; this will take about 14 minutes. When all broth has been absorbed, rice should be creamy but slightly firm to the bite. If necessary, continue to cook rice, using reserved mussel-clam cooking liquid and/or additional chicken stock.

6. Add thyme leaves and squid, and cook for 2 minutes. Add reserved lobster, shrimp, clams, and mussels, and season to taste with salt and pepper. Toss gently to mix and heat for 2 to 4 minutes. Add remaining 4 tablespoons butter and chopped parsley. Adjust seasonings and serve immediately.

Yield: 6 main-course servings
Time: 2 hours

COCOA CHRISTMAS COOKIES

4 cups all-purpose flour

1 cup unsweetened cocoa (preferably Valrhona, Callebaut, or Droste)

4½ teaspoons baking powder

2 teaspoons ground cinnamon

½ teaspoon freshly grated nutmeg

½ teaspoon ground cloves

½ teaspoon salt

1½ cups coarsely chopped plump, moist raisins

1 tablespoon orange juice

¾ pound (3 sticks) unsalted butter at room temperature

1¼ cups sugar

2 large eggs at room temperature

1 teaspoon vanilla extract

1 cup apricot jam

¼ cup milk at room temperature

1½ cups coarsely chopped walnuts, lightly toasted

1 cup confectioners' sugar

3 teaspoons lemon juice

1. In a large mixing bowl, combine flour, cocoa, baking powder, cinnamon, nutmeg, cloves, and salt. Whisk to combine and set aside. In a small bowl, combine raisins and orange juice; set aside.

2. Using a heavy-duty mixer with a paddle attachment, or by hand with a sturdy spoon, beat butter and sugar together until creamy. Add eggs 1 at a time, beating on medium speed for 1 minute after each addition. Beat in vanilla, jam, and milk. Set mixer to low and gradually add flour mixture, beating only until incorporated.

3. Stir nuts and reserved raisins into dough. Cover dough tightly with plastic wrap and chill at least 2 hours or as long as 2 days.

4. Preheat oven to 350 degrees. Using a tablespoon of dough for each cookie, roll dough between your palms to form walnut-size balls. Place balls 1½ inches apart on a nonstick or parchment-lined cookie sheet. Bake for 10 to 12 minutes, until tops look dry; the tops may crack, which is fine. Transfer cookies to a rack and repeat with remaining dough.

5. While cookies are baking, make a glaze: In a small bowl, combine confectioners' sugar, lemon juice, and 3 teaspoons warm water. Whisk until smooth. While cookies are still warm, dip tops in glaze and place on a rack to cool to room temperature. The cookies may also be painted with glaze using a feather pastry brush.

Yield: about 7 dozen

Time: 45 minutes, plus 2 hours for chilling dough

THE LAST WORD IN LUXURY AND SPEED

Foie gras, plump, extraordinarily rich duck liver, is an expensive, elegant indulgence. It's also surprisingly versatile. I prepare it year-round, changing its accompaniments with the seasons, but almost always I pair the warm liver with sweet fruit and something tart or acidic. The acidity balances the liver's richness, and the fruit is a supportive companion to its subtle flavor and silky texture. For a special indulgence, like New Year's Eve, I've created this dish of seared foie gras, roasted pears, honey, rosemary, and aged balsamic vinegar.

When I chose roasted pears to go with the foie gras, I decided to bolster their sweetness with a touch of honey. The rosemary was added to pull the dish back to the savory side. The idea of using balsamic vinegar as the sauce just seemed natural: Pears and balsamic vinegar are served together all over Italy.

If you're a first-time foie gras cook, you're about to learn that foie gras is the ultimate fast food—two minutes in the pan and it's done. But for it to be done properly, the liver shouldn't be too cold; if it is, the outside will cook, and the inside won't. To get the temperature right, slice the foie gras and keep it refrigerated until fifteen minutes before you're ready to cook. Then be certain that the pan is medium-hot and that the slices get only a minute of heat on each side.

As long as you are going all out—and serving foie gras is going all out—I urge you to try to finish this dish with a great authentic aged balsamic vinegar from Modena, Italy. At my restaurant I use rare twenty-five-year-old balsamic, although a fine twelve-year-old will give you the depth and layers of flavor this dish deserves. But if your balsamic vinegar isn't the best, don't give up. Just concentrate the flavor by boiling it down by half, then drizzle it over the foie gras and head for the table.

SEARED FOIE GRAS WITH CARAMELIZED PEARS AND BALSAMIC VINEGAR

2 tablespoons grapeseed or canola oil
3 large firm Bosc pears, peeled, halved, and cored
½ cup honey
3 3-inch sprigs fresh rosemary, each sprig cut into 3 pieces
¼ cup port, preferably white
1 fresh foie gras (see headnote), very well chilled
Coarse salt and freshly ground white pepper
2 tablespoons aged balsamic vinegar
6 sprigs fresh thyme
6 sprigs fresh chervil

1. Preheat oven to 450 degrees. Place a large ovenproof sauté pan over medium-high heat and add oil. When hot but not smoking, add pears. Immediately transfer pan to oven. Roast pears, turning often, until they begin to caramelize, about 10 minutes. Stir in honey and rosemary, and continue to roast until pears are golden and caramelized on all sides, 6 to 8 minutes more.

2. Transfer pan to stove top over medium heat and add port. Stir briefly, scraping bottom of pan, and coat pears with syrupy mixture. Turn pears into a colander and discard rosemary and any cooking liquids drained from pears. Keep pears warm until serving time.

3. Using your hands, carefully separate 2 lobes of foie gras. If there is any fat at separation point, trim and discard it. Warm blade of a sharp, thin knife in hot water, then dry blade. Cut each lobe of foie gras crosswise into ½-inch-thick slices. Keep blade warm as you work, dipping it again if necessary. (The foie gras may be sliced ahead of time, wrapped airtight, and refrigerated.

Remove slices from refrigerator 15 minutes before cooking.)

4. Heat a large nonstick sauté pan over medium-high heat. Season each slice of foie gras with salt and pepper. Working quickly, slip slices into pan. If necessary, work in batches; do not overcrowd pan. Sauté slices for 1 minute, then turn and sauté 1 minute more.

5. To serve, arrange 1 pear half in center of each of 6 warm plates. Top each half with slices of foie gras and drizzle with about 1 teaspoon balsamic vinegar. Garnish each plate with a thyme sprig and a chervil sprig. Serve immediately.

Yield: 6 servings
Time: 45 minutes

~⁀

ITALIAN PORK FROM AN AMERICAN OVEN

When my family and I vacationed in Cortona recently, we shopped in the local market, where we would buy sandwiches of sliced pork on warm focaccia for lunch. The pork was moist, had its own distinctive taste, and was thoroughly infused with the inviting flavors of the herb-covered Tuscan countryside. I was determined to recapture those flavors back home in New York.

To compensate for the subtle flavor of American pork, I wanted to use assertive flavors as a marinade and crust. Fennel had to be the main ingredient, as it is in Italy, and to that base I added onion, garlic, and the herbs that evoked memories of Tuscany. The challenge was to get this flavor into the pork and to keep the pork moist.

Where there's fat, there's flavor, so I chose a pork rib roast with a layer of fat on it. I first covered the fat with the chopped fennel and herbs; they promptly fell off in the oven. In my next attempt I pureed the ingredients in a food processor and then patted them onto the meat. They stayed put, and their flavors seeped into the meat as I let it marinate in the refrigerator. This crust also kept the roast moist as it cooked. The first bite took me back to Cortona.

FENNEL-CRUSTED PORK WITH WARM APPLE AND QUINCE COMPOTE

1 4½-pound pork rib roast, chine bone
    trimmed to ¼ inch thick
Kosher salt
1 cup chopped fennel (including some of the
    feathery tops)
½ cup chopped onion
6 cloves garlic, coarsely chopped
2 teaspoons finely chopped fresh thyme
2 teaspoons finely chopped fresh rosemary
    leaves
2 teaspoons finely chopped fresh sage
2 teaspoons finely chopped fresh oregano
2 teaspoons fennel seeds
1½ teaspoons coarsely ground white pepper
2 tablespoons butter
1½ teaspoons finely minced fresh ginger
2 large Rome or Cortland apples, peeled,
    cored, and cut into ¼-inch dice
2 large quinces, peeled, cored, and cut into
    ¼-inch dice
½ cup apple cider
Freshly ground white pepper

1. Using a sharp knife, score a crosshatch pattern on surface of roast. Rub skin with salt to taste and place pork in a roasting pan. In bowl of a food processor, combine chopped fennel, onion, garlic, thyme, rosemary, sage, and oregano. Pulse to chop. Scrape down sides and add fennel seeds and coarsely ground white pepper. Pulse until mixture is very finely chopped.

2. Pat fennel mixture onto surface of roast to form ¼-inch crust. Cover roast and pan with plastic wrap and refrigerate for 40 minutes.

3. Preheat oven to 350 degrees. Remove roast from refrigerator and let it rest at room temperature for 20 minutes. Discard plastic wrap and roast pork until internal temperature reaches 150 degrees for a pink center (or adjust cooking time according to taste). Begin to check temperature after 1 hour 30 minutes; cooking time will vary according to initial temperature of roast. Remove from oven, cover with aluminum foil, and let rest for 20 minutes before carving.

4. While roast is resting, prepare compote. Place a large skillet over medium heat and melt butter. Add ginger and stir until it softens but does not color, 1 to 2 minutes. Add apples and quinces, and raise heat to medium-high. Cook, stirring occasionally, until apples are very soft and mixture is lightly browned, 10 to 12 minutes. Mix in cider and reduce slightly, 1 to 2 minutes. At this point apples will have consistency of applesauce, and quinces will be tender but still hold their shape. Season with salt and freshly ground pepper, and keep warm.

5. To serve, place slices of roast and crust on each of 6 plates and serve with warm compote.

Yield: 6 servings
Time: 3 hours

WHAT JUNIPER BERRIES AND GINGER CAN DO

This is the third incarnation of a dish that started very simply and changed serendipitously. I had a pheasant that I was going to marinate, and I reached for juniper berries, knowing that juniper and game are a classic combination. I had it in mind to do something classic when, crushing the juniper berries, their powerfully fresh, bright fragrance forced me to take a detour. I headed straight for the ginger root, with its similarly crisp, clean fragrance.

I'm not usually given to these kinds of leaps. I like to know there's a precedent to back me up when I start inventing dishes, but the aromatic match was so strong, I went with it, adding onions and garlic to the marinade. The juniper and ginger turned what might have been an ordinary dish into something vibrant. I had never had a game dish like this one. It was almost refreshing, hardly the word I would choose to describe traditional game dishes, which are often heavily sauced, abundantly herbed, and paired with chestnuts, mushrooms, or brussels sprouts. I couldn't resist trying the combination on other birds.

I used the same marinade, cooking technique (pan-searing followed by oven roasting), and sauce (white wine and chicken stock flavored with the marinade's aromatic ingredients) with turkey to equally good effect. Finally, I tried it on chicken. Because chicken is so mild, the bright flavors of the marinade and sauce ingredients are even more vivid. Originally I served the pheasant with braised red cabbage, and I've found that it is just as fine with the chicken.

MARINATED CHICKEN WITH BRAISED RED CABBAGE

24 cloves garlic (about 2 heads), peeled
4 ounces fresh peeled ginger (a piece about 3 inches long)
5 tablespoons plus 2 teaspoons juniper berries
2½ cups roughly chopped onions, plus 1 thinly sliced onion
3 chickens (each about 3½ pounds), split in half and backbones removed
Coarse salt and freshly ground white pepper
5 tablespoons canola oil
4 ounces smoked bacon, cut into 4 pieces
2 teaspoons caraway seeds
1 large head red cabbage, cored and cut into slices ¼ inch thick
1 cup dry red wine
½ cup red wine vinegar
½ cup honey
¾ cup dry white wine
2 cups chicken stock
1 tablespoon unsalted butter

1. Thinly slice 19 cloves garlic and three-quarters of the ginger. Crush 5 tablespoons juniper berries with a mortar and pestle. In a very large mixing bowl, combine sliced garlic, sliced ginger, crushed juniper berries, and chopped onions. Season chicken with salt and pepper to taste, place in a bowl, and rub with mixture. Cover and refrigerate for 24 to 48 hours.

2. When ready to serve, prepare cabbage. In an 8-quart pot over medium heat, heat 1 tablespoon oil and add bacon. Sauté until well browned, about 6 minutes. Remove and discard bacon. Add sliced onion and sauté until lightly browned, about 5 minutes. Add caraway seeds

and sauté 2 minutes more. Stir in cabbage, red wine, vinegar, and honey. Add salt and pepper to taste. Cover and reduce heat to medium-low. Cook for 40 minutes, stirring occasionally. Uncover and continue to cook until liquid has reduced to a light glaze, about 30 minutes. Remove from heat and keep warm.

3. Meanwhile, prepare chicken. Preheat oven to 400 degrees. Remove chicken from refrigerator and allow to rest at room temperature for 15 minutes. Wipe off marinade and season with coarse salt to taste. In a large skillet over high heat, heat 2 tablespoons oil until almost smoking. Place 2 or 3 chicken halves in a skillet, skin side down, and sear until skin is browned, about 4 minutes. Turn and brown other side, 4 minutes more. Transfer to a shallow roasting pan and repeat with remaining chicken.

4. Finely chop remaining 5 cloves garlic and ginger. Grind remaining 2 teaspoons juniper berries in a spice grinder or pulverize with a mortar and pestle. In a small saucepan over medium-low heat, heat remaining 2 tablespoons oil and add garlic, ginger, and juniper berries. Sauté until softened but not colored, 8 to 10 minutes. Add white wine, increase heat to medium-high, and cook until wine evaporates. Add stock and increase heat to bring to a boil. Reduce heat to low and skim off any impurities from surface. Simmer until stock is reduced by half, 15 to 20 minutes. Remove from heat, cover, and keep warm. While stock is simmering, finish chicken.

5. Roast chicken for 20 minutes, turn pieces, and continue roasting until juices run clear when meat is pierced near bone, about 10 minutes. Remove from oven, cover, and keep warm. Strain sauce, discarding solids. Swirl in butter and season to taste with salt and pepper.

6. Place a chicken half on each of 6 plates. Spoon sauce over. Place a serving of cabbage alongside and serve immediately.

Yield: 6 servings

Time: 2 hours, plus 1 day to marinate chicken

ON A RARE NIGHT OFF, A SIMPLE DISH OUT OF THE FRIDGE

I recently created this pasta dish, spaghetti in a very creamy goat cheese sauce, on one of my rare nights out of the restaurant. I pulled an armful of ingredients from the refrigerator, gave them the once-over, and came up with this recipe. In the end I liked it so much that I refined it at my restaurant and have made it many times since, both there and at home.

The dish is quick to make—you can prepare it in the time it takes to cook the pasta—and most of the ingredients can be varied. The pasta is dried spaghetti, but penne or farfalle works well, too. While the pasta is boiling, I sauté the cremini mushrooms. Cremini are as easy to find as plain white mushrooms, but they have more taste. (The dish would be even better with shitakes or exotic mushrooms, such as chanterelles. Another choice for another day.)

When the pasta is al dente, I toss it with the rest of the ingredients: the sautéed mushrooms plus arugula, which can just as deliciously be radicchio or watercress; soft goat cheese, which can be replaced by half as much grated aged goat cheese for a more intense taste; great extra-virgin olive oil (essentially it is the sauce, so it should be the best that you can get); and some of the pasta's cooking water, which, just as in pesto, thins the sauce without diluting the flavor.

CREMINI MUSHROOM PASTA WITH WILTED ARUGULA, GOAT CHEESE, AND EXTRA-VIRGIN OLIVE OIL

Salt

1 pound spaghetti

10 tablespoons extra-virgin olive oil

2 pounds cremini mushrooms, trimmed and very thinly sliced

Freshly ground white pepper

2 tablespoons finely minced garlic

3 cups tightly packed arugula, washed, dried, and cut into thin strands

12 ounces soft fresh goat cheese at room temperature, crumbled

4 tablespoons chopped flat-leaf parsley

1. Place a large pot of salted water over high heat and bring to a boil. Add spaghetti and cook until al dente, about 10 minutes. While pasta is cooking, prepare remaining ingredients.

2. In a large nonstick sauté pan over high heat, warm 1 tablespoon oil. Add half of mushrooms and season to taste with salt and pepper. Sauté, stirring often, about 3 minutes. Add half of garlic and continue to cook, stirring, 3 minutes more. Transfer mushrooms and garlic to a bowl, cover to keep warm, and repeat, cooking remaining mushrooms and garlic in another tablespoon of oil.

3. When spaghetti is cooked, reserve about $1/2$ cup cooking water before draining pasta. Return pasta to cooking pot and add sautéed mushrooms, arugula, goat cheese, remaining 8 tablespoons oil, reserved pasta water, and parsley. Toss gently until arugula wilts and goat cheese melts into a creamy sauce. Season to taste with salt and pepper, and serve immediately.

Yield: 4 servings

Time: 25 minutes, plus preparation time

ELEGANT FARE FOR THE LAST SUNDAY OF FOOTBALL

I take football seriously, and so do the people who work with me, which is why I close the restaurant on Super Bowl Sunday and invite my staff and their families to eat, drink, and cheer their favorites on big-screen televisions set up around the dining room. I've always been a football fan (my hometown team is the Buffalo Bills), I've always had friends in to watch the game, and I've always cooked something special—but easy—for halftime.

Very often that has been these pan-roasted steaks with garlicky potato gratin. So that you don't miss a minute of the game, start cooking the gratin before kick-off. It will be done before halftime, so when there's a commercial, run into the kitchen and turn off the oven. (The gratin can stay inside.) Take the steaks out of the refrigerator then to bring to room temperature so they will cook perfectly. The minute the halftime whistle blows, run back and start the steaks.

I've chosen filets as much for their size as for their taste: Because they're small, three fit in a pan, leaving enough room for each to get a "steakhouse crust" from a home stove's heat. After I press cracked peppercorns into the steaks, I cook them in heavy skillets for six minutes on a side, and they're just the way I like them—rare. To test for doneness, press the steaks. If the dent you've made comes back slowly, they're rare; if it springs back more quickly, they're medium; and if it doesn't give at all (like a pigskin), they're well done.

You don't need a sauce for the steaks because the gratin is so creamy. I submerge thinly sliced potatoes in garlic-infused cream and bake them until they absorb the cream and develop a golden crust. You can dust the top with grated Gruyère if you like, or next time add mushrooms, butternut squash, or even artichokes to the potatoes.

PAN-ROASTED FILET MIGNON

6 teaspoons cracked white peppercorns
6 8-ounce filets mignons, each about
    1¼ inches thick
Coarse salt
2 tablespoons canola oil

1. Press peppercorns evenly into steaks, using 1 teaspoon for each filet. Season to taste with salt.

2. Pour 1 tablespoon oil into each of 2 heavy-bottomed 10-inch skillets and place over high heat. When oil just begins to smoke, place 3 steaks in each pan. Cook steaks 6 minutes on each side for rare, 7 minutes for medium-rare, and 9 minutes for medium. If necessary, turn heat down to keep them from burning.

3. Transfer steaks to a plate, cover with aluminum foil, and let rest for 5 minutes. Serve immediately.

Yield: 6 servings
Time: 20 minutes

POTATO-GARLIC GRATIN

Butter for greasing baking dish
4 pounds Yukon Gold or russet potatoes
Salt and freshly ground white pepper
½ teaspoon freshly grated nutmeg
2 small cloves garlic, peeled and minced
2 cups (approximately) heavy cream

1. Preheat oven to 400 degrees. Butter a 9 by 11-inch baking dish.

2. Peel potatoes and place in a bowl of cold water. Using a mandoline (which will keep slices together so they may be fanned out later) or a sharp knife, cut potatoes lengthwise into slices ⅛ inch thick. Place potatoes in a single layer in a dish, fanning them out so that each slice slightly overlaps its neighbor to cover bottom of dish. Sprinkle with salt and pepper to taste, nutmeg, and some garlic. Make as many layers as needed to use all potatoes.

3. Pour cream over potatoes half a cup at a time, pressing down firmly on potatoes after each addition to distribute cream evenly. When all cream is added, it should just cover potatoes when they are pressed; a little more or a little less than 2 cups may be needed.

4. Cover dish with aluminum foil. Poke a few holes in foil and bake for 1 hour. Remove foil and bake until potatoes have absorbed cream and top of gratin is golden, about 20 minutes more. Serve hot.

Yield: 6 servings
Time: 1¾ hours

RICK MOONEN

Rick Moonen is the executive chef and owner of Oceana in Manhattan.
He was photographed at the Fulton Fish Market at 5 A.M.
These columns were written with Dorie Greenspan.

CULINARY ALCHEMY: A SIGNATURE DISH WITH SIMPLE COMPONENTS

I've got a sentimental as well as a culinary attachment to this dish because it dates from my first days at Oceana. Now my signature dish, seared striped bass is essentially three simple components—the fish, whipped potatoes, and vinaigrette—but each, good alone, is out-standing with the others.

When I created this six years ago, striped bass was impossible to buy, although it is easier to find today. So back then I began with blackfish, and because the dish works with almost any firm-flesh fillet, over the years I've made the dish with mahi-mahi, red snapper, and even dorade.

The technique for cooking the fish is one I often use for fillets that are at least three-quarters of an inch thick. I preheat a dry ovenproof skillet to smoke-detector hot (a 10-inch pan works well), butter the fil-

let's skin generously, and slip the fish, skin side down, into the pan. (There's no need to butter the pan since the butter on the skin makes the fish self-basting.) As soon as I hear the fish sizzling and popping, I weight it down. Because the fillets have a tendency to scrunch up when they hit the heat—it's as though the fish were hunching its back—they need to be pressed against the pan so they can cook evenly. At the restaurant I keep a foil-wrapped brick in a small skillet at the ready for this job, but you can press them with a pancake turner and a little muscle.

After a couple of minutes on the stove, the fish goes into a very hot oven to finish cooking. Prepared this way, the fish stays moist, and the skin crisps enough to provide another texture for the dish.

I nestle the fillets into a mound of smooth, buttery whipped chive potatoes and then circle the potatoes with truffle vinaigrette, a sauce that uses both finely chopped fresh black truffles and aromatic truffle oil. I created this sauce for the fish, but it is completely complementary to the potatoes.

The vinaigrette, like all properly made sauces, resembles music. Here, the earthy truffles and the deep sherry part of the sherry vinegar are the bass; the shallots riff between the bass and the midrange; the midrange resonates with the white pepper and the grapeseed oil (which doesn't offer flavor but does contribute everything to the texture), and the high notes are played by the salt and the acid of the vinegar. Together, they create the well-balanced harmony I want in a sauce.

The sauce provides all the accompanying flavors the fish and potatoes need, but at the restaurant I like to add another texture by topping the fish with crispy fried straw potatoes. If you've got the time, slice Idaho potatoes into slender strands on a mandoline, soak in cold water, dry well, then fry them in grapeseed oil heated to 350 degrees. As they're fried, transfer them to a plate lined with paper towels to drain, then toss them with some salt. Just be sure to make more than you think you need—they beg to be snacked on.

SEARED STRIPED BASS ON WHIPPED CHIVE POTATOES WITH TRUFFLE VINAIGRETTE

1½ cups unsalted or low-sodium chicken stock or broth
⅓ cup finely chopped shallots
¼ cup sherry vinegar
Salt and freshly ground white pepper
¼ cup truffle oil (preferably Urbani)
½ cup grapeseed or other flavorless vegetable oil
1½ tablespoons finely chopped black truffles
4 Idaho potatoes (about 1¾ pounds), peeled and quartered
1 cup heavy cream
6 tablespoons unsalted butter, softened
1 cup finely chopped fresh chives
4 6-ounce fillets striped bass, with skin, each about 1 inch thick

1. Prepare truffle vinaigrette: In a small saucepan over high heat, bring stock to a boil. Boil until reduced to ½ cup. Place shallots in container of a blender, add hot stock, and allow to rest for 3 minutes. Add vinegar and salt and pepper to taste. With blender at medium-low speed, drizzle in truffle and grapeseed oils, blending until vinaigrette is emulsified. Add truffles and pulse just to mix. Set vinaigrette aside until needed; it may be prepared up to 8 hours ahead and kept at room temperature.

2. Prepare whipped chive potatoes: Put potatoes into a medium saucepan and add enough cold water to cover and 2 teaspoons salt. Bring to a boil over high heat, lower heat to medium, and simmer until potatoes can be pierced easily, about 15 minutes. When potatoes are almost cooked, in

a small saucepan combine cream and 4 table-spoons butter, and bring to a boil.

3. When the potatoes are done, drain and put back in pan. Return pan to warm, turned-off burner and add hot cream mixture. Using a sturdy whisk, break up potatoes and whip until smooth. Add salt and pepper to taste, stir in chives, and keep warm.

4. Preheat oven to 450 degrees. Prepare seared striped bass: Place a 10-inch ovenproof skillet over high heat. While heating, season both sides of fish fillets with salt and pepper to taste, and brush skin sides generously with remaining 2 tablespoons butter. Place fillets, skin side down, in hot skillet and immediately weight down with another, smaller skillet or flatten with a spatula. Remove second skillet after 1 minute. Cook 1 minute more, put pan in oven, and roast until fillets are cooked through but still moist inside, 3 to 5 minutes. Flip fillets so they are flesh side down and then remove to a warm platter.

5. To serve, place a mound of potatoes in center of each warm dinner plate, top with a fillet, skin side up, and surround with truffle vinaigrette. Serve immediately.

Yield: 4 servings
Time: 1 hour

A SHRIMP DISH WHERE THE REAL STAR IS BUTTER

I think the biggest compliment you can pay a chef is to grab a piece of bread and use it as a sponge for every last drop of sauce on your plate. Whenever I serve escargots, I love to hear the mmm's and aah's (and the slurps) of people as they polish off the last of the butter—the real star of the dish—with hunks of bread. It's high praise, and it's the praise you'll get when you serve these jumbo shrimp filled with a butter that's just as garlicky and even more herby than the one normally used for escargots.

I created this dish to showcase the rich flavors of that butter since everyone loves it, even though not everyone loves snails. Escargot butter, traditionally a combination of sweet butter, lemon juice, shallots, parsley, and lots of garlic, isn't meant to be subtle, and this recipe is even bolder.

I bumped up the herbs. Playing off the theme of fines herbes—a classic mix of parsley, chervil, chives, and tarragon—I substituted dill for the hard-to-find chervil and added thyme. I also gave it a shot of cayenne, kept the garlic flavor up front, and made enough of it so that each shrimp could be covered with a generous amount.

Shrimp are the perfect stand-ins for escargots. They're meaty, moist, sweet, just a little briny, and a natural with butter. Look for the biggest shrimp you can find. I use what are known as U-8 shrimp, the designation for shrimp that weigh in at fewer than eight to a pound. (You can use any large shrimp, but if you can find head-on white shrimp, labeled Gulf, Mexican, or Panamanian, you've hit pay dirt.) Jumbo shrimp are great for broiling, but remember to keep the broiler door open when you broil so that the heat comes only from the top; if you close the door, you'll be roasting, not broiling.

I serve the shrimp on toasted country bread, with the pan juices (the butter drippings mixed with white wine) poured over them. Then I add a crunchy, peppery watercress salad dressed with lemon juice to play against the richness of the dish.

Any way you eat this, you'll be happy, but here's the way I think you should go at it. Pull the shrimp, glistening with melting herb butter, out of their shells and really savor them. Don't be afraid to get in there and use your fingers. Put the shells on a side plate and enjoy your salad. Then pay the cook a compliment: Take your fork and give the bread a sleigh ride through the sauce.

BROILED JUMBO SHRIMP WITH HERBED ESCARGOT BUTTER

10 ounces (2½ sticks) unsalted butter, softened
½ teaspoon kosher salt
¼ teaspoon cayenne pepper
¼ cup fresh bread crumbs
3 tablespoons finely chopped shallots
1½ tablespoons finely chopped garlic
3 tablespoons finely chopped parsley
2 tablespoons finely chopped dill
2 tablespoons finely chopped chives
1 tablespoon finely chopped thyme
1 teaspoon finely chopped tarragon
12 jumbo shrimp, preferably with heads on
½ cup dry bread crumbs
2 teaspoons white wine
2 bunches watercress, stemmed, washed, and dried
1 tablespoon extra-virgin olive oil
2 teaspoons freshly squeezed lemon juice
Salt and freshly ground white pepper
4 slices ½-inch-thick country bread or 8 slices toasted brioche
4 to 8 lemon wedges for garnish

1. In work bowl of a food processor, combine butter, salt, and cayenne. Process until butter is satiny and doubled in volume, 3 to 4 minutes. Add fresh bread crumbs, shallots, garlic, parsley, dill, chives, thyme, and tarragon. Process to blend and set aside.

2. With scissors, cut away small legs on shrimp. Holding shrimp on their backs, use a serrated knife to slice each shrimp in half lengthwise. Remove center veins and small black sand sacs inside red tomalley near head. Place shrimp halves, shell down, in a single layer on a metal

baking tray or metal pie plate. Pipe or spoon an equal amount of herb butter down center of each shrimp half and dust with dry bread crumbs. Cover and refrigerate for 20 minutes or as long as 6 hours.

3. Preheat broiler. Uncover shrimp and, keeping broiler door open, broil until bread crumbs are golden and shrimp are cooked through, 3 to 4 minutes. Turn off broiler and remove tray of shrimp. Immediately pour wine around shrimp so that it mingles with pan juices and then return tray to turned-off broiler to keep warm.

4. In a medium mixing bowl, toss watercress with oil, lemon juice, and salt and pepper to taste.

5. To serve, place 1 slice country bread or 2 slices toasted brioche in center of each of 4 plates. Arrange 6 shrimp halves on top of bread and put mound of salad on plate. Stir pan juices and pour around plates and over bread. Garnish each plate with 1 or 2 lemon slices.

Yield: 4 first-course servings
Time: 1 hour

SALTING COD IN A ROBUST TWIST ON POT-AU-FEU

This is my fish version of the classic meat stew known as pot-au-feu in France, bollito misto in Italy, or New England boiled dinner here. In each of these the broth is savory, the vegetables generous, and the meat big and important. And every version has its pungent horseradish sauce.

In fact, it was the sauce that inspired me to make cod-au-feu. When I was the saucier at Le Cirque, we made bollito misto weekly, and I made the horseradish sauce. You'd think I'd tire of the dish, the sauce, or both, but when a combination is this good, you just want more. To turn this classic meat dish into a robust fish stew, the sauce would be key. So I kept its sharpness but added a handful of parsley to refresh the palate after the first hit of horseradish and to draw the sauce and other elements together.

The vegetables are pot-au-feu perennials, sturdy root vegetables. For the broth I like to use a good chicken stock, but this dish will be fine even if you use water. Just don't skip the bacon. You need its smokiness, fat, and fragrance; it provides the underlying warmth of the dish and ties it to its roots.

But the center of attention is the cod, which is poached atop the vegetables and served surrounded by them. I'm a fan of cod, fresh and salted. I love salt cod's texture—think flaky brandade—and wanted to get that into the dish but also keep the clean taste of fresh cod. I got both by salting fresh cod. Thinking about how meat is dry-aged and how its texture improves with aging, I lightly salted the cod and refrigerated it overnight. The salt removes some of the moisture, creates a flakier texture, and concentrates the flavor. These fillets hold their own against the root vegetables, stand up to the sauce, and make the dish every bit as satisfying as classic pot-au-feu.

Kosher salt

4 skinless cod fillets (each about 6 ounces),
 cut ¾ inch thick

1 small bunch parsley, stems reserved and
 leaves finely chopped

20 white peppercorns

4 sprigs thyme

2 cloves garlic, peeled and crushed

1 bay leaf

2 ounces double-smoked slab bacon, cut into
 1 by ¼-inch strips

½ small head green cabbage, cut into
 quarters, cored, and then cut into 1 by
 3-inch strips

3½ cups chicken broth or water

Salt

16 pearl onions, trimmed and peeled

4 small Yukon Gold potatoes, peeled and
 halved

3 medium leeks, white and light green parts
 only, trimmed, washed, and cut
 diagonally into ½-inch-thick slices

2 medium white turnips, peeled, halved, and
 cut into ½-inch-thick slices

2 medium carrots, peeled, trimmed, and cut
 diagonally into ¼-inch-thick slices

¾ cup crème fraîche

¼ cup bottled white horseradish, drained,
 with liquid reserved

2 tablespoons Dijon mustard

Freshly ground white pepper

1. On the day before serving, sprinkle a light dusting of kosher salt on both sides of each cod fillet. Wrap fillets in plastic wrap and refrigerate for 24 hours.

2. Preheat oven to 350 degrees. Make a sachet by placing parsley stems, peppercorns, thyme, garlic, and bay leaf in a double thickness of cheesecloth, folding into a packet and tying with kitchen string.

3. Place a 12-inch sauté pan with a tight-fitting lid over medium heat, or use a large flame-proof casserole. Add bacon and cook until it starts to render fat but doesn't color, about 1 minute. Place sachet in center of pan and spread cabbage evenly over surface. Add half of broth and salt to taste. Cover and bring to a boil. Reduce heat to low and simmer for 5 minutes. Layer onions, potatoes, leeks, turnips, and carrots in pan and add remaining broth. Cover and bring to a boil. Reduce heat to low and simmer for 10 minutes.

4. Place cod fillets on top of layered vegetables; the liquid will not cover fillets. Cover pan and place in oven. Bake until fish is opaque in center and starts to flake, 6 to 8 minutes.

5. While fish is baking, prepare horseradish cream: In a medium bowl, whisk crème fraîche until it holds peaks. Using a rubber spatula, fold in parsley leaves, horseradish, and mustard. Add a little of reserved horseradish liquid to thin sauce and sharpen its flavor; the sauce should have consistency of mousse. Season with salt and pepper to taste.

6. To serve, spoon an equal amount of vegetables and bacon into each of 4 wide soup plates. Place a fillet in center of each plate, spoon over some broth, and top with a generous spoonful of sauce.

Yield: 4 servings

Time: 45 minutes, plus 24 hours of refrigeration

WITH TUNA, A SECRET INSPIRED BY A BAGEL

Maybe you've had this experience. You're still half asleep, waiting in line to get your morning coffee and bagel. You wait and wait, just taking in all the great aromas, and then the guy behind the counter calls out, "Next!" with typical New York impatience, and it's you, you're next, and all of a sudden you're confused. "Give me an everything bagel," you say—it was the only thing you could think of—and it turns out to be perfect. It always is. It's got a ton of flavor and a taste that goes on forever.

That is the story behind my everything-crusted tuna: a thick hunk of tuna coated with the everything bagel's pebbly mix of dried garlic and onions, coarse salt, poppy and sesame seeds. A crust gives tuna flavor and shields it from too much heat, but the everything crust does more: It gives the tuna a strong personality. Once the tuna is dredged, it is panfried until the crust is beautifully browned and crunchy and the seeds and herbs are intensely flavorful. Then the tuna is finished in the oven.

To get the most out of this dish, buy premium-quality tuna and cook it only just enough. Ask the fishmonger to cut each steak like a brick, an even one inch thick. The tuna will look like beef, and, like beef, you'll want to keep it rare. Once fried it will be very rare. Put it in the oven for a minute, and it will be rare, and then for every minute after that you'll be cooking it to another level of doneness. Go easy. To my mind, tuna is best when it is cooked least.

EVERYTHING-CRUSTED TUNA WITH ROASTED RED PEPPER SAUCE

3 tablespoons dry minced garlic
3 tablespoons dry minced onion
3 tablespoons poppy seeds
3 tablespoons black sesame seeds
3 tablespoons white sesame seeds
2 teaspoons coarse salt
1 egg white, lightly beaten
4 sushi-quality center-cut tuna steaks,
    3 inches by 1½ inches by 1 inch thick
3 tablespoons olive oil
3 cloves garlic, peeled and thinly sliced
1 large shallot, peeled and thinly sliced
3 medium-size roasted red peppers, peeled
    and coarsely chopped
½ cup unsalted or low-sodium chicken stock
¼ cup white wine
Salt and freshly ground white pepper
3 to 4 tablespoons champagne vinegar
⅓ cup grapeseed oil
1½ cups canola or other vegetable oil

1. To make crust: Mix together garlic, onion, poppy seeds, sesame seeds, and coarse salt. Sprinkle some of this mixture on a plate. Dip tuna steaks in beaten egg white just enough to coat, then roll in crust mixture to cover thoroughly, adding more mixture if necessary. Put steaks on same plate on top of remaining mixture; set aside at room temperature.

2. Preheat oven to 450 degrees.

3. To make sauce: Warm olive oil in a large sauté pan over medium heat and add garlic and shallot. Cook, stirring, until soft but not colored, about 5 minutes. Add peppers, stock, and wine, season with salt and pepper, and simmer until

liquid is reduced by half, about 8 minutes. Carefully transfer mixture to a blender, add vinegar, and with machine running, pour in grapeseed oil. Blend just to emulsify. Adjust seasonings, adding water if sauce is too thick, and set aside in a warm place.

4. Have a metal baking pan ready; you will need it quickly after frying steaks. Pour canola oil into a 12-inch sauté pan and set over high heat; when oil reaches 350 degrees, slip tuna into pan. Fry for 1½ minutes on each side, until crust is well browned. Lift out steaks with a slotted spatula and place in baking pan. Transfer to oven and roast 1 minute for rare, 2 minutes for medium-rare, or 3 minutes for medium. Spoon some sauce onto each of 4 warmed dinner plates. Cut each steak in half on diagonal and place 2 pieces in center of each plate.

Yield: 4 servings
Time: 45 minutes

FISH STICKS AND TARTAR SAUCE FOR GROWN-UPS

Friday was fish day when I was growing up, and lots of times the fish was frozen fish sticks, the sauce was tartar, and the salad was coleslaw. With seven kids and a full-time job, my mom wasn't thinking fancy when Friday rolled around. But I enjoyed the crunch of the fish sticks' crust, the moistness of the fish, and the coolness of the slaw. And it didn't hurt that the tartar sauce was sweet and sharp. I had these things in mind when I created jumbo lump crab cakes with chipotle sauce. Crab cakes may be fancier, but they have the same appeal.

The secret to great crab cakes is proper seasoning and, of course, great crabmeat. They are seasoned with a cooked mayonnaise that includes onion and fresh bell peppers for sweetness, lime juice and Dijon mustard for zing, Tabasco for heat, and Vietnamese fish sauce (nuoc cham) for a complex saltiness. Finally, I fold in lots of fresh herbs for a clean, refreshing finish.

A word on crabmeat: It's expensive—but even more expensive if you don't buy the top grade. The best crabmeat, jumbo lump, has all large pieces of the choicest parts of the crab and the least cartilage. You pay more, but you get more crab for your money. If you buy less expensive lump or back-fin crabmeat with a lot of cartilage, you have to buy more to get enough meat.

I suggest preparing this dish as I do at the restaurant. Mix and shape the crab cakes. Chill them for one to six hours to firm them up. Make the chipotle sauce ahead, too. Chipotles are smoked jalapeño peppers (they usually come canned in adobo sauce), and they've got a rich, slightly sweet flavor with a soft, smoky heat. Mixed with lime juice, rice vinegar, and cilantro, then blended with vegetable oil, they give the sauce a depth of flavor that belies its lightness.

JUMBO LUMP CRAB CAKES WITH CHIPOTLE SAUCE

1½ cups vegetable oil, plus more for sautéing
½ cup finely diced red, green, and yellow bell peppers
¼ cup finely diced onion
2 egg yolks
2 tablespoons freshly squeezed lime juice
2 tablespoons Dijon mustard
1 teaspoon Tabasco
1½ teaspoons nuoc cham (Vietnamese fish sauce)
Salt and freshly ground white pepper
1 pound jumbo lump crabmeat, picked over to remove cartilage
½ to ⅔ cup fresh bread crumbs
2 tablespoons each of roughly chopped fresh dill, chives, and parsley
1 cup panko (Japanese bread crumbs)
1 chipotle pepper with 1½ teaspoons adobo sauce
1 teaspoon finely chopped garlic
1 teaspoon finely chopped shallot
¼ cup (packed) roughly chopped cilantro leaves
¼ cup seasoned rice vinegar
Juice of ½ lemon
Coleslaw, homemade or store-bought, for serving, optional

1. Prepare a saucepan of boiling water and a bowl of ice cubes and cold water. To make mayonnaise: Put ½ cup oil in a saucepan with peppers and onions, and cook over medium heat until oil simmers and vegetables are tender, about 7 minutes. Meanwhile, in a metal bowl, whisk together yolks, lime juice, mustard, Tabasco, and nuoc cham. Add vegetables to yolk mixture along with hot oil, by droplets, whisking steadily until mixture is smooth and slightly thickened. Season with salt and pepper. Put bowl over pan of boiling water and, still whisking, cook for 1 minute. Transfer bowl to ice-water bath. When mayonnaise is cool, cover and refrigerate until thoroughly chilled.

2. Put crabmeat in a large bowl and gently fold in 1 cup mayonnaise. Fold in ½ cup bread crumbs. Mixture should be lightly bound. If necessary, fold in more bread crumbs. Fold in dill, chives, and parsley.

3. Dust a plate with panko. Place a 2-inch-diameter ring mold, 1½ inches high, on panko and pack mold with crabmeat. Dust top with panko and tamp down crabmeat, pressing hard. Remove mold and transfer crab cake to another plate; repeat with remaining mixture. Cover crab cakes and chill at least 1 hour.

4. To make sauce: Put chipotle pepper, garlic, shallot, cilantro, vinegar, and lemon juice in a small food processor and pulverize. While machine runs, gradually pour in remaining 1 cup oil, blending until sauce is emulsified. Add salt and pepper to taste. Refrigerate. Bring to room temperature before serving.

5. Heat oven to 350 degrees. Pour ¼ inch oil into a large sauté pan and set over medium heat. When oil is hot, slip crab cakes into pan. Cook about 2 minutes on 1 side until brown, then transfer to a baking pan. Bake 5 minutes. Spoon coleslaw, if using, on each plate, surround with chipotle sauce, and top with 2 crab cakes.

Yield: 4 servings
Time: 1 hour, plus at least 2 hours of chilling

FOR AN OCEAN OF FISH,
JUST ONE SAUCE

If I had to choose my one "desert island" sauce, the only sauce I would be allowed to take to a place where I'd have lots of fish of different varieties, this vinaigrette would be it. It's an ideal companion to fish firm or soft, big-flavored or mild. It is easy to make, but it required the usual balancing act to develop.

When I develop a sauce, whether a simple sauce made from the cooking juices left in the pan, a butter sauce derived from a French classic, or a modern vinaigrette like this one, uniting soy, ginger, and orange, I often use wine as my reference. A good wine is balanced; its flavors are layered so that its fullness and complexity are revealed in stages, and its finish is round and complete. It is that same balance, mystery, and pleasure that I look for in a sauce.

Let's look at the components that make wine so satisfying. There's the acid, which is what you taste first. It opens your palate so you can fully appreciate the fruit. Then you get the fruit and, if there is some residual sugar in the wine, the sweetness. This is where the real fun begins and the nuances start to come through. Depending on the grape variety, where it is from and how it has been cellared, you will get different flavors. You may get spice or tropical fruit or earth, the way you often do with pinot noirs or what is sometimes referred to as an autumn leaf or barnyard taste in burgundies. The wine may be grassy or herbaceous, like sauvignon blanc, or flinty and tasting like minerals, like chablis.

After that you might taste the wine's age, the flavors associated with the grape's development, and the wood in which it was fermented.

You go through layer after layer of flavor until you come to the finish. This may be when you experience the wine's tannins, without which any wine would seem too lean, but it is certainly when you have the pleasure of recapping all the layers.

No analogy is ever a perfect fit, but the wine–sauce parallel is pretty close for this sauce in which the flavors are very deliberately layered. I start the sauce by warming some olive oil in a pan. Oil always provides the structure of a sauce; structure is what gives you body, and body is what gives you "mouth feel." Structure also develops legs. When you swirl a wine around in your glass and slender lines of wine remain after most of it has settled down, those are the legs. Legs hold up the wine or the sauce, and in this case, because the legs come from oil, they also carry the flavors throughout the sauce.

For the first thirty seconds the oil is heated with ginger, a perfume and spice giver. Then shallots are added for more perfume and spice. The Asian-flavoring trinity is completed when I toss the garlic into the warm, fragrant oil. Next I bring in the husky components: white wine for acidity; sherry vinegar for acidity and for its flavors of wood and age; soy sauce for richness and salt, which is the first flavor you catch in a sauce; and orange—whole for its fruit and the bitterness of the oils in its zest, and juice for sweetness and more fruit.

I cook these ingredients at a boil for twenty minutes to concentrate their flavors. Taste the sauce after this reduction, and you will be surprised: It is just too concentrated to appreciate. The flavors are closed. In a way it is like a bouillon cube, and as with a bouillon cube, it needs to be reconstituted.

To start putting things right, I stir in rosemary, which adds another layer of perfume; I don't add it earlier because it has a tendency to go from aromatic to medicinal over time. And then I add some previously reduced chicken stock, which will contribute to the sauce's structure.

I let everything steep a few minutes, strain the ingredients, and pour the liquids (which at this point are strong and bitter) into a blender. With the blender going, I add flavorless grapeseed oil, which dilutes and clarifies the muddled flavors in the reduction, provides the structure the sauce needs to live up to the name "sauce," and, most important, balances the flavors.

Taste the sauce now, and you'll have the same sensation you have with a good wine: There will be the bouquet, followed by the acidity, spice, sweetness, fruit, and age, and then the smooth, balanced finish.

Every time I prepare this sauce I think of the expression "mother sauce," the term French cooks use for a basic, essential sauce. In my kitchen, this vinaigrette is a mother sauce.

ORANGE-GINGER VINAIGRETTE

$1\frac{1}{3}$ cups unsalted chicken broth, preferably homemade

$\frac{1}{4}$ cup olive oil

2 ounces fresh ginger, peeled and cut into $\frac{1}{4}$-inch-thick slices

2 large shallots, peeled, trimmed, and cut into $\frac{1}{4}$-inch slices

4 cloves garlic, peeled and sliced

$2\frac{1}{2}$ cups freshly squeezed orange juice

$\frac{1}{2}$ cup white wine

$\frac{1}{4}$ cup soy sauce

$\frac{1}{4}$ cup sherry vinegar

1 orange, cut in half

2 sprigs fresh rosemary, each 3 to 4 inches long

2 cups grapeseed oil

Lemon juice

Salt and freshly ground white pepper

1. In a small saucepan over medium heat, reduce broth to $\frac{1}{2}$ cup. Set aside.

2. Place a large nonreactive skillet with high sides over high heat. When pan is hot, add oil and ginger. Sauté for 30 seconds, then add shallots. Sauté 30 seconds more, then add garlic. Sauté another 30 seconds, then add 2 cups orange juice, wine, soy sauce, and vinegar. Squeeze juice from orange halves into skillet, then add orange halves. Bring mixture to a boil and boil for 15 minutes. Add remaining $\frac{1}{2}$ cup orange juice and boil until liquid is reduced to 1 cup, about 5 minutes. Turn off heat and stir in rosemary and reduced broth. Allow mixture to steep for 5 minutes.

3. Pour mixture through a fine-mesh strainer placed over a bowl, pushing hard against solids to extract as much liquid as possible (about $1\frac{1}{2}$ cups). Discard solids and pour liquid into container of a blender. With blender at medium-low speed, slowly pour in grapeseed oil, blending until sauce is emulsified. Adjust seasonings, adding lemon juice, salt, and pepper to taste.

Yield: $3\frac{1}{2}$ cups (8 to 10 servings)
Time: 1 hour

FENNEL-CRUSTED TUNA WITH FENNEL SALAD

2 bulbs fennel, trimmed, halved, core removed, and thinly sliced on a mandoline
1 medium red onion, peeled, trimmed, and thinly sliced on a mandoline
1 tablespoon lemon juice
1 tablespoon blood-orange juice
2 tablespoons chopped chives
2 tablespoons extra-virgin olive oil
Kosher salt and freshly ground black pepper
4 tablespoons fennel seeds
3 teaspoons coriander seeds
1 teaspoon white peppercorns
2 egg whites
6 tuna steaks (each 7 ounces and about 1 1/2 inches thick)
Orange-Ginger Vinaigrette (see recipe above)

1. In a mixing bowl, combine fennel, onion, lemon juice, orange juice, chives, and 1 table-spoon oil. Toss to mix and season with salt and pepper to taste. Set aside.

2. Using a spice grinder, coffee mill, or mortar and pestle, finely grind fennel and coriander seeds, and peppercorns. Spread mixture on a plate. Whip egg whites just to break them up. Season tuna with salt to taste, brush 1 side with egg white, and then dip side into spice mix.

3. Place a 12-inch nonstick skillet over medium-high heat. Swirl remaining 1 tablespoon oil around in pan to coat bottom and place tuna steaks in pan, spice side down. Cook 2 minutes per side (for rare centers).

4. To serve, put equal portions of fennel salad on each of 6 serving plates. Place a tuna steak on top of each salad and drizzle with orange-ginger vinaigrette.

Yield: 6 servings
Time: 40 minutes

PESTO-TOPPED SALMON

2 tablespoons pine nuts
1/2 teaspoon finely chopped garlic
Salt and freshly ground white pepper
6 cups basil leaves, washed and dried
1/2 cup plus 1 tablespoon extra-virgin olive oil
3/4 cup fresh bread crumbs, plus extra for dusting salmon
6 boneless, skinless salmon fillets, each 6 ounces and about 1 1/4 inches thick at the center
1 teaspoon unsalted butter
Orange-Ginger Vinaigrette (see recipe above)

1. To prepare pesto: In a food processor, combine pine nuts, garlic, and salt and pepper to taste. Process to blend. Add basil and process until finely chopped. With machine running, add 1/2 cup oil in a slow stream, scraping down sides of bowl as needed and processing until mixture is smooth. A little at a time, add 3/4 cup bread crumbs to make a spreadable paste. Transfer to a bowl, press plastic wrap against surface, and refrigerate until needed.

2. Preheat oven to 400 degrees. Heat a 12-inch ovenproof nonstick skillet over high heat. Season salmon with salt and pepper to taste. Heat remaining 1 tablespoon oil in pan, add fillets, and cook for just 20 seconds on each side. Remove pan from heat, transfer salmon to a work surface, and wipe out pan.

3. Spread a ¼-inch-thick layer of pesto on 1 side of each salmon fillet. Dust pesto lightly with bread crumbs. Carefully put fillets in pan, pesto side down, and place pan over medium heat. Cook for 1 minute, adding butter to pan in bits during this time. Transfer pan to oven and roast salmon just until heated through and rare in center, about 3 minutes. If desired, serve on a mound of sautéed spinach. Surround salmon with orange-ginger vinaigrette.

Yield: 6 servings
Time: 20 minutes

IN SALMON, SMOKY MEETS SHARP AND SWEET

This dish was inspired by childhood trips to the ball-park, where I had smoky grilled hot dogs slathered with sharp mustard and topped with crunchy, slightly sweet relish. When I became a chef, I decided to create a dish with the same trio of flavors: smoky, sharp, and sweet.

It may seem like a leap from an all-beef frank to a velvety salmon fillet, but I think I have captured the essence of what we love in a hot dog by lightly smoking salmon and serving it with a sweet-sour cucumber rel-ish and a creamy horseradish-and-mustard sauce.

Smoking the salmon is mostly about fragrance: You pick up on the aroma immediately, but once you dig into the dish, the smoke's flavor recedes into the background. Smoking a fish in a home kitchen is easy. You can use a commercial stove-top smoker or improvise one with a heavy frying pan, a cake rack that fits into the pan (press one-inch balls of aluminum foil underneath the rack to give it needed height), and a lid. A wok is also perfect for this; because of its sloping sides, you can elim-inate the foil ball step.

Scatter applewood chips over the bottom of the pan, turn on the over-the-range exhaust system if you have one, and heat the chips until they smoke. Put the fillets on the rack and into the pan, cover the setup, remove it from the heat, and let the smoke waft around the salmon for 10 minutes. The fillets will still be cold and their edges will look a little dull, but their natural fats will have grabbed the smoke. Smoking does not cook the salmon—searing and roasting does—and the fish emerges fra-grant, perfectly moist, and seductively smoky.

The salmon, like a hot dog, requires cool condiments. The cucumber relish needs to chill until it is so crunchy that it is downright noisy when you eat it. The sauce—chilled, tangy crème fraîche jazzed up with horseradish and Dijon mustard—is bold enough to match the salmon's richness. This dish is a long way from the humble hot dog, but it satisfies in just the same way.

PAN-SEARED APPLEWOOD SMOKED
SALMON WITH CUCUMBER–RED
ONION RELISH

2 medium (each about 12 ounces) English
  cucumbers (also known as European or
  hothouse cucumbers), peeled
1 tablespoon kosher salt
½ medium red onion, peeled and thinly
  sliced
1½ tablespoons sugar
¼ cup rice wine vinegar
⅓ cup coarsely chopped fresh dill leaves
Salt and freshly ground white pepper
1 cup crème fraîche
¼ cup horseradish
3 tablespoons Dijon mustard
1 tablespoon olive oil
1 cup applewood chips (see headnote)
6 salmon fillets (7 ounces each and 1 inch
  thick), skin on
2 teaspoons unsalted butter, softened
Chopped chives for garnish

1. To make relish: Slice cucumbers in half lengthwise, scoop out seeds, and slice ¼ inch thick. Toss cucumbers with kosher salt and place in a colander. Weight down lightly, cover, and chill at least 30 minutes or as long as 12 hours. Drain cucumbers and toss with onion, sugar, vinegar, and dill. Season with salt and pepper, cover, and chill until needed. Relish can be refrigerated for 1 day.

2. To make horseradish cream: Whip crème fraîche with a whisk until as thick as mustard.

Fold in horseradish and mustard, add salt and pepper, and cover and chill until needed. Mixture can be kept in refrigerator for 6 hours.

3. To make salmon: Center a rack in oven and preheat to 450 degrees. If using a stove-top smoker, follow manufacturer's instructions for cold smoking. If fashioning your own smoker, place applewood chips in a wok or pan over high heat on top of stove. While they are heating, brush a cake rack with oil. Place salmon fillets skin side down on rack. When applewood chips start to smoke, after 5 to 10 minutes, put rack with salmon into wok (or into pan, raised on 1-inch balls of aluminum foil), and cover tightly. Remove from heat and let stand for 10 minutes. Remove salmon and season fillets with salt and pepper.

4. Place a 10-inch ovenproof sauté pan over high heat. When very hot, brush skin of fish generously with butter. Put fillets skin side down in sauté pan and immediately press with a spatula or place another skillet on top; stop pressing or remove top skillet after 1 minute. Cook 1 minute more, put pan in oven, and roast 4 to 5 minutes, or until fillets are cooked through but still moist inside.

5. To serve, place a mound of drained relish in center of each plate, surround with horseradish cream, and top with a salmon fillet, skin side up. Sprinkle each plate with chopped chives and serve immediately.

Yield: 4 servings
*Time: 30 minutes, plus up to 12 hours for chilling
  cucumbers*

CLAUDIA FLEMING

Claudia Fleming is the pastry chef at Gramercy Tavern
in Manhattan. She was photographed in a back room of the restaurant.
These columns were written with Melissa Clark.

THE ONE DESSERT A PASTRY CHEF CAN'T LIVE WITHOUT

It is near the end of a satisfying and complex restaurant meal—dessert time, the moment when many diners find themselves in the quivering grip of ambivalence. Do you go for the sweetness your palate so clearly craves? Or, fearing heaviness and excess, do you choose moderation and mutter, "No, nothing for me"?

The perfect dessert leaps this quandary by promising both sweetness and lightness (even if the lightness is more illusion than fact). And there is nothing in my repertory of some sixty desserts that does it better than buttermilk panna cotta. It is my own favorite, the one dessert I couldn't do without.

As remarkable as it is, this dessert is almost embarrassingly simple—just warmed sugared cream mixed with buttermilk and a touch of gelatin. I keep it on the menu all year long, changing its accompaniment to match the seasons. Ripe summer berries, autumnal figs,

and wintery blood oranges have all, in their turn, crowned the delicate custard. Recently I've kept the presentation simple and covered the custard with a Sauternes gelée. It's beautiful in a restrained way: The golden gelée, flecked with fragrant vanilla seeds, sparkles in a thin layer over the silken cream below. It adds a vibrant, elegant note without overpowering the tanginess of the buttermilk or the mellowness of the cream.

I got the idea from Tom Colicchio, the chef at Gramercy Tavern and my mentor. I noticed that he uses a Sauternes jelly with seared scallops. I love the way it shimmers and shines on the white plate, so I thought, "Why not add a similar element to my stark white panna cotta?" The only unusual ingredient is the leaf gelatin. It's sold in specialty markets, and I think it's easier to use than powdered. Just don't oversoak it; it should be softened but not so soft that it will fall apart when taken out of the water and squeezed dry.

This recipe makes seven panna cottas, which may

seem strange. It's dessert for six plus one for the cook the next day. At the restaurant, leftover panna cotta is one of the most coveted breakfasts of all.

BUTTERMILK PANNA COTTA WITH SAUTERNES GELÉE

1⅔ cups Sauternes
13 tablespoons sugar
1 2-inch piece of vanilla bean, halved
    lengthwise and seeds scraped out
2½ leaves gelatin
1¼ cups heavy cream
1¾ cups buttermilk

1. In a small saucepan, whisk together Sauternes, 6 tablespoons sugar, and vanilla seeds. Place saucepan over medium-low heat and reduce liquid at a bare simmer (turn heat to low if necessary) until it measures 1 cup, about 45 minutes.

2. Fill a bowl with cold water and add 1 gelatin leaf. Soak until softened, 3 to 5 minutes.

3. Meanwhile, in a saucepan over medium-high heat, warm cream with remaining 7 tablespoons sugar, stirring until it dissolves. Take pan off heat.

4. Remove gelatin leaf from water and squeeze dry in a clean dish towel. Add it to warm cream and stir until gelatin dissolves. Add buttermilk and stir well. Strain buttermilk mixture through a fine sieve into a glass measuring cup; pour mixture into seven 8-ounce ramekins, bowls, or parfait glasses. Chill until firm, about 3 hours.

5. While panna cottas are chilling, soften remaining 1½ gelatin leaves in a bowl of cold water for 3 to 5 minutes. Drain gelatin and squeeze dry. Add to warm Sauternes and stir until gelatin dissolves. Strain mixture through a fine sieve into a clean glass measuring cup and let cool to room temperature.

6. When panna cottas are set, stir Sauternes mixture to redistribute vanilla seeds. Very gently pour a thin stream of Sauternes down sides of ramekins to coat tops of custards (do this slowly to avoid puncturing creams). Chill until geleé is set, about 1 hour.

Yield: 7 servings
Time: 50 minutes, plus 4 hours of chilling

RHUBARB, ROSES, AND ROMANCE

I love the complex taste of rhubarb. Its mix of sweet and sour reminds me of the harshness and warmth of spring itself. Using it in a cobbler seems perfect; it's like a hint of the brilliance of the coming season cloaked in a wintery sort of dessert. In my cobbler, tender cream biscuits rest on top of the pieces of rhubarb, and the dish is baked until they melt into a bubbling pale red compote and the biscuits turn golden brown.

To add another sort of contrast, I garnish the steaming cobbler with something cool. At the restaurant I make goat's milk yogurt sorbet scented with rose water; at home you can get a similar effect for much less effort with a cool rose clabbered cream. Either way, the rose accents a touch of rose water that scents the rhubarb.

The combination was inspired by a pot of rhubarb-rose jam that a waiter brought back from London. I ate it by the spoonful, straight from the jar. The rose stirred memories of the crumbling stone walls I saw in England, which were covered with brave pink flowers and tiny brown shoots. To me, rose adds a little bit of romance wherever I use it. Now I can't think of rhubarb without thinking of reaching for the rose water. To best distribute the rose water—and the vanilla bean, which I also use in this dish—I like to rub them on the palms of my hands and then massage them into the rhubarb pieces. On days when I'm overwhelmed, it's a very calming, sensual way to spend a few minutes.

RHUBARB COBBLER

For the rhubarb:
> 2 pounds rhubarb, trimmed and cut into ½-inch pieces
> 1 cup sugar
> 2½ tablespoons cornstarch
> 1 2-inch piece of vanilla bean, split lengthwise
> ¼ teaspoon rose water

For the dough:
> 1⅔ cups all-purpose flour
> 3½ tablespoons sugar
> 1½ tablespoons baking powder
> ⅛ teaspoon salt
> 6 tablespoons cold unsalted butter, cut into ½-inch cubes
> ⅔ cup plus 1 tablespoon heavy cream
> 1 teaspoon turbinado (raw) sugar

1. Preheat oven to 375 degrees. In a large bowl, toss together rhubarb, sugar, and cornstarch. Scrape seeds from one side of vanilla bean (reserve other side for another use). Sprinkle rose water on your hands and smear vanilla seeds into one palm. Rub hands together to distribute seeds. Gently rub rhubarb with your hands to coat pieces with vanilla and rose water. (Or in a small bowl, stir together rose water and vanilla seeds, and toss with rhubarb.) Let rhubarb macerate for 20 minutes.

2. Meanwhile, prepare dough: In bowl of a food processor or electric mixer fitted with the paddle attachment, combine flour, sugar, baking powder, and salt. Pulse or mix to combine. Add butter and pulse or mix until flour resembles coarse meal. Add ⅔ cup cream and mix or pulse

until dough starts to come together, scraping down bowl and dough paddle when necessary.

3. Turn dough onto a lightly floured surface and gently pat together, incorporating any stray crumbs. Using a small ice cream scoop or a large spoon, form dough into 2-inch balls, then flatten slightly into biscuit shapes.

4. Put rhubarb in a shallow 2½-quart casserole in an even layer. Arrange biscuits on top, leaving about 1 inch in between them. Brush biscuits with remaining 1 tablespoon cream and sprinkle with turbinado sugar. Bake cobbler until rhubarb is bubbling and biscuits are golden brown, about 40 to 45 minutes. Serve warm with Rose Clabbered Cream (see recipe below).

Yield: 6 servings
Time: 1 hour 20 minutes

ROSE CLABBERED CREAM

1 cup clabbered cream
¼ cup rose jelly

Place clabbered cream in an electric mixer set on medium-high and beat until it thickens somewhat. Add jelly and continue to beat until stiff peaks form. Use immediately or chill.

Yield: 1½ cups
Time: 5 minutes

THE FUDGSICLE REFINED

At the end of a long meal I think most people are ready for something fun, and that's why I created this warm, gooey chocolate tart garnished with a fudgy sorbet. The tart, really a potent little chocolate soufflé, rests in a crisp crust of chocolate shortbread. Served warm from the oven, the tart has a soft and airy texture at the center, but a flavor that is as deeply chocolate as a dessert can be. The sorbet is an icy counterpoint, but it's no less intense.

I modeled the sorbet on what I imagine the perfect Fudgsicle should be: a scoop of frozen fudge. I simmer cocoa, water, and sugar together and reduce it into a thick chocolate syrup. Actually, I reduce the syrup a little more than it should be; a longer cooking time eliminates every trace of the grittiness and raw flavor that uncooked cocoa powder has. It also gives the finished sorbet more body and a silkier texture. To make up for my over-reduction, I whisk some water into the viscous syrup (which will allow the sorbet to freeze more easily). And I pump up the flavor a little more by adding some chopped extra-bitter chocolate.

At the restaurant I pair all this dark chocolate with a tiny, frothy chocolate malted shake, served in a shot glass. But for the home cook a suitable garnish that is a little more grown-up and infinitely more practical is a dollop of whipped crème fraîche. Plain whipped cream would be the obvious choice, but crème fraîche has a sharp flavor and a denser texture that cuts through all that chocolate better.

CHOCOLATE TARTS

For the filling:
  10 tablespoons unsalted butter
  5 ounces extra-bitter chocolate, such as
    Valrhona, chopped
  4 large eggs at room temperature
  7/8 cup sugar
  3 tablespoons all-purpose flour

For the dough:
  8 ounces (2 sticks) unsalted butter at room
    temperature
  1 cup confectioners' sugar
  1/4 cup unsweetened cocoa
  1 large egg at room temperature
  1 1/2 cups all-purpose flour
  1/2 cup ground almonds
  Whipped crème fraîche for garnish

1. To prepare filling: Put butter in a double boiler over simmering water and scatter chocolate pieces on top. Let mixture sit until butter and chocolate are melted. Remove boiler top from heat and stir until well combined. Transfer mixture to a large bowl and let cool.

2. In bowl of an electric mixer, briefly beat eggs to break them up. Add sugar and beat 5 minutes at high speed, until very pale and thick. Fold one-third of mixture into chocolate mixture to lighten it, then gently fold in remainder taking care not to deflate eggs. Sift flour over batter and carefully fold in. Cover filling and chill for 2 hours.

3. Meanwhile, prepare dough: Beat butter and sugar in an electric mixer until light and creamy. Add cocoa and beat until well combined. Add egg and beat until smooth.

4. Sift flour and almonds into cocoa mixture. Beat mixture on low speed until combined. Scrape dough onto a sheet of plastic wrap and form into a disk. Cover and chill until firm, about 1 hour.

5. Preheat oven to 350 degrees. On a lightly floured surface, roll dough to a thickness of 3/16 inch. Using a 3 1/2-inch round cutter, cut out 12 circles of dough and press them into individual 3-inch tart pans, trimming away any excess dough. Chill tart shells for 20 minutes.

6. Line shells with 5-inch squares of aluminum foil and fill with dried beans or rice as weights. Place shells on a baking pan and bake for 12 to 14 minutes, until set. Remove foil and weights, and cool shells on a rack.

7. Divide filling among tart shells and bake until puffed and slightly cracked on top, 12 to 14 minutes. Remove tarts from pans and serve immediately, garnished with whipped crème fraîche. Serve with chocolate sorbet (see recipe below).

Yield: 12 tarts
Time: 1 1/4 hours, plus 2 hours of chilling

⅞ cup sugar

¾ cup unsweetened cocoa powder

8½ ounces extra-bitter chocolate, chopped

1. In a medium saucepan, combine 2 cups water and sugar, and bring to a boil over high heat, stirring occasionally. Gradually add cocoa powder, whisking until smooth. Reduce heat to low and cook mixture at a gentle simmer for 30 minutes, until syrupy.

2. Put chocolate in a large bowl and add half of cocoa syrup, whisking until chocolate is melted and mixture is smooth. Add remaining syrup and whisk well. Strain mixture through a fine sieve and let cool. Stir in 1 cup water.

3. Chill sorbet mixture, covered, until very cold, at least 4 hours. Freeze in an ice cream maker according to manufacturer's instructions.

Yield: 1 pint

Time: 45 minutes, plus 4 hours of chilling

NUTTY, GRAINY CORNMEAL BISCOTTI

My favorite part of my job is playing with unusual flavors and coming up with interesting combinations. But sometimes I worry that I have gone too far. This was the case at first with these cornmeal biscotti, flavored with fresh rosemary and orange. I love the coarse texture and nutty flavor of cornmeal and the wonderful, grainy crunch it gives these biscotti, without making them too hard.

Rosemary has a natural affinity for cornmeal (really—think of how deliciously they are paired in polenta), and it is a natural digestive and appropriate to eat at the end of a meal. The rosemary lends a musky, pine flavor, one that cries out for a touch of refreshing brightness. That's where the orange zest comes in. (Adding the rosemary and zest to the warm, just-melted butter keeps the rosemary from turning brown and brings out the essential oils in both of them.)

In the end, those flavors and the others in these little biscotti—anise, almond, and hazelnut—blend into a mild harmony that isn't the least bit frightening. They are complex cookies and will hold their own no matter how often they are dunked. Although they're a fine match for coffee or tea, I prefer them with a glass of dessert wine. A dry Italian vin santo is a particularly nice complement.

CORNMEAL BISCOTTI

½ cup coarsely chopped blanched almonds
¼ cup coarsely chopped skinned hazelnuts
4 tablespoons unsalted butter
1 tablespoon minced rosemary
1½ tablespoons finely grated orange zest
1 cup all-purpose flour
½ cup coarse yellow cornmeal
½ cup sugar
1 teaspoon baking soda
1 teaspoon aniseed
3 large eggs

1. Heat oven to 350 degrees. Spread nuts out on a jelly roll pan and toast in oven, stirring occasionally, until lightly golden around edges, about 8 to 10 minutes. Let cool on a rack. Keep oven on.

2. In a small saucepan, melt butter over medium-high heat. Turn off heat and add rosemary and orange zest. Let cool.

3. In bowl of an electric mixer set at low speed, mix together flour, cornmeal, sugar, baking soda, and aniseed. Add 2 eggs, 1 at a time, mixing well after each addition. Add cooled, melted butter and mix to combine. Stir in nuts. Let dough rest for 5 minutes.

4. Form dough into a log 2 inches wide and place on a parchment-lined baking sheet. In a small bowl, mix 1 egg with 1 tablespoon water and brush over log, then bake until a deep golden brown, about 30 minutes. Let cool on a rack.

5. Reduce oven temperature to 200 degrees. Using a serrated knife, slice log on a diagonal into pieces ¼ inch thick. Arrange on 2 parchment-lined baking sheets and dry in oven until crisp, about 45 minutes to 1 hour. Let cool on a rack.

Yield: about 2½ dozen
Time: 2¼ hours

CLASHING FLAVORS CAN SOMETIMES WORK WONDERS

I offer this dessert—an Asian-accented sorbet in a tapioca soup—as a triumph of cooking dangerously. It is, in the end, soft and sharp, familiar and strange.

The dessert sounds harder and more complex to prepare than it is; bear with me. First, I simmer tapioca in milk, and as it reduces, it becomes a rich sauce containing tender tapioca pearls. I use both large- and small-pearl tapioca; it gives the dish the look of a bowl full of bubbles. Coconut milk, stirred in after cooking, lends a tropical flavor and thins down the tapioca mixture so that it has the texture of a light cream soup.

Then I reach out not just for a counterpoint to its creamy smoothness but also for sharp contrast in the sorbet: the bold flavor of passion fruit. But the biggest leap of faith is a cilantro syrup. Cilantro, as popular as it may be in Asia and elsewhere, is just not your ordinary dessert component. I transform the cilantro into a thin green-flecked syrup with a sharp, minty taste. In this quest for contrasts the cilantro works a miracle: It stands out against both the milky tapioca and the acidic passion fruit. You need only a few jewel-like drops of the syrup to make the point.

Since every dessert needs a textural contrast, I reprise the coconut in a caramelized golden brown tuile, which becomes a raft on which to float the sorbet. It's a practical presentation since the tuile keeps the sorbet from melting too quickly into the tapioca. And it's beautiful, too, with its vivid layers of gold, apricot, moon white, and green.

None of the components is particularly challenging to prepare. All can be made ahead. (The easiest shortcut is to buy a high-quality passion fruit sorbet.) The tapioca actually benefits from a night in the refrigerator; the resting time leaves it even more supple and silky. On serving day, you just assemble the components. The dessert may be risky in concept, but the results are a sure thing.

COCONUT TAPIOCA SOUP

5½ cups milk
1 cup sugar
¼ cup small-pearl tapioca
¼ cup large-pearl tapioca
1 13½-ounce can coconut milk
Cilantro Syrup (see recipe below)
Coconut Tuiles (see recipe below)
Passion Fruit Sorbet (see recipe below)

1. In a medium saucepan, place 2½ cups milk and ½ cup sugar. In another medium saucepan, place remaining 3 cups milk and remaining ½ cup sugar. Bring both mixtures to a simmer over high heat, stirring occasionally to dissolve sugar. Add small-pearl tapioca to saucepan with 2½ cups milk, and large-pearl tapioca to saucepan with 3 cups milk. Reduce heat to low and simmer mixtures, stirring frequently, until tapioca pearls are soft. This will take 35 to 45 minutes for small pearls and 50 to 60 minutes for large pearls.

2. When both tapioca mixtures are cooked, combine in a large bowl while still warm. Stir in coconut milk. Let mixture cool completely, then cover and chill for at least 10 hours and up to 24.

3. To serve, divide tapioca mixture among 6 soup bowls. Dot each serving with ½ teaspoon cilantro syrup. Float a coconut tuile in center of each bowl and place a scoop of passion fruit sorbet on tuile. Top sorbet with another tuile. Serve immediately.

Yield: 6 servings
Time: 1¼ hours, plus 10 hours of chilling

COCONUT TUILES

1¼ cups sugar
2½ tablespoons unsalted butter
7 egg whites at room temperature
2 cups shredded unsweetened coconut
¼ cup all-purpose flour

1. In bowl of an electric mixer set at medium speed, beat sugar and butter until mixture resembles wet sand, about 2 minutes. Gradually add egg whites and continue to beat until well mixed.

2. Combine coconut and flour, add to bowl, and mix well. Cover and chill at least 8 hours or overnight.

3. Preheat oven to 325 degrees. Use nonstick baking sheets or regular baking sheets with nonstick liners or parchment paper on top. For each tuile drop a heaping teaspoon of batter onto baking sheet, leaving 3 inches in between. Dip a small offset spatula or back of a spoon into cold water to prevent sticking and gently pat each mound of batter into a very thin, even 4-inch round. Bake until golden, about 15 minutes.

4. Using a plastic dough scraper or a spatula, remove tuiles from pans and cool on a wire rack. They may stick if cooled too much; return them to oven for 1 minute. Cool baking sheets between batches.

Yield: 3½ dozen
Time: 1½ hours, plus at least 8 hours of chilling

CILANTRO SYRUP

¼ cup tightly packed cilantro leaves
⅓ cup light corn syrup

1. Bring a small saucepan of water to a boil. Fill a bowl with ice cubes and water. Plunge cilantro leaves into boiling water for 15 seconds, drain, and immediately plunge into ice water. Remove from water and pat dry.

2. Combine cilantro and corn syrup in a blender or food processor and puree. Let mixture rest for 30 minutes, then strain, discarding solids.

Yield: ⅓ cup
Time: 40 minutes

PASSION FRUIT SORBET

1 cup peeled cubed pineapple
1 cup sugar
1⅓ cups unsweetened passion fruit juice or
    puree

1. Place pineapple and 2 tablespoons sugar in a food processor or blender and puree until very smooth. Let mixture rest for 1 hour.

2. Meanwhile, in a small saucepan over medium heat, combine remaining sugar with 1 cup water and simmer, stirring, until sugar dissolves, about 3 minutes. Remove from heat and allow to cool.

3. Strain pineapple mixture through a medium sieve (not a fine sieve). Measure ⅔ cup pineapple puree and discard rest.

4. In a large bowl, whisk together pineapple puree, passion fruit juice, and sugar syrup. Cover and chill at least 3 hours or overnight. Freeze in an ice cream maker according to manufacturer's instructions.

Yield: 1 quart
Time: 1¼ hours, plus chilling and freezing

⟜⟶

THE SWEETNESS OF CORN SET OFF BY THE TARTNESS OF BLACKBERRIES

A few years ago, I ordered an unusual dessert in a small Mexican restaurant. Sweet-corn ice cream sounded intriguing, but it turned out to be a disappointment, riddled with distracting icy kernels. Still, I love corn and was taken with the idea of a perfectly smooth corn ice cream.

Then I began wondering, "What would I pair it with?" Still under the influence of my Mexican meal, I toyed with the idea of refining a corn tortilla and came up with a twist on a French classic: a cornmeal crepe. The buttery crepes cried out for a tart counterpoint, and a minimally sweet blackberry compote adds just the right vibrancy to the dish. It looks beautiful, too, with its deep magenta drizzle of sauce.

As the dish developed, the flavor of the ice cream became elusive. At first bite, it's barely discernible. But it creeps up on you, growing more distinct and delicious as the ice cream melts into a rich custard sauce surrounding the crepe. At the restaurant, I trim the crepes into squares for a presentation like a floppy Napoleon. But you don't have to bother—and besides, this is such a summery dessert that you don't want it to appear too fussy.

CORNMEAL CREPES AND BLACKBERRY COMPOTE

½ vanilla bean, split lengthwise, seeds
    scraped off
2 cups milk
⅞ cup all-purpose flour
½ cup heavy cream
9 tablespoons sugar
3 large eggs
Pinch of salt
5 tablespoons cornmeal
Melted butter for pan if necessary
1 quart blackberries
Sweet-Corn Ice Cream (see recipe below)

1. Place vanilla seeds in a blender with milk, flour, cream, 6 tablespoons sugar, eggs, and salt. Blend until smooth. Pass mixture through a fine sieve and stir in cornmeal. Cover and chill at least 8 hours.

2. Heat a heavy, preferably nonstick 8-inch skillet over medium-high heat. (If not nonstick, brush with butter.) Add about 3 tablespoons crepe batter to pan and swirl so batter just coats bottom of pan. If too thick, pour excess batter back into bowl. Cook crepe until bottom is browned and small bubbles appear on top, about 45 seconds. Flip over and cook until browned on other side, about 30 seconds. Remove to a plate and repeat with remaining batter, buttering pan occasionally if crepes begin to stick. Makes about 30 crepes.

3. To make compote: Combine half of blackberries, 2 tablespoons water, and remaining 3 tablespoons sugar in a saucepan over medium-high heat. Cook, stirring occasionally, until blackberries give up their juice and sugar dis-

solves, about 5 minutes. Turn off heat and stir in remaining berries.

4. To serve, place a crepe on a plate and top with some compote, using a slotted spoon. Top with another crepe and more blackberries, then finish with a third crepe. Spoon some blackberry liquid around crepe and garnish with a scoop of ice cream.

Yield: 8 servings
Time: 45 minutes, plus 8 hours of chilling

SWEET-CORN ICE CREAM

4 ears of fresh sweet corn, shucked
2 cups milk
2 cups heavy cream
¾ cup sugar
9 large egg yolks

1. Using a large knife, slice corn kernels off cobs and place in a large saucepan. Break cobs into thirds and add to pot with milk, cream, and ½ cup sugar. Bring to a boil, stirring, then turn off heat. Using an immersion mixer, puree corn kernels. (If you don't have an immersion mixer, remove kernels with a slotted spoon, puree in a blender, and return to pan.) Let rest for 1 hour.

2. Bring mixture back to a simmer, then turn off heat. In a small bowl, whisk egg yolks and remaining ¼ cup sugar. Add a cup of hot mixture to yolks, stirring constantly so they do not curdle. Add yolk mixture to saucepan, stirring. Cook over medium-low heat, stirring constantly, until custard coats spoon, about 10 minutes.

3. Pass custard through a fine sieve, pressing down hard on solids. Discard solids. Let custard cool, then cover and chill at least 4 hours. Freeze

in an ice cream maker according to manufacturer's instructions.

Yield: about 3½ cups

Time: 45 minutes, plus 1 hour of resting and 4 hours of chilling and freezing

⁓

A HYBRID DESSERT INSPIRED BY CHEESE

This dessert incorporates the elements of a cheese course: fresh and dried fruit and the cheese itself. Its centerpiece is a tarte Tatin—a caramel-glazed, upside-down apple tart in a crisp puff pastry crust. While baking, the apples release juice, and it mingles with the caramel for an intense, buttery sauce.

It was harder to fit in the cheese. I wanted something simple to complement the tart, and it had to be more elegant than, say, the traditional cheddar on apple pie. I opted for a deliciously mild, creamy goat cheese from Coach Farm because it can be beaten to cloudlike lightness with cream to add fluffy contrast to the tart. On the plate it looks like a mild dollop of whipped cream. But there is no mistaking its tangy flavor—a cool piquancy against the caramel-coated apples.

For the third element, the dried fruit, I turned to golden raisins, which I plump in a hot bath of apple juice and verjuice. If you've never used verjuice, you're in for a pleasant surprise. It's grape juice made from unripe grapes, which makes it much more complex and less sweet than regular grape juice. Verjuice brings out the inherent grape flavor of the raisins without making them cloying. (It is also terrific for poaching other fruit.)

TARTE TATIN WITH GOAT CHEESE CREAM

½ cup sugar

8 tablespoons (1 stick) unsalted butter, softened and cut into 1-inch pieces

4 medium Granny Smith apples, peeled, halved, and cored

8 ounces puff pastry, thawed

6 ounces mild goat cheese at room temperature

¾ cup heavy cream

Golden Raisin Verjuice (see recipe below)

1. Preheat oven to 450 degrees. In a 10-inch ovenproof skillet over low heat, combine sugar with 3 tablespoons water and cook, stirring constantly, until sugar dissolves. Increase heat to high and cook until mixture is golden brown and caramelized. Remove skillet from heat and whisk in butter until melted and smooth. Arrange apple halves, cut sides up, over caramel.

2. Roll puff pastry to an 11-inch circle, trimming if necessary. Drape it directly over apples, tucking edges.

3. Place skillet in oven and bake about 25 to 30 minutes, until pastry is puffed and golden brown. Allow tart to rest until cooled, at least 1 hour.

4. Preheat oven to 400 degrees. Using an electric mixer, beat goat cheese until creamy. Add cream and beat until well combined. To serve, invert tart onto baking sheet and reheat in oven about 10 minutes. Serve warm tart garnished with goat cheese cream and golden raisin verjuice.

Yield: 6 servings

Time: 1 hour, plus 1 hour to cool

1 cup golden raisins
¾ cup white verjuice
½ cup apple juice
⅓ cup sugar
Seeds scraped from 1-inch piece of vanilla
　　bean

In a medium saucepan, combine all ingredients and bring to a simmer, stirring occasionally. Immediately reduce heat to low. Let mixture cook slowly, stirring occasionally and making sure it doesn't return to a simmer, until liquid is reduced by half, about 25 minutes. Let cool at least 15 minutes before serving.

Yield: 1 cup
Time: 35 minutes, plus 15 minutes to cool

THOMAS KELLER

Thomas Keller is the chef and owner of the French Laundry in Yountville, California. He was photographed by Monica Almeida on the veranda of the restaurant. These columns were written with Michael Ruhlman.

A SAVORY SUMMER

In New York City, it seems to me, restaurants are all about interior. Here in Yountville, California, it's the outdoors, the Napa Valley itself, that sets the tone and guides our expectations for what a restaurant should be.

The fresh produce is everywhere, especially as spring turns to summer. The grapes have only finished budding and are months away from harvest in the fall. But apricots have just arrived, and so have peas, spring garlic, cherries, and fuzzy green almonds. We're picking sugar snap peas from our garden, and our lettuces and herbs—thyme, tarragon, rue—have taken off. It may be the best place in America to be cooking at this very moment.

With so much to offer, it would be a pity to limit a meal to two or three large courses. But more than that, our interest in any single dish diminishes precipitously after the second or third bite. It's the same as stepping

into a hot bath: The initial sensation is jolting, but gradually you become used to the temperature and don't even think about it. That's why I like to present a series of five to nine intensely focused courses. I want my customers to experience the jolt, the new sensation on the palate, and then to move on to another one.

The first dish everyone receives upon being seated is what we call a cornet, a small cone filled with salmon tartare and crème fraîche. It looks like summer, a miniature pink ice cream cone. The cornet is an amuse-bouche *in the fullest sense. It first amuses the eye: People smile when they see it. And it amuses the palate: fresh salmon, seasoned with lemon-infused oil, a crunchy tuile cone, and cool crème fraîche flavored with minced red onion.*

The pleasure I derive from serving this dish remains, in part, a result of its origins, which occurred during a sad time in my life. I was leaving New York after ten years of cooking there. Rakel, the restaurant I'd owned with Serge Raoul, had failed with the economic down-

turn of the late 1980s. I'd become a restaurant consultant, a miserable experience, and then I'd accepted a job as chef at a restaurant called Checkers in Los Angeles, and would be moving to an unfamiliar city (a way station, as it turned out, on my journey to Napa).

My new boss wanted me to prepare a dish for a food and wine benefit in Los Angeles that would really wow people and introduce me to the community. I knew people would be standing, probably holding a glass of wine, so whatever I came up with couldn't require silverware. And it had to be original. There was a lot of pressure.

I'd been serving a simple garlic tuile—flour, eggs, salt, butter, garlic paste, and Parmesan—for a long time. I cooked it flat and served it with rabbit. We also baked it partly folded, as an American-style taco shell.

Shortly before I moved from New York, some friends took me to a favorite restaurant in Chinatown and, as always, to Baskin-Robbins for ice cream afterward. This food and wine party was in the back of my mind the whole time. I ordered an ice cream cone, and when it was extended to me in its holder, I didn't see a sugar cone—I saw a tuile. There it was: I would fill a tuile with tuna tartare. There's my dish, I thought.

On one level, I know, this was a mundane moment. But the fact is, that is often how inspiration arrives, not mysteriously but as a burst within the course of everyday events. How many ice cream cones had I eaten before without creating anything? Just then, though, anxious and depressed, my cone became my cornet, a festive opener that makes people happy.

At the restaurant I present the cornets in acrylic holders made for this purpose, but they would be just as striking served in a bowl filled with dry rock salt. It's an easy presentation, and it looks a little like a bowl of crushed ice, which seems like a perfect way to serve trompe l'oeil ice cream cones.

I now use salmon, but you can fill the cornets with almost anything. Eggplant caviar and roasted peppers or tomato confit is a vegetarian version. You could do it with meat—a julienne of prosciutto with some melon. The tuile is a vessel. Fill it with your imagination.

CORNETS OF ATLANTIC SALMON TARTARE WITH SWEET RED ONION CRÈME FRAÎCHE

4 ounces sushi-quality salmon fillet (belly preferred), very finely minced
¾ teaspoon extra-virgin olive oil
¾ teaspoon lemon oil
1½ teaspoons finely minced chives
1½ teaspoons finely minced shallots
Kosher salt
Freshly ground white pepper
½ cup crème fraîche
1 tablespoon finely minced red onion, rinsed and dried
7 tablespoons all-purpose flour
4 teaspoons sugar
8 tablespoons (1 stick) butter at room temperature
2 egg whites, chilled
1 to 2 tablespoons black sesame seeds
24 inch-long chive tips for garnish

1. To prepare salmon tartare: In a small bowl, combine salmon, olive oil, lemon oil, minced chives, and shallots. Mix well and season with ½ teaspoon salt and a pinch of pepper. Cover and refrigerate until well chilled, at least 30 minutes.

2. To prepare sweet red onion crème fraîche: In a small mixing bowl, whisk crème fraîche until it holds soft peaks, 30 seconds to 1 minute. Fold in onion and season to taste with salt and pepper. Cover and refrigerate until needed.

3. Preheat oven to 400 degrees. To prepare cornets: In a medium-size mixing bowl, combine flour, sugar, and 1 teaspoon salt. In a separate bowl, whisk butter until like mayonnaise in texture. Add egg whites to flour mixture, mixing with a wooden spoon until completely incorporated. Whisk in softened butter by thirds, until batter is creamy and smooth.

4. Make a 4-inch-wide circular stencil by cutting a hole in a large plastic lid or other piece of heavy plastic. Have ready a large baking sheet, a Silpat nonstick baking sheet liner or parchment paper, and 12 cornet molds (size 35, 4½ inches). Place liner or parchment on a baking sheet. Holding stencil flat, place a spoonful of batter in center of hole and spread evenly with an offset spatula. Batter should be just thick enough so that it is opaque with no thin spots; remove any excess batter. Lift stencil and repeat process until you have 12 rounds; leave 1½ inches between rounds. Sprinkle each round with ⅛ teaspoon black sesame seeds. Bake until batter is set and just beginning to brown, about 4 minutes.

5. Place baking sheet on oven door to keep rounds warm and flexible. Flip a round over, sesame side down, and place a cornet mold at one side. Form cornet by tucking dough up at bottom (small) end and rolling dough tightly around mold. Leaving cornet wrapped around mold, place it seam side down. Repeat with remaining rounds of dough, allowing rolled cornets to lean against each other to prevent them from rolling. Return baking sheet to oven and bake 2 to 3 minutes more to set seam and let them reach a golden brown. Remove from oven and cool slightly, then remove molds. Cool cornets on paper towels. Repeat entire process with remaining batter to make 12 more. Cornets may be stored in an airtight container for up to 24 hours.

6. To assemble, use a pastry bag or small knife to fill each cornet with ½ inch of red onion crème fraîche. Spoon about 1½ teaspoons salmon tartare over crème fraîche and mound so dome resembles ice cream in a cone. Press a chive tip against 1 side of tartare on each cone for garnish. Serve immediately.

Yield: 24 filled cornets
Time: 1 hour

FROM THE SEA, THE VINEYARD, AND TRADITION

Classic French cuisine has long had a reputation in this country for being stuffy and rigid, but the opposite, in fact, is true: Classic French cuisine is dynamic and infinitely renewable, a source I return to again and again for ideas and inspiration.

During my years at French Laundry, I have served hundreds of original dishes. They didn't just materialize out of air. Almost every one of them has a reference to something that came before it, and this dish is a good example of how a classic preparation can be transformed into something that feels both modern and regional.

I learned to make sole Veronique when I was a young cook, and it was straight out of Escoffier's 1903 text Le Guide Culinaire. A piece of sole is folded into a package and poached in a little fish stock, lemon juice, and wine; this liquid, called a cuisson, is reduced and mounted with butter to make the sauce, and the plate is garnished with very cold skinned grapes.

I fixed on this preparation because it uses grapes and I am cooking in the heart of the California wine country. Right now I'm using the perlette grape, a round green variety that keeps its crunch after you peel it and has a slightly acidic quality that enhances the fish and offsets the rich sauce.

I like the fact that a flat piece of fish is folded to give it more dimension. I decided to add another layer of complexity by stuffing this package. I couldn't stuff it with fresh grapes because of their size and water content, but dried grapes, I thought, would work perfectly. I use California raisins, bound with rich brioche, herbs, and butter. This simple notion of stuffing adds contrasting colors, flavors, and textures (most notably the chewy raisins) to what had been a plain piece of fish.

Then I wrap the fish in plastic and poach it in water—a great technique that's easy, efficient, and especially good for this dish. It lets the delicate stuffed fish hold its shape and makes it possible to cook many portions at the same time. (I use this technique, which I call "boil in a bag," for various poultry dishes as well.)

For the sauce I enrich a reduced fumet with hollandaise and cream. Then I glaze the dish under a broiler and garnish it with peeled seedless green grapes. Reduced to its essence, sole Veronique is fish and grapes. My sole Veronique has additional flavors and textures, but because I've stayed within the parameters of a classic French preparation, the dish doesn't feel confusing or overwrought. And now it is a quintessential Napa Valley dish, too.

FILLET OF SOLE VERONIQUE

2 1¾- to 2-pound whole gray sole, each cut into 4 fillets, and bones reserved for fish fumet

For the fish fumet:
 1 tablespoon canola oil
 3 ounces (1¼ cups) sliced button mushrooms
 ¼ cup sliced onion
 ¼ cup sliced leeks
 3 sprigs Italian parsley
 ¾ cup sauvignon blanc or other dry white wine

For the stuffing:
 ⅛ cup sultanas (golden raisins)
 ⅛ cup black raisins
 2½ cups diced brioche (¼ inch by ¼ inch) or Pepperidge Farm thinly sliced white bread
 1¼ tablespoons chopped Italian parsley
 1 tablespoon minced shallots
 2 tablespoons butter, melted
 Salt and freshly ground white pepper

For the hollandaise sauce:
 1 large egg yolk
 ¼ cup clarified butter
 ⅛ teaspoon lemon juice

For the glaçage:
 ¾ cup heavy cream
 ¼ cup unsweetened whipped cream
 16 green seedless grapes for garnish (peeled and cut in half if you wish)

1. To prepare fish fumet: Cut fish bones into 2-inch pieces and soak in cold water until all

traces of blood are gone, 1 to 2 hours. Heat canola oil in a 4-quart saucepan over medium heat. Add drained bones, cover, and allow to steam for 2 minutes. Add mushrooms, onion, leeks, parsley sprigs, wine, and 3 cups water. Bring to a boil, then reduce heat to low. Simmer, partly covered, for 30 minutes. (During this time, prepare stuffing.) Remove from heat and let fumet settle for 10 minutes. Place a clean kitchen towel over a bowl and pour fumet through towel; avoid straining sediment that has settled in bottom of pan. Pour 2 cups of fumet into a medium saucepan and set aside; refrigerate or freeze remainder for another purpose.

2. To prepare stuffing: In a small saucepan over low heat, combine sultanas and black raisins with ¼ cup water. Simmer until water is absorbed and raisins have plumped, about 8 minutes. In a large mixing bowl, combine brioche, chopped parsley, shallots, and melted butter. Drain raisins on paper towels and add to mixture. Season with salt and white pepper to taste, and set aside.

3. To prepare hollandaise sauce: In a 1-quart stainless steel mixing bowl or top of a double boiler, combine egg yolk with 1 tablespoon water. Place bowl over simmering water and whisk yolk until it thickens and resembles mayonnaise. Remove from heat and slowly whisk in clarified butter and lemon juice. Season to taste with salt and pepper.

4. To prepare glaze: Place saucepan of fish fumet over medium-high heat and bring to a boil. Reduce fumet to about ¼ cup. Add cream and reduce mixture to a total of ¾ cup. While mixture is still hot, whisk in hollandaise sauce, followed by whipped cream. Keep in a warm place; do not reboil.

5. Fill a large casserole half full of water, place over medium-high heat, and bring to a simmer. Place sole fillets between pieces of plastic wrap and pound lightly with a kitchen mallet to flatten to an even thickness. Place fillets on a flat surface, skinned side up. Season with salt and pepper to taste. Put equal amounts of stuffing on each fillet and roll fillets around stuffing. Place each rolled fillet on a piece of plastic wrap and roll tightly, securing each end with a knot. Transfer sole packets to simmering water and cook for 5 minutes.

6. To serve, cut one end of each sole packet. Lightly press uncut end, and rolled sole will slide out. Divide glaze evenly among 4 or 8 plates, place stuffed sole in center, and garnish with grapes. Serve immediately.

Yield: 8 as a first course or 4 as an entree
Time: 1½ hours, plus 1 to 2 hours for soaking fish
  bones

THREE-BEAN SALAD FIT FOR COMPANY

I've named this salad after those crocks of marinated green beans, garbanzo, and kidney beans in every American salad bar. But my three-bean salad is really something entirely different, a simple composition of dried beans and fresh beans: A base of pureed white beans is infused with truffle oil, topped with a mixture of fresh beans in a vinaigrette, and finished with field greens or fresh herbs.

The key to success is your bean technique. Dried beans must be properly rehydrated and then gently simmered, never boiled. If you boil the heck out of beans, they tend to explode. Soaking them in warm water and then gradually bringing the cooking liquid up to a gentle heat ensures even cooking and intact beans. Add salt toward the end of cooking rather than at the beginning, or it will inhibit rehydration.

The salad works well with any fresh beans—Blue Lake, haricots verts, yellow wax, fava, lima, or cranberry beans, to name some possibilities—cooked until they are firm but give no resistance to the teeth. To cook fresh beans—or any green vegetable, for that matter— I use a technique I call big-pot blanching: Cook your vegetable in so much water that the water does not lose its boil when you add the vegetables. Your water should be heavily salted, about a half cup for each gallon. The result is a vegetable of the brightest possible color.

If you've cooked your beans properly, you almost can't go wrong with this salad. It is seasonal, elegant, and fun—an interpretation of a salad-bar standard that is worthy, I think, of haute cuisine.

THREE-BEAN SALAD

1 cup dried marrow beans or other white beans, soaked overnight in 4 cups water at room temperature

5 cups plus 2 tablespoons vegetable stock or canned vegetable broth

1 shallot, peeled and halved, plus 1 teaspoon minced

1 small carrot, peeled

Bouquet garni: 3 sprigs parsley, 1 sprig thyme, and 1 bay leaf, wrapped in two 5-inch sections of leek greens and tied with string

Kosher salt and freshly ground white pepper

4 to 5 tablespoons white truffle oil

2 teaspoons sherry wine vinegar

1 cup trimmed haricots verts in 1-inch pieces

1 cup trimmed yellow wax beans in 1-inch pieces

½ cup shelled, peeled fava beans

1 tablespoon extra-virgin olive oil

1 teaspoon lemon juice

2 cups frisee or baby greens for garnish

1 tablespoon peeled, seeded, and diced tomatoes

1. To prepare bean puree: Drain white beans. In a large saucepan or casserole, combine beans with 4 cups water, place over low heat, and bring to a simmer. Remove from heat and let rest for 5 minutes. Remove any beans that float to surface. Drain and chill under cold running water. Return beans to saucepan and add 5 cups stock, shallot halves, carrot, and bouquet garni. Place over low heat and simmer for 20 minutes.

2. Add ¼ teaspoon salt and continue to cook until beans are completely tender, 25 to 30 minutes. There should still be some liquid remaining

in pan. Place a strainer over a bowl and drain beans, reserving liquid. Remove and discard carrot and bouquet garni. Using a food processor, puree beans. With machine running, slowly add reserved liquid through feed tube, adding just enough to make a smooth puree, then pass puree through a tamis or drum sieve. Measure 1 cup puree into a mixing bowl and set aside remainder for another use. Whisk in remaining 2 tablespoons stock, 2 tablespoons truffle oil, and 1 teaspoon vinegar. Puree should have a creamy consistency; add 1 more tablespoon truffle oil if desired. Season to taste with salt and pepper.

3. To prepare bean salad: Make an ice water bath by filling a large bowl with ice and water. Bring a large pot of water to a boil, adding ½ cup salt for each gallon. Add haricots verts and blanch until cooked but still firm to the bite, 2 to 3 minutes. Using a slotted spoon, immediately transfer beans to ice water bath. Bring water to a boil again and repeat with yellow wax beans and finally fava beans. Drain chilled beans and pat dry with paper towels.

4. In a small bowl, whisk together 2 tablespoons truffle oil, olive oil, lemon juice, and remaining 1 teaspoon vinegar. Season to taste with salt and pepper. Toss 1 tablespoon vinaigrette with salad greens and season to taste with salt and pepper. In a mixing bowl, combine remaining vinaigrette with blanched beans, diced tomatoes, and minced shallots. Season with salt and pepper.

5. To serve, use a spoon to smooth an even layer of puree in center of each serving plate. Arrange about ⅓ cup bean salad over puree. Gently stack a mound of greens over salad and sprinkle with a little additional salt.

Yield: 6 servings

Time: 2 hours, plus overnight soaking of beans

THE SPIRIT OF SUMMER, CAPTURED IN A SOUP

A single vegetable brought to its essence—that's the meaning of summer soup. Winter soups, with their soothing richness and warmth, tend to be a composition of ingredients—beef-vegetable, chicken-noodle, chowder, minestrone. But summer soups refresh rather than soothe. And with so many vegetables hitting their peak of freshness, my first urge for summer soups is to isolate each vegetable and make it more than what it is on the vine, to refine it to its purest form. (An exception is a bright gazpacho, whose many flavors blend into a single taste.)

The beauty of summer soups—one-main-ingredient soups served hot or cold—is that they're so easy. Zucchini, spinach, tomato, bell pepper: The less you change them, the better. The technique for all vegetables is the same; learn it, and you can transform any one of them into an extraordinary summer soup, whether it's pea or fennel, watercress or artichoke, tomato, carrot, or haricots verts. It's just a matter of cooking your vegetable, pureeing it in a blender, adjusting the consistency with stock or water, seasoning it, and straining. Some vegetables, like tomatoes and cucumbers, don't need to be cooked.

The principle is simple: Separate the flavor and color from what contains it, the cellulose. The tool that separates it is the chinois. The chinois, a fine-meshed conical sieve, is critical to these soups. It creates the texture of luxury. The chinois combines layers of fine mesh that catch even the smallest particles of fiber, producing a finely textured liquid that feels like silk or satin. Certainly you can heat your puree and serve it without straining, or you might pass it through a food mill and then through a strainer. But again, when you're looking for an essence of something, you must remove all the extraneous vegetable fiber that has no flavor.

My thinking about soups is so similar to my ap-

proach to sauces that I always wonder, Is sauce a soup or is soup a sauce? Which came first? If it's a great summer soup, it can be a great sauce, too. And vice versa. Sometimes we'll make a sauce that tastes so good, we decide to put it in a cup and call it soup. My favorite way is as opening canapes—two or three spoonfuls of intense flavor presented in small white bowls. A canape soup excites the senses and prepares you for the meal ahead. And these summer soups make the very best canapes because they focus on a single flavor. One sip of carrot soup should be as powerful in flavor as a mouthful of carrots.

Gazpacho is the perfect warm-weather soup, and the interpretation I offer here is intense and easy. The main technique is turning on your blender and then straining the liquid. The flavor is extraordinary because you're using fresh ingredients—cucumbers, onion, bell pepper, tomatoes—and overnight marination develops and blends flavors. Serve it in a chilled shot glass. Or serve it hot. Or think of it as gazpacho sauce: It goes perfectly with grilled chicken or fish, and I serve it at the restaurant as the sauce for an artichoke salad. (Put a little vodka in your gazpacho sauce, and it becomes the world's best Bloody Mary.)

GAZPACHO

1 cup chopped peeled tomatoes (see Note)
1 cup chopped peeled red onions
1 cup chopped green pepper
1 cup chopped English (seedless) cucumber
1½ teaspoons chopped peeled garlic
1½ teaspoons kosher salt
¼ teaspoon cayenne pepper
¼ cup tomato paste
1 tablespoon white wine vinegar
¼ cup plus 2 tablespoons extra-virgin olive oil
1 tablespoon fresh lemon juice
3 cups tomato juice
Sprig of thyme

1. In a large nonreactive mixing bowl, combine all ingredients, cover, and refrigerate overnight.

2. The next day, remove thyme. Using a blender, puree remaining ingredients until smooth. For a smoother texture the soup may be strained (this will reduce quantity). Refrigerate gazpacho until well chilled. Ladle soup into bowls and serve cold.

Yield: 2 quarts (8 to 16 servings)
Time: 10 minutes, plus chilling

NOTE: To peel fresh tomatoes, cut a shallow X on the bottom of each tomato, submerge in boiling water for 5 to 10 seconds to loosen the skin, and then chill under cold water. The skins will slip off easily.

PUREE OF ENGLISH PEA SOUP WITH WHITE TRUFFLE OIL

3 cups shelled English (green) peas (from
    about 3 pounds of pea pods)
1 cup sugar
1½ cups salt
¼ to ½ cup vegetable stock or canned
    vegetable broth
Kosher salt and freshly ground white pepper
¼ cup white truffle oil

1. To help peas retain bright color during cooking, place in a bowl, cover surface with ice, and toss peas and ice together to chill.

2. Fill a large stockpot with 6 to 7 quarts water and bring to a boil. Add sugar and salt. Lift a small batch of peas with a strainer, letting ice fall back into bowl. To keep vivid green color of peas it is important for water to return to a boil almost immediately, so add peas in small quantities. Cook peas until completely tender, 7 to 10 minutes.

3. While peas are cooking, fill a large bowl with ice water and submerge a colander in it. When peas are tender, transfer to colander as quickly as possible. Lift colander from ice bath and drain peas well. Using a food processor, puree peas, then scrape puree through a tami (for best results) or fine-mesh strainer. There should be about 2 cups puree.

4. Transfer to a blender and add ¼ cup stock and ¼ cup water. Blend until smooth. The color may lighten because of air blended into it but will darken after it sits. Check consistency of soup; if desired, add more stock or water. Add a pinch of kosher salt and pepper to taste, and blend again. Pour soup through a chinois or fine-mesh strainer. To serve cold, stir in oil and refrig-erate in a covered container. To serve hot, reheat gently over low heat and stir in oil just before serving.

Yield: About 3 cups (6 to 12 servings)
Time: 45 minutes

YELLOW PEPPER SOUP WITH PAPRIKA MOUSSE

3 large yellow or red bell peppers, seeded and
    cut into 1-inch pieces
1¾ cups heavy cream
Kosher salt
¼ cup crème fraîche
½ teaspoon paprika, or to taste

1. To prepare soup: In a medium pot over me-dium-low heat, simmer peppers gently in 1½ cups cream until tender and cooked through, 15 minutes. Puree cream and peppers in a blender for 2 to 3 minutes. Strain through a chinois, pressing to release all liquid. Season with salt. Set aside or refrigerate up to 2 days.

2. To prepare mousse: In a small bowl, whip crème fraîche and paprika until paprika is blended and mixture is stiff. Add salt to taste. Refrigerate until ready to use, up to 2 days.

3. To serve, whip remaining ¼ cup cream un-til it forms peaks. In a medium saucepan over medium-high heat, bring soup to a boil. Remove from heat and vigorously whisk in whipped cream to create a frothy consistency. Pour soup into hot soup cups and garnish with paprika mousse.

Yield: 4 first-course servings
Time: 30 minutes

A STANDARD OF THE
AMERICAN SHORE GETS CITIFIED

Every summer Mom took us to visit my aunt and uncle who owned a tavern in Gambrills, Maryland. There we ate soft-shell crab sandwiches: blue crabs just after they had molted, fried and served on two slices of bread with lettuce, tomato, and tartar sauce. I still love the multiflavored textural experience of a soft-shell crab sandwich—the crispy shell, the meaty interior, and the flavorful mustard, tomalley, and roe. I wanted to serve a version of the sandwich in the restaurant, and the trick was how to reinterpret this great rustic classic as something appropriate for people expecting to eat highly refined, French-inspired food.

It turned out to be easy. Instead of white bread I use a round of toasted brioche, rich and delicious. Tomato confit—wedges of slowly roasted tomato transformed into intense bursts of flavor—takes the place of the sliced raw tomato. Arugula is the lettuce, though any sharp Asian green or cress will provide a peppery counterpoint to the sweet crab. The sauce is still a tartar sauce, but one made with hard yolks, cornichons, and shallots, and refined by colorful, tiny vegetable dice.

I trim the crab to make its shape a little more elegant and proportionate to the brioche round. And I always check the quality of the crab; the shell should be no more resistant than silk (though if the shell is hard, it can be removed and discarded).

CHESAPEAKE BAY SOFT-SHELL CRAB SANDWICH

2½ teaspoons finely diced (1/16-inch) carrots
2½ teaspoons finely diced (1/16-inch) turnips
1 teaspoon finely diced (1/16-inch) leek greens
2 hard-boiled egg yolks
2 tablespoons hot chicken broth or water
3 tablespoons liquid from bottled cornichons
1 teaspoon Dijon mustard
½ cup canola oil, plus more for frying
3 tablespoons minced cornichons
1 tablespoon minced shallot
1 tablespoon minced parsley
Kosher salt and freshly ground black pepper
1 tablespoon capers
6 soft-shell crabs, cleaned and trimmed of
　　legs except for claws
All-purpose flour
Clarified butter for sautéing crabs, optional
6 brioche rounds, 2¼ inches in diameter and
　　¼ inch thick, lightly toasted
6 pieces Tomato Confit at room temperature
　　(see recipe below)
¼ cup baby arugula or thinly shredded
　　arugula leaves

1. To prepare sauce: Fill a medium saucepan half full of water and bring to a boil. Fill a large mixing bowl with water and ice. In a small strainer, combine carrots, turnips, and leeks. Submerge strainer in boiling water about 10 seconds, then plunge into ice bath a few seconds. Drain vegetables on paper towels. Set aside.

2. In container of a blender, combine egg yolks, broth, cornichon liquid, and mustard. With machine running, slowly drizzle in ½ cup oil to emulsify. Transfer to a small bowl and add blanched vegetables, cornichons, shallot, parsley,

and salt and pepper to taste. Refrigerate up to 2 days; bring to room temperature before serving.

3. To prepare capers: Pat dry with paper towels. In a very small saucepan over medium-low heat, heat about 2 inches oil to 250 degrees. Add capers and fry slowly for 12 to 15 minutes, until bubbles stop forming around them and they are dry and crunchy. Drain capers on paper towels. Set aside.

4. To prepare crabs: Cut off 2 large claws from each body and reserve. Using scissors, trim sides of each body for a smooth edge. In a large mixing bowl, combine about 1 cup flour with salt and pepper to taste. Dredge crab bodies and claws in flour, shaking off excess.

5. In a large skillet over medium heat, add clarified butter or canola oil to a depth of $\frac{1}{8}$ inch. Place crab bodies in skillet, shell side down, and adjust heat so crabs sizzle but butter or oil does not pop. Sauté crab bodies for 2 to 3 minutes, until golden brown and crusty. Turn bodies and add claws. Turn claws after about 1 minute. Cook about 2 minutes more. Remove crabs and drain on paper towels.

6. To serve, place a spoonful of sauce in center of each of 6 serving plates. Center a brioche round on sauce and top with a crab body. Place a piece of tomato confit on top of each body, folded if necessary, and finish with a stack of baby arugula. Sprinkle each dish with fried capers. Serve immediately.

Yield: 6 servings
Time: 50 minutes

TOMATO CONFIT

Kosher salt and freshly ground black pepper
6 whole ripe tomatoes
Extra-virgin olive oil
Sprigs of fresh thyme

1. Fill a medium saucepan half full of lightly salted water and bring to a boil. Fill a large mixing bowl with ice and water. Cut and discard cores from tomatoes and cut a shallow X through skin on bottom of each. Drop tomatoes into boiling water for a few seconds, then transfer to ice bath. Peel tomatoes and cut into quarters through stem; if large, cut into 6 pieces. Remove remaining pulp or seeds to leave a smooth tomato petal.

2. Preheat oven to 250 degrees. Cover a baking sheet with aluminum foil. Drizzle with oil and lightly sprinkle with salt and pepper. Place tomato petals on foil, insides facing down, and drizzle with more oil. Season tomatoes with salt and pepper and top each with a small thyme sprig.

3. Bake until tomatoes have partially dried but retain some juices, $1\frac{1}{2}$ to 2 hours. Discard thyme. Cover. Can be refrigerated until ready to use. Bring to room temperature before serving.

Yield: 24 pieces
Time: 2 $\frac{1}{4}$ hours

Red Snapper with Tomato–
Onion Compote and
Tomato Nage

MICHAEL ROMANO

Crab Spring Roll with
Tamarind Ketchup

JEAN–GEORGES VONGERICHTEN

Herring Salad with
Beets and Apples

Marcus Samuelsson

Milk Chocolate and
Cherry Tart

Daniel Boulud

Rhubarb Cobbler CLAUDIA FLEMING

Composed Salad with Fennel, Oven-Dried Pears, Walnuts, and Maytag Blue Cheese   Charlie Palmer

Quince Beignets
FRANÇOIS PAYARD

Seared Foie Gras with
Caramelized Pears and
Balsamic Vinegar

ALFRED PORTALE

Sautéed Skate with Lemon Risotto   DIANE FORLEY

Pan-Seared Applewood-Smoked Salmon with Cucumber–Red Onion Relish

RICK MOONEN

Summer Soups: Yellow Pepper, Gazpacho, and Purée of English Pea Soup

THOMAS KELLER
Photographer: Deborah Jones

Grilled Quail Salad with
Bacon and Camembert

WALDY MALOUF

Almond Brioche Toast

AMY SCHERBER

Candied Grapefruit Rind   PATRICK O'CONNELL

Marinated Salmon Wrapped in Avocado with Creamy Horseradish Oil   WYLIE DUFRESNE

Asian Duck Confit with Roasted Duck Breast and Wasabi Sauce

TADASHI ONO

Roasted Rabbit

CHRISTIAN DELOUVRIER

Sage Chicken in a Fried Potato Crust   MICHEL RICHARD

Sautéed Striped Bass with Basil-Scented Cherry Tomatoes and Basil Oil EBERHARD MÜLLER

Mussels and Cockles with a Spicy Coconut Broth PATRICIA YEO

Petrossian Egg   PHILIPPE CONTICINI

White Chocolate Sourdough Bread Pudding with Almonds   CHARLIE TROTTER   *Photographer: Tim Turner*

THE SECRET TO FEARLESS DUCK

People forget about duck at home; I don't know why. Duck is a rich, delicious meat; there are so many different things you can do with it, and it's easy to cook. For example, the key to perfect sautéed duck breasts— ones with nicely browned skin and a medium-rare interior—is cooking them over low heat so that the fat in the skin has time to render.

The sauce for the duck is simply corn juice heated with some corn and a little cream. Corn is a logical match for duck because it's one of the primary foods ducks eat. I add morel mushrooms to the corn because I love their woody, earthy qualities with the corn's sweetness. If you can't find fresh morels, dried are acceptable.

If you must buy a whole duck for this recipe instead of just the breast, consider yourself lucky. You'll have six legs left over and bones for stock. One of my favorite things to do with duck legs is to braise them: Sear them in an ovenproof pan; add stock or water, carrots, and onions; bring it to a simmer; cover; and cook in a 325-degree oven for an hour and a half. I mix the falling-off-the-bone meat with some cooked peppers, onions, and potato to make duck hash. Top it with a poached egg (a duck egg if you can find one) for a luxurious brunch dish.

PAN-ROASTED DUCK BREASTS WITH CREAMED WHITE CORN AND MORELS

7 large ears of sweet white corn, shucked
4 ounces morels
3 tablespoons butter
1 teaspoon finely minced shallots
1 teaspoon finely minced chives
1 teaspoon finely minced parsley
3 whole boneless duck breasts (Liberty Valley or Long Island), halved and trimmed of sinew and excess fat
Kosher salt and freshly ground black pepper
1 tablespoon heavy cream

1. Cut kernels from 4 ears of corn. Place in a blender, adding just enough water (1 to 2 tablespoons) to allow them to puree. Transfer puree to a chinois or fine-mesh strainer set over a bowl. Press lightly to extract juice but do not force puree through strainer. There should be about 1/3 cup corn juice; set aside.

2. Fill a medium saucepan half full of water and bring to a boil. Fill a bowl with a mixture of ice and water. Cut kernels from remaining 3 ears of corn; there should be about 2 cups kernels. Add to boiling water and blanch for 1 minute. Transfer kernels to ice bath, then dry on paper towels; set aside.

3. Trim stems from morels. Soak in warm water, changing water several times, until clear. If some mushrooms are larger than others, cut in half for a uniform size. Place a skillet over medium heat and add 1 tablespoon butter. Shake excess water from mushrooms and add to skillet. Sauté until liquid has evaporated and mushrooms are tender. If necessary, add 1 tablespoon water to pan. Add shallots, chives, and parsley, and sauté for 30 seconds. Remove from heat and set aside.

4. Remove small tender from each half of duck breast to allow even cooking. Score skin in a crosshatch pattern deep enough for fat to drain but not so deep as to cut meat. Season with salt and pepper to taste. Place a large skillet over low heat. Add breasts, skin side down, and sauté for 7 to 8 minutes, allowing most of fat to drain and skin to brown. Spoon out excess fat and turn duck breasts over. Sauté for 3 to 4 minutes to complete cooking. Transfer breasts to a platter lined with paper towels and let rest for 3 minutes.

5. While breasts are resting, transfer corn juice to a small, heavy saucepan. Place pan over medium heat and whisk until juice thickens. (Starch in corn will cause it to thicken quickly.) Do not allow it to boil, or it may curdle. When liquid has thickened, reduce heat to low and whisk in remaining 2 tablespoons butter and cream. Stir in blanched kernels and morel mixture. Keep warm.

6. To serve, divide creamed corn and morels among 6 plates. Top each portion with a duck breast and serve immediately.

Yield: 6 servings
Time: 45 minutes

THE DAYS OF FIGS AND HONEY

This is one of those great recipes because it's so easy and so satisfying. Hot figs and cold ice cream with honey—that's virtually all there is to it. You don't even have to make the ice cream; buy some, let it sit until it's pliable, and fold in the honey. To make it even simpler, drizzle the honey on top of the ice cream or add it to the pan when you cook the figs. However you want to incorporate the honey is fine, but it's important to use a honey of good quality, so taste a variety. In the Napa Valley there are a lot of wildflowers, so wildflower honey is the kind I like to use.

Summertime here also brings an overabundance of figs. The first crop arrives in late spring, the second in July. The later crop is high in sugar, perfect for this dish. I usually use Mission and Brown Turkey varieties, but any fig will work as long as it is ripe. The baking turns the fig into a sauce within its own skin.

The vanilla bean, cooked and served with the fig, provides additional flavor and visual components. Typically, the vanilla bean is incorporated into a preparation, but here it's a separate element. It's fun to scrape the seeds out of the pod and eat them with the ice cream and buttery sauce. I love the hot and cold combination in this dessert. It reminds me of hot fudge sundaes.

VANILLA-ROASTED FIGS WITH WILDFLOWER-HONEY ICE CREAM

For the ice cream:
  2 cups milk
  2 cups heavy cream
  ½ cup wildflower honey
  12 large egg yolks
  ¼ cup sugar

For the figs:
  18 ripe figs (Mission, Brown Turkey, Adriatic Green, or a combination), washed and dried
  4 vanilla beans, split lengthwise
  3 tablespoons unsalted butter
  1½ teaspoons sugar

1. To prepare ice cream: In a large saucepan, combine milk, cream, and honey. Place over medium heat and stir. When honey is completely dissolved, remove pan from heat and allow to cool.

2. With an electric mixer or by hand in a metal bowl, whisk egg yolks and sugar until thickened and lightened in color. Gradually whisk in warm milk mixture. Return mixture to saucepan and place over medium-low heat. Stir until mixture coats back of a wooden spoon and reaches 175 degrees; do not overheat. Immediately remove from heat and transfer to a mixing bowl. Chill bowl by placing it in ice water; allow mixture to cool to room temperature.

3. Strain mixture into a container, cover, and refrigerate at least 5 hours or overnight. Freeze in an ice cream maker according to manufacturer's instructions, then transfer to a covered container. Freeze for several hours or until hardened.

4. To prepare figs: Slice off and discard tops of figs. Cut split vanilla beans into 2-inch pieces. Make a small slit in top of each fig and insert a section of vanilla bean.

5. Preheat oven to 400 degrees. In an ovenproof pan large enough to hold all figs standing upright, melt butter over medium heat. Add sugar and stir to dissolve. Stand figs in butter and add any remaining vanilla bean pieces to pan. Place pan in oven until figs are thoroughly heated, about 10 minutes. Serve figs warm or at room temperature.

6. To serve, place a scoop of ice cream into each of 6 bowls. Arrange 3 of figs (with vanilla bean) around each scoop. Serve immediately.

Yield: 6 servings
Time: 30 minutes for ice cream, plus chilling and freezing, and 20 minutes for figs

WALDY MALOUF

Waldy Malouf is the chef and an owner of Beacon in Manhattan.
He was photographed in front of the restaurant's wood-burning oven.
These columns were written with Melissa Clark.

SUMMER HERBS: A SEARCH FOR PERFECTION

In the summer, herbs are so plentiful and full of flavor that I always find myself experimenting more than usual. But it is a risky business; these little things have very big flavors. They can easily overwhelm a dish or, in combination, fight each other so violently that the dish is left in ruins. So I don't use herbs indiscriminately or with abandon. No matter how casual the dish, there is rarely that handful tossed in at the last minute. I prefer a lighter, more subtle touch, one that lets the meat or fish or vegetable be the star and lets the herbs be a complement.

I tend to use the same technique with almost everything I cook with herbs, layering their flavors so they can be tasted in all their permutations. I like to start with a marinade or rub and then finish the dish with chopped fresh herbs—stirred into the sauce at the end of cooking, tossed into a salad that's served alongside, or just sprinkled on as a garnish. This lets you experience the herbs as they infuse the food while it marinates, as they cook and change in the heat, and in their natural state, lively and fresh, at the very end.

My roast chicken is a perfect example of that layering and of my summertime experimentation. It shows how a wintry dish can be transformed with herbs.

Putting a compound or flavored butter under the chicken skin before roasting is a traditional way to add seasoning. But instead of using just butter, I use a lighter mix of olive oil and butter. And instead of using only three or four herbs, I use ten. For something that sounds so simple, it turned out to be one of the harder dishes for me to develop. Deciding which herbs I would use was the easy part. I chose the ones whose flavors I knew would work well together. There are lots of fresh minty-flavored ones—cilantro, chervil, mint, and parsley—that give the dish its zesty, summery quality. The more complex, pronounced herbs—licorice-flavored tarragon, piney rosemary, and woodsy thyme—add depth. Chives, oregano, and sage round out the mix. But there is no basil. I find that it fights with tarragon and rosemary.

Figuring out the proper proportion of each herb was the tricky part. I probably made this dish twenty times before I settled on a combination I was truly happy with. Sometimes the rosemary would overpower everything, and I'd have a chicken that tasted like Vicks VapoRub. Other times the tarragon would be too strong, and I'd have licorice chicken. One mix ended up tasting grassy, like lawn mower clippings.

We kept charts in the kitchen and marked off how much of each herb we used in the butter mixture and how we would modify the next day's mix. All I wanted was a succulent chicken covered in a very crisp skin with a layer of herbs underneath. We forged on. Eventually, I got the chicken I imagined, and the herb mixture became one of the few things we measure in the restaurant kitchen, to ensure the right proportions.

I serve the chicken with a bread salad made with the same herbs I use in the butter compound, plus lightly sautéed wild mushrooms and fresh tomato. In the end it is the earthiness of the mushrooms that gives the chicken a final roundness and brings the entire dish together.

TEN-HERB ROASTED CHICKEN

1 3½-pound chicken
½ cup plus 2 tablespoons Ten-Herb Butter
(see recipe below), softened
Reserved herb stems from Ten-Herb Butter
½ cup chicken stock
¼ cup white wine
Herbed Bread and Mushroom Salad (see
recipe below)
2 tablespoons minced chopped herbs like
those in Ten-Herb Butter, for garnish

1. Rinse chicken and pat dry with paper towels. Place chicken on its back. Using a small, sharp knife, make 6 incisions into bird: 1 in meaty part of each drumstick (go through flesh), 1 at joints of thighs (go under skin), and 2 under skin of breasts (1 cut on each side). Turn chicken over and make an incision on upper part of each thigh.

2. Place ½ cup herb butter in a heavy-duty resealable plastic bag. Snip off a corner of bag and use it like a pastry bag. Squeeze butter from opening into incisions in chicken (try to use an equal amount in each incision). Massage herb butter into chicken. If any squeezes out of incision, wipe it into cavity.

3. Stuff cavity with reserved herb stems. Rub remaining 2 tablespoons herb butter all over outside of chicken.

4. Using a piece of kitchen string, truss chicken, beginning at neck and tying legs together. Place chicken in a bowl and cover. Let chicken marinate in refrigerator at least 4 hours or overnight.

5. Preheat oven to 425 degrees. Put a rack in a roasting pan and place chicken on rack, breast side up. Roast chicken for 30 minutes. Lower

oven to 300 degrees and add stock and wine to pan. Roast chicken 25 minutes more. Turn off oven and let chicken rest inside it for another 15 to 20 minutes.

6. Remove chicken from oven and pour off all chicken juices, reserving them. Spoon fat off top and measure drippings; you should have about ½ cup. Reserve for salad.

7. When ready to serve, carve chicken into 8 pieces. Place herbed bread and mushroom salad on platter and top with chicken. Garnish with chopped fresh herbs.

Yield: 4 servings
Time: 2 hours, plus 4 hours for marinating

TEN-HERB BUTTER

1 pound unsalted butter at room temperature
¼ cup extra-virgin olive oil
1½ teaspoons truffle oil
1 tablespoon lemon juice
1 teaspoon minced, seeded jalapeño
2 teaspoons kosher salt
½ teaspoon ground black pepper
1 teaspoon minced shallots
1 teaspoon minced garlic
½ cup chopped parsley, stems reserved
2 tablespoons chopped chives
1½ teaspoons chopped chervil, stems reserved
1½ teaspoons chopped cilantro, stems reserved
½ teaspoon chopped sage, stems reserved
½ teaspoon tarragon, stems reserved
½ teaspoon oregano, stems reserved
¼ teaspoon rosemary, stems reserved
½ teaspoon chopped fresh thyme, stems reserved
1½ teaspoons chopped mint

Place all ingredients except herb stems (reserve for chicken) in a food processor and blend well, or mix by hand until smooth.

Yield: 2¼ cups
Time: 20 minutes

2½ tablespoons extra-virgin olive oil

4 ounces wild mushrooms (a combination of cremini, shiitake, oyster, chanterelle, or portobello), stems removed and caps sliced

Salt and freshly ground black pepper

¾ cup freshly made 1-inch croutons (from 1 large slice toasted sourdough bread)

½ cup reserved pan drippings from Ten-Herb Chicken (see recipe above)

¼ cup diced, seeded tomato

2 tablespoons minced chopped herbs

1 teaspoon fresh lemon juice

1. In a small saucepan, heat 1½ tablespoons oil over medium-high heat. Add mushrooms and salt and pepper to taste, and sauté until mushrooms are tender, about 5 minutes. Transfer mushrooms to a bowl.

2. Add remaining ingredients to mushrooms and toss well. Serve immediately with chicken.

Yield: 4 servings

Time: 20 minutes

FROM A KITCHEN IN THE MEDITERRANEAN

My grandmother, who was from Lebanon, made leg of lamb whenever we all gathered for a family celebration. She would braise a whole leg with olives and lemon, and those flavors, so wonderfully Mediterranean, are one of my earliest taste memories. When I think of lamb, that dish instantly comes to mind. I wanted to recreate it at the restaurant, but I needed to cook smaller portions so they could be roasted to order, and I wanted to expand on the flavors just a bit.

I switched to thick triple lamb chops because they are tender enough to endure the kind of heat needed to get a nice crust. And still thinking Mediterranean, I hit on the idea of adding capers and anchovy to the olive-lemon marinade, making it almost a tapenade. All these strong, salty ingredients may sound like a very intense combination, but they really mellow as the lamb is roasted.

It's important to marinate the lamb at least four hours. During that time it is actually curing a little bit from the salt in the olives, capers, and anchovy. (You might notice that the marinade doesn't call for any added salt; it doesn't need it.) A mild curing makes meat a little more tender, but more important, it takes out water and concentrates fat, almost like dry aging. In the end the chop has a more moist and less grainy quality.

At the very end of cooking I deglaze the pan with wine, lemon juice, and stock (we use lamb stock, but you can use chicken or beef broth), then toss in some thinly sliced lemons and more olives. The liquids quickly reduce and form a simple sauce. The lemon slices and olives, which get nicely charred in the heat, add a final burst of flavor and look beautiful on the plate. To keep the Mediterranean mood, serve the chops with couscous or grilled vegetables. A bright sprinkling of chopped parsley is all the garnish you'll need.

ROASTED TRIPLE LAMB CHOPS WITH OLIVES AND LEMON

⅓ cup extra-virgin olive oil

3 tablespoons oil-cured black olives, pitted

1 tablespoon capers

2 teaspoons chopped parsley, plus extra for garnish

1 teaspoon chopped garlic

1 teaspoon chopped shallot

¼ teaspoon ground cumin

1 anchovy fillet

Freshly ground black pepper to taste

4 8-ounce, 3-bone racks of lamb, frenched by butcher

1 lemon

¼ cup white wine

¼ cup chicken stock

1 tablespoon fresh lemon juice

1. In a food processor, combine oil, 1 tablespoon olives, capers, parsley, garlic, shallot, cumin, anchovy, and pepper. Coat lamb with this marinade and place in a bowl. Cover and refrigerate at least 4 hours or overnight.

2. Thinly slice lemon and remove seeds. Cut slices into quarters. Set aside.

3. Preheat oven to 500 degrees. Arrange racks of lamb in a roasting pan large enough to hold them in 1 layer (or use 2 pans). Drizzle marinade left in bowl over lamb. Roast for 7 minutes.

4. Transfer lamb to a plate. Pour off fat from roasting pan and add wine, stock, and lemon juice. Return lamb to pan, browned side down.

5. Sprinkle lamb with remaining olives and lemon slices. Roast 7 to 9 minutes more, or to taste. Garnish with chopped parsley and serve.

Yield: 4 servings

Time: 30 minutes, plus 4 hours for marinating

REFINING A CLASSIC: SCALLOPED POTATOES

When I began devising the menu for Beacon, I wasn't sure what potato side dish to serve. I wanted to offer just one that everyone would love and that would work well with every entree. I considered french fries, home fries, mashed potatoes, and baked potatoes. Then I thought of scalloped potatoes and knew I'd hit on something just right. After all, there is a reason almost all Western cuisines have a baked cheese and potato dish laced with butter or cream.

To come up with the recipe I thought of all the marvelous potato gratins I'd eaten in my life. There is gratin dauphinois, *which is predominantly heavy cream and cheese, and* pommes à la boulangère, *scalloped potatoes with onion and stock. Everyone's mother made some sort of scalloped potatoes; I even loved them with Velveeta.*

I wanted to develop a signature version, based on a combination of the classic recipes. As much as I love the dish, it seemed that it could be refined a bit: I wanted one that was a little lighter and tasted more like potato than cream and cheese.

First, I halved the normal amount of heavy cream and substituted chicken stock; this added a subtle flavor and definitely elevated the texture. Then I began experimenting with the cheese. Aged Parmesan has a terrific pungency. Gruyère has a nice nutty flavor and is also a great melting cheese. I also use dry-aged goat cheese, which can be hard to find. Aged cheddar, Asiago, or more Parmesan will work in its place.

As for the star of the dish, I use Idaho potatoes, on the large side. It may be sexier to use Yellow Finn this or heirloom that, but all you really need is a dry starchy spud. Waxy varieties like red skin or fingerling don't absorb flavors or break down as well, and they make a runny, slippery gratin. Be sure to cut the potatoes one-eighth-inch thick. Thicker slices won't give you the in-

tegrated layers; with thinner slices the gratin nearly turns into mashed potatoes.

In the end, my gratin is a cross between scalloped potatoes and macaroni and cheese—probably the two ultimate comfort foods. Just what I wanted it to be.

POTATO GRATIN

6 unpeeled cloves garlic

1 tablespoon butter, softened

1½ cups heavy cream

1½ cups chicken or vegetable stock

1 sprig rosemary

1 sprig thyme

⅛ teaspoon freshly grated nutmeg

¾ teaspoon salt

Freshly ground black pepper to taste

4 medium baking potatoes, peeled

3 ounces Parmesan, grated (¾ cup)

3 ounces Gruyère, grated (¾ cup)

1 ounce aged goat cheese, grated (¼ cup)

1. Preheat oven to 350 degrees. Slice 1 clove garlic in half. Rub cut sides all over inside of 1½-quart shallow gratin or casserole dish. Brush inside of dish with softened butter.

2. Smash remaining 5 cloves garlic with side of a knife and place in a large saucepan. Add cream, stock, rosemary, thyme, and nutmeg. Bring mixture to a boil, reduce heat, and let simmer for 15 minutes. Strain mixture into a bowl, discarding garlic and herbs. Stir in salt and pepper.

3. Using a mandoline or food processor or by hand, cut potatoes into ⅛-inch-thick slices. Mix cheeses together in a small bowl.

4. Cover bottom of gratin dish with an overlapping layer of one-fourth of potato slices. Pour one-fourth of stock mixture over potatoes. Sprinkle with one-fourth of cheese mixture. Continue layering in this manner until all ingredients are used. With a spatula, press down hard on top of gratin to compact it.

5. Bake gratin for 60 to 70 minutes, until top is crusty and golden brown, and a knife cuts easily through potatoes. Transfer gratin to a rack and cool at least 10 minutes before serving.

Yield: 6 servings

Time: about 1½ hours

PEACHES AND BERRIES, ROASTED TO PERFECTION

There is one thing we almost never do to summer fruit: roast it. That is too bad because the intense heat reduces the sugary juices and concentrates the flavors. The flesh softens into something just this side of a compote but leaves the shape of the pieces intact.

All of this makes roasted fruit the perfect complement for a simple cake. This dessert is based on an English summer pudding, a layered confection of bread and fruit compote that is weighted and chilled. But instead of bread I used a fine-textured vanilla cake. The vanilla brings out the sweetness of the fruit, and to be sure it doesn't get lost in all that voluptuousness, I add the extract and a touch of the bean itself.

For the fruit I use a mixture of sliced peaches and blueberries, which reach their peak ripeness at the same time and don't need a lot of added sugar. And cooked together, their color is a purply blue with just a sunset smattering of red, orange, and gold.

After layering slices of cake with the roasted fruit, I chill it for several hours. The cake absorbs the delicious roasting pan juices, bonding with the fruit. It is at its best after eight to twenty-four hours, but you can make it up to two days ahead. The longer it sits, the moister it becomes, but after two days it begins turning to mush.

I like to serve this cake with a few slices of raw peach and a sprinkling of blueberries. Dressed in a light lemony glaze, they make a toothsome contrast to the tender cake. Add a drizzle of the pan juices, a generous dollop of whipped cream, and a sprig of mint—what's not to like?

ROASTED PEACHES AND BLUEBERRIES WITH VANILLA CAKE

6 large, ripe peaches, pitted and sliced
6 cups blueberries
1½ cups sugar
Juice of 1 lemon
¼ vanilla bean
8 tablespoons butter, cut in small pieces
2 large eggs
1 teaspoon vanilla extract
1 cup flour
1½ teaspoons baking powder
½ teaspoon salt
½ cup milk
Whipped clabbered or heavy cream for
   garnish
Mint sprigs for garnish

1. Preheat oven to 500 degrees. In a bowl, place peaches, blueberries, 1 cup sugar, and lemon juice, and toss to coat well. Pour all but 2 cups of fruit into a 9 by 13-inch baking dish. Cover reserved fruit and refrigerate.

2. Scrape seeds from vanilla bean and reserve. Bury vanilla pod in fruit in baking dish and arrange 4 tablespoons butter pieces on top. Bake for 30 minutes, stirring after about 15 minutes. Let cool on a rack; discard vanilla pod.

3. Lower oven temperature to 350 degrees. Grease and flour a 9-inch-round cake pan. In bowl of an electric mixer fitted with paddle attachment, cream remaining sugar and butter until very smooth. Beat in eggs, vanilla extract, and vanilla seeds. In a small bowl, combine flour, baking powder, and salt. On low speed, add flour mixture to batter in 3 stages, alternating with milk. Pour batter into prepared pan and bake for

25 minutes, until a tester inserted in middle comes out clean. Let cool, then unmold cake.

4. With a long serrated knife, carefully slice cake horizontally into 3 layers. Line a clean 9-inch cake pan with plastic wrap, leaving plenty of wrap overhanging. Place bottom layer of cake in pan, cut side up. Using a slotted spoon, layer half of cooled fruit over cake. Top with middle layer of cake and spoon on remaining fruit; reserve fruit juices. Cover with top cake layer, cut side down. Press down gently on cake and cover with overhanging plastic wrap. Chill cake at least 8 hours, preferably overnight.

5. When ready to serve, unmold cake and garnish each slice with a generous drizzle of reserved fruit juices, reserved raw fruit, and a dollop of whipped cream. Top with mint sprigs.

Yield: 10 to 12 servings
Time: 1½ hours, plus 8 hours of chilling

SHORT AND SWEET, BUT QUAIL CAN HOLD ITS OWN

Grilling quail is no more difficult than grilling chicken. Since you can buy cleaned, partly boned quail in specialty markets and good butcher shops, there is not much you need to do in the way of preparation. After marinating, the quails are just laid on the grill and flipped halfway through cooking. They are done in less than ten minutes, so it is easy to finish them just before serving.

But grilling can dry out these little birds, so it is important to add something to keep them moist. Classically, quails are larded with bacon slices. This is pretty impractical for a small bird being flipped on a grill, so I decided to use the bacon to stuff the quail instead. Although the bacon-stuffed quail was good, it wasn't transcendent. Plus the bacon needed to be cooked before being stuffed into the quail, so it didn't keep the bird as juicy as I thought it should be. I needed something else to lift the flavor and add succulence at the same time.

That's when I thought of cheese. Stuffing a bit of sheep's milk Camembert into the cavity, along with the bacon and a touch of fresh sage, is a simple way to add flavor and preserve the juices. The cheese melts and moistens the interior of the bird, coating it with a deliciously pungent flavor that works really well with the meat.

I serve the quail on a bed of zesty greens spiked with fresh herbs. The salad makes a bright contrast to the deep flavors of the meat, especially when mint is in the mix. It is also a very attractive way to serve the birds: nestled among the shiny dark greens.

GRILLED QUAIL SALAD WITH BACON AND CAMEMBERT

4 strips bacon, cooked and drained
4 fresh quails, partly boned and wing tips
    removed
2 ounces sheep's milk Camembert, cut into
    4 pieces
4 large sage leaves plus 1 teaspoon chopped
    fresh sage
6 tablespoons extra-virgin olive oil
Salt and freshly ground black pepper to taste
1 teaspoon chopped shallot
1½ tablespoons sherry vinegar
1 teaspoon chopped fresh parsley
2 cups salad greens
1 cup mixed leafy herbs such as basil, parsley,
    lovage, dill, mint, and sorrel
½ cup diced tomatoes

1. Cut 2 bacon strips in half. Stuff each quail with a half strip of bacon, a piece of Camembert, and a sage leaf. Place stuffed quail in a bowl and drizzle with 2 tablespoons oil. Add salt and pepper, and gently mix to coat quail. Marinate in refrigerator at least 30 minutes or overnight.

2. To prepare bacon vinaigrette: Chop remaining 2 strips bacon. In a small sauté pan over medium heat, add remaining 4 tablespoons oil and bacon. Sauté for 2 minutes. Add shallot and cook 1 minute more. Add vinegar, chopped sage, and parsley, and remove from heat. Season with salt and pepper.

3. To prepare quail: Grill quail, breast side down, about 4 minutes. Turn and grill 3 to 4 minutes more, until skin is crisp and juices run clear. Transfer quail to a platter and allow to rest for 2 minutes.

4. Meanwhile, toss salad greens and herbs with about two-thirds of vinaigrette. Divide salad among serving plates and top with quail. Drizzle quail with remaining vinaigrette. Garnish with tomatoes and serve immediately.

Yield: 4 appetizer servings or 2 main-course
    servings
Time: 50 minutes, plus at least 30 minutes for
    marinating

A WOOD-SMOKE TASTE AT HOME

When I started experimenting with the wood-burning oven at Beacon, I found that the combination of high heat and wood smoke worked extremely well with fish, especially trout. The only trouble is that most people, like me, don't have wood-burning ovens at home. But this recipe for trout was easy to adapt to a charcoal grill. Using firewood, or even wood chips, and indirect heat, anyone can make an ordinary kettle grill approximate a wood-burning oven.

I prefer real wood charcoal, but any kind will do, as long as you use plenty of it. If you are using a log, add it right after lighting the charcoal. Then let the fire burn for about an hour (depending on the size of the log) until the wood is practically reduced to ashes and the coals are beginning to die down. If you are using wood chips, soak a good-size handful in water while the charcoal lights. About ten minutes before you are ready to cook (the charcoal should be gray all over), add the soaked chips.

The fish has to cook over indirect heat, so remove the grilling rack and push the coals and wood over to one side of the grill. Then cover the grill, close the vents, and let it get really hot inside, like heating an oven. When the fish is put inside, on the half of the grill without coals, it will actually be roasting rather than grilling.

The sauce for the trout is also its marinade, which makes this dish extremely easy once the fire is lighted. A simple chervil vinaigrette, seasoned with shallots and champagne vinegar, lends a subtle herby onion flavor to the trout. Because the sauce is made in a blender, you don't have to chop any of the ingredients finely; just throw them all in together.

I like to blend the herbs with only half of the olive oil and then stir in the other half by hand. This is purely for looks. The sauce isn't fully emulsified, so it breaks on the plate. The effect is like a pale green pool surrounding dark islands of herbs. Spooned over the fish, it is so striking that no other garnish is needed.

WOOD-ROASTED TROUT WITH CHERVIL VINAIGRETTE

1 cup chopped chervil
¾ cup chopped flat-leaf parsley
3 tablespoons roughly chopped shallot
3 tablespoons fresh lemon juice
2 tablespoons champagne or white wine vinegar
1 cup olive oil
2 teaspoons kosher salt
Freshly ground black pepper
4 boned trout, skin on and heads removed

1. Light grill using plenty of charcoal. If using firewood, add it and let wood and charcoal burn for about 1 hour, or until most of firewood is burned up. If using wood chips, soak them in water at least 20 minutes, then add to the coals after they are completely gray. Let chips burn for 10 minutes. Move charcoal and wood to one side of grill for indirect grilling.

2. Meanwhile, prepare vinaigrette. In a blender, puree chervil, parsley, shallot, lemon juice, and vinegar with ½ cup oil. Transfer mixture to a small bowl and stir in remaining oil, 1 teaspoon salt, and pepper to taste.

3. Sprinkle inside of trout with remaining 1 teaspoon salt and pepper to taste. Spoon about half of vinaigrette on trout, inside and out. Rub vinaigrette into fish. Cover trout and refrigerate for 15 to 30 minutes.

4. Spray 1 side of a 15-inch-square piece of

aluminum foil with cooking spray. Cover side of grill that has no charcoal underneath with foil, sprayed side up. Place fish on foil and cover grill. Check fish after 10 minutes. (They do not have to be turned.) Fish are done when flesh is opaque and skin is crisp. Serve immediately with remaining vinaigrette as sauce.

Yield: 4 servings

Time: 40 minutes, plus about 1½ hours preparing the grill

A LATE-SUMMER COMMUNAL FEAST

Sometimes a good dish is really just a lucky accident. I stumbled on the idea for my Hudson Valley succotash several summers ago while I was working on a cookbook. My co-author, Molly Finn, and I had bought bags and bags of fresh vegetables at the farmers' market and were developing recipes. At the end of the day we were surrounded. There were bowls full of roasted corn and dappled cranberry beans, which we had cooked earlier in the day, and a cluster of perfectly ripe tomatoes. And as usual when recipes are being developed, there was also plenty of leftover chopped onion—in this case sweet red onions and scallions.

In the face of all these ingredients, I immediately thought about making a succotash. But I was tired after cooking all day, and our families were hungry. They were so hungry, in fact, that they descended on the bowls of vegetables and started nibbling. At that point Molly and I gave up on the idea of cooking anything else, and we all began to fill our plates. What had been just a table filled with individual vegetables turned into a communal feast—an instant self-serve succotash.

Ever since that summer, I've served this succotash when I could get good seasonal vegetables and felt like taking a day off. There's hardly any cooking involved, and even that can be done several hours ahead. Otherwise, the vegetables are left alone. And so is the cook.

HUDSON VALLEY SUCCOTASH

6 ears of corn, shucked
2 cups fresh shelled cranberry beans
    (1½ pounds in the pod)
3 medium tomatoes
2 tablespoons extra-virgin olive oil
1 tablespoon chopped basil
Salt and freshly ground pepper to taste
2 cups chopped red onions
¾ cup chopped scallions
4 tablespoons butter

1. Bring a large pot of water to a boil. Add corn and cook for 3 minutes. Drain corn, reserving ¼ cup cooking liquid. Let corn cool and then cut ears in half crosswise. Cut kernels off by standing a half ear up on a cutting board on its flat (cut) end and scraping off kernels with a knife. Reserve corn kernels and cooking liquid until ready to serve.

2. Bring a medium saucepan of water to a boil. Add beans and cook about 12 to 15 minutes, or until tender. Drain beans, reserving 1 cup cooking liquid.

3. Cut tomatoes in half crosswise and remove seeds. Cut tomatoes into ½-inch dice. Toss in a bowl with oil, basil, and salt and pepper. Put onions and scallions in separate serving bowls.

4. When ready to serve, place beans, their reserved cooking liquid, and 2 tablespoons butter in a small saucepan. Cook over medium heat until butter melts. Season with salt and pepper. Transfer to a serving bowl.

5. Place corn, its reserved cooking liquid, and remaining 2 tablespoons butter in a small saucepan. Cook over medium heat until butter melts, season with salt and pepper, and transfer to a serving bowl.

6. Serve bowls of vegetables while beans and corn are still warm. Let people mix ingredients on their plates as they wish.
    Yield: 6 servings
    Time: 45 minutes

AMY SCHERBER

Amy Scherber is the owner of Amy's Bread in Manhattan. She was photographed outside the bakery. These columns were written with Dorie Greenspan.

PIZZA WITH A "PUSH BUTTON" CRUST

As much as I like pizza, I have never been able to serve it at my two bakeries. We just don't have enough space, time, or people to get the pizza out for lunch, and pizza doesn't keep. But I often make it at home, where I get professional results in an ordinary oven. This recipe is straightforward, just like the others I'll be sharing— some from the bakeries, others from my home files. They use no difficult techniques, but there are secrets.

With this pizza, the tricks are in stretching the dough and intensifying the flavor of the tomatoes. Otherwise, the recipe does not call for anything esoteric. You can get everything needed, from the equipment to the ingredients, in a supermarket.

This pizza, topped with garlic, basil, ricotta, and the last of the season's corn and tomatoes, is made in a jelly roll pan and can be turned out by a first-timer. And it delivers what I think every good pizza must: a thin, crisp-bottomed crust that's tender to the tooth but strong enough to support its topping, a topping full of flavor, but not too heavy or too thick, too juicy or too dry, and has a mix of ingredients that keep their tastes and textures under fire.

The crust, made from what I call a push-button dough, takes sixty seconds to make in a food processor and sixty minutes to rise. It's just as easy to shape. There's no tossing in the air or rolling it out; to get a perfect crust, dip your fingertips in olive oil and then press, prod, push, and poke the dough along the bottom of the pan. If the dough gets springy, as yeast doughs will, you just let it alone for a few minutes, then press on. Patience is the key here: The thinner the crust, the crispier.

While the crust is rising, I roast tomatoes for the topping to concentrate their flavor, a small step that makes a big difference. All kinds of tomatoes, from cherry to plum to beefsteak or heirloom, work here. Just roast them until they are slightly softened, a little wrinkly, a bit less juicy, and very flavorful.

As for the corn, after you slice the kernels off the cob, run the back of the knife against the cob to press out the sweet milk. You won't get much, just enough to coat the kernels, but it will bring additional sweetness to the topping and keep the corn from drying out in the oven.

With the key components prepared, construction goes quickly. Strew the crust with garlic and basil, season it with salt and pepper, lay down a layer of tomatoes and corn, then spoon on some ricotta. A drizzle of good olive oil, and it's oven-ready.

When tomatoes and corn are gone for the year, I keep the crust but change the topping to black olives and roasted red peppers or sauteed scallions and diced potatoes, or just broccoli, Parmesan, and ricotta.

LATE-SUMMER PIZZA

Extra-virgin olive oil
¾ cup plus 1 tablespoon warm water
    (105 to 115 degrees)
1½ teaspoons active dry yeast
2 cups unbleached all-purpose flour
5 tablespoons coarse cornmeal
Kosher salt
1¼ pounds large tomatoes or cherry
    tomatoes
Freshly ground white pepper
2 ears of bicolor or sweet white corn, husked
3 cloves garlic, peeled and thinly sliced
15 large basil leaves, cut into thin strands
¾ cup ricotta cheese
Pitted imported olives, optional

1. Lightly coat a mixing bowl with oil and set aside. In bowl of a food processor, combine water, 2 teaspoons oil, and yeast, and process to combine. Add flour, 2 tablespoons cornmeal, and 2½ teaspoons salt. Process until dough forms a ball,

about 10 seconds. Process 5 seconds more, then transfer dough to a lightly floured counter. Knead for 30 seconds and shape into a ball. Place dough in an oiled bowl, cover with plastic wrap, and set aside to rise for 1 hour.

2. While dough is rising, preheat oven to 350 degrees. Core large tomatoes and slice them ¼ inch thick, or cut cherry tomatoes in half. Arrange on a 12 by 17-inch nonstick or parchment-lined jelly roll pan. Season well with salt and pepper. Roast tomatoes until slightly softened, 25 to 30 minutes. Transfer pan to a cooling rack and increase oven temperature to 400 degrees.

3. Using a sharp knife and working over a large bowl, cut kernels off corn cobs. With back of knife, scrape milk from cobs into bowl. Season with salt to taste.

4. Brush a 12 by 17-inch nonstick or parchment-lined jelly roll pan with a little oil and dust with remaining 3 tablespoons cornmeal. Lift dough from bowl, stretch it slightly, and place in center of pan. Dip your fingers in oil and begin to press dough out from middle of pan to edges. If dough springs back, let it rest for 5 minutes. Continue to pat it out until dough is thin and covers entire surface of pan. Cover with oiled plastic wrap, oiled side down, and allow to rest for 15 minutes.

5. Sprinkle garlic and basil evenly over dough. Top with roasted tomatoes and scatter with corn kernels. Drop teaspoons of ricotta about 2 inches apart in rows over pizza. Drizzle with a little oil and season with salt and pepper. Top with olives if desired.

6. Bake until crust is golden and top is bubbling, 20 to 30 minutes. Cool for 3 minutes, then cut into squares.

Yield: 4 servings (8 servings as a snack)
Time: 1 hour, plus 1 hour for rising

A COOKIE THAT TRANSCENDS THE AGES

When I was a child, my mother made lunch boxes that were the envy of my friends, mostly because they always included a homemade cookie, often these butterscotch cashew bars. As a youngster, I liked these cookies simply because they were sweet. But as a professional baker, I appreciate them for the contrasts they set up as the butterscotch almost fuses with the nuts in the topping. The taste of salty toasted cashews against the foolproof caramel topping is one delightful counterpoint, and the texture of the lightly crumbly crust against the firm and chewy topping is another. My grown-up self sees the bars as a sophisticated sweet, while the kid in me sees a great snack.

For all their character and appeal, these bars are quick to make. The crust is really just a brown-sugar shortbread and can be made by hand or in a mixer. The trick is to mix the dough only until it is crumbly, not until it forms a ball. Similarly, restraint is key when pressing the crust into the pan. Don't pack it, just pat it, so that it keeps its crumbliness and maintains its melt-on-the-tongue tenderness. If you press the crust down too tightly, it will be tough.

To keep the shortbread crust crisp, bake it on its own, without the topping, until it is lightly browned and just firm. As it cools, combine the topping ingredients in a saucepan and cook; then spread this mixture over the crust and scatter it with salted cashew pieces or, if you're feeling flush, whole nuts. The size of the nuts doesn't matter, but the salt does. It's the salt in the recipe that creates the surprising contrast of flavors, the one that makes this cookie fresh and fun.

CASHEW BUTTERSCOTCH BARS

8 ounces (2 sticks) plus 5½ tablespoons unsalted butter, softened, plus butter for greasing pan

¾ cup plus 2 tablespoons packed light brown sugar

1¾ teaspoons kosher salt

2½ cups all-purpose flour

10 ounces butterscotch chips, preferably Hershey's

½ cup plus 2 tablespoons light corn syrup

2½ cups salted cashew pieces

1. Center a rack in oven and preheat oven to 350 degrees. Butter a 13 by 18-inch jelly roll pan, including sides.

2. To make crust: In a mixer fitted with a paddle attachment or in a bowl with a rubber spatula, beat 8 ounces plus 2 tablespoons butter and brown sugar together until smooth. Stir salt into flour, then add flour to butter and sugar mixture. Mix until dough is well combined but still crumbly; if dough is mixed until a ball forms, crust will be tough.

3. Pat dough evenly along bottom of buttered pan, taking care not to pack dough down. Place pan in oven and bake for 5 minutes. With a fork, prick dough deeply all over. Return pan to oven to bake until dough is lightly browned, dry, and no longer soft to touch, about 7 minutes. Transfer to a cooling rack; do not turn off oven.

4. To make butterscotch topping: In a large saucepan, combine remaining 3½ tablespoons butter, butterscotch chips, corn syrup, and 1 tablespoon plus 2½ teaspoons water. Place over medium heat and cook, stirring constantly, until butter and butterscotch chips are melted, about 5 minutes. Pour topping over crust and use a spat-

ula to spread evenly all the way to corners. Sprinkle cashew pieces on top, pressing down lightly.

5. Bake until topping is bubbly and cashews are lightly browned, 11 to 13 minutes. Transfer to a rack and cool completely before cutting into 2 by 3-inch bars.

Yield: 36 bars
Time: 45 minutes

A BALANCING ACT LEADS TO A VARIETY OF QUICK BREADS

I count my plum-honey quick-bread recipe as my first professional culinary triumph—and try to forget that it was developed in a state of panic. I was a college student and had been hired as the summer cook and housekeeper for a family that did not have a clue how inexperienced I was. I listened as I was told that I would be responsible for lunches, dinners, and fresh baked sweets for breakfast, then ran to the library to read every cookbook. Thirty cookbooks and a little practice later, I learned the quick bread secret: Get the balance between the wet and dry ingredients right, and you can vary the fruits, nuts, and spices with abandon. This meant I could make a different quick bread every day, and I did.

Since quick breads are called "quick" because they are leavened with baking powder, not slow-acting yeast, check your baking powder supply—and the expiration date on the tin—before you start. Use double-acting baking powder, which releases its first round of leavening power when it comes in contact with moisture, and its second when it is exposed to the oven's heat.

Most quick breads, including mine, are put together using the one-two method: One set of ingredients, the wet, is added to a second set, the dry, in a bowl large enough to hold everything in the recipe. I use unbleached all-purpose flour as the basic dry ingredient because it produces a light, tender texture. Sometimes I add a touch of whole wheat flour for its fragrance, but for fiber and toothsomeness I prefer to round out the flour with oats. I have tried quick-cooking and instant oats and have been disappointed with both: they dissolve into the batter. But old-fashioned oats, with their big, puffy flakes, have staying power. In fact, their staying power is so strong that I soak them for a few minutes in milk before mixing them into the batter.

While the oats are soaking, I mix together the other wet ingredients. In this recipe I use milk for its sweet flavor, but when you are experimenting on your own, you might substitute fruit juice or buttermilk. Similarly, I've chosen honey as the sweetener because I like the way it goes with so many kinds of fruit, but you can use sugar or even maple syrup. The eggs are there partly for additional leavening, partly for moisture, but mostly for richness and body, and so they should not be tampered with. Nor should you change the vegetable oil, which helps give the quick bread its characteristic moist, tender, not-too-tight structure.

When the two sets of ingredients are ready, use a wooden spoon or a rubber spatula to stir everything together gently with a few quick strokes. It's crucial to the texture of the bread that you go easy here. Barely mixed is better than fully combined. Working once again with a quick, light touch, stir in the fruit and oats. If the mixture looks lumpy, that's fine.

PLUMS-AND-HONEY QUICK BREAD

Vegetable oil

¾ cup old-fashioned (not quick-cooking)
    oats

1 cup milk

2¼ cups unbleached all-purpose flour

1 tablespoon double-acting baking powder

1 teaspoon salt

½ teaspoon ground cinnamon

¼ teaspoon baking soda

¾ cup honey

2 large eggs, lightly beaten

14 ounces black plums (about 3 large or
    5 small), pitted and cut into ¼-inch dice

1. Center a rack in oven and preheat oven to 350 degrees. Oil a 9 by 5-inch loaf pan.

2. In a small bowl, combine oats and ½ cup milk, and allow to soak for 5 minutes.

3. In a large bowl, whisk together flour, baking powder, salt, cinnamon, and baking soda. In another bowl, whisk together remaining ½ cup milk, honey, 6 tablespoons oil, and eggs. Pour liquid ingredients over dry ones and stir until partly moistened. Add soaked oats, any milk remaining in bowl, and plums, and stir gently until batter is moistened. Do not overmix. Pour into pan.

4. Bake for 50 to 60 minutes, or until a toothpick inserted in center of loaf comes out clean. Transfer to a cooling rack for 5 minutes, then unmold. Allow to cool to room temperature before slicing. To store, wrap tightly in plastic wrap.

Yield: 1 loaf; 8 to 10 servings
Time: 1¼ hours

A NEW FRUIT HERE, A NEW SPICE THERE

The basic recipe can easily be varied with these substitutions.

Orange-apricot-cardamom: Replace the plums with diced orange and dried apricots; replace the ground cinnamon with 2 teaspoons ground cardamom.

Peach-cinnamon: Replace the plums with diced peaches, but keep the ground cinnamon.

Pear-ginger: Replace the plums with diced pears; replace the ground cinnamon with 1 teaspoon ground ginger.

~

A SPICY GRILLED CHEESE SANDWICH, BUILT TO LAST

You can think about sandwiches in two directions: from the inside out or from the outside in. You can decide on the filling and then choose the bread, or if you're like me, you can choose the bread and then decide what to put between the slices.

Whether you're going from bread to filling or filling to bread, to build a perfect sandwich you have to consider taste and texture. The basic rules are simple. For texture, pair soft breads with soft fillings (so the egg salad doesn't go flying out of the toast) and sturdy breads with firmer fillings (think roast beef or turkey), so you get a "chew" of equal density from the outside in. When you want to bend the rules, you can put a firm filling on a softer bread. Similarly, big-flavored breads go best with fillings that can stand up to them.

My favorite grilled cheese sandwich starts with country sourdough bread (a good toasting bread) spread with a zesty mixture of chipotle peppers and tomato paste. From the bottom up it has two slices of sharp New York State cheddar, red onions, fresh cilantro, a layer of ripe tomatoes, two more slices of cheese, and then another slice of bread spread with the chipotle paste.

You might want to use a different cheese, change the cilantro to parsley, omit the onions, or replace chili sauce with mayonnaise. You can play around with the inner elements as long as you don't change the order in which they are layered. Order is all when you grill this sandwich, as you'll see.

At the bakeries we use a press, which packs the sandwich down, toasts the bread, warms the innards, and melts the cheese. At home you can put the sandwich in a sauté pan and weight it with a small pot. Either way, you'll discover that the cheese melts on both sides and, even better, melts around the tomatoes, cilantro, and onions, forming a cocoon that keeps these delicate ingredients juicy but away from the bread. There is no sogginess ever.

This recipe makes two sandwiches, but it can be multiplied indefinitely. You can even assemble and refrigerate the sandwiches up to eight hours ahead.

SPICED-UP GRILLED CHEESE SANDWICH

1 6-ounce can tomato paste
2 canned chipotle peppers
1 tablespoon adobo sauce (the sauce in which the peppers are canned)
1 tablespoon molasses
4 large slices sourdough bread, cut ¾ inch thick
4 ounces New York State cheddar cheese, cut into 8 thin slices
4 thin slices red onion, cut in rings
¼ cup coarsely chopped cilantro
1 large or 2 small tomatoes, sliced ¼ inch thick

1. In a blender or small food processor, combine tomato paste, peppers, adobo sauce, and molasses. Puree until smooth.

2. Taste spread to determine spiciness, then place desired amount on each slice of bread. Refrigerate extra sauce.

3. On each of 2 slices of bread, place 2 slices cheese. Top with onion rings, then sprinkle with cilantro. Add tomato slices and top with remaining cheese. Put slices of bread, pepper side down, over sandwiches.

4. If using a sandwich grill, follow instructions. Otherwise, place a large skillet or sauté pan over medium heat for 30 seconds. Put sandwiches in pan and weight with a clean, heavy pot. When bread has begun to toast and brown, and cheese is melting, in 1 to 2 minutes, flip sandwiches over and toast other side.

Yield: 2 sandwiches
Time: 15 minutes

YESTERDAY'S LOAF COULDN'T BE SWEETER

Almond toast is a traditional French teatime snack with an American-style rags-to-riches history. Created by French bakers to use up day-old brioche, this easy sweet is simply sliced stale bread spread with a rich almond-butter "cream" and baked until the topping is golden and the bread toasted.

But what started as a make-do sweet became a beloved staple at many bakeries in France, as well as at mine in New York. In fact, to keep a steady supply of almond toast on the shelves, we bake surplus loaves of brioche and set them aside for a day to dry out. At home you can use any kind of egg bread, like challah, or a top-quality white bread or even split croissants.

For the light, characteristically fluffy almond topping you need only butter, eggs, ground almonds, and sugar. The topping will be fluffiest if you start with room-temperature butter and eggs; they beat to their fullest volume when they are not chilled. And you will get the tastiest topping using almonds with the skins on; the skins add deep flavor and a toasty color. You can buy almonds already ground or grind them easily in a food processor or blender. (A little confectioners' sugar keeps them from turning to an oily paste instead of a powder.)

Since fluffiness is most important, the topping has to be made with an electric mixer fitted with a whip or beaters. This is really the only way to get it sufficiently aerated, and it's the air that helps the baked topping form its fine crust.

Some bakers soak the bread in a sugar syrup flavored with kirsch before they cover it with the almond mixture, but I don't. I think the syrup is too sweet and masks some of the toast's flavor and much of its fragrance. I just spread the topping over the dry bread, lay the slices on a cookie sheet, sprinkle them with sliced almonds, and bake them until the bread is lightly toasted and the topping is puffed and golden. To support the topping, the bread should be cut three-quarters of an inch thick.

The minute the slices are baked, they have to be transferred to a rack to cool, to keep their toasted crunch. It's also important to let them cool completely. It is an exercise in willpower, but the toast, whether you eat it out of hand or with fork and knife, tastes much better when it is cool.

ALMOND BRIOCHE TOAST

½ cup whole unsalted almonds, skins on and toasted
¼ cup confectioners' sugar
8 ounces (1 stick) butter, softened
½ cup granulated sugar
2 large eggs, slightly beaten
8 slices day-old pan-loaf brioche, sliced ¾ inch thick, or challah slices or day-old croissants, sliced as if for sandwiches
8 tablespoons sliced almonds

1. In a blender or bowl of a food processor fitted with a metal blade, combine whole almonds and confectioners' sugar. Process just until nuts are powdery; do not make a paste. Set aside.

2. In bowl of a mixer fitted with a whip or beaters, combine butter and granulated sugar. Beat until light and fluffy. Add powdered almonds and mix just to blend. Add eggs and beat just until mixture is fluffy. (Overmixing will break down almond cream.)

3. Position oven racks to divide oven into thirds and preheat oven to 350 degrees. Line 2 baking sheets with parchment.

4. Place about 3 tablespoons almond cream in center of each slice of bread. Spread almost to, but not touching, edges. Sprinkle each with 1 tablespoon sliced almonds.

5. Divide slices between baking sheets and bake for 5 minutes. Rotate pans top to bottom and front to back, and continue baking until topping begins to brown and crust is golden, about 6 minutes more. (If using croissants, remove top halves, spread filling and almonds on bottoms, bake partly without tops, and replace tops for last 4 minutes of baking.) Transfer toast to a cooling rack immediately. Cool before serving.

Yield: 8 slices

Time: 30 minutes

⁓

A PUMPKIN PLEASURE DOME FILLED WITH SPICES AND PECANS

There can't be another bread that smells better as it is baking, or that looks more inviting when you cut into it, than this pumpkin spiral. The shape was inspired by a bread that Toy Dupree, who has been working with me at the bakeries from the start, saw Pueblo women making in beehive ovens in Taos, New Mexico. Over the years I have refined and changed the recipe, and now it is the quintessential fall bread, spiced with cinnamon, ginger, and cloves, studded with pecans, and coiled around on itself until it gently domes in the center, evoking the shape of those Pueblo ovens.

The dough for this rich, tender, slightly sweet bread is soft, moist, and fun to work with—it takes very light kneading and is best made in two simple stages. I mix the yeast with honey, pumpkin puree, cornmeal,

milk, egg yolks, and some flour. The resulting mixture, called a sponge in baker's lingo, gives the yeast a chance to lighten the heavier, wetter ingredients in the dough before more flour is added.

After fifteen minutes or so, when the yeast is activated and the sponge is bubbling, it is time for Stage 2: adding the remaining flour and all the aromatic spices. After kneading a few more minutes, you can start to appreciate the dough's fragrance and texture. The last step of mixing is to work in a stick of melted butter before kneading some more.

As dense as this dough may seem, it is delicate enough to require kid-glove treatment. All the words that are associated with kneading—pound, punch, slap, knock—are the wrong words here. I knead with a light push-and-pull motion until the dough becomes soft, supple, and silken; then I let it rest for twenty minutes before giving it another gentle knead to incorporate toasted pecans. Pecans are latecomers; I don't want their sharp edges to tear the strands of gluten, the bread's structure-giving element, that the initial kneading produced. When the pecans are in, the bread rises until it doubles in volume and is ready for shaping.

PUMPKIN PECAN SPIRAL

1 tablespoon plus 1 teaspoon active dry yeast
½ cup honey
1 cup unsweetened pumpkin puree
½ cup milk at room temperature
2 large eggs, separated
⅓ cup minus 2 teaspoons coarse cornmeal,
    plus extra for dusting
4 cups bread flour
1 teaspoon ground cinnamon
½ teaspoon ground ginger
½ teaspoon ground cloves
2½ teaspoons kosher salt
4 ounces (1 stick) unsalted butter, melted
1 cup pecan pieces, toasted

1. To make sponge: In a large mixing bowl, combine yeast and ¼ cup very warm water, and stir to dissolve. Allow to stand for 3 minutes. Add honey, pumpkin puree, milk, egg yolks, cornmeal, and 1⅔ cups flour. Stir briskly with a whisk until well blended. Let sponge stand at least 15 minutes but no longer than 30, until it begins to rise slightly.

2. In a medium bowl, combine remaining 2⅓ cups flour, cinnamon, ginger, cloves, and salt. Whisk to blend well and add to sponge. Using your fingers, stir, scraping sides of bowl and folding dough over itself until it forms a shaggy mass. Knead dough until it becomes smooth and somewhat elastic, about 5 minutes. Gradually add melted butter, kneading it in until well combined.

3. Turn dough onto a lightly floured surface and knead until very smooth, about 5 minutes. (Dough will be sticky at first but will become soft, supple, and springy.) Shape into a loose ball, cover with plastic wrap, and let rest for 20 minutes.

4. Gently stretch dough into a rectangle about 6 by 8 inches and scatter with toasted pecans. Press nuts in slightly and fold dough in thirds. Gently knead until nuts are evenly distributed, about 3 minutes. Shape dough into a loose ball and place in a lightly oiled bowl. Cover tightly with plastic wrap and allow to rise at room temperature until it has doubled in volume, about 2 hours.

5. Dust 2 large baking sheets with cornmeal; set aside. When dough has doubled, move to a lightly floured surface and divide into 3 equal pieces. Shape each into a rope 24 inches long. To elongate rope, roll it and stretch gently, resting dough briefly once. Beginning at one end, coil rope to form a flat spiral resembling a large cinnamon bun; spiral should be coiled tightly enough so that a slight dome (½ inch high) forms in center.

6. Transfer spirals to baking sheets and cover with oiled plastic wrap. Let rise at room temperature until doubled in volume, 1½ to 2 hours.

7. Position oven racks to divide oven into thirds; preheat oven to 425 degrees. Mix 2 egg whites with 2 teaspoons water. When loaves have doubled, brush surfaces with egg wash. Place sheets in oven; with plant sprayer, mist tops and sides of oven about 6 times. (This will help bread spring up and enhance color.) Quickly close oven door.

8. Bake for 15 minutes, then reduce oven temperature to 350 degrees. Continue to bake until loaves are golden brown and surface feels firm when pressed lightly, 20 to 25 minutes more. Loaves should have a thin, soft crust. Transfer to a rack to cool completely before slicing and serving.

Yield: 3 loaves
Time: 1¼ hours, plus 3½ hours for rising

REINVENTING BREAD
AND CHOCOLATE

Pain au chocolat, the French after-school treat, and its Italian cousin, bread slathered with Nutella, inspired me to create these chocolate rolls. I wanted a bread that wasn't too sweet but wouldn't need butter or jam. A bread that would be rich and, in its own way, decadent. Something that would be perfect for breakfast or as an afternoon pick-me-up.

The result is a tender chocolate roll, generously studded with tart-sweet dried cherries and bittersweet chocolate. The dough itself is rich, slightly moist, and, since I use cocoa powder and brewed coffee, neither very chocolaty nor very sweet. So the sweeter chocolate chunks and tangy cherries stand out more. Its soft crumb lets the melted chocolate bits ooze into the bread.

Chocolate chips will work here, but hand-chopped pieces of good bittersweet chocolate are best. The darker and more bittersweet the chocolate, the greater and more exciting the contrasts in taste and texture.

The dough is easy to make because there are no starters, sponges, or stages; just put everything in a bowl and then knead, let it rest, knead again, let it rise, and cut into pieces. The tricky part is shaping the dough into rolls. Make some room for yourself on a counter, and cup your hand over a piece of dough, like a cage. With your fingertips firmly on the counter, rotate your hand clockwise against the counter. You should feel the dough move in the opposite direction. Keep rotating the dough until it is firm and covered by a tight skin.

DECADENT CHOCOLATE-CHERRY ROLLS

2 teaspoons active dry yeast
3 cups unbleached all-purpose flour
⅓ cup unsweetened cocoa powder
⅓ cup granulated sugar
1½ teaspoons kosher salt
1 cup warm brewed coffee
1 large egg, separated
1 tablespoon unsalted butter, softened
8 ounces bittersweet chocolate, coarsely chopped
1 cup dried tart cherries

1. In a large mixing bowl, combine yeast and ½ cup very warm water. Stir to dissolve yeast and let rest for 3 minutes. In a medium bowl, combine flour, cocoa, sugar, and salt. Whisk to blend, then set aside.

2. Stir coffee, egg yolk, and butter into yeast mixture. Gradually add flour mixture, stirring until flour is moistened and binds into a shaggy mass. Dough should be sticky; if it feels stiff, mix in up to 2 tablespoons water.

3. On a lightly floured surface, knead dough until smooth and elastic, 7 to 8 minutes. Shape into a loose ball, cover with plastic wrap, and let rest about 10 minutes.

4. Flatten and stretch dough gently to form a rectangle about 1 inch thick. Scatter chopped chocolate and dried cherries on top. Fold rectangle into thirds like a business letter, then knead 2 to 3 minutes, until chocolate and cherries are distributed. If some pieces pop out of dough, they can be incorporated after first rise.

5. Shape dough into a loose ball and place in a lightly oiled bowl along with any loose chocolate and cherries. Cover bowl tightly with plastic wrap

and let rise at room temperature until dough has doubled in volume, 1 to 2 hours.

6. Line 2 large baking sheets with parchment. Gently transfer dough to a lightly floured work surface and press in any loose chocolate and cherries. Divide into 12 equal pieces. Shape pieces into rolls by forming a cage with your hand over the dough and rotating dough against table to tighten it. Place 6 rolls on each baking sheet, evenly spaced. Cover loosely with oiled plastic wrap and let rise at room temperature until doubled in volume, about 1 hour.

7. About 15 minutes before baking, position oven racks to divide oven into thirds and preheat oven to 400 degrees. When rolls have doubled, mix egg white with 1 teaspoon water. Brush each roll gently with egg wash, coating entire surface. Slide baking sheets into oven and, using a plant sprayer, mist top and sides of oven with water 6 to 8 times. Quickly close oven door.

8. Bake for 10 minutes, reduce oven temperature to 350 degrees, and rotate pans top to bottom and front to back. Bake until tops of rolls feel firm but not hard, and bottoms are only lightly browned, 10 to 15 minutes more. Cool on a rack before serving.

Yield: 12 rolls
Time: about 1 1/2 hours, plus 2 3/4 hours for rising
and cooling

PATRICK O'CONNELL

Patrick O'Connell is the chef and an owner
of the Inn at Little Washington in Washington, Virginia.
He was photographed with one of his dalmatians at the Inn.
These columns were written with Marian Burros.

MUSSELS WITH A SOUTHERN ACCENT

I have always loved transferring the primitive, soulful character of southern food to something that is delicate and refined. It's how I maintain a sense of place in my cooking, what the French call cuisine terroir, *here in back-country Virginia. In these recipes I bring you some of the flavors of my region, combined in unusual ways and presented in dishes where you wouldn't expect to find them.*

In the early days of the Inn, we served mussels the traditional way, in the shells. But as the years passed and things became more "elegant," dealing with shells didn't seem appropriate. So I combined steamed, shelled mussels with orecchiette, because the pasta has an indentation that's just right to hold a small mussel. And I adapted a lighter version of Alfredo sauce made with the steaming liquid. The sauce shouldn't be too thick; it

should roll off the pasta. (It thickens on the pasta, so make it a little thinner than you like.)

Like many of my dishes, the regional touch comes from an indigenous ingredient—in this case, collard greens. I cut them into julienne strips and fry them, which makes them look like seaweed. Most people need three tastes before they can identify that little southern flavor.

Actually, the first time I encountered fried collards was in Hong Kong, where they were served as a crispy nibble with drinks. I couldn't identify them at all. I thought they were some kind of weird seaweed. It was that association that made me think of serving them with mussels instead of a more traditional green like crispy spinach or parsley.

Collards stand up to frying much better than spinach or parsley because they are so sturdy. In fact, you can fry them as much as eight hours in advance. The fried collards turn emerald green and provide a striking contrast to the creamy white of the pasta and sauce, and add a pleasant crunch to the sensual softness of the dish. They're an intriguing note in taste, texture, and appearance.

MUSSELS WITH ORECCHIETTE

1½ pounds (about 40) mussels
2 shallots, peeled and chopped
2 cloves garlic, minced
3 sprigs thyme
½ bay leaf
3 sprigs parsley
¾ cup dry white wine or vermouth
2 cups heavy cream
½ cup plus 6 pinches of finely grated
 Parmigiano-Reggiano cheese
Salt and freshly ground white pepper
Freshly ground nutmeg
36 orecchiette
Extra-virgin olive oil
Crispy Collard Greens (see recipe below) for
 garnish

1. Discard any mussels with broken shells. Scrub mussels with a brush under cold running water and discard any that are not tightly closed.

2. In a saucepan large enough to hold mussels after they open, combine shallots, garlic, thyme, bay leaf, parsley, and wine. Place over high heat and bring to a rapid boil. Add mussels and steam about 3 minutes. Transfer opening mussels to a bowl and remove from shells.

3. Strain liquid into a small pan and bring to a boil. Reduce by half and set aside. In another small pan, bring cream to a boil and reduce by half. Add ¼ cup mussel liquid to cream, adding more as desired for sauce consistency and flavor.

4. Place sauce in a large saucepan. Add ½ cup cheese and season with salt, pepper, and nutmeg. Keep warm.

5. Bring a large pot of lightly salted water to a boil and add orecchiette. Boil until tender, 8 to 10 minutes. Drain well.

6. Bring sauce to a simmer, add mussels, and heat until warm. Add orecchiette and stir to mix well. Sprinkle with oil and adjust seasonings. Spoon into 6 serving bowls. Top each with a pinch of cheese and a mound of collard greens.

Yield: 6 appetizer servings
Time: 30 minutes

CRISPY COLLARD GREENS

½ cup collard green leaves, washed,
 thoroughly dried, and cut into very thin
 strips
Oil for deep-fat frying
Salt

1. In a deep fryer, wok, or medium saucepan, bring at least 2 inches of oil to 350 degrees. Set aside a plate covered with absorbent paper.

2. Add collard greens to hot oil and fry just long enough to make them curl, about 30 seconds. Transfer to a plate to drain and salt lightly to taste.

Yield: 6 servings as a garnish
Time: 10 minutes

A SOUP THAT TRACES ITS HERITAGE TO A MOUNTAIN HOLLOW

Many people think that the whole notion of preserved ancestral dishes exists only in Europe. But it exists here, too. In Virginia the traditions can still be found in the hollows and foothills of the back country. Hollows—they're called hollers locally—are not as big as towns, but each one has a name and six to twelve families in residence. Your hollow is your cultural heritage.

In the early days a young country girl who worked for me talked about what she cooked for her daddy up in her hollow. I was fascinated by her descriptions. She had an uncanny sense of taste. In fact, her palate was better than those of many graduates of culinary schools. While she was happy to do cutting and chopping, she would not do any cooking because, she said, she cooked only for her daddy.

Finally, after several years, I succeeded in getting her to cook lunch for me. She made her daddy's favorite soup in about fifteen minutes, using only a paring knife and a stockpot. We christened it Turnip Comfort.

It is really a chowder, the deeply nourishing, satisfying kind that warms you through and through. Little cubes of turnips and potatoes give it a rugged texture, and the broth is similarly sturdy and rich, even though its base is water, not stock. The turnips have a hearty sweetness that melds so well with the potato that the soup doesn't need stock; in fact, stock would probably just muddy the flavors.

You can make the soup a day in advance, but it is so quick, it's good for the last minute. Just cook some diced country bacon, which gives the broth a deep, smoky note, and then sweat a little onion, add the turnips and potatoes, and cover it all with water. In a remarkably short time the flavors meld and the starch in the potato naturally thickens the soup. Some torn-up collards provide color, and a few drops of cream marry the flavors and add a little luxury.

The longer the soup cooks or rests, the thicker it will be; eventually it will turn into a porridge. I prefer it cooked only until the turnips and potatoes are spoon tender. But it depends on how you like it. If you make it ahead and rewarm it, you'll have to thin the broth with a few drops of water or cream to return it to a chowder.

Either way, the taste of Turnip Comfort is reminiscent of an earthy European peasant soup, the kind you just can't find anymore.

TURNIP COMFORT

4 ounces lightly smoked thick country bacon, cut into ½-inch dice (1 cup)
2 cups onions cut into ½-inch dice
2 cups peeled potatoes cut into ½-inch dice
2 cups peeled turnips cut into ½-inch dice
1 bay leaf
½ cup torn collard leaves
¼ cup heavy cream
Salt and freshly ground white pepper

1. Place a large saucepan over medium heat and add bacon. Cover and cook slowly until bacon is thoroughly cooked and lightly brown on edges, about 4 minutes. Remove from heat and pour off all but 1 tablespoon fat.

2. Return pan to medium heat and add onions. Sauté until onions are translucent but not brown, about 4 minutes. Add potatoes and turnips, and stir well. Sauté for 2 minutes. Add bay leaf and enough water to just cover vegetables, about 4 cups. Bring to a boil, reduce to a lively simmer, and simmer until potatoes are very tender, 15 to 20 minutes.

3. Add collard greens and simmer until they are tender but still retain their color, about 3 minutes. Add cream and season with salt and

white pepper to taste. Remove, discard bay leaf, and serve hot.

Yield: 4 servings
Time: 35 minutes

CHILDHOOD CAKE, GROWN-UP FLOURISH

As a kid I always loved my mother's pineapple upside-down cake. But as a chef I knew it needed a drastic makeover to take it into the next century. Losing the maraschino cherry was a no-brainer. Getting rid of the cake's clunkiness was trickier.

I remembered a caramelized Alsatian apple crepe we used to serve, and I tried substituting thinly sliced fresh pineapple. Its acidity made the dessert more refreshing, and surprisingly, all of the flavors I remembered from childhood were preserved in something light and delicate. The crepe is a six-inch disk with thin slices of pineapple laid on top in concentric circles and covered with an alluring golden glaze. The caramelization created in the skillet tastes just like the gooey brown sugar topping on the American classic.

The beauty of the dish is that you are unaware of the crepe. It's like a film holding the pineapple together. People are sometimes afraid to make crepes because they think they have to be paper-thin. It's not necessary for this dish—it will be equally delicious if they are more like pancakes.

Flipping them will take a little practice. The trick is to jerk the pan forward with a quick flipping motion, then catch the crepe as it lands upside down; people usually don't thrust the pan forward with enough oomph. If you're worried about watching the first few fall on the floor, ask the cat to stand by when you practice, or

put a plate over the pan, invert the pancake onto the plate, then return to the pan, pineapple side down.

It would seem like torture if you had to make the crepes while your guests were waiting, but there's really no point. Just lay them on greased cookie sheets and warm them just before serving.

PINEAPPLE UPSIDE-DOWN CREPES

For the crepe batter:
   2 cups all-purpose flour
   6 tablespoons unsalted butter, melted and
      cooled
   4 tablespoons sugar
   3 large eggs
   Pinch of salt
   1 cup milk, or as needed

For the topping:
   2 large ripe pineapples, peeled, cored, and cut
      lengthwise into quarters
   6 tablespoons butter, plus 3 teaspoons for
      greasing pan
   1 cup toasted coarsely ground macadamia
      nuts
   ½ cup sugar
   ¾ cup heavy cream, or as needed
   ½ cup 151-proof rum
   10 to 12 miniature scoops vanilla,
      buttermilk, or coconut ice cream

1. To make batter: Combine flour, butter, sugar, eggs, and salt in a food processor or blender. With motor running, add enough milk to make a fluid batter, which may be covered and refrigerated up to 24 hours.

2. Line a large baking sheet with parchment paper and set aside.

3. Slice pineapple quarters crosswise, 1/8 inch thick.

4. In a 7-inch nonstick pan over medium heat, melt 1/4 teaspoon butter, spreading with a spatula. Remove pan from heat and allow to cool slightly.

5. With pan off heat, ladle about 3 tablespoons batter on pan and roll around until bottom is evenly coated. Sprinkle with 1 tablespoon macadamia nuts.

6. Return pan to medium heat. Just as crepe sets but while still wet on top, remove pan from heat and arrange pineapple slices in an overlapping circular pattern, completely covering surface of crepe. Use a skewer or a fork to arrange any pineapple slices that fall out of place. Shake crepe slightly to keep it from sticking to pan.

7. Return pan to heat and sprinkle pineapple with 2 teaspoons sugar and about 1/2 tablespoon cold butter cut in bits. Use a rubber spatula to loosen edge of crepe and check underside. When bottom is golden brown, loosen crepe by running a rubber spatula around edges and carefully flip crepe over in pan. Continue cooking until sugar underneath begins to turn a light caramel color. Add 1 tablespoon cream around edges of crepe and tilt pan so that cream blends with sugar and runs under edges of crepe.

8. Spray a flat metal surface such as the bottom of a cake pan with nonstick cooking spray. Place sprayed side over crepe and invert skillet to remove crepe. Slide crepe onto prepared baking sheet. Repeat process, wiping pan clean between crepes, to make 10 to 12. Sheet of crepes may be covered and refrigerated up to 4 hours.

9. To serve, reheat crepes in a 350-degree oven until hot, about 4 minutes. Transfer to serving plates. Pour rum into a small pitcher or gravy boat and set aflame. Top crepes with burning rum. Garnish each plate with a miniature scoop of ice cream.

Yield: 10 to 12 servings
Time: 1 1/4 hours

THE SHORTEST ROUTE TO RISOTTO

Simpler is usually better when it comes to risotto. All too often American versions are cluttered with so many fancy ingredients that the purity of the dish is lost. A good risotto is meant to be as comforting and nourishing as a bowl of porridge.

Many people think they don't have time to make a dish that requires standing over the stove and stirring constantly for twenty minutes while gradually adding stock. But here is a simple restaurant trick that allows you to partly cook the rice in advance and chill it to prevent overcooking—a sort of instant risotto base. It can then be quickly reheated and finished by adding hot liquid and any additional ingredients just before serving.

This delicious base can be kept in your refrigerator for those times when you don't feel like cooking but crave a comforting meal. I encourage home cooks to set aside one day a week—perhaps Sunday afternoon—for cooking large batches of food that can be enjoyed throughout the week.

The risotto base can be flavored a number of ways at the last minute to make a first course or main dish, or for a dinner party. Shredded collard greens, fresh sage leaves, or strips of thinly sliced prosciutto can be tossed in to make this dish more substantial.

The amount of liquid for a risotto varies, so don't

depend on an exact measure. When finished, the center of the rice should be al dente, *the mixture loose enough to slide on a tilted plate. The dish will continue to thicken as it rests, so serve it immediately.*

MAKE-AHEAD RISOTTO WITH
SAGE AND PROSCIUTTO

For the make-ahead risotto:
   2 cups chicken stock
   2 tablespoons unsalted butter
   2 tablespoons extra-virgin olive oil
   ½ large onion, minced
   1 cup Arborio rice

To finish preparation:
   1½ cups (approximately) chicken stock
   7 leaves fresh sage
   1 collard green leaf, trimmed and rib
      removed, torn into pieces
   1 tablespoon unsalted butter
   1 thin slice prosciutto, cut into thin strips
   Salt and freshly ground black pepper.

1. To prepare risotto: In a small saucepan, bring stock to a boil, reduce heat, and keep stock at a simmer.

2. In a medium saucepan, combine butter and oil. Place over medium heat until butter has melted. Add onion and sauté until translucent. Add rice and stir until evenly coated with butter.

3. Reduce heat to low. Slowly add simmered stock, ⅔ cup at a time, stirring constantly until rice absorbs liquid, 4 to 5 minutes with each addition. When all stock has been absorbed, remove risotto from heat. Immediately pour onto a baking sheet to stop cooking, and cool as quickly

as possible; rice grains will still be a bit raw at center. Refrigerate, uncovered, until chilled, then transfer to a covered container. Partly cooked risotto may be refrigerated for up to 2 days.

4. To finish preparation: In a small saucepan, combine about 1½ cups chicken broth with sage and collard greens. Bring to a boil, reduce heat, and keep stock at a simmer.

5. In a medium saucepan over medium-low heat, melt butter and stir in risotto until warm. Hold sage and collard greens to the side with a spoon while pouring in ½ cup stock. Stir until stock is absorbed, 4 to 5 minutes with each addition. Repeat until all stock has been absorbed. Add prosciutto with final addition of stock. Adjust amount of stock as needed; risotto should be very creamy and rice grains tender but firm. Season to taste with salt and pepper, and serve immediately.

Yield: 2 servings
*Time: 40 minutes: 25 minutes for the make-ahead
   risotto, 15 minutes to finish the dish*

SWEET REWARDS OF A
WATCH ON THE RIND

For more than twenty years we've been serving candied grapefruit rind after dinner at the Inn. Our guests seem to find the chewy texture and bittersweet flavor irresistible. It's the perfect last bite after an extravagant meal or equally good with afternoon tea. And all you need are grapefruit and sugar.

The story of how we began serving the rind centers on one of the oldest inhabitants of our tiny town who died at 107 a few years ago. Mattie Ball Fletcher, affectionately called Mother Ball by everyone, was known for her cooking, her herb garden, and her outspokenness. When we opened, she was in her mid-eighties and was our primary supplier of herbs, which she grew just a few doors away.

Mother Ball didn't believe in waste. She was appalled when she learned that we threw out the rinds of the grapefruit we used for our tarts, so she offered to candy them for us. But she was not about to explain her technique. "Folks think it's a secret," she said, "but there's no secret to it. It's just right much work." Eventually even she knew she was too old to candy the rinds, and she finally confided the recipe to one of our kitchen assistants who delivered meals to her from the Inn.

We still make the rind the way Mother Ball did, but we've streamlined the recipe. When we blanch the rind to get rid of the bitterness, we line up three pots instead of using the same one over and over as she did.

We also slice the rind into more delicate strips that are all the same size, unlike Mother Ball's. (Scraps can flavor cookies or tea cakes.) But we candy the rinds the same way, coating them first in sugar syrup and then tossing them in dry sugar.

Around Christmastime the candied rind makes a wonderful gift or stocking stuffer, placed in small decorative boxes or wrapped in transparent bags and tied with ribbons. Candied grapefruit rind keeps for weeks in a cool, dry place and can be made easily and economically in large batches for gifts.

CANDIED GRAPEFRUIT RIND

4 large pink unblemished grapefruit
6 cups sugar

1. Fill three 4-quart saucepans with water. Place over high heat and bring to a boil. Cut each grapefruit vertically (through stem end) into 8 wedges. Peel rind from each wedge and reserve.

2. Trim off pointed ends of rind wedges and cut each wedge into strips 1½ to 2 inches long and ¼ inch wide. Discard irregular trimmings.

3. When water boils, submerge strips in 1 pot, keeping them down with a spoon. Return water to a full boil, then boil rind for 2 minutes. Drain rind immediately, then place in a second pot of boiling water. Return water to a boil and boil for 2 minutes. Drain. Place rind in third pot of water, boil 2 minutes, and drain well.

4. In 1 pot combine 5 cups sugar and 5 cups water. Boil over medium heat until sugar has dissolved. Add rind to sugar syrup, making sure it is submerged. Boil, stirring occasionally, until candy thermometer reads 238 degrees. Rinds should be translucent.

5. Drain rinds and transfer to a wire rack placed over a cookie sheet or waxed paper. Allow to dry in a single layer in a warm, dry place overnight, until barely sticky.

6. In a large bowl, toss rinds with remaining 1 cup sugar, coating evenly. Store in a covered container at room temperature. If rinds become moist or sticky, toss in sugar again.

Yield: 3 cups
Time: 1 hour

BRINING WORKS WONDERS
FOR POULTRY

Brining is a centuries-old method of food preservation, with the most basic formulas using salt, water, and sugar. In the past couple of years there has been a surprising resurgence of interest in the technique. Chefs are brining everything from salmon to pork loin, but most commonly the method is being used for turkeys and chickens.

Why has this suddenly come into vogue? Probably because of a never-ending quest by chefs for intensified flavors. Many of these old recipes were developed in the absence of refrigeration, and they used salt, acid, or sugar to preserve meats and, at times, to mask off-tastes. With these treatments the food often acquired another dimension. Many of the exotic tastes and the layerings of flavors in these old inventions of necessity suddenly seem novel and nostalgic in this era of technological sterility.

We first began to use a brining technique during the holidays many years ago when we had a tradition of giving an open house for the entire town. We roasted three suckling pigs after soaking them overnight in an aromatic solution of salt, sugar, water, and plenty of spices. The roast pigs were such a delicious success that we were inspired to begin experimenting with brining other foods, and we found that the process also had a miraculous effect on poultry, both turkey and chicken.

We always use a brine with our Thanksgiving turkeys and whenever we have roast chicken for the meal for staff members. The technique prevents the bird from drying out during roasting and imparts a beautiful flavor with a lot of depth. The sugar in the brine helps a turkey or chicken take on a rich amber color as it cooks. The combination of salt, water, and a panoply of herbs and spices cures and flavors the bird.

Salt alone could be used, but the brining liquid works much faster. The salt draws out fluid from the tissues and concentrates the flavor. The liquid in the brine replaces the moisture drawn out by the salt, so the meat is much juicier. Any spices in the brine also penetrate all the way through the meat. The result is a tender and succulent bird that needs no additional seasoning.

Water for the brining mixture should be brought to a boil before the salt, sugar, and aromatic seasonings are added. But be sure to cool it to room temperature before adding the bird, and keep it refrigerated or in a very cool place to prevent bacterial growth. The brine can be made well in advance.

BRINED CHICKEN

For the brine:

½ cup kosher salt

1¾ cups sugar

1 cup honey

3 sprigs each fresh parsley, dill, thyme,
    tarragon, sage

1 sprig fresh rosemary

1 tablespoon mustard seeds

1 tablespoon fennel seeds

1 cinnamon stick

2 large bay leaves

4 cloves

½ tablespoon juniper berries

½ tablespoon cardamom pods

1 tablespoon black peppercorns

1 lemon, halved and squeezed lightly

3 star anise

½ tablespoon whole allspice

For the chicken:

1 3- to 4-pound chicken

1 cup sliced carrots

1 cup sliced celery

1 cup sliced onion

2 tablespoons unsalted butter, melted

1. In a large stockpot or roasting pan large enough to hold chicken, place 1 gallon water. Bring to a boil, then remove from heat. Add all ingredients for brine and stir. Let cool to room temperature.

2. Add chicken to pan, cover, and refrigerate overnight.

3. Preheat oven to 350 degrees. Drain chicken well and discard brine. Cut off and discard wing tips. In a roasting pan, place carrots, celery, and onion. Place chicken on top of vegetables. Brush chicken with melted butter.

4. Roast chicken until thigh joint temperature reaches 150 degrees, about 1 hour. Baste with pan juices at least every 15 minutes. Watch carefully to avoid burning; if parts become well browned, cover with aluminum foil. When chicken is done, remove from oven and allow to rest 10 minutes before carving.

Yield: 4 to 5 servings

Time: about 1¼ hours, plus overnight brining

AN INTENSE SAUCE ADDS PUNCH TO FILET MIGNON

Like a classic string of pearls, filet mignon is always appropriate for a special occasion. And when it is accessorized with an intensely flavored red wine reduction, rings of charred onions, and colorful pendants of crisp zucchini, this seductive dish can go anywhere.

This intense sauce, made with balsamic vinegar, red wine, and butter, is one of my favorite tastes. It combines beautifully with the sweetness of the charred onions and really punches up the flavor of an otherwise bland cut of beef. The sauce is a deep aubergine color with a satin texture and a high-gloss sheen. And since it is so vibrantly flavored and wonderfully concentrated, a little goes a long way.

The charred onions help balance the acidity of the sauce. The slices of zucchini provide another textural component. Searing them helps prevent the usual mushy texture and watery taste commonly associated with steamed or boiled zucchini. Actually, onions would even be delicious on a burger.

Most components in this dish lend themselves to advance preparation, and that includes the butter sauce. A trick for holding a butter sauce up to several hours is to keep it in a thermos. The onions and zucchini can be cooked ahead and then reheated in the oven just before serving.

FILETS MIGNONS ON CHARRED ONIONS AND ZUCCHINI WITH BALSAMIC VINEGAR SAUCE

For the sauce:
    1⅛ cups cabernet or pinot noir wine
    1 cup balsamic vinegar
    1 shallot, peeled and halved
    2 tablespoons unsalted butter, cut into
        4 pieces
    4 tablespoons salted butter, cut into 8 pieces
    Salt and freshly ground black pepper

For the filets mignons and vegetables:
    Extra-virgin olive oil
    1 large white onion, peeled and sliced
        ¼-inch thick
    2 medium zucchini, trimmed and cut
        diagonally into ¾-inch-thick slices
    Salt and freshly ground black pepper
    4 5- to 6-ounce trimmed filets mignons

1. To prepare sauce: In a small, heavy-bottomed saucepan, combine wine, vinegar, and shallot. Place over medium heat, bring to a boil, and reduce to a syrupy consistency, about ⅓ cup. Remove from heat and discard shallot.

2. While sauce is still hot, whisk in unsalted and salted butter, 1 piece at a time. If desired, add 1 or 2 drops of water to thin sauce to taste. Season with salt and pepper to taste. Keep warm until ready to serve.

3. To prepare filets mignons and vegetables: Place a heavy cast-iron skillet over high heat until very hot. Add only enough oil to leave a film; place onion slices in skillet in 1 layer. Cook until lightly charred on bottom, but do not blacken. Turn over with tongs or a spatula, and char on other side. Onions should be soft. Transfer to paper towels.

4. Season zucchini slices with salt and pepper. Return skillet to high heat. When very hot, add a light film of oil and place zucchini in skillet in 1 layer. Sear for 2 to 3 minutes, until surfaces against pan blister. Turn and cook about 1 minute, until light golden. Remove from heat and transfer to paper towels.

5. Brush filets with oil and season with salt and pepper to taste. Return skillet to high heat. When skillet is very hot, sear filets for 2 minutes on each side (for rare), or to taste.

6. To serve, arrange 3 zucchini ovals on each of 4 warm plates so they touch in center. Arrange 3 or 4 onion rings over zucchini. Place a filet on top of onion. Spoon 3 small pools of sauce on each plate. Top each filet with a few more onion rings and serve immediately.

Yield: 4 servings
Time: 45 minutes

TADASHI ONO

Tadashi Ono is the chef at Sono in Manhattan.
He was photographed at the pottery wheel in his basement office
at the restaurant. These columns were written with Mark Bittman.

JAPANESE AND FRENCH TRADITIONS, IN A NATURAL BLEND

Fusion cooking is a term that is thrown around a lot these days. Most of the time it means a muddled mix of disparate influences, but at its best it is a clear bridge between two very different culinary philosophies.

Japanese cooking is generally based on the idea of taking the natural essence of an ingredient—its sweetness, its richness, or its ocean flavor—and setting it off with a contrasting taste. For example, the Japanese way with lobster, which is sweet, is to serve it with ginger or lemon, both of which are strong and have a kick. Classic French cooking more often looks at that same ingredient and tries to enhance it, to increase its sweetness or richness. That is why the French often serve lobster with butter sauces.

Fusion cooking takes both approaches into account, and since I was born in Tokyo and did most of my training in classical French kitchens, it's a natural

leap for me. I want to see an ingredient's basic nature, to know it, so that I don't overwhelm it but instead make the minimal contribution to show it at its best.

Salmon, for example, is so rich and flavorful that to enhance those qualities would be overkill. I cut through its richness and intensify its flavor by curing it lightly with ginger and salt, and then serve it with a tiny bit of green tea powder, which is grassy and tannic and an ideal counterpoint. I also pan-roast the fish, which keeps its flavor strong and makes its skin really crisp, a contrast to the tender flesh.

With the salmon I serve a rice dish that smacks of the sea and also borrows a little from Italy, not France. It's much like risotto in both technique and texture, but I take a shortcut, steaming the rice first so that the final preparation, gradually adding stock, is quick and easy.

For the Japanese accent, I also make it with different kinds of seaweed, like kombu, ogo, tosaka, wakame, or nori, all of which are available in Asian and natural food markets. At its most basic, this is a simple dish of fish and rice, a combination at home in either Eastern or Western culture. But the Asian touches unify the flavors and techniques around another theme: the essence of the ocean.

PAN-ROASTED SALMON FILLET WITH SEAWEED RISOTTO

4 6-ounce salmon fillets, skin on and scaled
4 slivers of ginger (each about 1 by ¼ inch), peeled
Salt and freshly ground black pepper
1 onion, peeled and quartered
1 carrot, peeled and cut into chunks
1 celery stalk, cut into chunks
1 3-inch piece kombu
1 cup short-grain rice
½ cup dried seaweed such as wakame, ogo, or tosaka, or a combination
1 teaspoon macha (green tea powder)
1 sheet nori
2 tablespoons extra-virgin olive oil
4 teaspoons salmon roe, optional

1. Cut a slit in middle of skin of each salmon fillet and insert a piece of ginger. Sprinkle skin side of salmon with salt and pepper, wrap loosely, and refrigerate at least 1 hour, preferably overnight.

2. Combine onion, carrot, and celery in a saucepan with 4 cups water. Simmer about 1 hour, then turn off heat and add kombu. Let sit 10 minutes; drain and reserve 3 cups (add water if necessary). Keep warm.

3. While stock is simmering, combine rice with 1¼ cups water and a pinch of salt in a small saucepan; bring to a boil, cover, and turn heat to low. Cook for 15 minutes, or until water is absorbed.

4. Soak seaweed in cold water to cover for about 10 minutes. Combine macha and 1 teaspoon salt, and set aside. Preheat oven to 500 degrees. Toast nori briefly in a dry skillet or over an open flame, just until darkened on both sides, 1 or 2 minutes total; crumble and set aside.

5. Combine rice and about half of stock in a saucepan over medium-high heat. Cook, stirring, until liquid is absorbed; drain seaweed and add, along with about half of remaining stock. Turn heat to low and stir occasionally.

6. Put oil in a large ovenproof skillet, preferably nonstick (you may have to use 2 skillets), and turn heat to high. When oil smokes, add salmon, skin side down. Cook about 30 seconds, shaking pan to make sure fillets don't stick. Transfer to oven and roast for 5 minutes, or until fish is medium-rare to medium.

7. Just before serving, stir remaining stock into rice and turn heat back to high. Cook, stirring, for 1 minute, until mixture is creamy and resembles risotto. Stir in crumbled nori. Remove ginger from salmon skin and fill slit, if you like, with roe. Serve salmon with rice and sprinkle a tiny bit of green tea salt over all.

Yield: 4 servings
Time: 1½ hours, plus at least 1 hour for refrigeration

SHRIMP COOKED IN THEIR SHELLS, AND EATEN THAT WAY, TOO

Whether to peel shrimp before cooking them is debated endlessly among cooks, but even when the nonpeelers win, the shrimp are almost always shelled before they are eaten. The shells, like fish skin, are tough when raw, almost rubbery, and usually virtually inedible. Yet proper cooking can make them crisp and delicious, a lot like soft-shell crab.

My technique is similar to methods common in China, where shrimp are often stir-fried in their shells, and Japan, where unpeeled shrimp are simply salted and grilled.

A great deal of the shrimp's flavor is actually contained in the head and shell, and the head is full of delicious buttery juices. The French know this since they use the heads and shells to make sauces. I set out to create a dish in which the shrimp do the talking, one that features the head and shell as much as the meat and expands on the classic Asian treatments. So I liberally season the shrimp with salt, then sear them in olive oil in a very hot skillet so they are extremely crisp. I then toss in shishitoh peppers, a Japanese variety with just a touch of heat but good flavor. (Long frying peppers are a fine substitute.) Chili paste and orange and lemon zest add the last flash of flavor. I serve this dish as an appetizer, unaccompanied, but it would make a fine main course, followed by a salad.

Good shrimp are essential, but they needn't be live or even "fresh" (as opposed to frozen). I believe good frozen shrimp are often better because freezing techniques have become so good. Look for frozen Pacific white shrimp, sold with the heads on in Chinatown and some local markets.

This dish is not complicated; the most time-consuming step is trimming off the tops of the heads, the sharp end of the tails, and the spiny legs. If you like, you can also extract the veins with a toothpick.

The beauty of "soft shell" shrimp is how an uncomplicated preparation presents them in a nearly natural state, demonstrating their true complexity. Once you taste them, you will understand shrimp in a way you never did before.

PAN-GRILLED SHRIMP WITH PEPPERS

2 to 3 pounds shrimp, shells and heads on
Salt
3 tablespoons extra-virgin olive oil
20 shishitoh peppers or 8 long green frying
    peppers, cut into 1-inch pieces and
    seeds removed
1 teaspoon chili paste, or to taste
1 tablespoon orange zest
1 tablespoon lemon zest
Juice of 1 lemon

1. Using a small, sharp knife, cut off only the top of each shrimp's head, including eyes. Also cut away sharp end of tail and tough front legs. If you like, use a toothpick or needle to poke through middle hinge of shell, just below top of each shrimp's back, and slowly draw toothpick out to remove vein. Sprinkle shrimp liberally with salt.

2. Heat a large skillet over high heat for 1 minute. Add oil, and when it smokes, add shrimp. Cook, undisturbed, for 1 minute, or until underside is crisp and pink. Turn and cook a minute longer, and add peppers. With heat still high, cook, stirring occasionally, 1 or 2 minutes more.

3. Add chili paste and zests, and cook for 30 seconds, stirring. Turn off heat, sprinkle with lemon juice, and serve.

Yield: 4 servings
Time: 30 minutes

DUCK: THE MOST SUCCULENT PART

One of the French dishes that have always amazed me is duck confit. I loved it as soon as I first tasted it in 1988 when I came to work at La Caravelle as a saucier. At my previous restaurant job the cooking was very high-end nouvelle, and I had never encountered anything as rustic as these slow-cooked duck legs. They were a revelation: How could duck be so tender and crisp at the same time, and so wonderfully flavored with nothing to it but meat?

Not long after that first taste I started trying to find a way to use the same concept in a dish with Asian flavors.

Duck, of course, is common in several Asian cuisines, but there is no tradition I know of where it is cooked like confit. The traditional French method of simmering duck legs in rendered fat tenderizes them. My method is not traditional, but it is easy—you can almost ignore the bird as it simmers—and after the duck has been refrigerated for a day, you can crisp the skin right before serving.

The classic French method calls for curing the meat in salt and spices like thyme and allspice for a day or more before cooking it. The salt cure preserves the duck, but I dispense with that step. The French idea is that the salting draws out unnecessary water, which is replaced first by salt and later by fat. But I think it also takes out some of the juices and therefore some of the duck's natural flavor.

Instead, I simply season the duck, add the spices to the fat, and cook it, which gives the meat plenty of flavor. Two of the classic French seasonings for confit, thyme and cloves, work perfectly in my Asian-oriented version. To those I add two ingredients identified with Asian cooking, star anise and ginger. The ginger becomes the dominant flavor and really gives the confit spirit.

Many chefs use confited legs in one dish and the duck's breast in another, but I combine them. For one thing it's much easier to buy a whole bird than parts. I prefer an ordinary Peking duck for this dish because more expensive ducks are no more flavorful in confit. You can use the fat and excess skin from the duck to make your own fat for the confit. Just combine them in a saucepan with a tablespoon or two of water to keep them from burning, and cook over low heat until the fat is mostly liquid, with a few pieces of skin floating in it. (Or you can buy duck fat at some markets.)

I bake the confit in a covered saucepan because it's very easy to regulate oven heat. From that point on, the legs must be handled gently. If you refrigerate them in the fat, let them come to room temperature before reheating so that the fat softens and the meat can be removed without falling apart.

The breast is already tender and is best served medium-rare, so it doesn't make sense to confit it. I simply roast it on the bone, as I cook all my meat, so that it stays juicy. Since the breast takes only a few minutes to cook, the timing with the reheated confit is nearly perfect.

To make the Asian theme of this dish more complex, I create a quick sauce based on wasabi and watercress. The watercress mimics the wasabi flavor and some of the same heat, and their colors also match. Fresh wasabi is hard to find and very expensive; wasabi powder works fine. A touch of soy sauce completes the sauce, which cuts through the richness of the duck while intensifying its flavor.

We serve the duck with buckwheat spaetzle, but any fresh egg noodles, tossed with a little butter, would be a lovely side dish.

ASIAN DUCK CONFIT WITH ROASTED DUCK BREAST AND WASABI SAUCE

1 4- to 5-pound duck
Salt
2 cups duck fat, or a bit more
10 nickel-size slices ginger
3 cloves
5 star anise
3 sprigs thyme
Freshly ground black pepper
1 tablespoon plus 1 teaspoon extra-virgin
    olive oil
1 small bunch watercress, stems removed
1 tablespoon wasabi powder
¾ cup duck or chicken stock
2 teaspoons soy sauce

1. Preheat oven to 200 degrees. Cut legs off duck. Cut off second and third joints of wings. Cut breast with its ribs off backbone. Cover and place in refrigerator. (Discard wing tips and backbone or use for stock.) Salt legs well and put in a saucepan with duck fat, ginger, cloves, star anise, and thyme. Bring to a boil. Make sure meat is submerged in fat (add more if necessary), then cover pan with aluminum foil and bake for 4 to 5 hours, or until meat offers almost no resistance when pierced with a thin-bladed knife or skewer. Cool, then refrigerate, fat and all, for at least a day. Bring to room temperature before proceeding.

2. Preheat oven to 450 degrees. Score skin of breast in a crosshatch pattern at ¼-inch intervals and season well with salt and pepper. Put 1 tablespoon oil in an ovenproof skillet over high heat, wait 1 minute, then brown duck on skin side about 2 minutes, moving it occasionally so that it doesn't stick. Transfer to oven. Roast, skin side up, about 15 minutes, or until meat is medium-rare (an instant-read thermometer will register about 130 degrees). Keep warm.

3. While breast is roasting, make sauce: Blanch watercress in boiling salted water to cover about 30 seconds. Drain, rinse in cold water, and squeeze dry. Place in a blender with salt, pepper, wasabi, stock, soy sauce, and remaining 1 teaspoon oil, and puree until smooth. Taste and adjust seasoning—it should be quite hot. Transfer to a small saucepan and warm very gently; do not allow to boil.

4. Remove legs from fat and brown skin under broiler or in a skillet over medium-high heat, less than 5 minutes. Cut breasts off bone and slice thin. Arrange on a plate with some confit and spoon wasabi sauce around.

Yield: 2 to 4 servings
Time: 24 hours (1 hour of active work)

PORK STAYS TENDER UNDER A PANKO BLANKET

Crisp-fried pork is a classic Japanese dish today, but it is actually a very early example of fusion cooking. Sometime early in the twentieth century Europeans brought veal Milanese to Japan. The flavor and style of the breaded and fried veal cutlets became widely popular, but the dish could not be duplicated without importing meat since there is almost no veal in Japan. So it was adapted using pork and Japanese bread crumbs, called panko, and Worcestershire, steak sauce, or ketchup.

In Japan, and in many Japanese restaurants in New York, the pork cutlets are deep-fried and served as a lunch dish. Their appeal is obvious, especially when the dish is done right. The meat remains tender inside the crunchy panko coating, and the sauce offsets the pork's mildness.

Almost any cut of pork can be used, from the tenderloin to the shoulder or the loin. I prefer to cut pork tenderloin into medallions. I found that deep-frying them is unnecessary; the meat can be fried in a skillet and just needs to be turned once. The cooking time is only five minutes. As long as the pork is not overcooked, it remains moist and tender, protected by the panko coating.

In adapting this dish for my menu, the tricky part was the sauce. I wanted to draw from tradition but also make something that had great character of its own. I started with tomato paste and chicken stock, added garlic that had been slowly cooked in olive oil, and ended with both Western and Eastern accents: Dijon mustard and soy sauce. The result is much fresher and brighter tasting than either Worcestershire sauce or ketchup.

It is also rich enough to serve on white rice, the traditional and perfect accompaniment. At the restaurant I also serve the dish with root vegetables such as burdock, lotus, daikon, carrots, or turnips that have been parboiled until nearly tender, stir-fried in light oil, *and finished with a little sesame oil and sugar. Another possibility is a green salad or the kind of "coleslaw" often served in Japan—shredded cabbage lightly dressed with oil and rice vinegar.*

CRISPY PORK CUTLETS WITH SPICY TOMATO SAUCE

10 large cloves garlic, peeled
½ cup extra-virgin olive oil
1½ pounds pork tenderloin
2 tablespoons tomato paste
2 cups chicken or vegetable stock
¼ cup Dijon mustard
2 tablespoons soy sauce
Canola, grapeseed, or other neutral oil
Flour
1 cup milk
2 cups (approximately) panko

1. Preheat oven to 200 degrees. Combine garlic and olive oil in a small ovenproof dish and cover with aluminum foil. Bake until garlic is very tender, about 45 minutes. Leave oven on. Remove garlic and mash with a fork. Set aside 1 tablespoon oil; reserve remainder in refrigerator for other uses such as sautéing or vinaigrettes.

2. Remove any gristle from pork and slice 1 inch thick. Put slices between 2 sheets of plastic wrap and pound gently with a mallet, side of a cleaver, or bottom of a pot until meat is ¼ to ½ inch thick. (Pork is so tender that this will not take much effort.)

3. Put reserved olive oil in a small saucepan and turn heat to medium-high. Add tomato paste and cook, stirring constantly, until fragrant, about 2 minutes. Stir in stock and cook over medium heat, stirring occasionally, until reduced by about

half and fairly thick, about 10 minutes. Stir in garlic, mustard, and soy sauce to thicken sauce; keep warm.

4. Cook pork while sauce is reducing or after it is finished. Pour neutral oil to a depth of ½ inch in a skillet over medium-high heat. Dredge each piece of pork lightly in flour, dip in milk, then press into panko. When oil is hot (a pinch of flour will sizzle), add a few pieces at a time to skillet; do not crowd. Cook for 2 or 3 minutes per side, or until nicely browned. As medallions finish cooking, drain on paper towels and keep warm in oven. When all are cooked, nap with sauce and serve, preferably with white rice.

Yield: 4 servings
Time: 1½ hours

FOR THAT CRUNCH TIME BEFORE THE FOOD ARRIVES

When we were planning our menu at Sono, we had to decide what to offer people while they waited to order. We wanted to serve something like bread, but not the usual sourdough because of the menu's Japanese overtones. In Japan a starchy food would never be served until the end of the meal. Starches are considered inexpensive fillers, which reduce full appreciation of the main dishes. In New York, though, people expect bread when they sit down in a restaurant.

So my pastry chef, Christine Chang, and I came up with a paper-thin crunchy flatbread. It has a lot in common with both Indian papadum and Japanese rice crackers, but it is a bread with no real roots, a supercrisp cracker that is fun to eat. We serve large irregular sheets of the flatbread arranged vertically in a holder so that diners can break off crunchy bits to nibble.

The bread is made with a plain dough of white flour and water, which is easily put together by hand, in a mixer, or in a food processor. To flavor it we most often use a mixture of black and white sesame seeds, as in the recipe below. They add crunch along with flavor. At other times we add dried shiso, which tastes a little like minty basil; dried crumbled nori; or curry powder.

You can also try saffron, which would lend the dough a beautiful color, or anise, or ground cardamom or cumin, or any combination. We serve the flatbreads on their own, but you can serve them with a dip, like miso thinned with a little white wine or a mayonnaise flavored with soy sauce.

This is not a delicate dough, and it need not be handled carefully. It just has to be allowed to rest thoroughly after it is mixed and before it is rolled out, so that it relaxes. To roll it out, you can use a rolling pin or a pasta machine. Once the dough is laid on a baking sheet, you can stretch it out even thinner before baking it. Since this recipe makes six large sheets, you can freeze extra dough for as long as a couple of weeks if you like. Defrost it in the refrigerator overnight before rolling it out.

SESAME FLATBREADS

2 cups all-purpose flour
½ tablespoon sesame seeds, preferably white and black mixed
1 tablespoon sugar
1 teaspoon salt
1 tablespoon lime juice
1½ tablespoons olive oil

1. The dough can be made by hand, in a mixer equipped with a dough hook, or in a food processor. By hand or with a mixer, mix dry ingredients together in a bowl. Stir in lime juice and oil, then gradually add about ¾ cup water, mixing well until you have a fairly sticky but not too soft dough. Knead until dough is smooth and elastic, using as little additional flour as possible. Dough should be somewhat sticky, like pizza dough. To make dough in a food processor, combine flour, sugar, salt, lime juice, and oil, and pulse once or twice. With machine on, gradually add about ¾ cup water, enough to make dough gather into a ball. Process for 15 seconds or so longer, then knead sesame seeds in by hand with as little additional flour as possible. Dough should be somewhat sticky, like pizza dough.

2. Gather dough into a ball, wrap in plastic, and refrigerate at least a couple of hours, preferably overnight.

3. Preheat oven to 350 degrees. Cut dough into 6 pieces and rewrap 5 of them. Roll out remaining piece with a pasta machine or rolling pin on a lightly floured surface until dough is as thin as possible without tearing it. Rolling with a pin will leave edges thicker than center. (Irregularities of thickness are a pleasant feature.) Put dough on a dry cookie sheet, stretching it as much as you can and anchoring edges by pressing them to sheet. If small tears occur, ignore them. Patch large tears or start over.

4. Bake for 10 to 15 minutes, or until golden brown. Break into pieces and eat immediately. You can bake breads all at once or store remaining dough in refrigerator for several days.

Yield: 6 flatbreads
Time: 1 hour, plus at least 2 hours of chilling

A GLOSSY COAT OF MISO FLAVORS A STEAK

During the last few years, fish marinated in miso has become a popular dish in restaurants all over town. It's not hard to understand why. The preparation is instantly appealing: The miso transforms the texture of the fish while adding an intriguing interplay of sweet, salty, and tangy flavors.

But equally popular in Japan, and hardly ever seen here, is meat glazed with miso. Miso is, of course, the delicious Japanese paste made from fermented soybeans and sometimes other grains like rice and barley. It is intensely savory, as powerful a flavoring as Parmesan. But you wouldn't want to use it in a marinade with meat; you don't want to permeate the flesh with flavor as much as complement it. A glaze for pan-grilled steaks seems an ideal way to do that.

Miso, it turns out, works perfectly in place of long-cooked meat stock. It provides the same depth of flavor but with almost none of the effort: A package of miso is one of the great convenience foods.

The glaze begins with aromatics softening in butter—garlic and shallots in the French style, but ginger as well—and continues with a reduction of red wine. Its character is transformed by two ingredients: mirin, Japanese sweet cooking wine; and toban djan, Japanese chili bean paste. (Both are sold at Asian markets, but you can substitute equal parts of water and honey for the mirin and a spicy Asian chili paste for the toban djan.) I prefer country-style miso, which is made with rice and soy; it is medium-bodied and slightly sweet (or use half light and half dark miso).

When you top a cooked steak with the glaze and run it under the broiler, it becomes glossy, quite sweet, and a little crisp—perhaps comparable to the most sophisticated ketchup you can imagine. Because I chop the aromatics rather than mince them, they remain somewhat

chunky and a little crunchy, giving the glaze additional texture.

With the steak I serve a simple seared, unseasoned eggplant, which can be used to mop up the delicious juices from the meat and glaze. It has the creamy texture that you usually look for when cooking eggplant, but without a lot of oil or stirring.

BEEF WITH MISO-CHILE SAUCE

1 pound eggplant (preferably 4 small)
3 tablespoons butter
2 tablespoons chopped shallots
1 tablespoon peeled and not-too-finely
    minced ginger
1 teaspoon not-too-finely minced garlic
1/4 teaspoon toban djan or other chili paste
    (see headnote)
3/4 cup dry red wine
2 tablespoons mirin
2 tablespoons country-style miso or a mixture
    of light and dark miso (see headnote)
3 tablespoons extra-virgin olive oil
Salt and freshly ground black pepper
4 6- to 8-ounce steaks, preferably rib eye,
    sirloin, or hanger steaks, or use an
    equivalent amount of filet mignon
1/4 cup chopped chives

1. Preheat oven to 450 degrees. If you are using small eggplants, cut in half the long way and make a 1/4-inch crosshatch pattern on flesh side. If you are using 1 large eggplant, cut 1/2- to 1-inch-thick slices and make 1/4-inch crosshatch pattern on both sides.

2. In a small saucepan, put 2 tablespoons butter and turn heat to medium-high. When it

foams, add shallots, ginger, and garlic, and cook, stirring, about 30 seconds; don't let vegetables become too soft. Stir in chile paste and cook, stirring, another 30 seconds or so, until mixture is uniformly colored. Add wine and reduce, stirring occasionally, until pasty but not dry. Stir in mirin and cook until most of it is absorbed. Stir in miso until well blended, dark, and glossy. Turn heat very low and keep warm.

3. In a large skillet, put 2 tablespoons oil and turn heat to medium-high. Place eggplant in pan, skin side down, and cook until it begins to brown. Turn heat down a bit and cook 2 minutes more, then place in oven for 5 minutes or so, until tender.

4. Meanwhile, put remaining 1 tablespoon butter and 1 tablespoon oil in a large skillet and turn heat to high. Season steaks with salt and pepper and, a minute later, sear them on both sides until rare-to-medium, according to taste, about 2 to 3 minutes per side. Set aside in a warm place and turn on broiler.

5. Stir any liquid that has accumulated around steaks into miso sauce, then glaze steaks generously with sauce. Run steaks under broiler until sauce bubbles and begins to burn a little bit, 2 to 5 minutes. Serve steaks with eggplant, garnished with chives.

Yield: 4 servings
Time: 40 minutes

GIVING RICE PUDDING A COCONUT MILK TWIST

Many people are surprised to find rice pudding, a classic American comfort food, on my menu. But to me it seems a natural choice. Rice is tremendously important in Japanese cuisine, and I knew we could create a rice pudding that departed from the ordinary. What Christine Chang, our pastry chef, and I came up with follows the typical technique, which is to simmer rice in sweetened milk until it is soft and creamy, but the result has a flavor and texture that are completely unexpected.

My simmering liquid is half coconut milk, which is richer than milk and adds its own flavor. I use short-grain sushi rice, which becomes softer and creamier than long-grain rice and, because of its high gluten content, has a chewier texture. I cook the rice until it can hold a shape. The result is less like American rice pudding than a creamy version of Asian sticky rice.

It is best to simmer the rice in a wide-bottomed pot so that the liquid can evaporate quickly; this keeps the rice from becoming too mushy, and it leaves the core of each grain distinct as the entire mixture becomes creamy. The technique is very much like that for risotto—the pudding requires near-constant stirring, too—and, in fact, the results are not dissimilar.

At the restaurant we lay shallow five-inch rings on a nonstick surface and pack the pudding into the rings, smoothing the top. At home it's probably easier to spoon the pudding into custard cups or ramekins. They can sit at room temperature for a few hours or be refrigerated for up to a day. Just before serving we grate a layer of palm sugar on top and caramelize it with a propane torch; at home, brown sugar can substitute. Caramelize it under the broiler (set the rack as close to the heat source as you can and watch carefully).

Traditionally, rice pudding is topped with whipped cream, but instead of adding more creaminess and sweetness, I created a tart, bright green syrup with lime juice and zest that adds a spark of color and cleanses the palate of the pudding's richness.

COCONUT RICE PUDDING
WITH LIME SYRUP

1½ cups sugar
4 limes
3 cups whole milk
3 cups canned coconut milk
1 vanilla bean
¾ cup short-grain (sushi) rice
1 teaspoon salt
6 teaspoons palm or brown sugar

1. Set a small pot of water to boil. In a separate pot, combine ½ cup sugar and ½ cup water and bring to a boil. Cook for a few seconds, until sugar dissolves. Zest limes and place zest in boiling water for 10 seconds, no more; drain through a strainer and plunge into ice water to chill. Set aside. Juice limes and add to sugar syrup. Cook over medium heat, stirring only occasionally, until it darkens and thickens, about 20 minutes. Let cool, then stir in lime zest and set aside.

2. Put rice in a deep bowl and run cold water on it, stirring by hand. Drain and repeat until excess starch is removed and water runs clear. In a wide, deep, heavy-bottomed saucepan, combine milk and coconut milk, then turn heat to medium-high. Split vanilla bean lengthwise and scrape out seeds; add to milk along with rice, remaining 1 cup sugar, and salt. When liquid begins to boil, adjust heat so that it bubbles steadily but not vigorously; if mixture begins to brown, turn heat down a little more. Stir occasionally at first, then more and more frequently, until mixture becomes thick and much like oatmeal, about 25 minutes total.

3. Spoon pudding into 6 ramekins and let cool to room temperature (you can refrigerate for up to a day, but these are best at room temperature). Before serving, sprinkle top of each pudding with palm or brown sugar and use a propane torch or run under a broiler until sugar bubbles and begins to burn. Serve drizzled with lime syrup.

Yield: 6 servings
Time: about 1 hour

CHRISTIAN DELOUVRIER

Christian Delouvrier is the executive chef of Lespinasse
in Manhattan. He was photographed in the lobby of the St. Regis Hotel,
where the restaurant is located. These columns were written with Melissa Clark.

ENRICHING SALMON WITH A SIMPLE TECHNIQUE AND A GENTLE TOUCH

Salmon confit with arugula is a luxurious dish—so luxurious that it is best in small portions. I love it as an appetizer or, at the restaurant, as a small course on the tasting menu. Like so many dishes that appeal to me, it relies on perfect, simple ingredients and classical French technique.

The idea of making a confit out of fish came from my sous-chef, Neil Annis. The fish cooks gently in hot oil, so the flesh doesn't shrink or fall apart but instead takes on a silken richness. The flavor intensifies, and even the color turns a deeper shade of rose. In a classic confit, duck is cooked in its own rendered fat, but I didn't think duck fat would work well with salmon. Salmon is an oily fish; the added flavor of poultry fat would only be a distraction. So instead, I decided to try olive oil, which is light enough to let the true flavor of the

salmon shine through. In the finished dish, it is undetectable.

In April and May, I like to use wild salmon from the Copper River. It's a beautiful fish, with dark pink flesh that's a little less fatty than other types of salmon. Other times of the year I use a farmed salmon from Scotland, which is also very good.

To make the confit, we heat the oil on the stove, then place the pan on a heated marble slab (it's really a plate warmer). That keeps the oil at the right temperature, about 140 degrees, for the whole night. At home you can simply heat the oil in a heavy pan, then take it off the heat; the fish will cook before the oil cools down.

Once I had the technique for cooking the salmon, the rest of the dish was easy. I keep it very spare, using only four elements on the plate. I place a rectangular chunk of the salmon on a little pile of baby arugula, which is a bit sour and cuts through the fatty fish. I never use a vinaigrette; the juices from the salmon coat the greens and keep the flavors focused. But I do drizzle a one-hundred-year-old balsamic vinegar around the edge of the plate, and together with the salmon juices, it is essentially a deconstructed dressing.

I use a very good vinegar, so concentrated it's almost like a syrup. It can be very, very expensive, as much as $130 a bottle, so in this recipe, I give you a trick. By reducing regular balsamic vinegar, you can create a thick liquid that imitates the texture and sweet flavor of the aged vinegar.

But there is another ingredient that simply can't be skimped on: the coarse sea salt I sprinkle on top of the salmon. I use sel de Guerande, a moist, gray salt from France. It's not difficult to find (even some supermarkets have it), and it's not terribly costly, about $2 for a nine-ounce canister. Sel de Guerande is unlike any other salt; it retains some of the mineral flavors of the sea and has an almost foamy sort of crunch. And in the end, the sea salt is what brings the dish to life.

SALMON CONFIT IN OLIVE OIL WITH ARUGULA AND BALSAMIC VINEGAR

⅓ cup balsamic vinegar
4 1-inch-thick pieces skinless salmon fillet (2 to 3 ounces each)
1 sprig fresh parsley
1 sprig fresh thyme
1 bay leaf
1 quart extra-virgin olive oil
2 cups (about 1½ ounces) baby arugula, washed and dried
Coarse gray sea salt (sel de Guerande) to taste

1. In a small saucepan, bring vinegar to a simmer over high heat. Turn heat to low and simmer mixture until reduced by half, about 10 minutes. Let cool and set aside.

2. Rinse salmon and pat dry. Using string, tie parsley, thyme, and bay leaf into a bundle.

3. In a large, deep skillet, preferably cast iron, combine oil and herb bundle. Cook over medium-high heat until oil reaches 140 degrees. Remove pan from heat and immediately add salmon pieces. Let salmon rest (carefully turning it once) until it turns opaque on outside but is still rosy inside, about 3 to 4 minutes total. Transfer salmon pieces to a paper towel–lined plate to drain and pat top of pieces with paper towels. Discard herb bundle.

4. To serve, divide arugula among 4 plates. Place salmon on top of arugula and sprinkle with sea salt. Drizzle a teaspoon of reduced balsamic vinegar around each plate. Serve at once.

Yield: 4 appetizer servings
Time: 20 minutes

A ROBUST RABBIT WITH TOUCHES OF SPRING

In France one of the most traditional ways to serve rabbit is hunter's style, a robust stew made with mushrooms, onions, and herbs—the sorts of foods a hunter might come upon on his way home through the woods. It's a hearty dish that was popular when I was growing up; my mother and grandmother often made it, and I still do. But at the restaurant I treat this rustic dish with an elegant touch. Instead of stewing pieces of the meat in a sauce, I roast the rabbit quickly at a high temperature so the skin becomes crisp and brown while the meat remains succulent. My sauce is enriched by the rabbit trimmings, tomato, garlic, carrot, and herbs.

And I serve it on a particularly creamy polenta made with milk and Parmesan. It's as rich and soft as a buttery potato puree, an extravagant partner for the lean rabbit meat. Polenta is, of course, not so typical in France; mashed potatoes or rice would be served instead, and you could do that, too.

As the weather begins to warm, I look forward to bringing touches of spring to the plate with vegetables like blanched asparagus tips sautéed in butter until the ends crisp, and morels, gently stewed with olive oil and herbs. But even with all those embellishments, at heart this is still a simple dish. Its success depends on having a fresh, young rabbit; frozen ones tend to toughen during cooking. And because the meat is extremely lean, it's important not to overcook. The rabbit can even be taken off the heat a little early, when it's still slightly pink near the bone. Then it can finish cooking as it rests under a sheet of foil.

ROASTED RABBIT WITH POLENTA

3 tablespoons extra-virgin olive oil

2 tablespoons butter

2 rabbits, hind legs and forelegs separated from loins, hind legs cut in two at joints, and trimmings reserved

Kosher salt to taste

4 white button mushrooms, quartered

1 large onion, chopped

1 carrot, sliced

12 cloves garlic, smashed and peeled

1½ tablespoons tomato paste

¾ cup white wine

2 medium tomatoes, cubed

1 bunch tarragon

1 bunch thyme

3 shallots, sliced

For the polenta:

5 cups milk

1 cup quick-cooking polenta

1 teaspoon salt, or to taste

½ cup grated Parmesan cheese

3 tablespoons butter

1. In a large, deep skillet over high heat, heat 1 tablespoon oil and 1 tablespoon butter. Add rabbit forelegs, trimmings (except liver), and salt. Cook over high heat, stirring, until golden brown on all sides. Add mushrooms, onion, carrot, 4 cloves garlic, and tomato paste, and cook, stirring, until vegetables are tender, about 10 minutes. Add ½ cup wine and simmer until it evaporates. Add tomatoes, ½ bunch tarragon, ½ bunch thyme, and water to just cover. Simmer until reduced by half, about 1 hour. Strain, pressing on solids. Discard solids.

2. Place loins on a work surface with cavities

facing up. Lay remaining ½ bunch thyme and ½ bunch tarragon and 8 cloves garlic on centers of each loin. Roll up loins so that filling is enclosed and tie with kitchen twine.

3. Preheat oven to 450 degrees. In a large ovenproof skillet over high heat, heat remaining 2 tablespoons oil and 1 tablespoon butter. Add loins and hind legs, and sear until golden brown; add salt to taste. Place skillet in oven and roast 5 minutes. Turn rabbit pieces, lower temperature to 425 degrees, and roast until meat is slightly pink at bone, 15 to 20 minutes. Transfer rabbit to a platter (reserving skillet and its drippings) and cover with aluminum foil to keep warm. Let rabbit rest for 10 to 15 minutes.

4. To finish sauce, place skillet with drippings over medium heat. Add shallots and sauté until tender, about 5 minutes. Add remaining ¼ cup wine and cook until it evaporates. Add sauce and simmer for 10 minutes. Strain sauce, pressing hard on shallots.

5. While sauce simmers, prepare polenta: In a medium saucepan, simmer milk. Add polenta and salt, whisking well, until polenta absorbs milk but is still soft, 5 to 7 minutes. Stir in cheese and butter. Keep warm.

6. Cut twine off loins and remove garlic and herbs. Carve loin meat off bones. Arrange loin and leg meat over polenta. Pour sauce around meat and serve.

Yield: 4 servings
Time: 1½ hours, plus 1 hour of simmering

MINUTE RISOTTO (ALMOST)

To many cooks, risotto is a dish with heavy connotations: It takes time and attention—lots of attention—and often emerges from all that simmering and stirring in a slightly leaden state. What you want from risotto is more ethereal, something that is luxuriously rich, yet airy and light. And if you can get there without all the work, so much the better.

I can assure you, it is possible.

First, no restaurant has time to make risotto the traditional way, which requires twenty straight minutes of standing at the stove as you sauté the rice and then slowly add hot broth. The usual chef's shortcut calls for cooking the rice partway, then chilling it and finishing the dish by simmering and stirring just before serving.

My method is not like that at all; in fact, I've actually eliminated the stirring altogether. My final cooking time is less than six minutes, and I get such terrific results—firm grains suspended in a creamy sauce—that even if I had the time, I wouldn't go back to the traditional method. I learned my shortcut from some colleagues who had worked in the south of France. They apparently picked it up from some Italian cooks they met there. Since then, I've seen this method used in kitchens here and in France.

Early in the day we simmer Arborio rice in white wine, then let it cool. When an order for risotto comes into the kitchen, we simply finish the rice by simmering it in a good chicken broth, then adding a touch of Parmesan cheese along with whatever flavorings we are using that day. A spoon never comes near the pot except to dish up the finished risotto.

I go a step further by embellishing it with a cloudlike ring of foamed liquid spooned over the top at the last minute. While the foam reinforces the flavors in the risotto, it also does something far more important: It lifts the earthiness of the rice and contributes to the sensation of lightness.

Turning liquids into foams is a technique I began to see in Paris restaurants several years ago. Usually used as a playful garnish, foams can also add a lot of flavor to a dish, especially if you start out with an intense liquid. For example, with a black truffle risotto I make a foam of chicken broth scented with black truffle oil; for a tomato risotto I infuse the broth with pesto and basil oil. You can experiment with oils infused with other flavors in the foam, like citrus, or other herbs or spices, or you can flavor the broth itself.

I prepare the foams using a commercial immersion blender fitted with a ruffled blade, which is a perfect whipping tool. At home, you can get the same results with a standard immersion blender if you add frozen butter to the broth as you whip it.

Risotto is a perfect base for showcasing seasonal ingredients. By itself, it has a relatively neutral taste, but any addition gives it more dimension. In winter, I like fresh black truffles. Their magnificent fragrance and lingering flavor are best set off by a starch, which makes risotto a perfect partner. I also love the way the dish has the stark black and white color scheme of a chessboard.

As the weather warms, I look forward to a springtime risotto with asparagus and lemon. I prepare butter with Meyer lemon juice and zest, and use that for both the risotto and the foam. I add blanched, sliced asparagus and zest from the lemon at the end of cooking. To give the foam an added boost, I add lemon oil.

In the summer, I use beautiful ripe tomatoes in my risotto. As good as they are on their own, I intensify the flavor—and eliminate some of the moisture that would otherwise dilute the risotto—by roasting them in an herb-infused olive oil as you would with confit.

The possibilities for flavoring risotto are endless, as long as you stick to a few basic principles. One is to keep whatever you may add small, not much bigger than the grains of rice. Another is to precook the vegetables and stir them in at the end of cooking to heat them up.

In the fall, you can switch to vegetables like butternut squash and puree them before folding them in at the last minute.

WINTER BLACK TRUFFLE RISOTTO

4 ounces (about ¾ cup) Arborio rice
½ cup white wine
6 tablespoons unsalted butter
2 ounces fresh or jarred black winter truffles
2½ cups strong chicken broth
2 tablespoons crème fraîche
1 tablespoon black truffle oil
⅓ cup freshly grated Parmesan cheese
Salt and freshly ground pepper to taste

1. In a medium saucepan over medium heat, combine rice and wine. Simmer until wine is absorbed, then let cool.

2. Cut 2 tablespoons butter into ½-inch dice and place in freezer. Reserve remaining butter at room temperature.

3. Using a stiff brush, clean truffles. If using jarred truffles, rinse well. Using a truffle slicer, mandoline, or sharp knife, slice 8 thin slices off largest truffle. Coarsely chop remaining truffles and set aside.

4. Return rice to stove and add 1¼ cups broth to pan. Simmer until rice is *al dente* and most of liquid is absorbed, about 6 to 7 minutes.

5. While rice is cooking, prepare foam. In another saucepan, simmer remaining 1¼ cups broth. Add crème fraîche and oil, and remove pan from heat. Using an immersion blender, whip mixture, adding frozen butter cubes gradually. Continue to whip until very foamy, about 2 minutes.

6. Stir cheese into rice and remove from heat.

Stir in chopped truffles and remaining 4 table-spoons butter, then add salt and pepper. Divide risotto among 4 bowls and top with truffle slices. Rewhip foam if necessary and spoon it on top of risotto and around inside edges of bowls. Serve immediately.

Yield: 3 to 4 servings as an appetizer or side dish
Time: about 1 hour

SUMMER TOMATO BASIL RISOTTO

For the tomato confit:
    2½ cups extra-virgin olive oil
    3 cloves garlic, peeled
    2 tablespoons coriander seeds
    1 bay leaf
    1 sprig thyme
    4 large ripe tomatoes, cored, halved, and
        seeded

For the risotto:
    4 ounces (about ¾ cup) Arborio rice
    ½ cup white wine
    6 tablespoons unsalted butter
    2½ cups strong chicken broth
    2 tablespoons pesto
    2 tablespoons crème fraîche
    1 tablespoon basil oil
    ⅓ cup freshly grated Parmesan cheese
    Salt and freshly ground pepper to taste

1. To make tomato confit: Preheat oven to 200 degrees. In an 8 by 8-inch pan, combine oil, garlic, coriander, bay leaf, and thyme. Place to-matoes, cut side down, into oil. Cover pan with aluminum foil, poking a hole or two to let steam escape. Bake tomatoes for 2 hours, until very ten-der and skins pull away from flesh easily. Let cool. Peel tomatoes and chop. Discard oil and season-ings. Makes about 2 cups.

2. To make risotto: In a medium saucepan over medium heat, combine rice and wine. Sim-mer until wine is absorbed. Let cool.

3. Cut 2 tablespoons butter into ½-inch dice and place in freezer. Reserve remaining butter at room temperature.

4. Return rice to stove and add 1¼ cups broth to pan. Simmer until rice is *al dente* and most of liquid is absorbed, about 6 to 7 minutes.

5. While rice is cooking, prepare foam. In an-other saucepan, simmer remaining 1¼ cups broth and pesto. Strain through a fine sieve into a clean bowl and add crème fraîche and oil. Using an immersion blender, whip mixture, adding frozen butter cubes gradually. Continue to whip until very foamy, about 2 minutes.

6. Stir ⅓ cup tomato confit and cheese into rice and season with salt and pepper. Divide risotto among 4 bowls. Rewhip foam if necessary and spoon on top of risotto and around inside edges of bowls. Serve immediately.

Yield: 3 to 4 servings as an appetizer or side dish
Time: about 1 hour, plus 2 hours for confit

APPLES WITH A RICH SURPRISE

The combination of foie gras and apples has always had a powerful appeal to me. I even used to serve a foie gras "burger" in which the fruit acted as the bun for the meat. It was more than a culinary conceit: The sweet and tangy apple set off the rich and fatty duck liver to perfection. These days I'm putting those two partners together again in a new marriage that's more traditional but just as extraordinary. The foie gras is still seared so it has a great crisp edge, but the apples are more like a throne than a bun.

Roasted apples and foie gras are a very old Périgord dish, a reminder of my childhood near Toulouse and the boudin noir, *or spicy blood sausage, we ate with sautéed apples. Foie gras has the same saltiness and certainly the same richness. Traditionally, the dish is simple and unadorned: The apples are roasted in duck fat until they practically fall apart, then halved and stuffed with seared foie gras and baked again.*

My variation is more refined. I start with Gala apples, which have a beautiful color and shape, and bake them until they are only slightly softened. I fill them with a puree of roasted Golden Delicious apples, my favorites for their honeyed, slightly floral taste. The foie gras sits on that bed, and tiny cubes of Granny Smith apples in a sauce with dried sour cherries finish the dish, along with a tart cranberry sauce.

I also use two kinds of vinegar to balance the sweetness and richness of the dish. Cider vinegar adds a jolt of flavor; sherry vinegar brings up the flavor of the little sauté of Granny Smith cubes.

As much as I consider this dish a celebration of apples, its heart is the seared foie gras. I use a whole lobe, trimmed and cut into thick slices. Don't be afraid to pull it apart to remove the unsightly large veins. Foie gras is forgiving, and you can pat it back into shape if it's slightly damaged.

The pan for searing it must also be very, very hot to get the crisp edge. And the slices should be cooked only a minute or so; the longer you cook them, the more fat they will lose, and the smaller they will become. And they should be more than just a garnish for these luxurious baked apples.

ROASTED APPLES WITH SAUTÉED FOIE GRAS

- 1 cup frozen cranberries
- ¼ cup plus 5 teaspoons sugar
- 1 Grade A duck foie gras (about 1 pound)
- 8 Golden Delicious apples, cored
- 8 tablespoons melted butter
- 8 Gala apples
- Salt and freshly ground black pepper to taste
- 2 Granny Smith apples, peeled, cored, and cut into ¼-inch cubes
- ¼ cup chopped dried cherries
- 1 tablespoon sherry vinegar
- 2 teaspoons cider vinegar

1. Combine cranberries and ¼ cup sugar in a small pan. Cook, stirring and mashing, about 15 to 20 minutes. Let cool and then puree in a blender or food processor. Strain, pressing on solids, and set aside.

2. Rinse foie gras and pat dry. Using a small, sharp knife, trim away large veins and membranes. Cut foie gras crosswise into 8 slices about 1½ inches thick. Refrigerate.

3. Preheat oven to 350 degrees. Arrange Golden Delicious apples in a baking pan and drizzle each one with ½ tablespoon butter and ½ teaspoon sugar. Bake until very soft, 35 to 40 minutes. Let cool, then peel apples and puree. Strain and set aside.

4. While Golden Delicious apples are baking,

prepare Galas. Slice off just enough of bottoms so apples will stand upright. Slice 1 inch off tops, then use a melon baller to hollow out tops and centers, reserving flesh and leaving a ¼-inch border. Brush apples and tops with 2 tablespoons butter. Return apple flesh to apples to help them keep their shape, and replace tops. Bake until tender but not mushy, about 20 minutes. Discard apple flesh. Cover shells and tops with aluminum foil to keep warm. Leave oven on.

5. Season foie gras slices with salt and pepper on both sides. Place a large ovenproof skillet over high heat. Add foie gras and cook until well browned but still firm in center, 30 seconds a side. Transfer to oven and bake for 1 minute, until center is soft.

6. Put remaining 2 tablespoons butter in a small skillet, add Granny Smith cubes, cherries, and remaining 1 teaspoon sugar, and sauté for 2 minutes. Add sherry vinegar and cook until evaporated, 1 to 2 minutes.

7. Reheat apple puree in a small saucepan. Fill each apple shell with puree. Stir cider vinegar into remaining puree and spoon about 1½ tablespoons in center of 8 plates. Stand apple shells in puree and lay a slice of foie gras in each apple. Spoon a bit of apple-cherry mixture over foie gras. Place tops on apples at an angle to expose foie gras. Drizzle cranberry sauce around plate and serve.

Yield: 8 servings
Time: 2 hours

A SPIN ON THE PERFECTION OF CRÈME BRÛLÉE

Crème Brûlée is all about contrast, about the way the crackling crust of hot caramelized sugar yields to the creamy richness of the cold custard underneath. It's a perfect dessert made with just vanilla, but I wanted to take it to another level. Literally.

What I conceived is a layering of two separate flavored custards under that crunchy crust. A spoon scooped into this crème brûlée captures not just the caramelized topping but also a base of chocolate and a center of coffee custard. The flavors almost cascade.

Odd as it may sound, I took my inspiration for layering from a fish terrine made with a base of pale ivory fish mousse under an intense orange lobster mousse. To combine them neatly, the bottom layer is frozen before the top layer is added. I wasn't sure if this technique would work with custards, which are thin and runny compared with firm mousses. My pastry chef, Chris Broberg, put my concept to the test.

First, he made a dark chocolate custard—like the most intense chocolate pudding you can imagine—and froze it in ramekins overnight. The next day, he poured a coffee custard over the tops, then baked the ramekins until the edges were set. Once they cooled, we could see that our little trick had worked. The top layer solidifies before the bottom layer melts.

The advantage to this crème brûlée is that most of it can be—in fact, must be—made in advance. The custards can be baked up to two days ahead (though one day is optimal), then caramelized just before serving.

I like to keep the caramel layer very, very thin, just a hint of crackle across the top. We use a miniature blowtorch to caramelize the sugar, but a broiler works very well. Watch the custards very carefully, moving them around if they begin to caramelize unevenly, and pulling any from the heat before they get too dark. Bitterness from burning ruins the contrast.

CHOCOLATE-COFFEE CRÈME BRÛLÉE

For the chocolate custard:

3½ tablespoons sugar

1 tablespoon plus 1 teaspoon unsweetened cocoa powder

1 cup heavy cream

2 large egg yolks

¼ vanilla bean, halved lengthwise and seeds scraped out and reserved

For the coffee custard:

2 large egg yolks

2½ tablespoons sugar

1 tablespoon instant coffee

1 cup heavy cream

¼ vanilla bean, halved lengthwise and seeds scraped out and reserved

3 tablespoons extra-fine granulated sugar

1. To prepare chocolate custard: Whisk together 2 tablespoons sugar and cocoa in a small bowl. Bring cream to a simmer in a small saucepan. Add cocoa mixture and whisk well. Return to a simmer, then turn off heat and let cool.

2. In a medium bowl, whisk together egg yolks, remaining 1½ tablespoons sugar, and vanilla bean scrapings with seeds. Whisk in cooled cream mixture. Strain custard through a fine sieve and divide among six 4-ounce ramekins or custard cups. Cover with plastic wrap and freeze for at least 8 hours or overnight.

3. Preheat oven to 350 degrees. To prepare coffee custard: Whisk together egg yolks, sugar, and instant coffee in a medium bowl until coffee dissolves. Whisk in cream and vanilla bean scrapings with seeds. Strain mixture, then pour into ramekins over frozen chocolate custard.

4. Arrange ramekins in a baking pan and place on oven rack. Pour enough very hot water into pan to reach two-thirds of the way up sides of ramekins. Cover baking pan with aluminum foil and prick in a few places with a knife. Bake for 40 to 45 minutes, until custards are set around edges but still slightly jiggly in center. Transfer ramekins to a rack and let cool. Cover and refrigerate at least 6 hours or overnight.

5. Just before serving, sprinkle a thin, even coating of extra-fine granulated sugar on each custard. Using a preheated broiler or kitchen blowtorch, caramelize sugar. It will take about 30 seconds with a blowtorch or 1 to 2 minutes under a broiler.

Yield: 6 servings

Time: about 2 hours, plus overnight freezing and chilling

DEPTH AND COMPLEXITY
IN A CLASSIC SAUCE

When I first learned how to make this dish, I was a young assistant sauce chef at Café de la Paix in Paris. The head sauce chef, a man named Charles Lejay, was very particular about this preparation, a classic of French cooking. In fact, I had to watch him make it for months before he would let me near the stove.

The dish is entirely about building a sauce; every step adds a layer of depth and complexity. The lobster is simmered in the shell, which releases its flavors into the base of the sauce. The simmering liquid—a heady base of wine, tomatoes, shallots, garlic, and herbs—builds and condenses, and is set aflame with Armagnac. The innards of the lobster (the tomalley and, if it is a female, the coral) are whisked in for their briny nuance, and the sauce is finished with a nugget of butter and more Armagnac.

The result is light and satiny, nothing like the thick glaze you might expect. The balance of aromatic, acidic, and sweet ingredients stands up to and harmonizes with the lobster, while the butter adds smoothness and softness.

My version here is even lighter than the preparation I was taught or the one I make now at the restaurant. There, I can use many more lobsters to make the sauce (the meat from some goes into other dishes, like lobster salad). Using more lobsters means I can simmer the sauce longer and develop a deeper flavor. If you simmered the sauce that long at home, it would extract more flavor, but it would ruin the wonderful lightness. I choose delicacy over potency.

I have also made the dish simpler in other ways. I use a good chicken stock instead of a fish stock (Chef Lejay insisted on stock made with only sole bones). I serve the meat in its shell, and sometimes I ask the fishmonger to cut up the lobster for me. Finally, at home I pair the lobster with the simplest of partners—rice, crusty bread, or just a spoon. You won't want to miss a drop of the sauce or compete with its dazzle.

LOBSTER À L'AMÉRICAINE

4 tablespoons olive oil

2 lobsters, about 1½ pounds each, claws separated from bodies and cracked; tails cut into 1-inch medallions, bodies split lengthwise, innards and roe reserved (your fishmonger can do this)

Salt and freshly ground pepper

4 tablespoons Armagnac

½ cup sliced shallots (2 to 3)

6 cloves garlic, smashed and peeled

6 sprigs tarragon

6 sprigs thyme

2 carrots, sliced

2 celery stalks, sliced

2 small leeks, white part only, sliced

6 tablespoons tomato paste

1 cup white wine

3 cups chicken stock

12 plum tomatoes, halved lengthwise

3 tablespoons unsalted butter, softened

Pinch of cayenne pepper, or to taste

Chopped herbs, such as parsley and tarragon, for garnish

1. In a large skillet at least 2½ inches deep, heat 1 tablespoon oil until smoking. Add lobster claws and salt and pepper to taste, and sauté until shells turn bright red, about 10 minutes. Transfer claws to a plate and add another tablespoon of oil to pan. Add tail medallions and salt and pepper, and cook until meat is browned and shells are bright red, about 7 minutes. Transfer medallions to a plate and repeat with lobster bodies, cooking

until shells turn bright red all over, about 12 minutes.

2. Return claws and medallions to pan with bodies and add 2 tablespoons Armagnac; flame with a match or by shaking pan over a high flame until it ignites. Let flames die down, then transfer claws and medallions to a plate, leaving bodies in pan. Add remaining oil, shallots, garlic, tarragon, thyme, carrots, celery, and leeks. Sauté until vegetables soften, about 10 minutes. Add tomato paste and wine, and cook, stirring, until liquid evaporates. Add stock and tomatoes, and let mixture simmer until thickened, about 40 minutes. Let cool, then strain through a sieve, pressing hard on solids.

3. In a bowl, mash together butter, reserved lobster innards, and remaining 2 tablespoons Armagnac.

4. Place sauce in a large, clean skillet and add claws and medallions. Heat sauce over medium heat until lobster pieces are hot. Whisk in lobster butter, cayenne, and salt and pepper to taste. Serve lobster in sauce garnished with chopped herbs.

Yield: 4 servings
Time: 2 1/4 hours

A SOPHISTICATED AND SUBTLE RICE PUDDING FROM FRANCE

When I was a child, I would spend Sundays in my grandmother's kitchen in Toulouse, watching her prepare dinner on a coal-burning stove. In fact, seeing her take command of those meals was one of my first inspirations to become a cook. Of all the delicious dishes she made, one of our favorites was a dessert she called riz au lait. *Although I usually translate it as rice pudding, that term doesn't really describe her marvelous confection.*

Made without eggs, her dessert did not firm up like a typical custard-based pudding. Instead, she kept it soft and soupy, cooking the rice with plenty of milk and sugar until it swelled and fattened, hardly resisting the tongue when you ate it. The sauce was creamy and gently flavored with vanilla and a bay leaf. Nourishing and plain-looking, it was still, in its way, a sophisticated and subtle creation.

My grandmother spent hours and hours simmering the rice. She left it all morning long on one side of her hot cast-iron stove, which kept the mixture at the right temperature, just below a boil. Since she was usually nearby preparing the rest of the meal, she often stirred and checked the rice, adding cold milk if the mixture got too hot or too dry. Slowly, the rice drank up most of the liquid, absorbing its sweet flavor along the way.

Of course, this method is quite impractical for a restaurant kitchen and for most cooks at home, too. So my pastry chef, Chris Broberg, and I adapted it. First, we blanch the rice with the bay leaf to begin the cooking and rid the rice of excess starch. Then we transfer the rice and bay leaf to a baking dish, adding milk, sugar, and a vanilla bean, and half-submerge the baking dish in hot water. A sheet of parchment is set directly on top of the rice and left there while it bakes.

The water bath keeps the rice from cooking too quickly, while the parchment holds the moisture in, en-

suring that the rice plumps up before the liquid evapo-rates. The rice still has to bake for two hours, but you don't have to stir or even watch over it at all. As the rice cooks, the parchment paper catches the steam and rises slightly, turning brown. If you let the parchment rest on the rice after pulling it from the oven, the brown color (which is really just caramelized milk on the surface) bleeds into the milky white pudding. So to keep the color pristine, peel the paper off the rice as soon as it comes out of the oven.

MARIE LOUISE'S RICE PUDDING

½ cup long-grain rice
1 very small bay leaf or ½ large bay leaf,
    preferably fresh
1 quart milk
1 cup sugar
½ vanilla bean, split in half crosswise
½ cup crème fraîche

1. Preheat oven to 350 degrees. Put rice and bay leaf in a small saucepan and add 2 cups water. Bring to a boil, then immediately drain rice. Transfer rice and bay leaf to an 8-inch-square baking pan and stir in milk, ½ cup sugar, and vanilla bean.

2. Cut a piece of parchment paper to fit inside pan and place it directly on top of rice mixture. Place pan inside a larger baking pan and fill larger pan with enough very hot water to reach halfway up sides of small pan. Bake rice until very tender and much (but not all) of liquid is absorbed, about 2 hours.

3. Meanwhile, prepare caramel syrup: In a small saucepan over medium-high heat, combine remaining ½ cup sugar with 2 tablespoons water. Cook, stirring, until sugar dissolves. Raise heat to high and let mixture cook without stirring until it caramelizes and turns a very deep amber, about 7 minutes. Carefully add ⅓ cup water (it will sputter). Simmer caramel, stirring, until mixture is smooth. Set aside to cool.

4. As soon as rice comes out of oven, peel off parchment paper. Transfer pan to a rack to cool. Remove vanilla bean and bay leaf.

5. Using a whisk or an electric mixer, beat crème fraîche until it holds soft peaks. Fold into cooled rice mixture. Serve rice pudding in bowls with a drizzle of caramel syrup on top.

Yield: 6 to 8 servings
Time: about 2½ hours

WYLIE DUFRESNE

Wylie Dufresne is the chef at 71 Clinton Fresh Food in Manhattan. He was photographed on the roof of his house near Union Square. These columns were written with Jack Bishop.

SEAFOOD SAUSAGE WITH SEAFOOD ON THE OUTSIDE AS WELL AS THE INSIDE

It has become nearly impossible to surprise food-savvy New Yorkers. The collective attitude might be summed up as "Been there, tasted that."

What's a chef to do? My shrimp-stuffed squid is one answer. This dish starts with familiar ingredients but defies expectations about appearance and texture. When the squid comes to the table, no one quite knows what to expect. The first slice into the whole squid reveals the bright orange chunks of shrimp, thin strips of basil, and tiny nuggets of sautéed garlic. But the real surprise comes with the first bite. The squid is soft, the filling is firm, and the shrimp pop—even crunch—in your mouth.

By this point my intentions are probably becoming clear: The dish is a riff on a traditional seafood sausage. But with traditional seafood sausage, the filling is creamy and mousselike, while the wrapper is taut, even

a little tough. Sausage snaps when you bite into it. My shrimp-stuffed squid reverses the usual textures of the wrapper and filling. Chopping the shrimp coarsely ensures that they have plenty of texture. A tiny amount of toasted bread crumbs in the filling adds some crunch. I use panko, the Japanese bread crumbs sold in many markets, but any coarse crumbs will do.

A few notes about buying and cooking squid. The dish starts with whole squid that have been cleaned. You want fairly small squid, about five inches long. If the bodies have any flaps attached, cut them off. The squid bodies should be perfectly smooth, tapered cylinders. At most markets you can buy just the squid bodies. If you're buying squid with the tentacles still attached, however, don't worry. At the restaurant I marinate the tentacles overnight in olive oil, garlic, and thyme. I grill them and put them on the plate with the stuffed squid as garnish.

At the restaurant I also serve the squid with a dollop of fennel puree, which is nothing more than chopped fennel steamed until very soft, then pureed with salt and a little butter. It adds a nice contrast—though, again, it isn't necessary.

But the sauce made from blood orange juice is essential. A friend calls this reddish orange sauce the world's best Russian dressing. Although the color and consistency are similar to Russian dressing, the flavors are quite different. Blood oranges are sour, sweet, and musky all at once, making them an ideal foil for seafood and the basil in the stuffing.

Finally, it is worth remembering the adage about squid: Cook it either a minute or an hour. If you cook the squid just a little too long, it will turn rubbery. And once it is tough, it takes an hour of braising or stewing to make it tender again.

In this dish the plump alabaster squid bodies look as if they had been poached. In reality they are placed in a hot skillet, which is then quickly transferred to an oven that has been preheated. Any juices exuded by the squid evaporate in the hot pan, so there is no chance that the filling will become soggy. Although it may seem easier to cook the squid completely on top of the stove, sautéing will cause it to brown and overcook before the filling is done. In the oven, heat attacks the squid from all sides without causing much change in color. Frequent turning also helps keep the squid from browning.

SHRIMP-STUFFED SQUID WITH BLOOD ORANGE EMULSION

For the emulsion:

1 cup blood orange juice
$\frac{1}{2}$ large egg yolk
Salt
1 teaspoon sherry vinegar
$\frac{1}{3}$ cup grapeseed oil

For the squid:

4 tablespoons extra-virgin olive oil
2 medium cloves garlic, minced very fine
12 ounces medium shrimp, peeled and
  deveined
2 tablespoons coarse bread crumbs, toasted in
  a dry skillet until golden brown
10 basil leaves, cut into thin strips
Cayenne pepper to taste
6 cleaned squid bodies, each 5 inches long

1. To make emulsion: Strain juice into a small saucepan. Bring to a boil, lower heat, and simmer briskly until thickened and reduced to $\frac{1}{4}$ cup, about 8 minutes. Cool completely.

2. Whisk egg yolk and a pinch of salt together in a small bowl. Whisk in reduced juice and vinegar. Slowly whisk in grapeseed oil until sauce is emulsified. Adjust seasonings.

3. To prepare squid: Heat 2 tablespoons olive oil in a small skillet. Add garlic and cook over medium-low heat until lightly colored, about 2 minutes. Remove from heat.

4. Cut each shrimp into 6 or 7 pieces and place in a bowl. Stir in cooled garlic and oil, bread crumbs, basil, salt, and cayenne. Refrigerate until chilled, at least 30 minutes.

5. Gently stuff shrimp mixture into each squid body until all but last $\frac{1}{2}$ inch of each squid

is filled; don't pack. Thread a toothpick through open end of squid to seal.

6. Preheat oven to 450 degrees. Heat remaining 2 tablespoons oil in a large ovenproof skillet over medium-high heat. Add squid, cook for 30 seconds, and turn. Transfer pan to oven and cook, turning squid every 2 minutes, until squid are opaque and filling is warm and firm, about 6 minutes total. (Do not overcook.) Remove skillet from oven and let pan rest for 1 or 2 minutes. Remove toothpicks.

7. Drizzle blood orange emulsion over 6 individual plates. Place 1 squid on each plate and serve immediately.

Yield: 6 first-course servings
Time: 1½ hours

CRISPY RISOTTO CAKES

The kitchen in my restaurant is so small that conventional risotto simply isn't practical. All that last-minute work doesn't make sense when three cooks are standing in a space smaller than a Ford Expedition.

Parcooking the rice, the strategy most restaurants use, wasn't the answer. Risotto prepared this way still needs at least ten minutes of attention. In the end I modified a classic technique for cooking leftover risotto. Thrifty Italian cooks refrigerate extra risotto until it becomes a solid mass that can be shaped into patties and sautéed in olive oil. These sautéed rice cakes are usually served as a light meal, perhaps with a little salad.

I started playing with the idea of risotto cakes and realized I could use them as the starch base on my main-course plates. Just like mashed potatoes or polenta, risotto cakes work with countless main courses: grilled shrimp, seared scallops, sliced steak, chicken breasts.

I pack as much flavor into the risotto as possible by seasoning the rice with black olives, shallots, and Parmesan. These Mediterranean flavors work year-round and match up well with scallops. I also drizzle a little basil-infused olive oil on plates. (I make my own, but you can buy basil oil in the supermarket.) At other times I've stirred pureed peas into my risotto cakes. The flavor is remarkable, and so is the color. This summer I'll add caramelized corn kernels, scallions, bacon, and maybe even lobster. As long as the rice firms up when it's chilled, you can add almost anything you like.

Nobody really thinks about the consistency of risotto; it's always creamy. But cooked in a hot pan, risotto cakes develop a thick, golden brown crust that's down-right crunchy, with an exterior as crisp as a lace cookie. The contrast with the creamy interior is addictive.

Two tips: Risotto cakes hold together best if the rice is overcooked a bit to release as much starch as possible. Because starchiness is desirable, there's no need to stir. Once the stock boils, simply throw the cover on the pot and walk away. Exactly seventeen minutes later, the rice will be done. And although the risotto can be made and the cakes browned on the same day, I get better results when the rice has chilled overnight.

SEARED SCALLOPS ON BLACK OLIVE RISOTTO CAKES

2 tablespoons unsalted butter
3 medium shallots, minced
1 cup Arborio rice
3½ cups chicken stock
Salt and cayenne pepper to taste
⅓ cup grated Parmesan cheese
½ cup pitted and chopped Niçoise olives
Flour
5 tablespoons grapeseed oil
16 medium sea scallops (about 1 pound),
    tendons removed
Basil-infused olive oil

1. In a large saucepan melt butter, add shallots, and cook over medium heat until translucent, about 4 minutes. Stir in rice and cook, stirring constantly, until grains are coated with fat, about 2 minutes. Stir in stock, salt, cayenne, and half of cheese. Bring to a boil, then lower heat, cover, and simmer until rice is creamy, 17 minutes. Uncover and stir rice vigorously. Add olives and remaining cheese, and stir until all liquid cooks off.

2. Scrape rice into a 9-inch-square pan lined with parchment paper. Tap pan against counter to level rice. Cool to room temperature, about 1 hour. Cover and refrigerate until firm and chilled, at least 6 hours.

3. Preheat oven to 400 degrees. Using a 3½-inch biscuit cutter, cut 4 disks out of cooled rice.

(Scraps can be reworked and used to make an extra disk.) Lightly dust rice cakes with flour.

4. In a 12-inch nonstick skillet over medium-high heat, heat 2 tablespoons grapeseed oil. Slide cakes, smooth side down, into hot pan and cook until crisp and well browned on bottom, about 3 minutes. Flip cakes over and transfer pan to rack in center of oven. Bake until second side is crisp and well browned, about 7 minutes.

5. While rice cakes are in oven, season scallops with salt and cayenne. Heat remaining grapeseed oil in a large skillet over high heat. Add scallops and lower heat to medium-high. Cook until bottoms are golden brown, about 2 minutes. Turn with tongs and cook until second side is golden, 1½ to 2 minutes. Transfer scallops to a platter lined with a paper towel.

6. When rice cakes are golden brown, transfer to a platter lined with a paper towel. Place 1 rice cake, bumpy side up, on each plate. Stack 4 scallops in a pyramid on each cake. Drizzle a few drops of basil oil on each plate and serve.

Yield: 4 servings
Time: 45 minutes, plus 7 hours of chilling

LOOKING TO ASIA FOR A BREAD-CRUMB CRUST

I grew up on the Lower East Side of Manhattan. Since I am now cooking in the old neighborhood, I wanted to pay homage to the local foodstuffs. The most popular dish on the restaurant's menu—sea bass with edamame and rye-bread crust—does just that. Although it may sound exotic, its roots are right here where Jewish, Asian, and Latino cuisines dominate.

I've always liked a crust on fish. When done right, the crunch of the crust balances perfectly with the tender fish. Breading is the most common choice, and for me, rye was a natural. I had envisioned the fish with chopped fava beans, but they are seasonal and expensive. I wondered if edamame, or green soybeans, which look like favas but are available inexpensively year-round in Asian markets, would work.

To my surprise the two geographically distinct ingredients—which inhabit the same culinary turf in Manhattan—came together beautifully. The chewiness of the chopped soybeans stands up to the powerful crunch of the toasted rye crumbs. The soybeans are salty and earthy, and actually taste better with rye bread than favas, which are somewhat bitter. The sweet, oniony flavor of minced chives ties together the rye and edamame.

Most coatings for fish are applied before cooking. But this crust is actually spooned over the fish once it has been sautéed. Really, it's just a simple loose topping.

Meaty sea bass fillets are my first choice for this dish, but striped bass and red snapper are excellent substitutes. Be sure to buy skin-on fillets; the skin becomes cracker-crisp and adds another texture to the dish.

A few tips about cooking fish: Score the skin side of the fillets to prevent curling when the fish hits the hot pan. Also, heat the pan really well; if the pan is too cool, the fish is almost guaranteed to stick. I follow the 70-30 rule when cooking skin-on fillets: Place the fil-

lets in the pan skin side down and cook 70 percent of the way, then flip them and finish on the second side. This ensures that the skin is really crisp.

At the restaurant, I serve the fish over chive-flavored mashed potatoes and drizzle some chive oil onto plates with a little mushroom juice. But this is just icing on the cake. The pairing of rye bread and edamame creates such an intriguing and flavorful topping that nothing more is needed.

BLACK SEA BASS WITH EDAMAME AND RYE-BREAD CRUST

3 ounces fresh or frozen soybeans in pods
  (edamame)
½ cup coarse rye bread crumbs
2 teaspoons unsalted butter, melted,
  plus 1 tablespoon unmelted
4 skin-on black sea bass fillets (each about
  7 ounces)
Salt and cayenne pepper to taste
2 tablespoons grapeseed oil
4 teaspoons minced chives

1. In a small saucepan, bring several cups of water to a boil, add soybeans, and cook for 1 minute. Drain and transfer to a bowl of ice water until cool. Drain and peel, discarding pods. Finely chop soybeans to yield ¼ cup. (Once prepared, the chopped soybeans can be covered and refrigerated overnight.)

2. Preheat oven to 350 degrees. Toss rye crumbs and melted butter on a small baking sheet. Bake, tossing once or twice, until crumbs are well browned, about 12 minutes. Transfer to a plate lined with paper towels to blot up excess butter. (They can be set aside at room temperature for several hours.)

3. With a paring knife, score each fillet 3 times on skin side to prevent fish from curling when it hits pan. Season both sides of fish with salt and cayenne.

4. In a skillet large enough to hold fish comfortably in 1 layer, heat oil over medium-high heat. When oil is hot, lay fish skin side down. Cook until fillets are golden brown on bottom, about 4 minutes. Flip and continue cooking on second side until fish is opaque in center, about 2 minutes.

5. As soon as you flip fish, melt remaining 1 tablespoon butter in a small skillet. Add soybeans and toasted crumbs, and mix well. Cook until hot, about 1 minute. Stir in chives and add salt to taste.

6. Put fillets, skin side up, on individual plates, spoon a little topping over each, and serve immediately.

Yield: 4 servings
Time: 30 minutes

HOW ONE GOOD DISH CAN BEGET ANOTHER

At any given time, there are dozens of sauces, oils, purees, and stocks in my storage bins and walk-in refrigerator. Like most chefs I'm always trying to find new uses for these flavoring agents. Most of these experiments never make it into the dining room. But sometimes, I get lucky and create something memorable. My chive-flavored mashed potatoes are one example.

These sweet, oniony potatoes actually began with some leftovers. Margins are so tight in this business that chefs must use every part of every ingredient that comes into the kitchen. Of course, just throwing a bunch of scraps into a pot won't help any chef. The idea is to take a by-product from one dish and use it to make a second dish taste better.

One day while straining pureed chives from a chive oil I had just made, I wondered if there was a use for the chives. Yes, they had given up some flavor and color, but they still smelled and tasted pretty good. I folded the chive pulp into mashed potatoes and was pleasantly surprised by the result. The chives dyed the potatoes bright green and gave them a lovely herb flavor. I liked these potatoes so much I started making chive puree for its own sake. To get as much chive flavor as possible, I stopped straining the oil. The by-product from one dish suddenly had its own raison d'être.

The thick green puree is equally good folded into grits or polenta. Other soft green herbs, especially parsley and basil, can be used in the same fashion. Just grind the herbs in a blender with a pinch of salt and add enough oil to make a thick puree. (Blanch basil first to set its color.)

I serve my chive mashed potatoes beneath a piece of sautéed sea bass, but the potatoes are delicious with steak or poultry.

Many people ask me why restaurant mashed potatoes are so much smoother than the ones they make at home.

The secret is a combination of technique and fat. I gently boil my potatoes whole—not cut into chunks—so that less surface area is exposed to the water and they don't become soggy. Drier potatoes absorb butter and cream better, and will feel lighter on the tongue. Ideally, potatoes should be boiled in their skins so that they absorb even less water, but given the bother of peeling hot potatoes, I take the skins off before cooking. Once the potatoes are drained, I let them rest in a colander for several minutes to give off as much steam as possible.

Any self-respecting chef will tell you that a potato masher is not the best tool for the job. I hate to sound like a snob, but you must use a ricer, which turns boiled potatoes into fine, feathery bits.

As for the fat, the chive puree has a fair amount of oil, so I use a restrained amount of butter. A dairy product—cream, half-and-half, or whole milk—lightens the texture of the potatoes so they almost melt in your mouth. When richness is my goal, I use cream. When it is lightness, a quality more appropriate in warm weather, I use milk.

CHIVE MASHED POTATOES

1½ cups coarsely chopped chives
Salt to taste
½ cup grapeseed or other neutral oil, or more
    as needed
3 pounds Yukon Gold potatoes, peeled
4 tablespoons unsalted butter, softened
¾ cup heavy cream, half-and-half, or whole
    milk, heated

1. To make the chive puree: Place chives, a pinch of salt, and oil in a blender. Blend, stopping occasionally to scrape down sides, until chives form a smooth puree, 2 to 3 minutes. If necessary, drizzle in more oil until chives break down. Set aside. (The puree can be scraped into an airtight container and refrigerated for up to 3 days or frozen for up to a month.)

2. Put potatoes in a medium pot and add enough water to cover by at least 2 inches. Add salt, bring to a boil, lower heat, and simmer until a skewer glides easily through potatoes, 30 to 35 minutes. Drain potatoes and let rest in strainer to dry, about 5 minutes.

3. Run potatoes through a ricer and into an empty pot set over low heat. Beat in butter with a wooden spoon. When butter melts, beat in hot cream with a spoon. Season with salt. Beat in chive puree, adjust seasonings, and serve immediately.

Yield: 6 servings
Time: 55 minutes

A LITTLE GREEN MOUND
WITH A SURPRISE INSIDE

This dish is somewhat mysterious when it comes to the table. A small dome of avocado scored with fine ridges, it looks almost like a small green sea creature or the model for a Frank Gehry building. There's no hint of what's contained within: a mound of bright pink fish cut into tiny cubes. But the dish has more than just a visual surprise and preppy colors going for it. The flavors are thoroughly unconventional, yet in perfect harmony.

Tuna tartare is a restaurant workhorse, and pairing tuna with avocado is common in sushi restaurants. I wanted to play off that idea but came up with something a bit different.

Salmon seemed like a good candidate, but I worried that it might be too fatty with the avocado. In the end the solution was to balance the richness of the two main ingredients with some crunch, some acid, and some heat. The contrasts of textures and flavors and expectations make this dish everything a good appetizer should be: sexy but not insanely rich, with just enough heat and acidity to cleanse the palate.

The seasonings in the filling—lime juice, Tabasco, pickles, and chives—are hardly quiet. Used judiciously, none is overpowering.

The crunch comes from two sources. In the filling, it's pickled radishes. I pickle red radishes in a sweet and spicy brine made with rice vinegar. But you can also use the pickled daikon radishes sold in Asian markets, or even cornichons, to provide the same crisp texture and tang.

Garnishing the avocado with flaked sea salt adds crunch to the exterior. The snowflake crystals of Maldon sea salt have an airiness that makes them perfect in this dish, but any coarse salt will do. A squirt of lime juice adds more acidity. The heat of the Tabasco hits the back of the mouth and erases any lingering flavors.

At the restaurant, I serve the avocado-wrapped salmon with a squirt of creamy horseradish sauce. I grind fresh horseradish in a food processor or blender along with a dash of rice vinegar and salt until it is very fine, then drizzle in homemade mustard oil to make a thick mousselike emulsion. (You can do the same thing at home with neutral grapeseed oil.) The floral, spicy flavor of fresh horseradish brings all the elements on the plate together. It is worth spending five extra minutes to make the sauce.

. . .

Avocado and seafood have a natural affinity, and you can use this presentation technique with any number of fillings. The method remains the same: Prepare the seafood filling, slice the avocado, and stuff and shape individual portions. Here are a few suggestions:

Tuna tartare: To preserve the bright red color of fresh tuna, eliminate the lime juice, which would turn the fish white. Tuna isn't as fatty as salmon, so the pickled radish will supply enough bite.

Scallop seviche: Chop top-quality sea scallops a bit more coarsely than the salmon to give them a rougher texture. Marinate the chopped scallops in a little lemon juice, olive oil, minced red onion or shallot, salt, and fresh herbs for about an hour. The slight firming caused by the acid makes the scallops a toothsome contrast to the creamy avocado. For an Asian flavor cut down on the salt and add a splash of soy sauce.

Poached shrimp: Chop and lightly dress the shrimp. (I like the fruity flavor of an orange vinaigrette.) Add scallions and herbs to round out the filling.

Crab: Make a light salad of peekytoe or Jonah crabmeat. But don't use mayonnaise—it will be too rich with the avocado. Instead, toss the crabmeat with a mustard vinaigrette, diced seeded tomatoes, shallots, and fresh herbs.

I sometimes change the portion size and presentation of this dish at the restaurant when two people want to share it. Once the stuffed avocado has been unwrapped, slice it in half crosswise to reveal the bright filling inside.

MARINATED SALMON WRAPPED
IN AVOCADO

1 12-ounce salmon fillet with skin, pin
    bones, and gray area removed (about 8
    ounces when trimmed)
4 teaspoons minced chives
4 teaspoons minced pickled radish or
    cornichons
2 teaspoons lime juice
2 teaspoons extra-virgin olive oil
Table salt to taste
¼ teaspoon Tabasco sauce, or to taste
2 medium ripe Haas avocados
Cracked black pepper to taste
Flaked or coarse sea salt for garnish
6 tablespoons Creamy Horseradish Oil
    (see recipe below)

1. With a very sharp knife cut salmon into thin slices, then chop it to texture of coarsely ground meat. Place in a bowl and stir in chives, radish, lime juice, olive oil, table salt, and Tabasco. Taste and adjust seasonings.

2. Working with 1 avocado at a time, cut in half lengthwise. Twist to separate into 2 halves. Remove and discard pit. Cut off and discard ½ inch from top of each half. Carefully peel away and discard skin, trying not to gouge flesh with fingertips. Place halves pit side down. With tip of a sharp knife, slice each half lengthwise as thin as possible, holding sides of avocado as you work so

it keeps its shape. You should be able to cut each half into at least 12 slices.

3. Lay an 18 by 12-inch sheet of plastic wrap flat on a work surface. Slide side of knife under sliced avocado half, transfer to plastic, and turn pit side up. Press lightly with an open hand to fan slices slightly. Season with table salt and pepper.

4. Spoon a quarter of salmon mixture over center of avocado half. Lift opposite corners of wrap over fish and repeat with 2 remaining corners. Grasp all 4 corners of wrap in one hand; with other hand, grasp avocado and flip, twisting and pulling on corners of wrap to tighten it around underside of avocado. Twist avocado several times, pinching plastic tight under avocado and pushing avocado slices into original shape. Repeat with remaining avocado halves and salmon, forming each half in its own piece of plastic. (Can be refrigerated for 1 hour.)

5. Lay wrapped avocado on side and slice off twisted portion of wrap just below avocado. Turn avocado so that salmon filling faces up. Gently peel back wrap. Place small plate over avocado and flip avocado onto plate so green side faces up. Repeat with other avocado halves. Sprinkle lightly with coarse salt. Drizzle horseradish oil around edges of plates and serve immediately.

Yield: 4 first-course servings
Time: 45 minutes

3 ounces fresh horseradish, peeled and cut
    into chunks
½ teaspoon rice vinegar
Pinch of salt
½ cup (approximately) grapeseed oil or other
    neutral oil

1. Place horseradish, vinegar, and salt in a
food processor and grind, stopping to scrape
down sides of bowl several times, until horseradish is quite fine, 1 to 2 minutes.

2. With processor motor running, add oil
through feed tube in a steady stream and process
just until mixture forms a creamy emulsion,
about 1 minute. (Once mixture has sauce consistency, stop adding oil.) Adjust seasonings. Horseradish oil can be refrigerated in an airtight
container for several days. Shake or whisk before
using.

Yield: about ¾ cup
Time: 5 minutes

NOTE: You will need only about half this sauce for
the marinated salmon wrapped in avocado. The rest
can be served with grilled fish, steak, or cold asparagus, or used on roast beef or lamb sandwiches.

A FLAVORFUL TWIST ON
A SPRING TRADITION

*I devised this dish by thinking of the ways lamb is tra-
ditionally served. Lamb and fava beans are a classic
springtime pairing. The gutsy flavor of the meat also
works well with fruit. And rosemary and lamb are a
natural combo. So no single element in my lamb with
fruit dressing is unusual, but the combination is: tender
meat with sweet fruit, bitter favas, licoricelike fennel,
and piney rosemary.*

*The dressing is really more of a warm salsa than
anything else. It is very lightly cooked so that each component retains its flavor and texture. The grapes have
some snap and the fennel some crunch, while the favas
are creamy and the dried fruit is chewy. The colors—
green, orange, red, and pink—are vibrant and appealing. The dressing changes from bite to bite, depending
on whether you get apricots, cherries, grapes, favas, or
fennel on your fork. And each ingredient makes the
lamb taste a bit different.*

*The dish can be altered in countless ways. Lima
beans or peas can take the place of the favas. Shallots or
yellow onion can replace the red onion, and green grapes
or even raisins are an easy substitute for red grapes. So
are local fresh apricots, peaches, and cherries.*

*At the restaurant I butcher a whole lamb saddle
and then cut the boneless loin into six-ounce portions.
Once cooked, the meat is sliced and fanned out over the
plate. At home you have two options to feed four people:
Cook two whole boneless loins (each weighs twelve to
fourteen ounces) or use twelve individual loin chops. I
think the sliced loin looks nicer, and I find that diners
would rather not deal with the bones.*

*To use boneless loin, buy two racks of lamb and ask
the butcher to remove the loin from each rack. Make sure
every bit of fat has been trimmed from this torpedo-
shaped cut. Since you've purchased the entire rack, be
sure to take the flap of meat that the butcher cuts away*

from the bones—it can be used for shish kebab. The bones are yours, too; save them for stock. Ideally, I would grill either the whole loins or the individual chops. The light char and smoky flavor that lamb picks up on the grill are a perfect complement to the dressing.

Otherwise, you can sauté the loin or chops in clarified butter (as I do in the restaurant) or in a neutral oil like grapeseed. Two caveats about sautéing: Be prepared to make a mess on your stove top and to put a powerful exhaust system to full use.

GRILLED LOIN OF LAMB WITH
FAVA AND FRUIT DRESSING

¼ cup diced fennel
7 ounces fava beans, shelled (about ½ cup)
2 boneless loins of lamb (12 to 14 ounces
    each), trimmed of all fat, or 12 loin lamb
    chops, trimmed of excess fat
Salt and freshly ground white pepper
2 tablespoons unsalted butter
¼ cup minced red onion
3 tablespoons diced dried sour cherries
3 tablespoons diced dried apricots
16 seedless red grapes, quartered lengthwise
2 teaspoons minced rosemary

1. Bring water to a boil in a small saucepan. Add fennel and blanch until crisp-tender, about 2 minutes. Drain and set aside. Bring more water to a boil in a saucepan, add favas, and blanch for 1 minute. Drain. When cool, slip favas out of tough outer skins and set aside.

2. Heat grill. Season lamb with salt and pepper to taste. Grill lamb, turning once, until instant-read thermometer inserted deep into meat registers 125 degrees for medium-rare, about 8 minutes. Transfer lamb to a plate and let rest for 5 minutes.

3. Meanwhile, melt butter in a medium skillet. Add onion and sauté over medium heat until translucent, 2 to 3 minutes. Add dried fruit and cook for 1 minute. Add 2 tablespoons water and cook until water evaporates, about 1 minute. Add fennel and cook until heated through, another minute. Add grapes and favas, and cook until warm, about 1 minute. Add rosemary, and salt to taste.

4. Divide fruit dressing among 4 plates. If using loin, slice ¾ inch thick. Place sliced loin or grilled chops over dressing and serve immediately.

Yield: 4 servings
Time: 45 minutes

A LOBSTER ROLL WITH FINESSE

In formal restaurants lobster is always served out of the shell. A claw might float in a rich broth, or the tail might be served as an entree. But the meat from the knuckles—the jointed, tubular segments that connect the lobster claws to the lobster body—is difficult to remove from the shell and does not make a very good presentation. More often than not, the knuckles are saved for salad.

Lobster salad is too precious to serve to the staff, so I started making an amuse-bouche—*one of those little giveaways that the chef sends out before the meal—with lobster knuckle salad on tiny rounds of toasted brioche. This finger food was so delicious that I decided to supersize the idea and make regular lobster sandwiches. To get that much lobster meat, you need to use whole lobsters. But I still call it a lobster knuckle sandwich.*

I bind the lobster meat with a little homemade mayonnaise. Instead of the standard lemon juice, I use fresh ginger juice to emulsify the egg yolk. The heat of the ginger keeps the lobster salad from tasting too rich. I don't like too much mayonnaise—lobster is decadent enough, so you don't want to go overboard with egg yolks and oil. The mayo is really just a binder and a vehicle for the ginger. Add only as much as you need to hold the lobster meat together. This recipe provides more ginger mayonnaise than you need. The extra can be served with any seafood or used on a turkey club.

I also flavor the lobster with chervil and chives. The light anise flavor of chervil complements the lobster, while the chives add a mild hit of onion. I prefer to keep the focus on the lobster, but you can add some diced celery or radish for crunch. Diced apple or avocado are two other possibilities.

As for the bread, I like the rich flavor of brioche, but any soft bread will do just fine. You can even use sliced white bread. After all, this recipe is basically a souped-up lobster roll.

LOBSTER-KNUCKLE SANDWICHES

1 large egg yolk
2 tablespoons ginger juice (see Note)
½ teaspoon Dijon mustard
Salt
Splash of red wine vinegar
⅔ cup grapeseed oil
2 lobsters (each 1½ pounds)
1 tablespoon chopped fresh chervil
1 tablespoon chopped fresh chives
Pinch of cayenne pepper
8 slices brioche, toasted

1. Whisk together egg yolk, juice, and mustard in a medium bowl. Add salt to taste and vinegar, and whisk again. Slowly whisk in oil until mayonnaise is smooth. Adjust seasonings. (The mayonnaise can be refrigerated for a day.)

2. Bring a large pot of highly salted water to a boil. Add lobsters and cook for 11 minutes. Transfer to a bowl of ice water. When cool, crack open shells and remove meat from tail, claws, and knuckles. Cut meat into ¼-inch cubes. (You should have about 2 cups.)

3. Place lobster in a medium bowl. Stir in enough mayonnaise to moisten it, no more than ¼ cup. (Reserve remaining mayonnaise for another use.) Stir in chervil, chives, and cayenne. Add salt to taste.

4. Spoon lobster salad onto 4 slices of toasted bread. Top with remaining slices and serve.

Yield: 4 sandwiches
Time: 1 hour

NOTE: To obtain ginger juice, wrap several ounces of finely grated fresh ginger in cheesecloth and squeeze hard. Or place grated ginger in a fine sieve and press with the back of a spoon.

MICHEL RICHARD

Michel Richard is the chef and owner of Citronelle in
Washington, D.C. He was photographed in the East Wing of the National
Gallery of Art by Susana Raab. These columns were written with Marian Burros.

A HAWAIIAN INSPIRATION

*A few years ago when I was working in Los Angeles, I
complained to a friend about flavorless tomatoes. My
friend, who happened to be a chef from Hawaii, told me
that he adds a julienne of pineapple to tasteless tomatoes
to make up for the missing acidity and sweetness.*

*I liked the idea, so I tried adding a pineapple puree
to a vinaigrette that I was serving over a tomato salad.
It worked: The bland tomatoes suddenly seemed to have
a lot of flavor. I served that salad for years but never
told anyone about the pineapple; I was cooking real
French food, after all, and that combination sounded
oddly Polynesian.*

*When I returned to cook in Washington, I thought of
using the tomato-pineapple combination in a dessert. I
reasoned that both are botanically fruits, and I already
knew that they go very well together. My cold "fruit"
soup flavored with maple syrup and lime and topped
with a basil crème anglaise was a big hit—until people*

*learned that tomatoes were in it. So I tried using
rhubarb instead; it has the acidity of a tomato, and I
liked its crunchy texture. Rhubarb and pineapple seem
to need each other the way strawberries and rhubarb do,
but they make a much more unexpected combination.*

*This dish is more like a compote than a soup, but un-
like most compotes, the fruit is cooked as little as possible so the flavors and textures remain distinct. In fact,
it's so much like a bowl of fresh fruit that I call it a
salad. At the restaurant I top it with basil crème
anglaise; I like adding an herbal touch to fruit desserts,
and since I love Provençal flavors, I reached for basil.
At home, though, I just whirl some vanilla ice cream
with some basil in a blender and chill it again. The
differences are very slight because the basil is what's important here; all it needs is a creamy cold base.*

*As surprising as the flavors are, the dessert couldn't
be easier to make. But there are a couple of things to keep
in mind: The rhubarb must be cut very small to retain
some crunch, but cook it all the way through. Don't be*

tempted to cook the pineapple at all; the dessert would lose its fresh flavor if you did. When you are blanching the basil, if you have the ice cream ready in the blender you can put the basil directly into the blender.

PINEAPPLE-RHUBARB "SALAD" WITH BASIL CREAM

  5 tablespoons packed brown sugar
  2 cups finely diced (¼ inch) peeled rhubarb
      (about 3 stalks, 10 inches long)
  1 rounded cup finely diced (¼ inch)
      ripe fresh pineapple
  20 large basil leaves
  ¾ cup (approximately) good-quality vanilla
      ice cream, slightly softened

1. Place a medium sauté pan over high heat and melt sugar. Add rhubarb and sauté about 30 seconds, then reduce heat to low. Cover and cook until rhubarb is softened but still firm, 2 to 3 minutes more. Transfer rhubarb to a mixing bowl and add pineapple. Set aside or cover and refrigerate up to 24 hours; bring to room temperature before serving.

2. Prepare a bowl of ice water. Bring a small pan of water to a boil and add basil leaves. Blanch leaves for 30 seconds, then transfer to ice water to stop cooking. In a blender, combine ice cream and basil leaves. Puree until mixture is smoothly blended. If necessary, freeze until mixture is thick but can still be poured from a spoon.

3. To serve, divide fruit mixture equally among four ½-cup serving dishes. Top each with a spoonful of basil–ice cream mixture and serve immediately.

Yield: 4 servings
Time: 20 minutes, plus freezing if necessary

POLENTA'S SECRET: CREAM OF WHEAT

When I was a child in the Champagne region of France, my mother served us a dessert called gâteau de semoule. *It may sound exotic, but it's really just a cake made of semolina, the same as the American breakfast cereal Cream of Wheat. Its grainy, creamy texture was so soothing.*

Years later I was working in Paris for Gaston Lenôtre, the great pastry chef; he mixed semolina with olive oil and Parmesan to make gnocchi alla Romana. *They were tender and light, and I much preferred them to regular gnocchi, which I find too gummy. I suppose those two memories are the reason I make my polenta with Cream of Wheat instead of cornmeal. I prefer the smoother texture of Cream of Wheat to the rougher texture of cornmeal, probably because it reminds me of my childhood and Lenôtre. In this dish I combine my mother's cooking method with the way polenta is made, fortifying the grain with eggs and other flavors, then chilling it and slicing it into rectangles.*

I like to give the polenta the anise flavor of fennel combined with the sweetly grassy, slightly peppery flavor of basil. I serve it sliced with foie gras and duck jus. Most people don't want to cook foie gras at home, so I've created a red pepper sauce. Peppers sweeten when you cook them, and the sauce adds brightness to polenta's creaminess.

HERB POLENTA WITH RED BELL PEPPER SAUCE

For the herb polenta:
    4 tablespoons extra-virgin olive oil
    1 cup milk
    1 clove garlic, finely chopped
    ½ cup regular (10-minute) Cream of Wheat
    2 large eggs
    ¼ cup plus 2 tablespoons finely grated
        Parmigiano-Reggiano cheese
    1 cup well-packed thinly shredded spinach
        leaves
    12 large basil leaves, thinly shredded
    2 tablespoons finely chopped parsley or
        chervil
    Salt and freshly ground black pepper
    Sprigs of fresh oregano for garnish

For the red bell pepper sauce:
    1 large red bell pepper
    ½ anchovy, chopped, or ½ teaspoon anchovy
        paste, optional
    2 cloves garlic, chopped
    2 tablespoons extra-virgin olive oil
    ¼ cup chicken stock or broth, or as needed
    ½ teaspoon sugar
    Salt and freshly ground black pepper

Vegetable oil for baking sheet

1. To prepare herb polenta: Line an 8 by 8-inch pan with plastic wrap and set aside. In a medium saucepan, combine oil, milk, and garlic. Place over high heat and bring to a boil, then remove from heat and whisk in Cream of Wheat until well blended. Return to high heat and whisk until thickened but still pourable. Remove from heat and whisk in eggs. Return to heat and stir in ¼ cup cheese, spinach, basil, parsley, and salt and pepper to taste. Stir mixture until thickened and no longer pourable.

2. Immediately spoon mixture into plastic-lined pan, smoothing with a piece of plastic wrap to make a flat, even surface. Cover and refrigerate until chilled and solid, 2 to 24 hours.

3. While polenta is chilling, prepare red bell pepper sauce: Preheat a broiler. Place red bell pepper under broiler, turning occasionally until blackened on all sides. Let cool. Peel and seed pepper, cut into pieces, and place in a blender. Add anchovy, garlic, and olive oil, and process until smooth. Add just enough stock to make a thick but fluid sauce. Transfer mixture to a small saucepan over medium-low heat. Season with sugar and salt and pepper to taste. Bring to a simmer, remove from heat, and keep warm.

4. Preheat a broiler. Remove polenta from plastic and cut into 12 rectangles. Place on an oiled baking sheet and allow to return to room temperature. Sprinkle with remaining 2 tablespoons cheese. Broil until polenta is heated and cheese is lightly browned. Place 2 pieces of polenta on each of 6 plates and top with sauce. Garnish with oregano sprigs and serve immediately.

Yield: 6 servings
Time: 45 minutes, plus 2 to 24 hours of chilling

A SHARP KNIFE AND
THE RIGHT SEASONINGS

When I had my first restaurant in Los Angeles twenty years ago, every time I sent a piece of tuna out to the dining room, the dark portion would return to the kitchen. No one liked the dark part, because it tastes more fishy than the rest of the tuna. So I started cutting out that section, which meant I had leftover pieces.

First, I tried making tuna tartare; even though it may be on every menu today, no one would touch it then. So I decided to turn the chopped-up tuna into patties, sear them briefly and serve them on sliced brioche as "tuna burgers." They turned out to be very popular and are still on our lunch menu today, made from the whole fillet.

Since then, lots of chefs have started making them. Mine are different in a couple of ways: They are flavored with fresh herbs and seasonings mixed into the patty, and the fish is cut with a very sharp knife, not a food processor. A food processor will leave you with a very dense, heavy patty.

There are several other techniques for preparing the tuna burger that make the difference between one that tastes exceptional and one that is just run-of-the-mill. Be sure to use a small pan and just one tablespoon of oil; if the pan is too big, there will not be enough oil and the burger will burn. Sauté the garlic over very low heat to remove the raw taste without burning it, and chop the basil with a very sharp knife so it does not blacken. (Don't cut it on a wooden surface; use marble, plastic, or stone. Otherwise it will oxidize.)

Unfortunately, even today some people still want their tuna well done, but when you overcook it, it tastes like cardboard. A brief sear leaves it soft and creamy.

I serve the burgers on a slice of brioche, because I find most burger buns too soft. French bread isn't good, either; it's too hard. The texture of brioche is just right, and its flavor is so much richer. Toast it on one side only, so the untoasted side can sop up the juices of the burger.

TUNA BURGERS

1½ pounds fresh tuna fillet
4 cloves garlic, minced
6 tablespoons extra-virgin olive oil
2 anchovies, minced
¼ cup minced basil
Salt and freshly ground black pepper
6 tablespoons good-quality mayonnaise
½ teaspoon soy sauce
2 cups mesclun
1½ tablespoons red wine vinegar
8 slices brioche or 4 hamburger buns
1 tablespoon grapeseed or canola oil
1 large ripe tomato, trimmed and cut into
    4 slices

1. Using a large, sharp knife, thinly slice tuna. Chop until it is texture of hamburger and presses into a compact ball. Place in a large mixing bowl.

2. Add garlic, 4 tablespoons olive oil, anchovies, basil, and salt and pepper to taste. Mix well, shape into 4 circular patties, and set aside. (Patties may be placed on a baking sheet lined with waxed paper, covered, and refrigerated for as long as 8 hours. Remove from refrigerator 30 minutes before sautéing.)

3. If preparing rare burgers, preheat oven to 300 degrees. (Other burgers will not need finishing in oven.) In a small bowl, combine mayonnaise with soy sauce. In a mixing bowl, combine mesclun with 2 remaining tablespoons olive oil and vinegar. Toast brioche or buns on one side and spread with seasoned mayonnaise.

4. Place a small nonstick sauté pan over medium-high heat and add grapeseed oil. Add burgers and sauté 1 minute a side for rare, 1½ minutes a side for medium-rare. Transfer rare

burgers to oven for 2 or 3 minutes to be sure centers are not cold. To serve, place a slice of tomato on a slice of brioche and top with a tuna burger and a portion of mesclun. Place a second slice of brioche to one side. Repeat to make a total of 4 burgers and serve immediately.

Yield: 4 servings
Time: 30 minutes

PEACHES HARD AS ROCKS? THE ANSWER'S IN THE LOBSTER POUND

A long time ago my wife came back from the market and gave me some peaches that were as hard as a rock, as they too often are. I decided to slice them very, very thin and mix them with a crisp salad. The flavor wasn't right, so I tried the peaches in a coleslaw instead. Because we often serve lobster with fruit, like papaya, I put this coleslaw with it. The flavors are sweet and sharp, and it's a very refreshing summer dish.

Although we do not have sweet salads in France, when I came to the United States I fell in love with coleslaw. Unripe peaches are not dripping with juice, but they do have a little peachy flavor and good, firm texture. Cut into julienne strips, they are a perfect replacement for cabbage. The sweet and sharp flavors are so unexpected.

I make the dressing with yogurt instead of oil because my wife and I are always trying to lose some weight. Yogurt also has acidity and creaminess. When the peaches sit in the dressing overnight, it wilts them. And I mix in ginger and chives for some savory flavor—I don't want it to taste like fruit salad.

The soft texture of the lobster and the crispness of the peaches make a very good balance in a very elegant dish. I steam the lobster, then massage the meat with olive oil and warm it in a very low oven to keep it very, very moist. (If you have guests, you can steam and shell the lobster early, then finish the dish in minutes.) I also drizzle the lobster with lemon juice and maple syrup for sweetness and extra flavor. Sugar would only taste sweet here, but maple syrup has a burned caramel flavor and adds extra complexity to the lobster.

You can also use sautéed scallops because scallops, like lobster, are sweet and tender.

I garnish the dish with a fresh herb, usually chervil for a little anise flavor, but anything but cilantro will do. And just to make the coleslaw look like a mimosa salad, like a flower, I sprinkle it with sieved hard-cooked egg yolk, heated in a microwave to dry it out so it doesn't clump. It looks very elegant although it doesn't add much flavor.

LOBSTER WITH PEACH COLESLAW

For the coleslaw:
  ½ cup plain whole-milk yogurt
  2 teaspoons sugar
  Juice of ½ small lemon
  ½ teaspoon finely grated fresh ginger
  4 unripe peaches (1¼ pounds), peeled and
    cut into ⅛-inch julienne strips
  Salt and freshly ground black pepper

For the lobster:
  2 lobsters (1 to 1½ pounds each)
  2 teaspoons extra-virgin olive oil
  Salt and freshly ground black pepper

  1 tablespoon maple syrup
  1 tablespoon lemon juice
  1 hard-boiled egg yolk
  2 teaspoons chopped chives
  Chervil and curly parsley for garnish

1. To prepare coleslaw: In a medium bowl, combine yogurt, sugar, lemon juice, and ginger. Add peaches and salt and pepper to taste. Cover and refrigerate for at least 2 hours, preferably overnight.

2. To prepare lobster: Preheat oven to 300 degrees. Place a rack in a large steamer (or a roasting pan that has an inch of water) and bring water to a boil. Steam lobsters for 4 minutes. When lobsters are cool enough to handle, carefully remove meat from knuckles and claws so that it remains intact. Break tails from bodies. Leaving tails in shells, cut tails in half lengthwise. Massage meat with oil and add salt and pepper to taste. Place in a glass baking dish with tail meat facing up. Bake for 4 minutes, or until meat has turned white and is no longer transparent.

3. Mix maple syrup with lemon juice and set aside. Put egg yolk through a sieve and dry it for 10 seconds in a microwave oven on high.

4. In center of each of 4 plates, place a portion of coleslaw and sprinkle with egg yolk and chives. Remove lobster tails from shells and rub with a little more olive oil. Arrange a lobster claw, knuckle, and half a tail around coleslaw. Drizzle with maple syrup mixture and garnish with chervil and curly parsley.

Yield: 4 servings
*Time: 40 minutes, plus at least 2 hours of
    marinating*

A COAT OF BASIL FITS NICELY ON A LOIN OF LAMB

The first time I tasted basil, in a soup, it became my favorite herb—and it wasn't even fresh. Before the 1970s in France, it was almost impossible to find fresh herbs. They didn't become plentiful until the development of nouvelle cuisine. When I discovered fresh basil, it changed my life.

In July and August I use a lot of it, and I love to use it as a coating on a roasted loin of lamb. When the meat is sliced, there is the beautiful green of the crust and the gorgeous pink of rare lamb, the colors arranged on a pale creamy bed of quickly cooked fennel. When I make this, I hope it transports my guests in Washington to Provence.

I like this combination much better than the traditional lamb persillade. Persillade is a mixture of a lot of butter, bread crumbs, parsley, and garlic. The crust is too thick and too rich, and it doesn't stick very well to the lamb. I use egg to help the basil crust adhere to the lamb; that makes the lamb easier to cut. I also warm the basil quickly in oil before adding it to the bread crumbs to set the color and improve the flavor.

There are three steps to cooking the loin, a cut you can get by asking your butcher to debone a rack of lamb to obtain the loin. I sauté the meat to brown and caramelize the outside, then I roast it a bit, coat it with the basil crust, and roast it again. Doing this in stages means the basil crust keeps its bright color, as it doesn't have to be cooked so long.

The anise flavor of the fennel makes a good marriage with the basil. To keep the flavor and crunch of fennel, I barely cook it.

LAMB LOIN WITH BASIL CRUST AND FENNEL

For the lamb:
  20 large basil leaves, washed and completely dried
  1 cup vegetable oil
  ½ cup fresh bread crumbs
  2 cloves garlic, peeled
  Salt and freshly ground black pepper
  2 12-ounce boneless lamb loins, silver skin and fat removed
  2 tablespoons extra-virgin olive oil
  ½ cup chicken broth
  3 tablespoons flour
  1 large egg, beaten

For the fennel:
  8 ounces (1 small bulb) fennel, sliced into fine julienne (⅛ inch or less)
  2 tablespoons extra-virgin olive oil
  2 teaspoons Pernod, pastis, or other anise-flavored liqueur, or 1 teaspoon aniseed
  2 teaspoons sugar
  Juice of 1 lemon
  Salt and freshly ground black pepper

4 sprigs thyme for garnish

1. To prepare lamb: In a small saucepan, heat oil to 300 degrees. Place half of basil leaves in oil until they turn dark green, 30 to 50 seconds. Transfer to paper towels to drain and repeat with remaining basil.

2. In a food processor, combine basil, bread crumbs, garlic, and salt and pepper to taste. Blend thoroughly until mixture is fine in texture and bright green. Set aside.

3. Preheat oven to 300 degrees. Season lamb with salt and pepper to taste. In a large sauté pan over very high heat, heat olive oil and add lamb. Sauté until well browned on all sides, about 5 minutes. Transfer to flameproof baking pan and roast for 12 minutes, turning 2 or 3 times.

4. Remove lamb and keep warm; it may be held for up to 1 hour. Discard fat from pan and place pan over medium heat. Stir in broth, scraping bottom of pan well, and allow liquid to reduce by half. Season with salt and pepper, and strain into a small saucepan. Set aside.

5. Roll lamb in flour to coat evenly; pat to remove excess flour. Spread basil–bread crumb mixture across a baking sheet. Brush lamb evenly with beaten egg and roll in bread crumb mixture, pressing firmly so crumbs will adhere. Return lamb to a 300-degree oven until crust is very lightly browned and lamb is reheated, about 5 minutes. While lamb browns, prepare fennel.

6. In a medium saucepan, combine fennel, oil, Pernod, sugar, and lemon juice. Place over medium heat and sauté until fennel is slightly wilted, about 1 minute. Remove from heat and season with salt and pepper to taste.

7. To serve, place saucepan with lamb juices over low heat to warm. Cut each lamb loin into 6 slices. Divide fennel among 4 plates and arrange slices of lamb on top. Drizzle lamb juices around plates and garnish with thyme sprigs. Serve immediately.

Yield: 4 servings
Time: 1 hour

FRIED CHICKEN WITH MORE CRUNCH FOR THE MONEY, FROM POTATOES

I have thought a lot about fried chicken because Americans love it. The idea for a potato crust on it came to me from frozen Tater Tots. I loved their crunch and thought if I coated the chicken with potatoes instead of bread crumbs, the crunch would be better. It's more work, but it's more than worth it. I had to play with the recipe a few times before I got it right. The hardest part was getting the potatoes to stick to the skinless chicken. The potatoes are diced very small because that adds so much more texture. You don't want them to be uniform because you get a better crunch if the pieces are different sizes. I use a mandoline to cut fine strips and then a very sharp knife to cut tiny cubes, but you can do it all with a knife.

At first I tried potato starch, but it didn't adhere, so I switched to flour. I also wanted to marinate the chicken to give it more flavor and sophistication. An oil-based marinade also kept the coating from sticking, so I had to change to a dry rub with sage, cumin, and garlic. They all add interesting notes that are not found in traditional fried chicken. I mix the chicken and the dry rub with my hands in order to massage the seasonings into the flesh.

Wrapping the chicken in plastic film also helps the coating adhere. When I first tried it, it was very tricky to remove the plastic without having some of the coating come with it. So I tried putting the wrapped pieces in the freezer for an hour, and that was all it needed. The plastic was easy to remove.

I prefer to make this dish with boneless chicken because it cooks more quickly and is easier to eat. I fry only a few pieces at a time so that the temperature of the fat does not cool down too much. In the restaurant I use clarified butter, but at home I do it in grapeseed oil because it is healthier. I have to admit, though, that the clarified butter gives it more flavor.

SAGE CHICKEN IN A
FRIED POTATO CRUST

3 skinless, boneless chicken breast halves
3 skinless, boneless chicken thighs
½ cup loosely packed chopped sage
1 teaspoon minced garlic
1 teaspoon ground cumin
2 pounds (2 to 3 large) baking potatoes
7 tablespoons all-purpose flour
2 tablespoons lightly beaten large egg white
Freshly ground black pepper
2 large eggs, lightly beaten
Grapeseed oil for deep frying

1. Cut each chicken breast half into 3 pieces and each thigh into 2 pieces. In a bowl, combine chicken, sage, garlic, and cumin. Cover and refrigerate for 2 hours.

2. Using a mandoline or sharp knife, slice potatoes lengthwise into ⅛-inch-thick julienne, then crosswise into ⅛-inch dice. Rinse, then pat dry between cloth towels. Roll in towels to squeeze out moisture. In a medium bowl, combine potatoes with 4 tablespoons flour and beaten egg white. Set aside.

3. Scrape garlic and sage from chicken pieces and pat dry with paper towels. Season with pepper to taste and dust with remaining flour.

4. Place a 10-inch square of plastic wrap on a work surface. Evenly spread about 2 tablespoons potato in center of plastic. Dip a piece of chicken in beaten egg and place in center of potato. Top with about 1 tablespoon potato and wrap plastic securely so that potato covers chicken completely. Repeat with remaining chicken, egg, and potatoes to make a total of 15 packets. Place in freezer for 1 hour.

5. Preheat oven to 200 degrees. Preheat at least 4 inches of oil in a deep fryer to 325 degrees. Unwrap 3 chicken packets and deep-fry until potatoes are crisp and golden brown, 5 to 8 minutes. Transfer to baking sheet lined with paper towels and keep warm in oven. Repeat with remaining packets. Serve hot.

Yield: 4 servings
Time: 1¼ hours, plus 2 hours of refrigeration and 1 hour of freezing

A TANGY SLICE OF SUMMER IN A TERRINE

Some people might call my tomato terrine a tomato pudding, but it is more a salad, with very thin layers of highly seasoned tomato slices and bread. It is the perfect first course in summer. The terrine has so many origins: Mexican pico de gallo with its highly seasoned tomatoes; Italian panzanella, the bread salad; and a salad my mother always made.

The idea first came to me when I was making a summer pudding with layers of brioche, strawberries, and cassis. As it sits in the refrigerator overnight, all the juices soak through the bread and blend together into a pudding that bursts with the flavors of the fruit and cassis.

My mother's tomato salad had no bread but great flavor. It was seasoned with onion, parsley, garlic, red wine vinegar, and peanut oil, and she made it four or five hours in advance so the flavors would meld. I use basil and olive oil, but we didn't have those in the Champagne region. I adopted those ingredients when I went to work in the south of France and combined them with red onion and red wine vinegar.

For this salad the tomatoes have to be skinned. You can do this with a blowtorch, charring the skin until it can be slipped off, as we sometimes do, or you can blanch them in boiling water until the skins loosen and will easily slide off. Just don't put in more than two at a time, or the tomatoes will remain in the water so long that they will cook and turn mushy.

Some people blanch garlic when they use it in a dish that won't be cooked, but I prefer to sauté it because that adds a bit of flavor while removing the harshness.

The bread must be very dense to stand up to all the liquid. That's why I use brioche, but you can use another dense bread like challah or pain de mie, *the French sandwich bread, which has a dense texture and is made with milk and butter.*

SUMMER TOMATO TERRINE

4½ pounds (about 10 large) ripe field
    tomatoes
7 tablespoons extra-virgin olive oil
5 cloves garlic, finely chopped
1½ cups finely diced red onion
7 tablespoons red wine vinegar
Salt and freshly ground black pepper
1 unsliced loaf brioche, pain de mie, or other
    fine-textured white bread
1½ cups minced Italian parsley

1. Bring a large pot of water to a boil. Using a slotted spoon, dip tomato for a few seconds and remove. Repeat until skin cracks, then set aside to cool. Repeat with remaining tomatoes. Slip off skins and cut tomatoes in half. Remove cores and seeds. Cut flesh into ¼-inch dice and place in a large bowl.

2. In a small sauté pan over low heat, heat 1 tablespoon oil, add garlic, and sauté just until softened, not browned. Add to tomatoes with onion, vinegar, and remaining 6 tablespoons oil. Season with salt and pepper, and toss to mix well.

3. Line an 11½ by 4 by 3-inch terrine with plastic wrap. Remove crust from bread and cut loaf lengthwise to make a slice ¼ inch thick to fit bottom of mold. (If necessary, use more than one slice, fitting them together in an even layer.) Spoon one-third of tomatoes evenly across bread and sprinkle with one-third of parsley.

4. Top with another ¼-inch layer of bread. Add one-third of tomatoes and one-third of parsley. Repeat with last layers of bread, tomato, and parsley, and top with bread. Spread any juices over bread. Cover with plastic wrap and place a brick or similar weight on top. Refrigerate overnight.

5. To serve, lift terrine from mold and remove plastic wrap. Using a serrated knife, cut terrine into slices ½ inch thick. Serve 2 slices as a side dish or 3 as a first course.

Yield: 6 to 10 servings

Time: 45 minutes, plus overnight refrigeration

EBERHARD MÜLLER

Eberhard Müller, formerly the executive chef and an owner of Lutèce, is now the executive chef at Bayard's in Manhattan. He was photographed on his organic farm on Long Island, New York. These columns were written with Jack Bishop.

FOR ANYONE WHO LOVES TOMATOES, WELCOME TO PARADISE

Most chefs wait for the morning produce delivery. I walk out the back door of my farmhouse and pick my own. My wife and I own an eighteen-acre organic farm nestled amid the vineyards of the North Fork of Long Island. We run a small business supplying organic produce to restaurants, including mine.

As a chef my inspiration begins with these glorious farm-fresh fruits and vegetables. They are my passion. Here, I'll be creating dishes inspired by what is ripening and ready for harvest. I begin with tomatoes: vivid red Costoluto Fiorentinos, Ruffled Yellows, Green Zebras, and Purple Cherokees. Their flavors are intense. In fact, these tomatoes are so good that I don't eat tomatoes the rest of the year. The rock-hard kind available in December just can't compare.

Presented with such a bounty so delicious on its own, most cooks are content simply to slice ripe tomatoes and

maybe dress them with a little vinaigrette. While this is a fine use for summer tomatoes, it's not the only one. For instance, I like to slow-roast tomatoes in a 250-degree oven: I peel, halve, and seed the tomatoes, then season them with garlic, olive oil, salt, and pepper in a baking dish. After three or four hours in the oven the tomatoes become tender, less watery, and incredibly sweet. I eat them as a snack or serve them with grilled meats or fish.

If you want to use more heat and less time, make a tomato gratin. But instead of masking that great tomato flavor with butter and cheese, simply layer peeled and sliced tomatoes in a baking dish with olive oil, garlic, thyme, and sliced fresh bulb onions. (These onions, recently dug, don't have papery skins and are especially juicy and flavorful.) I like to spoon the juicy, almost jellied tomatoes over bread for an easy appetizer or over a piece of grilled fish for an instant sauce.

You can pump up the tomato flavor without cooking, too. In my tomato tartare I peel, seed, and dice a vari-

ety of tomatoes and put them in a sieve to let the excess liquid drip away. I season the drained tomatoes and serve them straight up in a martini glass. And I pour the liquid into small glasses and serve this sweet juice as a sort of tomato chaser. The tartare may look like a salsa, but instead of the in-your-face flavors of chilies and cilantro, I add celery and chives. These subtle seasonings keep the focus squarely on the tomatoes.

Most serious cooks overlook cherry tomatoes, which is a big mistake. They, too, have a sweet, delicious flavor. Just don't confuse locally grown heirloom cherry tomatoes with the tough specimens sold in supermarkets. The heirlooms have much thinner skins and more acidity than bland commercial varieties. I also like cherry tomatoes because they hold their shape when cooked. For instance, I make a quick sauce for sautéed striped bass by deglazing the pan with sherry vinegar and then adding some homemade basil oil. The tomatoes, which I halve or quarter for easier eating, are then warmed in the sauce and spooned over the fish. Although I like to use striped bass in this dish—partly because it's caught in the waters near our farm—grouper or even snapper can be handled in the same fashion.

When tomatoes are at their peak, be greedy. Have your fill. Then wait, hard as it may be, until tomato season rolls round again. It's worth it.

SAUTÉED STRIPED BASS WITH BASIL-SCENTED CHERRY TOMATOES

2½ cups lightly packed fresh basil leaves, roughly chopped, plus 16 fresh basil leaves, julienned, for garnish (use both green and purple basil if possible)
⅔ cup extra-virgin olive oil
1 striped bass fillet, skinned (about 2¼ pounds)
Salt and freshly ground white pepper
Flour for dusting fish
4 to 5 tablespoons grapeseed oil
⅓ cup sherry vinegar
12 ounces cherry tomatoes, halved or quartered, depending on size

1. Place 2½ cups chopped basil in a medium saucepan. Add oil and set over medium-low heat. Cover and heat until basil wilts and oil is extremely fragrant, about 3 minutes. Remove from heat and set aside, covered, for at least 20 minutes and up to 1 hour.

2. With a sharp knife, cut fish on an angle into ¼-inch-thick scallops, starting about 2 inches from tail end and working toward head end, with slicing angle toward tail. Trim ragged edges.

3. Heat oven to 200 degrees and place serving platter in oven. Season fish with salt and pepper to taste. Dust 1 side very lightly with flour and press into fish.

4. Heat 3 tablespoons grapeseed oil in a large skillet over high heat until barely smoking. Place several scallops, floured side down, in skillet and sauté until crisp and golden brown on underside, about 2 minutes. Flip over and cook for 5 seconds on other side. Transfer fish, browned side up, to a plate lined with paper towels. Blot up excess oil.

Arrange fish, browned side up, on warm platter in oven. Meanwhile, repeat process with remaining scallops, adding more grapeseed oil to skillet as necessary.

5. When all scallops are sautéed, wipe pan clean with paper towels. Add vinegar, 2 tablespoons water, and salt and pepper to taste. Turn off heat but keep pan over burner. Strain basil oil into hot pan but do not stir. Add tomatoes and warm slightly, less than 1 minute.

6. Remove platter from oven and spoon tomato mixture over fish. Garnish with julienned basil and serve immediately.

Yield: 4 servings
Time: 45 minutes

TOMATO GRATIN

Coarse sea salt or kosher salt
1 medium clove garlic, minced
2½ pounds tomatoes (use several kinds in a
    variety of colors), cored and scored on
    blossom end
4 tablespoons extra-virgin olive oil
½ cup thinly sliced fresh bulb onions
1 tablespoon whole fresh thyme leaves
Freshly ground white pepper

1. Sprinkle salt liberally on minced garlic. Press garlic-salt mixture into cutting board with side of chef's knife. Continue mincing and pressing until garlic breaks down and forms a smooth paste. Set aside.

2. Bring a large pot of water to a boil. Add tomatoes and heat for 15 seconds to loosen skins. With a slotted spoon transfer tomatoes to a large bowl of cold water. Soak until just cool, about 1 minute, remove from water, and then peel. Slice ¼ inch thick, keeping slices from each tomato together.

3. Heat oven to 350 degrees. Smear 1 tablespoon oil over bottom of a 12 by 6-inch (or similar size) gratin dish. Sprinkle half of onions, garlic paste, and thyme into dish, then sprinkle with salt and pepper to taste. Place each whole tomato in dish, spreading slices just a bit. Distribute remaining onions, garlic paste, and thyme over tomatoes. Drizzle with remaining 3 tablespoons oil and sprinkle with pepper to taste.

4. Bake until oil and juices start to bubble, about 25 minutes. Lower heat to 300 degrees and continue baking until tomatoes are very tender and just beginning to brown, about 25 minutes. Serve warm or at room temperature.

Yield: 4 to 6 appetizer or side dish servings
Time: 1¼ hours

BASIL OIL

My method for making basil oil for tomato dishes is pretty unconventional. Most chefs blanch the basil, rinse it under cold water, and then blend it with extra-virgin olive oil. After letting the basil and oil steep, they strain out the solids to obtain a vibrant green oil.

While the results on the plate are stunning, I find that this method sacrifices flavor for color. Blanching and rinsing basil washes away too much taste.

I prefer to warm olive oil and chopped basil in a saucepan, heating the oil to just above body temperature for a few minutes. Gentle heat speeds the transfer of flavor compounds from the basil to the oil. I then take the pan off the heat, cover it, and let the basil steep for at least 20 minutes. When strained, the oil looks like ordinary olive oil, but the flavor and aroma are almost intoxicating.

When I have more time, I steep basil oil by the method used to make sun tea. I place chopped basil and extra-virgin olive oil in a covered glass jar and let the mixture heat outside in the sun for a few hours. No matter which method you try, the oil is best used the day it is made.

~⌒

A TART REINTERPRETED: THE FRENCH CLASSIC IS RUSTIC IN GERMANY

Growing up, I lived above my parents' bakery in the Black Forest region of Germany. Out back was an orchard where we grew pears, apples, apricots, plums, and peaches for use in the family business. The weather in southwestern Germany isn't ideal for fruit trees, and at the end of the summer we often had a lot of peaches that were ripe but still firm. They weren't great for eating out of hand, but they were perfect for tarts.

In that part of Germany, fruit tarts are made with brioche, a buttery yeast dough, rather than the shortbread pastry used in French and American baking. The difference is enormous. In the oven the brioche dough develops a crunchy, well-browned crust while the inside remains tender and springy. Brioche also does a much better job of absorbing fruit juices than a crumbly shortbread-style crust, and because the dough isn't terribly sweet, the fruit—in this case, peaches—really shines.

Soft, sweet peaches make a delicious tart, of course, but not such a pretty one; they lose their shape and exude a lot of juice when they are baked. That is why I prefer peaches that are firm but ripe, with no green spots. When they are baked, their flavor improves and their texture becomes creamy, but they still hold their shape.

I don't complicate this tart—it's more or less my parents' recipe: just brioche, a light sprinkle of ground almonds and bread crumbs to absorb excess juices, and fruit. Don't think of it as the typical elegant dessert; this tart is a much more rustic affair, almost like a deep-dish pizza. In fact, in Germany it is a midafternoon snack.

Brioche tart dough works well with other summer fruits, too, especially plums and apricots. With plums, which I don't peel, I sprinkle the tart shell with ground hazelnuts, bread crumbs, sugar, and cinnamon. Apricots already have a strong almond flavor, so I just use bread crumbs and sugar. When I have both plums and peaches, I arrange them in a single tart. The acidity of the plums heightens the sweetness of the peaches. The combination is brilliant. Brioche tastes best warm, so I time the tart so that it comes out of the oven just as we're sitting down to dinner.

Although the tart can stand on its own, I like to add a dollop of crème fraîche or ice cream.

BRIOCHE PEACH TART

1½ cups all-purpose flour plus extra for
    dusting work surface

¼ cup plus 2 teaspoons sugar

1 packet (¼ ounce) rapid-rise active dry yeast

⅛ teaspoon salt

2 large eggs at room temperature

¼ cup milk, slightly warmed

9 tablespoons unsalted butter at room
    temperature, diced

4 ripe but firm peaches

1 tablespoon finely ground almonds

1 tablespoon bread crumbs

1. To make brioche dough: Place flour, ¼ cup sugar, yeast, salt, eggs, and milk in bowl of a standing mixer fitted with a dough hook. Beat on medium speed, scraping down sides of bowl once or twice, until dough is smooth, about 10 minutes. Add 8 tablespoons butter and continue beating and scraping down sides of bowl until it is completely incorporated and dough is smooth again, about 5 minutes. Dust top of dough lightly with flour, cover bowl with a damp towel, and let dough rise in a warm place until almost doubled, 1½ to 2 hours.

2. Preheat oven to 400 degrees. Punch down dough and divide in half. (Wrap one piece and set aside for another use; it can be refrigerated for several days or frozen for several weeks.) Roll the other half out on a heavily floured work surface into an 11-inch circle, dusting frequently with flour to prevent sticking. Lay dough over a rolling pin and transfer to a 9-inch fluted tart pan with a removable bottom. Press dough into bottom and sides, trimming any excess with a sharp knife. Let rise until slightly puffed, 15 to 20 minutes. Lightly prick with a fork.

3. Meanwhile, bring a large pot of water to a simmer. Add peaches for 30 seconds, then remove with a slotted spoon to a large bowl of cold water. Soak peaches just until cool, about 30 seconds. Drain and peel. Halve, pit, and cut each peach into 8 wedges.

4. Mix almonds, bread crumbs, and 2 teaspoons sugar in a small bowl. Sprinkle all but 2 teaspoons of almond mixture over dough. Arrange peach slices on dough so that they overlap. Sprinkle with remaining almond mixture, dot peaches with remaining 1 tablespoon butter, and place pan on rimmed baking sheet.

5. Place on bottom rack of oven and bake for 10 minutes. Lower oven setting to 350 degrees and bake until tart is golden brown on top, 25 to 30 minutes. Remove from pan immediately (crust will steam and soften if left in pan) and transfer to a wire rack. Cool briefly and serve warm.

Yield: 6 to 8 servings
Time: 3 hours

TRANSFORMING CORN'S SWEETNESS WITH SOME HEAT AND SOME TANG

When I moved to the United States eighteen years ago, corn was a discovery to me, but it seemed shockingly sweet and one-dimensional. I now love all that sweetness, but it took me a while to figure out how to deal with it. Over the years I have learned that spiciness and acidity are necessary to balance corn sugars. That's why I add chilies to the batter for corn fritters and lime or lemon juice to corn chowder.

I use both those ingredients in my savory corn soufflé, which is a perfect vehicle for appreciating old-fashioned corn flavor. Any hot chili can be used, but a super-hot habañero keeps the corn and sweet bell peppers from tasting cloying. (Wear gloves while you chop it because it will burn your skin.) The acidity comes in the form of grated lime zest and a few drops of lime juice. To understand the importance of some acidity, taste the soufflé base before adding the lime juice. It will seem flat and underseasoned. Add the lime juice and taste again. The flavors will be rounder, fuller, and more complex.

Fresh herbs, especially mint, cilantro, basil, and tarragon, will also make corn taste less sweet and more interesting. That's why I infuse mint into the milk for this soufflé. It adds a bracing but not overwhelming bite.

Serve this soufflé in small portions as a first course, or spoon out larger portions for brunch or a light supper.

SWEET CORN SOUFFLÉ WITH PEPPERS AND MINT

½ cup milk
1 sprig mint
2½ cups corn kernels (cut from 5 ears of sweet corn)
3 tablespoons unsalted butter, plus extra for pan
1 red bell pepper, stemmed, seeded, and diced
1 yellow bell pepper, stemmed, seeded, and diced
1 red habanero chili, stemmed, seeded, and diced
Salt and ground white pepper to taste
1 tablespoon flour, plus extra for pan
4 large eggs, separated
½ lime

1. Place milk and mint sprig in a medium saucepan and heat until warm. Remove from heat and let steep about 15 minutes.

2. Puree 2 cups corn kernels in a food processor until smooth.

3. Melt 1 tablespoon butter in a large skillet, add peppers, and cook over medium heat until softened, about 5 minutes. Season with salt and pepper, and remove from heat.

4. Fill a large roasting pan with 1 inch of water and place in middle of oven. Preheat oven to 375 degrees.

5. Remove mint from milk and discard. Return saucepan to medium-low heat, add 2 remaining tablespoons butter, and bring to a simmer. When butter melts, slowly whisk in flour and cook, whisking frequently, until mixture is smooth and quite thick, about 5 minutes. Remove pan from heat and let cool 1 or 2 minutes.

Whisk in egg yolks. Grate zest of lime and add to mixture, stirring to incorporate. Stir in pureed corn and ¼ cup corn kernels. Stir in sautéed peppers and season with salt, pepper, and a few drops of lime juice. At this point the mixture should be somewhat spicy and a bit overseasoned. Scrape mixture into a large bowl. (It can be covered and refrigerated for several hours.)

6. Butter and flour a 2-quart soufflé dish.

7. With an electric mixer, whip egg whites until stiff but not overbeaten. With a rubber spatula gently fold egg whites into corn mixture. Scrape into soufflé dish and sprinkle with remaining ¼ cup corn kernels.

8. Place dish in a water bath in oven and bake until well browned and puffed, about 1 hour. Serve immediately.

Yield: 6 first-course servings
Time: 2 hours

WHERE FENNEL'S CONCERNED, START WITH BABIES AND TREAT THEM TENDERLY

Unlike the swollen, tough fennel bulbs you find in supermarkets, tiny young fennel is tender and has a more intense flavor. The bulbs are small enough to fit into a child's palm. A few slivery slices of these young bulbs will add real personality to a leafy salad, but when you're serving fennel on its own, I think its licorice kick needs to be tamed. I usually add some acidity in the form of citrus or white wine, as in the Italian salad made with sliced fennel and oranges.

And although I like fennel raw, I think it is more intriguing cooked. Grilled or roasted fennel can be lovely, but neither of these cooking methods does much to improve the texture. Like celery, fennel can be stringy. I often marinate it in lemon juice, salt, and olive oil, which helps break down some fibers, but many still remain after cooking.

And that's one reason that I prefer to braise fennel. A brief browning in a pan on the stove top adds color and flavor, and then I deglaze the pan with wine, add chicken stock, and place it in the oven. The fennel absorbs the liquid and becomes totally tender, almost creamy. Best of all, the stringy fibers melt away in the moist heat.

I often braise fennel with thin baby leeks since their sweetness takes up some of the anise flavor. A moderately sweet white wine, like a dry Riesling, adds acidity and reinforces the sweetness. Like fennel, leeks become amazingly tender when braised.

Baby fennel and baby leeks can be found at farmers' markets, but this recipe can be adapted for larger vegetables. Just peel off the outer layers from larger fennel bulbs and cut them in half from top to bottom. With larger leeks, strip away several outer layers. In either case, use fewer vegetables so that the leeks and then the fennel will fit in the pan in a single layer for browning.

Braised fennel and leeks work well with fish such as striped bass and swordfish, or they can be part of a vegetarian platter, perhaps with roasted or sautéed potatoes and roasted peppers.

BRAISED BABY FENNEL AND LEEKS

12 baby leeks (¼ inch thick or less) or 8
    small leeks (no thicker than ½ inch)
16 baby fennel bulbs (about 2½ ounces each
    when trimmed)
6 tablespoons extra-virgin olive oil
Kosher salt and white pepper to taste
¾ cup white wine, preferably dry Riesling
¾ cup chicken or vegetable stock

1. Preheat oven to 400 degrees. Trim dark green portions and roots from leeks. Starting at light green ends, halve leeks lengthwise almost to (but not through) root ends. Wash leeks in successive bowls of cold water until clean. Pat dry. Trim stalks and cut a thin slice from bottom of fennel bulbs.

2. Heat 3 tablespoons oil in a large ovenproof skillet or braising pan. Add salt, pepper, and leeks, and cook over medium-high heat, turning once, until lightly browned, about 4 minutes. Transfer leeks to a platter.

3. Add remaining 3 tablespoons oil to pan and heat briefly. Add fennel and cook, turning once, until lightly browned, about 7 minutes. Add wine, place leeks on top of fennel, and add any juices on platter. Simmer about 1 minute. Add stock, bring to a boil, cover, and transfer pan to oven.

4. Braise fennel and leeks for 20 minutes. Remove cover and continue cooking until vegetables are extremely tender and most of liquid has evaporated, about 15 minutes. Adjust seasonings and serve immediately.

Yield: 6 to 8 servings
Time: 1 hour

GETTING ALL THE ROASTED PEPPERS WITH LESS OF THE WORK

Like most chefs, I've spent countless hours charring peppers over an open flame, steaming them in a covered bowl, and then scraping off their skins and pulling out every last seed. Although tedious, this process is magical. Roasting transforms crunchy, crisp peppers into soft, smooth vegetables that melt in your mouth.

But I've found that stewing sliced peppers in lots of olive oil creates a similar texture with just a fraction of the work. This cooking method also captures the peppers' flavorful juices, which are lost when they are roasted. With a combination of orange, yellow, and red bell peppers, the juices and the oil emulsify to create a brilliant orange sauce, and it has a great taste.

The sauce moistens the peppers if you want to serve them as a side dish. But there is also enough sauce to spoon over grilled striped bass or bluefish, or roasted or grilled chicken. Fresh peppers exude plenty of juice, and you need all the oil in this recipe to thicken it to a sauce consistency.

To balance the sweetness of the peppers I also use Hungarian wax peppers, which have pure pepper flavor with minimal sweetness or heat, and a red jalapeño, which adds heat. The Hungarian peppers are long, thin, and yellowish green, and are sold at farmers' markets. The red jalapeño tastes fruitier than chilies picked green.

This dish starts with garlic and cipolline onions (or

any freshly dug onions without papery skins). But in-stead of sautéing these aromatics, I sweat them in a cov-ered pot so they don't overpower the peppers. When they're in season, locally grown peppers are as sweet as candy and far superior to the insipid hothouse Holland peppers available anytime. Don't buy green ones, though. They have an unpleasant, bitter flavor. And don't bother with purple peppers; their color is only skin deep, and their green flesh is bitter.

SWEET AND SPICY PEPPER STEW

⅔ cup extra-virgin olive oil
12 small fresh cipolline onions, stalks and
    roots trimmed, bulbs thinly sliced
    (1 generous cup)
Salt and freshly ground white pepper
2 medium cloves garlic, minced
4 pounds orange, yellow, and red bell
    peppers, halved, stemmed, seeded, and
    thinly sliced
2 Hungarian wax peppers, halved, stemmed,
    seeded, and thinly sliced
1 red jalapeño pepper, halved, stemmed,
    seeded, and thinly sliced

1. Place oil and onions in a large braising pan or casserole. Turn heat to medium, season with salt and pepper to taste, cover, and cook until softened, 4 minutes. Stir in garlic, cover, and cook until garlic is softened, about 1 minute.

2. Add bell peppers (they will mound high in pan) and 2 tablespoons water, cover, and cook, stirring once or twice, until peppers begin to re-lease their liquid, about 6 minutes.

3. Stir in wax peppers and jalapeño, cover, and continue cooking, stirring several times, un-

til peppers are tender but not mushy, about 10 minutes. Adjust seasonings. Serve hot, warm, or at room temperature.

Yield: 8 side-dish servings
Time: 45 minutes

⌒

A SIMPLE EGGPLANT DISH THAT TASTES LIKE EGGPLANT

Everyone knows how beautiful deep purple eggplants can look in the market, but they are even more elegant in the field: row upon row of dark green plants with flaw-less, shiny purple ornaments suspended beneath the leaves.

They are completely alluring. And yet so few people want the bother of them. Unlike most other vegetables, which can pretty much go directly from the produce bin (or the field) into the pot, eggplant takes some thought and attention. It needs to be drained or roasted, and the larger varieties can be bitter if they're not handled prop-erly.

I wanted to figure out a way to create an eggplant dish that really tasted like eggplant—not like garlic or tahini or any of the other flavors that are traditionally used with it—and was still simple enough for everyday cooking. Roasting is a good start: It is an easy way to draw off excess liquid and some of the bitterness. Once the eggplants cool, I open them up and remove the seeds, which leaves just a few spoonfuls of meaty flesh. This might seem wasteful, but it is worth it; the flavor and texture are greatly improved.

Next, to draw off even more moisture, I sauté the eggplant in olive oil until it is nearly dry. This extra step transforms the roasted eggplant into a smooth, thick puree without using a food processor. I keep the season-ing simple: a little minced shallot or fresh onions, some garlic, and fresh herbs.

I am careful to keep the garlic flavor mild, though, by sprinkling the raw clove with coarse salt and then working the mixture with the side of a chef's knife un-til the garlic breaks down. With garlic paste you never get chunks of garlic in the puree.

This recipe starts with an unbelievable amount of eggplant: eight to ten pounds for just eight servings. But once the skin, seeds, and water are gone, you're left with pure, concentrated eggplant flavor without a trace of bitterness. In fact, my eggplant "puree" actually tastes sweet. (It tastes even better if you can give it a few hours' rest; with time the herbs really perfume the egg-plant.) I serve the puree as a side dish for grilled fish, but on a casual late-summer afternoon, it's hard to re-sist spreading it over a slice of grilled bread.

EGGPLANT PUREE WITH MIXED HERBS

5 large eggplants (each 1½ to 2 pounds),
   green caps trimmed
1 large clove garlic, minced
Coarse sea salt
6 tablespoons extra-virgin olive oil
2 shallots or fresh cipolline onions, minced
½ cup minced curly parsley
⅓ cup minced chives
3 tablespoons minced garlic chives
4 mint leaves, minced
Salt and freshly ground white pepper

1. Preheat oven to 400 degrees. Prick egg-plants all over with a paring knife and place on a large rimmed baking sheet. Bake, turning once, until eggplants are collapsed and completely soft,

about 1½ hours. Let cool. Meanwhile, sprinkle garlic with sea salt and use flat blade of a chef's knife to mash to a coarse paste. Set aside.

2. Halve eggplants lengthwise and remove seeds with a large spoon. Scoop flesh out into a large bowl, discarding skins. Mix eggplant with spoon to break up large chunks.

3. Place 4 tablespoons oil and shallots in a large casserole. Turn heat to medium and cook until softened, about 3 minutes. Stir in garlic paste and eggplant, and cook, stirring occasion-ally, until excess liquid evaporates and eggplant thickens, 15 to 20 minutes.

4. Remove from heat and stir in remaining 2 tablespoons oil and herbs. Season with salt and pepper to taste. Serve hot, warm, or at room tem-perature.

Yield: 8 side-dish or appetizer servings
Time: 2½ hours

WITH HERBS AND MORE HERBS, VINAIGRETTE GOES BEYOND SALAD

Home cooks rarely think of vinaigrette as a sauce. In most kitchens vinaigrette has only one use: as a dressing for salad greens. But if you bulk up oil and vinegar with plenty of good mustard and fresh herbs, the familiar vinaigrette turns into something else entirely and has a consistency almost like pesto. That shouldn't be such a surprise: Vinaigrette is a cold sauce, after all, just like pesto, aioli, and tapenade.

My favorite herb vinaigrette calls for as much minced herbs as oil. This sauce is too thick for drizzling over lettuce, but it naps a piece of poached fish perfectly. For my herb vinaigrette I use bits of every herb growing behind my farmhouse. Minced basil, mint, chervil, garlic chives, parsley, cilantro, and chives create a vibrant sauce bursting with fresh herb flavor.

Of course, you can trade some complexity for simplicity and use fewer herbs. Substitute more of another herb with similar intensity if you can't track down every herb in the market. And remember that freshness is as important as variety. Dull herbs make a dull dressing.

Another key to great herb flavor is good mincing technique. The first thing I teach young cooks in my restaurant is how to handle herbs. Most cooks rock a chef's knife through herbs, grinding them down into the board. This motion bruises the cell structure and causes flavorful oils to be lost. If your cutting board is dyed green every time you mince herbs, you're doing something wrong. You want that flavor in your food, not the cutting board.

When I mince or chop herbs, I use a slicing motion. I pull the front of the knife backward through a pile of herbs, rather than pressing down and pushing the knife forward. (Using the front of the knife is important. When most cooks mince, they grind the herbs with the heavy back end of the knife.) I keep slicing the herbs until they reach the texture I'm looking for. When I'm

done, my cutting board is clean. Minced this way, herbs have tremendous clarity of flavor. Even though my vinaigrette calls for seven herbs, you can taste each one.

Because halibut is lean but meaty, it is the perfect fish for this sauce. I poach the halibut rather than grill or sauté it so you can really taste the herbs. The poaching liquid is a quick broth flavored with vegetables as well as white wine and vinegar for acidity.

You can easily play around with the vegetables in the broth, adding fennel, celery, tomatoes, or even lemongrass. Or subtract vegetables to make things simpler: Just leeks, carrots, and a bay leaf will do if that's all you have on hand. The idea is to use a fair amount of vegetables—as well as wine and vinegar—so that the broth is strong enough to flavor the fish.

POACHED HALIBUT WITH HERB VINAIGRETTE

- 2 medium leeks, white and light green parts only, halved lengthwise, cleaned, and cut crosswise into several pieces
- 2 medium carrots, peeled
- 1 medium onion, thickly sliced
- 1 medium clove garlic, peeled
- 2 tablespoons kosher salt
- 15 white peppercorns
- 1 bay leaf
- 1 cup white wine
- ⅓ cup white vinegar
- Sprigs of fresh thyme and basil
- 2 tablespoons Dijon mustard
- 1 tablespoon sherry vinegar
- 1 teaspoon red wine vinegar
- Salt and freshly ground white pepper
- ⅓ cup extra-virgin olive oil
- 3 tablespoons grapeseed oil
- Lemon juice to taste
- 4 tablespoons minced chives or garlic chives or a mixture of both
- 2 tablespoons minced parsley
- 2 tablespoons of minced herb mixture (choose 2 to 4): basil, mint, cilantro, and chervil
- 4 halibut fillets (8 to 9 ounces, about 1½ inches thick), skin on

1. Combine leeks, carrots, onion, garlic, kosher salt, peppercorns, and bay leaf in a medium casserole with 6 cups water. Bring to a boil, lower heat, cover, and simmer until vegetables are soft, about 20 minutes. Add wine and white vinegar, cover, and cook for 10 minutes. Add thyme and basil sprigs. Turn off heat and let cool to room temperature. Strain broth.

2. Whisk mustard, sherry and red wine vinegars, and salt and pepper to taste with 4 teaspoons water in a bowl. Whisk in oils until dressing is emulsified. Add a few drops of lemon juice. Whisk in herbs. Let stand at least 10 minutes. (It can be covered and set aside for 1 hour.)

3. Pour broth into a large, deep skillet. Add halibut. (Liquid should just cover pieces; if not, add water.) Bring to a simmer over medium heat; by then fish should be opaque and firm. (If not, turn off heat and cover pan.) Peel off skin. Divide fish among 4 plates and spoon vinaigrette over.

Yield: 4 servings
Time: 2 hours

PATRICIA YEO

Patricia Yeo is the executive chef at AZ in Manhattan. She was photographed at the restaurant. These columns were written with Jack Bishop.

CARAMEL ABANDONS THE DESSERT MENU FOR A STEAK

In most restaurants caramel is sticky and sweet and part of dessert. But Asian influences dominate my cooking, so sugar plays a more complex role. Following a tradition popular in Southeast Asia, I use caramel as the base for a savory glaze for steaks.

I start by heating sugar until it melts and turns amber. I then add lemongrass, garlic, shallots, ginger, and chilies, and, in effect, sauté the aromatics in caramel rather than oil to release their flavor. After that I add fish sauce. The caramel bubbles, and the aroma released by the fish sauce is intense; we jokingly call this potent concoction "dead whale sauce." The finished glaze doesn't really taste fishy, though. Like salt, fish sauce is a flavor enhancer; it makes foods taste richer without calling attention to its presence.

Although the glaze contains half a cup of sugar, it isn't really sweet, either. When sugar becomes caramel, *it takes on bitter, burnt notes. The fish sauce and aromatics firmly push it into the savory category.*

I like to use the caramel glaze on hanger steak, the long, thick piece of meat that hangs from the cow's sternum. Like skirt steak, it has a wide grain and rich, gamy flavor. A cow yields a single hanger steak that weighs one and a half to two pounds. Ask your butcher to remove the fat and gristle from the steak. In the process he will have to divide the meat into two long pieces, each big enough to serve two. Hanger steak can taste livery if cooked past medium-rare. It will also be too chewy unless you slice it across the grain. The glaze can also be used on other types of steak, like a whole tenderloin or individual fillets. It also works well with tuna, salmon, foie gras, and pork. It's an easy way to add Southeast Asian flavor.

Even though the glaze is not terribly sweet, the sugar does turn grilling into something of a challenge. To prevent flare-ups, I let the fire die down a bit once the grill has been preheated and then cook the steak over moder-

ate heat. I also oil the grill rack to prevent the meat from sticking. (The steak can also be seared in a cast-iron skillet for a couple of minutes on all sides and then finished in a 450-degree oven; about five minutes there will yield medium-rare meat.) I serve the steak with chickpea fries, but it also goes well on a bed of arugula.

The glaze can also be turned into an oil-free salad dressing with tons of flavor: Whisk four parts of it with one part lime juice. I drizzle the dressing over sliced roast beef, carrots, red peppers, celery, mint, cilantro, parsley, basil, and mâche to make Thai beef salad. I also use it to make a slaw from underripe mango, jicama, and Granny Smith apples.

GRILLED HANGER STEAK WITH LEMONGRASS–CARAMEL GLAZE

1 stalk lemongrass, tough top and bottom
　　portions removed, tender center portion
　　halved and very thinly sliced
　　(about 3 tablespoons)
2 medium cloves garlic, peeled
2 slices unpeeled ginger, each about ¼ inch
　　thick
1 shallot, roughly chopped
1 jalapeño pepper, roughly chopped
½ cup sugar
¼ cup fish sauce
1 hanger steak (1½ to 2 pounds), trimmed of
　　fat and gristle and cut into 2 pieces
Vegetable oil for grill rack

1. Place lemongrass, garlic, and ginger in a food processor and process until coarsely ground. Add shallot and jalapeño, and process until finely ground. Scrape into a bowl.

2. Place sugar in a medium heavy-bottomed saucepan and turn heat to medium-high. Cook, breaking apart lumps with a wooden spoon, until sugar melts and turns amber, about 5 minutes. Stir in lemongrass mixture and cook, stirring constantly, until very fragrant, about 1 minute. (Caramel will seize up a bit at first.) Add fish sauce and simmer to blend flavors, about 30 seconds. Remove from heat and let cool to room temperature.

3. Massage mixture into meat. Let stand at room temperature for 30 minutes.

4. Light gas grill or heat charcoal fire until very hot. Lower heat to medium-high or let coals cool slightly. Dip a wad of paper towels in oil and, holding towels with tongs, lubricate grate thoroughly. Cook steaks, turning 3 times to brown all 4 sides, about 9 minutes for medium-rare. Transfer to a cutting board and let rest for 5 minutes. Slice crosswise and serve immediately.

Yield: 4 servings
Time: 1½ hours

A NEW SOURCE OF COMFORT

When chefs get their hands on classic comfort foods, they often wind up with macaroni and cheese enriched with half a dozen European cheeses or meatloaf with foie gras. The high style obliterates the simple pleasure.

For me, nothing says comfort quite like bar food— casual, classic things like Buffalo wings. But there is no way my restaurant could serve deep-fried chicken wings tossed with hot sauce, accompanied by blue cheese dip and celery sticks. And I didn't want to dress them up beyond recognition.

My solution replaces the chicken wings with boneless quail and the hot sauce with an Asian-inspired ginger glaze. I buy the quail butterflied, with the breast and thigh bones removed; only tiny leg and wing bones remain. Most butchers sell the birds that way, and I just cut them in half lengthwise to make them easier to eat and quick to cook. We deep-fry the quail, but at home they can be panfried. Just two minutes in hot oil crisps the skin and leaves the meat perfect: rosy at the bone. Don't cook them more, or the meat will taste like liver.

As soon as the quail come out of the hot oil, I lacquer them with an incredibly simple glaze made with pineapple juice, dried chilies, brown sugar, and fresh ginger. The pineapple and brown sugar give it great body and sweet stickiness, while the sliced ginger and chilies provide heat and punch. I use dried Thai bird chilies, which are quite spicy, but any small dried chilies are fine. With the ginger, more is definitely better here. In the restaurant we use ten pounds of ginger a day. The skin has a lot of flavor, so simply slice the unpeeled ginger into thin coins; these, along with the chilies, are strained out when the glaze has reduced sufficiently.

I serve the lacquered quail on a bed of greens with thick rings of pineapple that have been flavored with vanilla, brandy, and honey, and roasted in a hot oven until tender. I usually sprinkle the platter with chopped toasted macadamia nuts and sliced fresh water chestnuts or julienned jicama.

At home, I serve the lacquered quail alone, to be eaten with fingers. Lacquered quail are too messy for a fancy cocktail party but are ideal for a casual event, like a gathering to watch football on a Sunday afternoon. If you make the glaze before the game, you can actually fry and lacquer the quail during a commercial break.

GINGER-LACQUERED QUAIL

2 cups pineapple juice
2 small dried chilies, such as Thai bird chilies
1/4 cup light brown sugar
1 2-inch piece unpeeled ginger, thinly sliced
4 partially boned, butterflied quail
Canola oil for frying
Salt and freshly ground black pepper
All-purpose flour for dredging

1. Combine pineapple juice, chilies, sugar, and ginger in a medium skillet and bring to a boil. Lower heat and cook at a bare simmer for 30 to 40 minutes, until liquid reduces to about 1/3 cup. (Mixture will darken and thicken considerably.) Strain into a clean bowl. (It can be refrigerated for 1 week. Bring to room temperature before using.)

2. Cut each quail in half from neck to tail. Place half of glaze in a medium bowl and set aside.

3. Heat about 1/4 inch oil in a large skillet until shimmering. Season quail generously with salt and pepper to taste, then lightly dredge in flour and shake off excess.

4. Add 4 quail halves to hot oil and fry, turning once, until well browned, 2 to 3 minutes.

Transfer to glaze and toss with tongs to coat. Put glazed quail on a platter. Pour remaining glaze in bowl and repeat with remaining quail. Serve immediately.

Yield: 4 appetizer portions
Time: 1 hour

◠

A SECRET INGREDIENT
LIFTS A SEAFOOD SOUP

As I child I often visited my grandmother in Malaysia during the holidays, when the house was full of people who needed to be fed. In the morning she would soften rice noodles in hot chicken broth, drain and oil them, and put them in a large bowl on the counter. Throughout the day everyone would duck into the kitchen, put noodles in a soup bowl, add chopped cilantro, and then ladle in some spicy coconut broth.

It was the broth, based on a traditional Malaysian street food called laksa, *that made the noodles so delicious. With every slurp you could taste chilies, coconut, ginger, garlic, and seafood. It was aromatic and heady, capable of clearing your sinuses.*

The secret ingredient is ground dried shrimp, a seasoning that is ubiquitous in Southeast Asia as well as parts of Latin America and Africa. Dried shrimp are much more pungent than the fresh kind, and more fibrous. They add a meaty texture, almost like ground pork, and have a flavor similar to stock made from shrimp shells. I toast the ground shrimp with ginger, garlic, and chilies to bring out their nutty flavor. My grandmother used to add candlenuts or macadamias to accomplish the same thing. Coconut milk brings together all the flavors and really enhances the toasted shrimp.

My broth is delicious with noodles, but at the restaurant I have taken it in a different direction. Given the seafood base, it seemed like a natural for mussels and tiny green-tinged New Zealand cockles, although small littleneck clams are delicious, too.

You can buy dried shrimp in Asian and Hispanic markets. Small shrimp, which are less expensive than large, are fine for this recipe because they will be ground, but look for whole shrimp rather than pieces. If you're brave, chew on one—it should taste like shrimp. An ammonia flavor or odor means the shrimp are past their prime. My grandmother stored dried shrimp in a jar on the counter, but I keep them refrigerated.

The mussels and cockles can be served as a first or a main course. Grilled flatbread is an excellent accompaniment, but any bread can be used to soak up the broth. If the seafood is served as a main course, I would follow with something crunchy, like a green papaya or jicama salad.

MUSSELS AND COCKLES WITH SPICY COCONUT BROTH

2 cups dried shrimp

1 3-inch piece unpeeled ginger, sliced thick

3 medium cloves garlic, peeled

2 medium jalapeño peppers, stemmed and sliced

4 tablespoons canola oil

1 teaspoon paprika

4 cups chicken stock

1 14-ounce can coconut milk

1 lemongrass stalk, top and bottom portions removed and center portion smashed with bottom of saucepan

1 long piece lemon peel

48 mussels (about 2½ pounds)

36 New Zealand cockles or very small littleneck clams (about 1 pound)

Chopped cilantro for garnish

Lemon wedges for garnish

1. Place dried shrimp in a bowl and cover with boiling water. Soak until softened, about 30 minutes. Drain and place in a food processor with ginger and garlic. Process until finely ground. Add peppers and grind for several more seconds.

2. Heat 2 tablespoons oil in a large saucepan until shimmering. Add shrimp mixture and sauté over medium heat until dry, about 4 minutes. Drizzle remaining 2 tablespoons oil over mixture and sprinkle with paprika. Continue cooking until mixture is lightly browned, about 8 minutes.

3. Add stock, coconut milk, lemongrass, and lemon peel, and bring to a boil. Lower heat and simmer gently to blend flavors, about 30 minutes. Discard lemongrass and peel.

4. Put mussels and cockles in a large casserole or Dutch oven. Turn heat to high. Pour simmering coconut broth over seafood. Cover and steam just until mussels and cockles open, about 6 minutes.

5. Divide mussels and cockles among individual bowls. Ladle broth over seafood and garnish each serving with cilantro. Serve immediately with lemon wedges.

Yield: 4 servings as a main course or 8 as a first course

Time: 1½ hours

SUBTLE CHANGES ADD DEPTH

Egg drop soup was the first thing I learned to cook for myself. I was about ten years old and had been watching my mother make this Chinese classic as long as I could remember. The basic recipe is so easy—you just drizzle eggs into a boiling broth—that even a child can make it for lunch. But I find that it can actually be a very sophisticated dish.

Like most chefs, I don't like to cook the same thing over and over, though, so I enhanced my latest version with peas and crabmeat. Soy sauce is traditionally used to season egg drop soup, but I've never liked how it muddies the color of golden chicken broth. Fish sauce adds the same salty Asian flavor without turning the stock brown. This minor substitution alters the soup's character. Leftover chicken is often added to it, but fish sauce makes seafood a better call.

Both chopped shrimp and crab work fine, but crab is more appealing. The tender strands of crabmeat hide amid the feathered eggs. You can taste the crab, but you can't quite see it.

The eggs will feather best if you beat some cold stock into them before drizzling them into the broth. Then stir with a fork so they don't clump together.

Don't bother making this soup with anything other than top-notch ingredients. At the restaurant we use double chicken stock made from backs and bones simmered in chicken stock, not water. You can use regular-strength stock, but it should be homemade (premium store-bought stock counts as homemade). As for the crab, peekytoe is sweeter than regular blue-crab meat. When I lived in California, I used Dungeness crab, which is also delicious. No matter what kind you use, remember that a little goes a long way. The eggs, not the seafood, should be the focus.

EGG DROP SOUP WITH PEAS AND CRAB

2 tablespoons canola oil
2 shallots, very thinly sliced
½ medium clove garlic, very thinly sliced
4 cups plus 2 tablespoons chicken stock
2 tablespoons fish sauce
Freshly ground black pepper
½ cup julienned sugar snap peas or frozen
    sweet peas, thawed
½ cup lump crabmeat, preferably peekytoe
2 large eggs
Chopped cilantro and/or pea sprouts for
    garnish

1. Heat oil, shallots, and garlic in a large saucepan over medium-low heat until softened but not browned, about 3 minutes. Add 4 cups stock and bring to a boil. Add fish sauce and pepper to taste. Add peas and crab, and cook until heated through, 1 to 2 minutes.

2. Meanwhile, in a medium bowl, lightly beat eggs with remaining 2 tablespoons stock just until smooth.

3. Let soup return to a rolling boil and slowly drizzle in beaten eggs, mixing soup gently with a fork. Cook until eggs feather, about 30 seconds. Ladle soup into individual bowls, garnish with chopped cilantro and/or pea sprouts, and serve.

Yield: 4 servings
Time: 20 minutes

JUICY? FLAVORFUL?
THESE ARE PORK CHOPS?

Ham is all the things that modern pork isn't: flavorful, moist, and appealing. Pork is bred to be lean, but fat gives pork moisture and juiciness. Ham is meat from the pig's leg, usually cured in a mixture of water, salt, sugar, and spices, a process that adds tons of flavor and keeps the meat juicy.

My restaurant can't serve a huge fifteen-pound ham studded with cloves, but I figured that I could borrow from that idea to make pork chops more succulent. Curing meat in a salt solution, also called brining, takes time but is an easy way to transform bland and dry pork. The chops become so flavorful that they need no sauce, although they go well with fruit, and I serve them with prunes marinated in Armagnac.

I start with extra-thick center-cut loin chops. Thicker chops are easier to cook because you can put a really good crust on them before the interior dries out. Center-cut loin chops are best because they are tender and meaty. For the brine I start with apple juice, which is sweeter than water, and then add a sweet apple, onion, spices, and the all-important salt. The salt does two jobs: It makes the meat taste better and improves its texture. Just as salt makes a hot dog plump, it helps the chops absorb the brine and makes them especially juicy.

When cooked, these chops have the sweetness and saltiness of good ham. Their texture is also like ham, plump and firm. For best results I let the pork chops sit in the brine for twenty-four hours. If you're in a rush, you can double the amount of salt and reduce the brining time to six hours.

When it is time to cook the chops, I prefer to sear the meat in a cast-iron skillet and then move the chops, pan and all, to a hot oven to cook through. The cast-iron pan gives the meat a great crust. At the restaurant we weight the chops with a second pan as they sear, which guarantees a perfectly even, mahogany crust. I finish the chops in the oven so that the interior can continue to cook without causing the crust to get too dark.

I like pork served medium-rare, when it is still pink at the bone; after four or five minutes on top of the stove and seven minutes in the oven, thick pork chops will have reached this stage. If you want your pork cooked more, just increase the oven time by a minute or two.

Because brined pork chops are like ham and go so well with fruit, I serve each one with a couple of pitted prunes that have been steeped in tea and Armagnac. The prunes enhance the apple and spice flavors in the pork. The prunes require just ten minutes of work but should marinate for a week. Plan ahead and consider making a double or triple batch. Having extra prunes might encourage you to cook pork more often and without disappointment.

APPLE-BRINED PORK CHOPS

1 sweet apple, roughly chopped
1 small onion, peeled and roughly chopped
3 cups apple juice
Kosher salt
5 black peppercorns
1 cinnamon stick
1 star anise
1 bay leaf
4 center-cut loin pork chops
1 tablespoon canola oil
Freshly ground black pepper
Prunes Marinated in Armagnac and Tea
   (see recipe below)

1. Place apple, onion, juice, 2 tablespoons salt, peppercorns, cinnamon, star anise, and bay leaf in a medium saucepan. Bring to a boil, remove from heat, and let cool to room temperature.

2. Place pork chops in a deep nonreactive baking dish. Pour apple mixture over and cover dish tightly with plastic wrap. Refrigerate for 24 hours, turning chops once.

3. Preheat oven to 450 degrees. Set a 12-inch cast-iron pan over high heat. Add oil and heat until almost smoking. Remove chops from brine, pat dry, and season generously with pepper and lightly with salt. Add to hot pan and lower heat to medium-high. Sear until golden brown, 2 to 3 minutes. Turn chops and sear on second side until golden brown, about 2 minutes.

4. Carefully transfer pan to hot oven and roast chops for 7 minutes (meat will still be pink near bone). Remove from oven and let chops rest in pan for 5 minutes. Serve immediately with marinated prunes.

Yield: 4 servings
Time: 20 minutes, plus 1 hour for brine and 24
hours of brining

PRUNES MARINATED IN ARMAGNAC AND TEA

½ cup Armagnac
½ cup strong brewed tea
¼ cup sugar
12 pitted prunes

Bring Armagnac, tea, and sugar to a boil in a small saucepan, stirring occasionally to dissolve sugar. Place prunes in a heatproof container and pour liquid over them. Let cool to room temperature. Cover and refrigerate for at least 1 week. Lift prunes from marinade with a slotted spoon just before serving.

Yield: 4 servings
Time: 10 minutes, plus 1 week of marination

SWEET AND SPICY ON BREAD, OR ON TURKEY

I grew up in England and have always been partial to chutneys. Most Americans think these Indian-inspired condiments are sticky and sweet, but chutneys can have a range of textures and heat, with lots of flavor in every small spoonful. At my restaurant I serve chutneys with flatbreads at the start of each meal. At home, I'm just as likely to incorporate chutneys into the main part of the meal. Either way, they are ideally suited to entertaining around the holidays.

I make different chutneys every day, but the breads are usually a combination of something crunchy, like pita crisps or rosemary matzo, with something doughy, like focaccia, onion roti, or nan. And there are always three chutneys: one sweet, one savory, and one spicy. I have twenty-five in my repertoire, so they are constantly changing. Fruits, vegetables, and legumes are mainstays in the recipes. Although most American cooks associate the word "chutney" with Indian cuisine, I use the term more loosely to include almost any sauce you might smear on bread or serve with a main course.

These are three of my favorites. Any of them would work as a dip, and all are good complements to poultry, particularly turkey. My dried cherry and shallot chutney and my pear and dried cranberry chutney are excellent choices for the holiday season. The cherry chutney has shallots briefly sautéed for crunch.

The cranberries in the pear chutney hint at tradition, but it is far from the usual sauce. It is fairly acidic, which helps cut the sweetness of many holiday dishes. To make it, I cook the pears in verjuice—unfermented juice pressed from unripe wine grapes. Verjuice is more acidic and less sweet than wine, but not so sharp as vinegar. (You can buy it in most specialty markets.) Apple cider vinegar can be used instead.

My lentil and cauliflower chutney is much different, a traditional Indian recipe redolent with warm spices and toasted flavors, but not really hot. It is great spread on bread like roti or with turkey. And at any time of year it also works with fish. You might even want to eat it from a spoon.

I find plenty of more mundane uses for chutneys, too, like adding mustard (both whole grain and Dijon) to my pear chutney to turn it into a sandwich spread. It is just the thing for leftover turkey.

DRIED CHERRY AND SHALLOT CHUTNEY

2 tablespoons canola oil
10 large shallots, thinly sliced
2 cups dried sour cherries
2 cups port
Salt to taste

1. In a large saucepan over high heat, heat oil until shimmering. Add shallots and cook, stirring occasionally, until slightly softened and beginning to brown, about 4 minutes.

2. Add cherries and port, and bring to a boil. Lower heat and simmer until liquid has evaporated, cherries have plumped up, and shallots are red, about 30 minutes. Add salt to taste. Chutney can be refrigerated in an airtight container for up to 2 weeks.

Yield: 4 cups
Time: 45 minutes

LENTIL AND CAULIFLOWER CHUTNEY

¼ cup canola oil
1 medium red onion, diced
2 tablespoons minced ginger
2 teaspoons curry powder
1 teaspoon black mustard seeds
1 cup red lentils
1½ cups white wine
2 cups small cauliflower florets
½ cup diced canned tomatoes
Salt to taste
1 teaspoon ground Aleppo pepper (or a pinch of cayenne pepper mixed with 1 teaspoon paprika)
¼ cup minced fresh cilantro
Juice of ½ lime

1. Heat oil in a Dutch oven or large casserole over medium-high heat. Add onion and ginger, and cook until softened, about 2 minutes. Add curry powder and mustard seeds, and stir until fragrant, about 1 minute.

2. Add lentils and 1 cup wine. Bring to a boil, lower heat, cover, and cook until lentils absorb wine and swell up, about 5 minutes.

3. Add cauliflower, tomatoes, remaining ½ cup wine, salt, and Aleppo pepper. Cover and cook, stirring occasionally, until lentils and cauliflower are tender but not mushy, 15 to 20 minutes. (If needed, add more water to pan to prevent scorching.)

4. Remove pan from heat and let cool to room temperature. Stir in cilantro and lime juice, and adjust seasonings. Chutney can be refrigerated in an airtight container for up to 3 days.

Yield: 4 cups
Time: 1 hour

CRANBERRY-PEAR CHUTNEY WITH WALNUTS

2 tablespoons canola oil

1 medium onion, diced

4 ripe Bartlett pears, peeled, cored, and cut into small dice

1 cup dried cranberries

1¼ cups verjuice or apple cider vinegar

2 tablespoons brown sugar

1 cinnamon stick

1 star anise

2 bay leaves

½ cup chopped toasted walnuts

Salt to taste

1. Heat oil in a Dutch oven or large casserole over medium-high heat. Add onion and sauté until softened, about 2 minutes. Add pears and cook until softened, about 2 minutes.

2. Add cranberries, verjuice, sugar, cinnamon, star anise, and bay leaves. Bring to a boil, lower heat, and cook until liquid evaporates, 10 to 12 minutes. (Pears should be tender but not mushy.) Stir in walnuts and salt. Chutney can be refrigerated in an airtight container for up to a week. Discard spices before serving.

Yield: 4 cups

Time: 30 minutes

AN ASIAN INFLUENCE HELPS THE POTATO KNISH LIGHTEN UP

Before coming home to New York a few years ago, I was working in San Francisco, and I missed all those local specialties New Yorkers take for granted. Bagels, pastrami, and potato knishes just don't travel well. Though I wasn't willing to make my own pastrami and bagels, I figured I could do something about my yearning for a good potato knish. I started tinkering with the dough but couldn't get it right. My knishes were always heavy and pasty.

On a lark, I tried spring roll wrappers, which were much lighter and more sheer. When I filled my first wrapper with mashed potatoes, I knew I was on to something. The wrapper fried up flaky and crisp, a perfect contrast to the rich, creamy filling. Street food vendors may not recognize my creation, but it's still a knish, maybe even better.

Back in New York, I continued to refine the recipe, cutting the knish into bite-size pieces and adding a garnish of crème fraîche and caviar. This elegant knish has become a signature at my restaurant, and it's a great party appetizer.

There are several secrets. I use Yukon Gold potatoes for their buttery flavor and golden color. When I tried enriching the potatoes with milk or cream, the filling turned thin and runny. I had better luck with crème fraîche. The filling became dense and creamy, almost like custard, with that great crème fraîche tang.

I leave the potato skins on and cook the potatoes whole, with the water at a bare simmer, to keep them from becoming soggy. Grated onion and salt and pepper complement the potatoes. Use more salt than you think you need, as potatoes can absorb a lot of seasoning.

I use standard-issue spring roll wrappers, which are sold in many supermarkets as well as most Asian markets. Frozen wrappers are fine; just let them thaw on the counter for half an hour or until they are pliable. Just don't buy egg roll wrappers. They are much too thick and doughy for this recipe.

Once the knishes are fried, I trim a thin slice from either end and cut each knish into thirds. That way I can stand the pieces up like little smokestacks, crowning each with crème fraîche and caviar.

YUKON GOLD POTATO KNISHES WITH OSETRA CAVIAR

1½ pounds Yukon Gold potatoes, scrubbed
½ medium onion, peeled
Salt and fresh black pepper to taste
¾ cup crème fraîche
12 spring roll wrappers, each about 6 inches square
1 large egg, beaten
Canola oil for frying
2 ounces (approximately) osetra caviar

1. Place potatoes in a large saucepan and cover with cold water. Bring to a boil, lower heat, and cook at barest simmer until a skewer glides easily through potatoes, about 1 hour. Drain, let cool slightly, and peel. Run potatoes through a food mill and into a bowl. Grate onion on large holes of a box grater directly into bowl with potatoes. Season with plenty of salt and some pepper. Stir in ½ cup crème fraîche. Let cool to room temperature. (Potatoes can be covered and refrigerated for up to 1 day.)

2. Set 1 wrapper on a work surface with a corner facing you. Spread scant ¼ cup potatoes about 2 inches above bottom corner so potatoes form a 1-inch-wide strip that extends almost from one side of wrapper to the other. Fold bot-

tom corner of wrapper over potatoes. Roll wrapper, folding in sides to enclose potatoes. When you get three-quarters of way to top, brush remaining edges with beaten egg and continue rolling to seal. Repeat with remaining wrappers and filling. (Knishes can be refrigerated, uncovered, for up to 1 day.)

3. Heat 1 inch of oil in a large, deep saucepan until very hot but not quite smoking, about 375 degrees. With tongs, add several knishes and fry, turning once or twice, until golden brown all over, about 1 minute. Remove from oil and drain on paper towels. Fry remaining knishes in batches.

4. With a serrated knife trim a thin slice from either end of each knish. Cut each knish crosswise into 3 pieces. Arrange pieces with 1 cut side up on a platter. Top each piece with a dollop of remaining crème fraîche and a little caviar. Serve immediately.

Yield: 8 to 12 appetizer-size servings
   (36 pieces in all)
Time: 2½ hours

PHILIPPE CONTICINI

Philippe Conticini is the head chef at the Petrossian Boutique and Café in New York. He was photographed by Owen Franken at Petrossian in Paris. These columns were written with Amanda Hesser.

TO TRULY TASTE, TASTE THE UNEXPECTED

I can give you the easy description of my job. I am a chef and pastry chef for Petrossian restaurants in New York and Paris. But my palate lies somewhere between the worlds of savory and sweet. I've never quite been able to separate the two. Sweet flavors end up in entrees; salt and spices find their way into my desserts. My menus are fairly conventional, but the fine print might cause you alarm. With a skate dish I serve in Paris, there are capers and praline. In a cake that I serve in New York, there is tuna.

Yes, tuna.

I have a little problem, you see. I began as a pâtissier, *and it has indelibly marked my work as a chef. With pastry, I was always the experimental type, inclined to use spices like cumin and pepper to make sweets that would have horrified Lenôtre. But once I*

saw how well they worked, it was liberating. Possibilities suddenly sprang up everywhere.

Now that I am also a chef, I apply the same principle to cooking. I use classic techniques, of course. But when it comes to flavor, I erase all tradition and open my mind to any seasoning. With these recipes, I'm going to try to explain this unusual approach. It will take a leap of faith to try some of the combinations I throw out. When you see cod and spice bread together in the same dish, you may shudder. But I hope you will see it as an opportunity to revise the way you think about flavor.

I thought my tuna cake would be a good place to begin. It is indeed a cake, not a "cake." It has flour and oil and is leavened with eggs and baking powder, but it is not at all sweet. Rather than flavor it with sugar and something like vanilla essence, I have used fleur de sel, curry powder, and tumeric. In place of nuts and chocolate, I've added tuna and onions.

The tuna is first marinated overnight in red wine,

coconut extract, lime juice, garlic, coriander, mint, and onion. The next day a standard cake batter is assembled with flour and spices moistened with eggs and crème fraîche. Then the tuna mixture is folded in, and everything is baked in a cake pan.

Think of it as you would a quiche. You can serve a few slices with a salad for lunch or do as my fiancée and I do when we entertain: We slice the cake and serve it as an hors d'oeuvre with champagne. It was actually her creation. She had it in her mind to make a savory cake to serve with aperitifs. When everyone tasted it, they oohed and aahed. I have since changed it a bit, intensifying the spices and lightening it with more baking powder. Now it's a standard at our house. The cake is soft and crumbly, and has a delicacy that belies its aroma, which is heady with tuna and spices, just as you would expect a strong curry dish to be.

SAVORY TUNA, COCONUT, AND LIME CAKE

½ cup red wine
8 ounces good-quality canned light tuna
½ cup sliced onion
½ cup extra-virgin olive oil
1 teaspoon coconut extract
1 tablespoon fresh lime juice
1 clove garlic, peeled and minced
1 teaspoon roughly chopped parsley
1 teaspoon roughly chopped cilantro
¼ cup roughly chopped mint
Butter for cake pan
1½ cups flour, plus additional for pan
2 tablespoons baking powder
2 tablespoons turmeric
1 teaspoon fresh black pepper
1 tablespoon curry powder
1 teaspoon fleur de sel
5 large eggs
1 large egg yolk
3 tablespoons crème fraîche

1. In a glass or ceramic bowl, combine wine, tuna, onion, oil, coconut extract, lime juice, garlic, parsley, cilantro, and mint. The mixture should be rough, not uniform. Cover and refrigerate overnight.

2. Preheat oven to 350 degrees. Butter and flour a 9-inch cake pan. In a medium bowl, stir together flour and baking powder. Add turmeric, pepper, curry powder, and fleur de sel, and mix well. In another bowl, combine eggs, egg yolk, and crème fraîche. Add to flour mixture, stirring well. Add tuna mixture and marinade, and stir gently, being careful not to break up tuna too much, until blended.

3. Pour into cake pan and bake until a knife inserted in center comes out clean, about 45 minutes. Let cool for 5 minutes. Remove from pan and continue cooling on a rack. Serve at room temperature.

Yield: 4 servings

Time: 1 hour 10 minutes, plus overnight marinating

~⌒~

CAVIAR'S COMPANION FINDS NEW EMPLOY

If there is a single unifying element to the savory side of my menu, it is the blini. Every main course I make owes something to it—even though you will rarely find the classic little buckwheat pancake on the plate.

I realized the possibilities of blini batter a few years ago when I was looking for a way to give my dishes a Russian feeling. I was agreeably surprised by this simple combination of buckwheat flour, cream, egg whites, leavening, salt, and sugar. Buckwheat flour has a low gluten content, so it makes a much thinner and more delicate mixture than, say, an American pancake batter. Folding in whipped egg whites and cream makes it lighter, too. When you use blini batter as a coating, it clings without being cakey or starchy and puffs up beautifully when it's fried, almost like tempura. If you add more egg white and cream and use it as a cake batter, the result is moist and less chewy than if you had used regular flour.

But modifications like those were just the beginning. I have come to see the blini and its ingredients as something like a foundation. The challenge is to take those blocks and arrange them a different way in each dish. With sautéed chicken, for example, I serve a small blini cake that is filled with squab juices and cream. It is akin to a molten chocolate cake with a crisp, delicate shell and an almost liquid interior. With roasted lamb I make a traditional blini the size of a pancake and fill it with fruit chutney. I fold tarragon into the batter and make thin, crisp waffles to go with roasted pigeon. I even make blini-inspired beignets, which I stuff with cod.

But one of my favorite uses of blini batter is this crispy rouget appetizer. I season it with five-spice powder and paprika, and use it as a coating for small fish fillets. When they're fried slowly, flesh side down, the blini batter puffs and curls the fish into a C shape, like truite au bleu. After draining the fillets I sprinkle them with crushed hazelnuts, black pepper, fleur de sel, a few thin slivers of candied orange peel, and some drops of hazelnut oil and balsamic vinegar. It's a seasoning mixture I would use on a dessert, but it works here, too. The orange peel, for instance, adds sweetness and acidity, which really pushes the flavor of the fish.

Although the blini batter is delicate on the palate, it is very sturdy, so you can pick up the rougets and eat them like a very elegant fish and chips. You may even want to wrap them in a napkin.

½ cup all-purpose flour

¼ cup buckwheat flour

½ teaspoon salt

½ teaspoon sugar

2 large pinches of five-spice powder

1 large pinch of paprika

1 teaspoon fresh yeast

¾ cup milk

1 large egg yolk

2 teaspoons heavy cream

2 large egg whites, beaten until stiff but not dry

Vegetable oil for frying

12 small fillets rouget or red snapper

Freshly ground balck pepper

Fleur de sel

¼ cup extra-virgin olive oil, or to taste

2 tablespoons balsamic vinegar

24 strips candied lemon peel

¼ cup finely chopped hazelnuts

1. In a medium bowl, combine flours, salt, sugar, five-spice powder, and paprika. In a small bowl, whisk together yeast and ¼ cup milk; let rest for 10 minutes. Whisk in egg yolk. Add to flour mixture and whisk until smooth. Whisk in remaining ½ cup milk.

2. In a small bowl, whisk cream until it holds a soft peak. Fold beaten whites into batter. Fold in cream. Let batter rest at room temperature for 30 minutes.

3. Fill a deep, heavy pan with 3 inches of vegetable oil. Heat to 375 degrees. Season rougets with pepper to taste. To fry, dip flesh side of rouget into batter, making sure not to get batter on skin side. Carefully lower fish into hot oil; it will curl. Fry until batter is golden brown, then remove and drain on paper towels. Repeat with remaining fillets.

4. To serve, place 2 fillets on each plate, curled side up. Sprinkle with fleur de sel, olive oil, vinegar, lemon peel, and hazelnuts.

Yield: 6 appetizer servings

Time: 1 hour

⌐◡

CAVIAR, BEYOND THE SPOON

Caviar has a kind of season, and it usually falls around the holidays when people are feeling festive, social, and generous.

There's nothing wrong with this. Caviar makes one of the easiest hors d'oeuvres ever (open a tin, grab a spoon), and it rarely disappoints. While I use caviar in a number of appetizers and entrees, I don't sprinkle it around like salt. Caviar is a rare commodity and a delicacy, and I treat it as one. What I don't do is treat it with fear, which I think many cooks do. To them it is precious and untouchable. They serve it with that fancy little spoon and such reverence that it threatens to let them down. With caviar like sevruga, there are wonderful ways you can use its bitterness and salinity to flavor dishes. It is not a matter of aggressively seasoning with caviar but of accenting foods with its subtle touch. When you use caviar this way, you will be surprised at how little you need and how much is left for you to savor on your own afterward.

For parties we make countless tiny canapes with caviar. They accentuate rich, flavorful ingredients like smoked salmon, steak tartare, and eggs. Canapes are not meant to fill you up but to give you a quick, sharp burst of flavor that excites your palate. Good canapes are often salty to exaggerate the intensity of flavor and create a thirst—for more champagne, more punch, or more wine. When I make canapes, what I often do is simply adapt dishes that I would normally serve as a full course. That way you get the complexity of a dish distilled into a single bite.

Begin with steak tartare, a dish that is usually plated as a first course, and serve it on Asian soup spoons. The tartare is dressed with hazelnut oil, balsamic vinegar, sesame seeds, and fleur de sel. I sprinkle a small mound with crushed hazelnuts and a curry caviar vinaigrette. I top each spoon with a cluster of sevruga caviar and a chip of a buckwheat tuile. I use sevruga because the beef and curry vinaigrette are robust on their own. A more subtle caviar like osetra would be lost, as it would be in my other canapes. The sevruga adds a slight touch of salt and ocean flavor but is not fishy-tasting, so it can marry with something like beef.

Eggs, chicken, and quail are also easy to adapt as a canape. I soft-boil them until they are intact but soft like a water balloon. Then I dip them gently in blini batter and fry them. The batter puffs and crisps so that they look like large beignets. I cut them in half and sprinkle each side with sevruga caviar, fleur de sel, hazelnut oil, balsamic vinegar, pepper, crushed hazelnuts, and a few sprigs of herb salad. Call them gentrified deviled eggs if you like.

Another favorite of mine is something I call friantine, or little fried puffs of potato stuffed with caviar. This dish was actually inspired by one of my desserts. I make little balls of chocolate ganache and roll them in bread crumbs and fry them. When you bite into one, you get a flood of warm chocolate. I thought I could do the same thing with potatoes as long as the potatoes had the same kind of creamy liquid texture as the chocolate, so I made a potato puree that's just that way. I fill a tray of small circular molds with the puree, add a pocket of sevruga in the center, and freeze it. When the balls are hard, I take them out, roll them in egg and bread crumbs, and fry them until they're crisp and brown like Tater Tots. They can be made in a large batch and kept warm in the oven, and then just before passing them around, I put a little bit of sevruga on top of each. When you bite into a friantine, it is at first crispy like a potato chip, then the potato puree flows out like cream, ending with a flash of salt and sea from the caviar.

I also make a salmon tartare dressed with caviar, pepper, shallots, lime juice, and olive oil. I layer it in spoons or on pieces of toasted baguette with slices of smoked salmon and whipped cream seasoned with dill and more caviar.

I use sevruga in all these canapes. It is the least expensive caviar because its flavor is less delicate than the others. But I use it—particularly when it is "in season"—with prudence, not caution, and a liberal dose of creativity.

PETROSSIAN EGGS

½ cup all-purpose flour
¼ cup buckwheat flour
Salt
½ teaspoon sugar
1 teaspoon fresh yeast
¾ cup milk
1 large egg yolk
2 teaspoons heavy cream
2 large egg whites, beaten until stiff but not
    dry
Peanut oil for frying
6 large eggs
½ cup mixed parsley, chives, and chervil
Hazelnut oil
Balsamic vinegar
Finely crushed hazelnuts
Fleur de sel
Freshly ground black pepper
3 teaspoons sevruga caviar

1. In a medium bowl, combine flours, ½ teaspoon salt, and sugar. In a small bowl, whisk together yeast and ¼ cup milk; let rest for 10 minutes. Whisk in egg yolk, add flour mixture, and whisk until smooth. Gradually whisk in remaining ½ cup milk.

2. In a small bowl, whisk cream until stiff enough to hold soft peaks. Fold beaten egg whites into batter. Add cream and fold until smooth. Allow to rest for 30 minutes.

3. Fill a deep, heavy pan with 3 inches of peanut oil and heat to 375 degrees. Fill medium pan with 3 inches of water and bring to an active simmer. Add eggs and cook for 5 minutes. Transfer to a bowl of ice water to cool, then peel.

4. Using a slotted spoon, carefully lower 1 egg into batter. Coat well, then lift spoon and let as much batter fall off as possible. Lower egg into hot oil and cook just until golden brown. Drain on paper towels. Repeat with remaining eggs.

5. In a small bowl, combine herbs with a sprinkling of hazelnut oil and a few drops of balsamic vinegar. Season with salt to taste and toss.

6. Slice eggs in half and place on a platter; yolks should be almost liquid. Sprinkle with a little hazelnut oil, a pinch of crushed hazelnuts, fleur de sel, and pepper. Top each with ½ teaspoon caviar. Place a pinch of herb salad on each egg and serve.

Yield: 6 servings
Time: 1 hour, plus 30 minutes of resting

BEEF TARTARE WITH CURRY CAVIAR VINAIGRETTE

1 pound beef fillet, finely chopped
5 tablespoons sesame seeds
2 tablespoons plus ½ cup hazelnut oil
2 teaspoons balsamic vinegar
2 teaspoons fleur de sel
2 tablespoons curry powder
2 tablespoons honey
3 tablespoons lemon juice
1 tablespoon plus 2 teaspoons sevruga caviar
Finely crushed hazelnuts

1. In a small bowl, combine beef, 2 tablespoons sesame seeds, 2 tablespoons hazelnut oil, balsamic vinegar, and 1 teaspoon fleur de sel, and mix well.

2. Whisk together curry powder, honey, lemon juice, remaining 3 tablespoons sesame seeds, remaining ½ cup hazelnut oil, and 1 tablespoon caviar.

3. Fill 24 tablespoons halfway with beef tartare. Sprinkle with curry vinaigrette, remaining 1 teaspoon fleur de sel, and crushed hazelnuts. Dab with remaining caviar. Arrange on a platter.

Yield: 24 hors d'oeuvres
Time: 30 minutes

FRIANTINE (FRIED POTATO PURSES FILLED WITH CAVIAR)

1 medium (6 ounces) Idaho potato, peeled and cut into 2-inch pieces
1 medium (2 ounces) fingerling potato, peeled and cut into 2-inch pieces
⅓ cup milk
6 tablespoons butter at room temperature
Sea salt
¼ cup sevruga or osetra caviar
Peanut oil for frying
8 large egg yolks, lightly beaten
2 cups fine dry bread crumbs
Fleur de sel

1. In a saucepan with water just to cover, place Idaho and fingerling potatoes and boil until very tender, about 25 minutes. Meanwhile, in a small pan, heat milk until steaming; remove from heat and keep warm.

2. Drain potatoes and press through a ricer or food mill into a bowl. Whisk half of milk into potatoes, reserving half. Gradually whisk butter into potatoes; mixture should be quite liquid. Season to taste with salt.

3. Transfer potatoes to a mixer fitted with a paddle. Start mixing on low speed and over a minute gradually increase to medium-high. Mixture will thicken and rise as air is incorporated.

Add remaining milk and adjust salt. Continue mixing on high for 3 minutes, then let cool.

4. Using ice trays with round indentations or mini-muffin tins, spread a thin layer of potato puree in each of 24 indentations. Drop ½ teaspoon caviar in center, then top with a layer of potato puree, making sure to cover all caviar. Repeat with remaining potatoes and caviar. Chill until potatoes are firm, about 1 hour.

5. Place 2 inches of oil in a deep, heavy pot. Heat to 375 degrees. Preheat oven to 350 degrees. Place egg yolks in a bowl and bread crumbs in another bowl. Remove potatoes from molds; if they are very hard, allow to sit for a few minutes.

6. Roll potato balls, a few at a time, first in egg yolks and then in bread crumbs. Roll again in egg and crumbs. Carefully drop breaded potatoes into hot oil and fry until crisp and quite brown. Drain on paper towels, then transfer to a baking pan placed in oven. Heat for 5 minutes to finish warming in center. Place on a plate lined with a napkin. Sprinkle with fleur de sel and serve immediately.

Yield: 24 hors d'oeuvres
Time: 1 hour, plus 1 hour of chilling

SALMON AND CAVIAR QUENELLES

3 tablespoons sugar

½ cup Riesling wine

2 tablespoons lemon juice, or more as needed

¾ teaspoon unflavored gelatin

2 tablespoons green peppercorns in brine, drained and chopped

2 tablespoons minced shallots

1 tablespoon lime juice

3 tablespoons plus 3 teaspoons extra-virgin olive oil

Salt and freshly ground pepper

2 tablespoons plus 2 teaspoons sevruga caviar

12 ounces sushi-quality salmon, finely chopped

7 tablespoons heavy cream, whisked until stiff

2 teaspoons chopped dill, plus sprigs for garnish

1 baguette, ends trimmed and cut diagonally into twenty-four ½-inch-thick slices

Fleur de sel

4 ounces sliced white or red smoked salmon

1. In a small pan over low heat, melt 1 tablespoon sugar until light golden brown. Add wine, another tablespoon sugar, and 1 tablespoon lemon juice. Bring to a boil and stir in gelatin. Let cool, then refrigerate until jelled, about 6 hours or overnight.

2. In a small bowl, whisk together peppercorns, shallots, lime juice, remaining 2 tablespoons sugar, and 3 tablespoons oil. Season with salt to taste and stir in 2 tablespoons caviar. Place salmon in a medium bowl and mix in caviar mixture.

3. In a small bowl, fold together whipped cream, remaining 1 tablespoon lemon juice, and chopped dill. Season with salt and pepper to taste. Add more lemon juice if desired.

4. Lightly toast baguette slices. Sprinkle with oil and fleur de sel. Using 2 teaspoons, shape a quenelle of salmon tartare on each slice. Top with a dollop of caviar. Lay small, neat slices of smoked salmon on top of caviar. Dab a little wine jelly on some, and whipped cream on others. Finish with a sprig of dill.

Yield: 24 hors d'oeuvres
Time: 30 minutes, plus 6 hours of refrigeration

BROWNIES, FRENCH STYLE

When I first came to New York, I tried to taste as many breads and pastries as possible. American baked goods were new to me. I ate brownies, muffins, cinnamon rolls, and bagels (and just one cupcake). What surprised me most was how completely different they are from french breads and pastries. I had almost nothing to compare them with.

The more I ate, the more I wanted to bake them myself. So, for a few months I worked to understand how they are made. I bought American baking books, I experimented with recipes, and I was delighted to find that something that sounds as simple as a muffin is actually challenging. I spent the most time on brownies, and finally I reached the point where I understood the fundamental structure and began adding my own touches.

Most brownie recipes call for melting chocolate and combining it with eggs, butter, flour, and sugar, mixing it all up in a bowl, and pouring it into a baking dish. This process can be easily improved by using excellent chocolate and some spices or seasonings, with walnuts for crunch. But I wanted to work on the final texture of the brownie. I wanted it chocolaty and gooey but not heavy, so I reworked the technique.

I melt the chocolate and mix it with melted butter, cinnamon, fleur de sel, and candied orange zest. I add egg yolks and the dry ingredients. But then I make a Swiss meringue, beating egg whites and sugar until they are stiff, and I fold this into the chocolate as for a soufflé. I bake the mixture in a large buttered and sugared sheet pan. When the brownie mixture comes out of the oven, it is very puffed and light. I invert the pan onto a baking sheet so that the sugar crust that has formed is on top, and I let the brownie cake rest for eight hours before cutting. This is the crucial step. Those hours allow it to settle, giving it that dense chocolate texture. The sugar crust hardens, crackling when you bite into it.

And there is one more surprise: The meringue builds a tight web of tiny bubbles throughout the brownie so that each bite is as rich as a truffle and as light as a feather.

BROWNIES WITH CANDIED ORANGE ZEST

> Zest of 1 orange, cut into ⅛-inch strips
> Juice of ½ lemon
> Juice of ½ orange
> 2 tablespoons sugar, plus more for pan
> 10 ounces (2 sticks plus 2 tablespoons) butter, plus more for pan, at room temperature
> 11 large eggs at room temperature
> 2¼ cups confectioners' sugar
> 11 ounces best-quality chocolate (preferably 58 percent cacao)
> 1 tablespoon ground cinnamon
> ¼ cup chopped walnuts
> ½ teaspoon fleur de sel

1. In a small saucepan, combine orange zest, lemon juice, orange juice, and 2 tablespoons sugar. Bring to a boil and then simmer until zest is tender and liquid is reduced to a syrup, about 10 minutes. Let cool. Chop zest and reserve; there should be about 3 tablespoons.

2. Preheat oven to 450 degrees. Put parchment paper in a 10 by 15-inch baking pan with a ¾-inch rim. Butter and sugar paper. Separate 9 eggs, placing whites in bowl of a mixer and 7 yolks in a medium bowl. (Reserve remaining yolks for another use.) Add 2 whole eggs and ¼ cup confectioners' sugar to yolks, and whisk to blend.

3. In a double boiler or microwave oven, melt

chocolate and stir in butter until smooth. Whisk in yolk mixture. Stir in cinnamon.

4. Add remaining 2 cups confectioners' sugar to egg whites. Whisk with a mixer until stiff. Add about 1 cup egg whites to chocolate mixture. Fold until blended. Add chocolate mixture to whites in bowl. Fold until smooth. Fold in reserved orange zest and half of walnuts.

5. Pour into prepared baking pan and use a spatula to spread evenly to sides. Sprinkle with remaining walnuts and fleur de sel. Bake. When top is puffed, about 20 to 25 minutes, insert a knife tip into center; if it comes out clean, remove from oven. While cake is still hot, use a paring knife to trim sides that have puffed up over rim of baking sheet. Place another baking sheet lined with parchment paper on top of brownie, invert, and remove top sheet. Allow brownie to rest at room temperature for 8 hours, then cut into 12 rectangles.

Yield: 12 brownies
Time: 1½ hours, plus 8 hours for resting

INSPIRED BY THE IDEA OF COMMUNITY AND A GREAT CIGAR

One of the early breakthroughs in my creative life came when I discovered the plated dessert. Dessert was no longer a slice of cake or an individual soufflé but a synthesis of flavors and components. Over the years, however, this concept, too, fell short. The flavors and complexity were all there, but they seemed somehow diffuse. What creates synergy in a dish, as I slowly figured out, is not just the combination of flavors but how they are combined. And often with a dessert, a plate simply won't do. Because it's flat, it does not allow the components to mingle as they are eaten. And it makes it hard to get the proper range of flavors in each bite.

I played around with different dishes and bowls and finally decided on a glass. In a shallow one, like a martini glass, the flavors are like neighbors in a small community. They bump into one another, they interact, and they are concentrated. It is this proximity that makes this dessert work. It is basically a sundae, but I designed it with the aroma of my favorite cigar, Monte Cristo No. 5, in mind. I used to smoke one with a glass of pear eau de vie as the restaurant was closing. Together in my mouth I would get a peppery sensation and the aromas of tropical fruit, vanilla, dried fruit, spices, and tobacco.

It is impossible to re-create the full flavor, though, without tobacco, so I added some to the dessert. And I called it Alma-Ata after a city in Kazakhstan. I macerated a few pinches of tobacco—the kind bought loose in a pouch—in water thickened with flavorless cornstarch. After a few stirs, the leaves began to bleed. Tobacco can be quite spicy and bitter, so it is best to go easy with it and sweeten it lightly. (Still, on its own, it will seem inedible.)

That's where the glass is important. In it, I layer pineapple, passion fruit juice, caraway seeds, crushed pistachios, coconut milk, a slice of gingerbread-like pain d'épices, vanilla ice cream, black pepper, and the tobacco sauce. You will get a bit of each flavor with every spoonful, no matter which way you turn the glass. Admittedly, Alma-Ata is an odd concoction, but in your mouth will be that synergy—and the sense of what these lovely cigars taste like to me.

ALMA-ATA SUNDAE

1 ¼ teaspoons cornstarch dissolved in
        1 tablespoon water
¼ cup cigar or pipe tobacco
1 tablespoon sugar
1 cup diced (½-inch cubes) fresh pineapple
¼ cup passion fruit juice
¼ cup coconut milk
1 teaspoon crushed black peppercorns, or as
        needed
1 teaspoon caraway seeds, or as needed
1 teaspoon ground pistachio nuts, or as
        needed
4 ¼-inch-thick slices pain d'épice (available
        in fine bakeries)
4 small scoops vanilla ice cream
8 fresh mint leaves, torn into pieces
8 teaspoons pomegranate seeds or 2 teaspoons
        pomegranate juice
12 pieces candied orange zest

1. In a small pan, bring ¼ cup water to a boil. Whisk cornstarch mixture into water and cook until slightly thickened, about 1 minute. Cool completely; it should be opaque and have consistency of gravy. Add tobacco and sugar, and stir until mixture turns a pale caramel color. Pass mixture through a strainer into a bowl; do not press tobacco. Set tobacco sauce aside; discard tobacco.

2. In each of 4 tall martini or other wide-mouthed glasses, spoon ¼ cup pineapple. Into each glass drizzle 1 tablespoon tobacco sauce, ½ tablespoon passion fruit juice, and ½ tablespoon coconut milk. Sprinkle a few peppercorns, caraway seeds, and pistachio nuts on top.

3. Top with a slice of *pain d'épice;* it should lie horizontally. Place a scoop of ice cream in center and sprinkle with another ½ tablespoon each of passion fruit juice and coconut milk. Sprinkle with additional peppercorns, caraway seeds, and pistachio nuts. Top each glass with an equal portion of mint, pomegranate seeds or juice, and orange zest. Serve immediately.

Yield: 4 servings
Time: 30 minutes

SWEET AND A BIT SALTY: AN ENGINEER FINDS THE WAY TO A MAN'S HEART

I met my fiancée, Anne-Lise Menu, at a chocolate show where I was doing a demonstration. First she fell in love with my chocolate cake recipe and later with me. She is an engineer by profession and a wonderful home cook. We often banter about cooking ideas, and now and then it leads to something entirely new. Once I had her taste my molten chocolate cake, which is sprinkled with fleur de sel, the flaky, fine salt from Brittany. She thought I had made a mistake because it was salty. But once I explained how the salt carries the flavor of the chocolate, she began experimenting on her own.

One Sunday morning not long after, Anne-Lise told me she was going to make a dessert for me. She came up with this dish: banana croque-monsieur seasoned with the salt. When I tasted it, I was in awe. I asked her, "Do you realize what you've done?" She had no idea how good it was.

It is not a restaurant dessert, and yet it is no ordinary home dessert. It is what I call "gourmand"— yummy, that is. It is like the Little Prince: appealing to children and adults alike. For pastry chefs that is the ultimate goal. I don't use this recipe or anything like it at Petrossian. It is Anne-Lise's specialty; she cooks it for me every Sunday morning. Her croque-monsieur is nothing like the classic French sandwich of grilled ham and cheese, but I think it's classic in its own way.

Her sandwich is made with a rather coarse grain–flecked whole wheat bread whose outer layers are spread with butter and sugar. Inside, it is layered with thin slices of very ripe banana, a dash of cinnamon and ground ginger, and a healthy pinch of fleur de sel. As a finishing touch, there's a drizzle of sweetened condensed milk. The sandwich is then pressed closed and toasted in a sandwich griddle. The sandwich

warms through, the milk moistens the middle, and the outside gets crispy and caramelized.

Believe me, as the recipient of this otherworldly treat, I understand that I am one lucky man.

BANANA CROQUE-MONSIEUR

6 tablespoons butter at room temperature
8 slices high-quality multigrain country bread
8 teaspoons sugar
2 very ripe bananas, peeled and thinly sliced
4 large pinches of ground cinnamon
4 pinches of ground ginger
4 pinches of fleur de sel
8 teaspoons sweetened condensed milk
1 tablespoon grated lemon zest, optional

1. Heat a sandwich griddle or a large skillet on medium-high. Spread equal portions of butter on 1 side of each bread slice. Sprinkle 1 teaspoon sugar evenly over each slice.

2. Place 4 bread slices on a work surface, butter-and-sugar side down. Place bananas in equal portions on slices, leaving a ¼-inch border. Sprinkle a large pinch of cinnamon, a pinch of ginger, and a pinch of fleur de sel on each slice. Drizzle 2 teaspoons condensed milk over each slice.

3. Top each sandwich with a slice of bread, butter-and-sugar side up. Transfer sandwiches to griddle and cook until edges are crisp and well browned, and sandwiches are warmed through, about 4 minutes. (Alternatively, cook sandwiches in a skillet and use a large spatula to gently compress and brown them evenly, about 2 minutes on each side.) Garnish with lemon zest and serve hot.

Yield: 4 servings
Time: 20 minutes

A POPCORN TREAT YOU CAN'T FIND AT THE MOVIES

If you haven't already noticed, I have little fear about combining flavors that otherwise would probably never meet. How else would I have come up with this, a dessert of roasted apple, carrots, and popcorn?

The combination coalesced one day in my kitchen when one cook was peeling carrots, another was peeling apples, and another was making popcorn. I'm like a ghost floating around the kitchen. I taste, taste, taste. I saw them and thought about roasted green apples and their flavor, then about carrots Vichy, which are simmered with butter, salt, and a pinch of sugar. Popcorn interested me mostly for its texture, but I've used it before in savory dishes, like pigeon. It's inconspicuous until you taste it, and suddenly the popcorn becomes something else. Here I thought it would work the same way. Popcorn makes an obvious statement sprinkled on top, and with cooked apple and carrots it is swept into a river of flavors.

My cooks and I played around with the three, settling on treating the apple like a chicken. I start it out in a pan on the stove, sautéing it in butter, sugar, and lemon juice, and basting it. Once it begins cooking, I transfer it to the oven to roast and finish cooking, again basting it from time to time. Once it's out of the oven, I let it cool, then peel off the skin. The carrots, which are cut into julienne, are simmered in butter with sugar, lemon juice, and crushed coriander seeds. When they are tender, I strain them and reduce the cooking juices, adding a little coconut milk, olive oil, and fleur de sel, emulsifying the liquid as if it were a vinaigrette.

I serve this dessert as I do many others, in the style of a sundae. I spread the carrots and their "vinaigrette" in the bottom of the glass and place the apple on top. Then I sprinkle in olive oil, coconut milk, sesame seeds, pistachio, fleur de sel, and, of course, caramelized popcorn. You have to work at it as you eat, digging with a spoon

into the flesh of the warm apple, scooping up strands of carrot. It's soft, it's crunchy, it's sweet, it's savory. It's untethered and new, and that may be what's most pleasing of all.

CARROTS, APPLES, AND CARAMELIZED POPCORN

4 Golden Delicious apples
5½ tablespoons butter
7 tablespoons sugar
1 cup fresh lemon juice (about 4 lemons)
1 large carrot, peeled and julienned
12 ounces fresh carrot juice
2 teaspoons crushed coriander seeds
1 tablespoon plus about 2 teaspoons coconut milk
2 tablespoons plus about 2 teaspoons extra-virgin olive oil
Fleur de sel
2 teaspoons sesame seeds
1 tablespoon finely crushed pistachios
½ cup caramel popcorn

1. Preheat oven to 400 degrees. Using tip of a paring knife, make a shallow incision around circumference of each apple, about one-third of way from top; this is to prevent skin from exploding when baked. In a deep sauté pan over medium heat, combine 3½ tablespoons butter, 5 tablespoons sugar, and ½ cup lemon juice. Simmer for 1 minute. Add apples and tilt pan to spoon juices over them. Baste for 2 minutes, then transfer pan to oven.

2. Bake apples, basting occasionally, until very tender, about 30 minutes. Remove from oven and allow to cool to touch. Peel off skin, remove core, and set apples aside.

3. In a medium sauté pan, combine carrot, carrot juice, remaining ½ cup lemon juice, remaining 2 tablespoons sugar, remaining 2 tablespoons butter, and coriander seeds. Bring to a boil, partly covered, and cook until carrots are tender, about 5 minutes. Using a slotted spoon, remove carrots and set aside. Reduce juices until syrupy. Add 1 tablespoon coconut milk and 2 tablespoons oil, and season to taste with fleur de sel.

4. To serve, spoon a bed of carrots and pan juices into each of 4 tall, wide-mouthed glasses. Sprinkle ½ teaspoon coconut milk and ½ teaspoon oil in each glass. Add a pinch of sesame seeds and a pinch of pistachios. Top with an apple and spoon a little of apples' pan juices on top. Sprinkle with fleur de sel plus another pinch each of sesame seeds and pistachios. Top with a few kernels of caramel popcorn.

Yield: 4 servings
Time: 1 hour

CHARLIE TROTTER

Charlie Trotter is the chef and owner of Charlie Trotter's in Chicago. He was photographed in front of the restaurant's bar. These columns were written with Regina Schrambling.

WHAT HAPPENS WHEN MUSHROOMS MEET PEARS

Almost from the beginning, my restaurant has offered an all-vegetable tasting menu. I never call it vegetarian, because that word has too many political overtones. It just seemed to fit with what we do, and I like cooking with vegetables. They are so much more interesting than meat or fish in their texture and depth of flavor, and in the range of things you can do with them.

And so the first dishes are from an all-vegetable menu. It's fairly rigorous and involved cooking, dishes you might serve to guests on a weekend rather than make on a weeknight. Later we'll let our hair down a little and explore meat and simpler preparations. But in both cases the philosophy is the same. I always want a menu with complete balance, a menu where you can taste every element, and every element is complementary with every other one.

A vegetable menu has to build the same way a regular menu does and the way the wines served with it do: in flavor and intensity. And so I start with a smooth, satiny, very delicate puree of soft, unassertive cultivated exotic mushrooms. I add contrast with some texture, some spice, and some sweetness, and end up, in spite of the refinement, with this profound flavor.

Each element is completely familiar on its own, but all of them are put together in ways you might not have thought of. To begin, I sauté trumpet royale mushrooms for the base of the soup; some are pureed, some are left whole, so you taste them two ways. (You can substitute oyster mushrooms, which are from the same family, or button mushrooms; both have the same delicacy of flavor.)

Then I make a pear conserve for a contrasting taste. The first time I encountered this combination was in Italy, at a restaurant in Alba where the signature dish was porcini mushrooms with peaches. Since then I've used fruit-mushroom combinations in different dishes.

I finish the soup by drizzling cumin-infused oil around the inside edge of the bowl. I use onion and apple in the oil because spices like curry, cardamom, and cumin come to life with a little bit of sweetness behind them. When the oil hits the warm bowl, it is like a perfume wafting up. And when you eat the soup, you get tastes that are equally contrasting and complementary.

At the restaurant I embellish the dish quite a bit. Before I ladle the soup into the bowl, I cover the bottom with a puree made from a cup of spinach and a cup of green mixed herbs (parsley, basil, chives, and fennel fronds) that have been blanched in boiling water, shocked in ice water, and blended until smooth with a little olive oil and vegetable stock. It is an intense, explosive, but light element that you find as you spoon up the soup. Over that I lay pieces of salsify that have been poached in milk and then sautéed in olive oil so they have great texture and clear flavor.

The last touch is a paper-thin slice of pear, coated in simple syrup, seasoned with a little cumin and salt, and dried to a crisp in a 225-degree oven for about an hour. Even in the pared-down form here, the soup sets the tone for my style of meal: It is earthy but ephemeral.

MUSHROOM SOUP WITH PEARS AND CUMIN OIL

¾ cup grapeseed oil
1½ teaspoons finely chopped apple
1½ teaspoons finely chopped onion
1 tablespoon cumin seed
2 tablespoons extra-virgin olive oil
3 shallots, minced
3 Seckel or other small pears, peeled and diced
¼ cup verjuice (available in specialty food markets)
2 cloves garlic, minced
4 cups cleaned trumpet royale, oyster, or button mushrooms
2 tablespoons soy sauce
2 tablespoons white wine
Salt and fresh black pepper
Chervil leaves for garnish

1. To prepare cumin oil: Heat 2 tablespoons grapeseed oil in a small sauté pan over medium heat. Add apple and onion, and sauté until translucent, about 3 minutes. Stir in cumin, remove from heat, and let stand for 10 minutes. Place mixture in a blender and add remaining grapeseed oil. Blend until apple and onion are pureed. Refrigerate at least 8 hours.

2. To prepare pear conserve: Heat 1 tablespoon olive oil in a medium sauté pan over low heat. Add 1 minced shallot and sauté until translucent, about 5 minutes. Add pears and sauté until softened and lightly browned, about 20 minutes. Add verjuice and simmer until liquid has evaporated, about 5 minutes. Transfer to a blender, puree, and keep warm.

3. To prepare mushrooms: Heat remaining 1

tablespoon olive oil in a large skillet over medium-high heat. Add garlic and remaining 2 shallots, and stir for 1 minute. Add mushrooms and sauté until golden brown, 8 to 10 minutes. With a slotted spoon, remove about 1 cup mushrooms and keep warm. Add soy sauce and wine to pan, and cook until absorbed, 3 to 5 minutes. Put in blender, add 3 cups water, and puree until smooth. Return to pot to reheat. Season with salt and pepper to taste.

4. Divide pear conserve and reserved mushrooms among 4 shallow soup bowls. Drizzle about 1 tablespoon cumin oil around bottom edge of each bowl. (Reserve remainder for another use.) Carefully ladle soup around mushrooms, garnish with chervil, and serve.

Yield: 4 servings

Time: 1¼ hours, plus 8 hours of refrigeration for cumin oil

~~~

FOR FENNEL, A TREATMENT WORTHY OF A GOOSE

To me, a vegetable menu is a success if you eat it and then it dawns on you that it's only vegetables. You don't miss anything. One way to make this happen is to use different cooking techniques all through the meal. To follow my mushroom soup I serve fennel cooked as confit so that it develops ultrasucculent texture. To make it more of a complete dish, almost a warm salad, I pair it with rice flavored with some surprising elements.

I like to contrast things that have soul-satisfying flavor but are also delicate and not overly rich. And so the rice is an interesting type, kalijira from Bangladesh, which has a light, aromatic quality, similar to basmati or jasmine (which you can also use; just be sure to adjust the cooking time). I fold in shallots seasoned with vinegar and sugar for a sweet-and-sour effect. These and Kalamata olives contribute complex flavors to the rice. A mustard vinaigrette adds bite and also unifies everything on the plate.

Confit was originally more about preserving than cooking; it was done in southwest France so they could eat goose all through the winter. Here I do it because it renders such extraordinary flavor while the fennel becomes meltingly soft; it's a way to taste a vegetable in a way you might not ordinarily. You can also use celery instead. It's just important to submerge it in oil and cook it slowly, preferably in the oven where you have more control over low heat. To keep the dish light, blot off all the oil with paper towels before you assemble the salad. I'm a big advocate of taking that extra moment to blot liquid, whether it's the oil on sautéed halibut or the water on blanched haricots verts, because the final taste is cleaner and works more harmoniously with other elements like a sauce or a vinaigrette.

You can make this a meat dish by adding chicken or lamb, but it is best as part of a vegetable menu.

FENNEL CONFIT WITH KALIJIRA RICE AND OLIVES

3 shallots
2¾ cups plus 1 tablespoon extra-virgin olive
    oil
2 small bulbs fennel, trimmed
3 cloves garlic
2 bay leaves
2 sprigs thyme
2 teaspoons red wine vinegar
1 teaspoon sugar
1 cup kalijira, jasmine, or basmati rice
Salt
1 tablespoon butter
¼ cup pitted Kalamata olives, slivered
    lengthwise
1 tablespoon whole-grain mustard
1½ teaspoons Dijon mustard
1 teaspoon white wine vinegar
1 tablespoon balsamic vinegar
2 tablespoons vegetable broth
Freshly ground black pepper

1. Preheat oven to 250 degrees. Peel 2 shallots and place in a small baking dish. Add ½ cup oil and set aside. In a small, deep baking dish, combine fennel, 2 unpeeled garlic cloves, bay leaves, thyme, and 2 cups oil. Cover both dishes. Bake shallots until tender, about 1 hour. Bake fennel until very tender, about 1½ hours.

2. When shallots are baked, drain on paper towels and transfer to baking sheet. Sprinkle with red wine vinegar and sugar, and return to oven until dry, 2 to 3 minutes. When fennel has baked, remove from heat and keep warm.

3. Peel and mince remaining shallot and remaining clove garlic. Heat 1 tablespoon oil in a saucepan over medium-low heat and add minced shallot and garlic. Sauté until translucent, about 3 minutes. Rinse and drain rice and add to pan. Stir until thoroughly coated with oil. Add 1¼ cups water and a pinch of salt, bring to a boil, cover, and reduce heat to low. Simmer until water is absorbed, 10 to 15 minutes. Remove from heat and let stand, covered, for a few minutes. Chop roasted shallots. Fluff rice with a fork and fold in roasted shallots, butter, and olives. Keep warm.

4. While rice cooks, prepare vinaigrette: In a small bowl, whisk together mustards, vinegars, and broth. Slowly whisk in remaining ¼ cup oil. Season to taste with salt and pepper.

5. Cut each fennel bulb into quarters. Divide rice among 4 plates and place 2 pieces of fennel on each plate. Drizzle vinaigrette over and serve.

Yield: 4 servings
Time: 2 hours

CONTRASTS COME TOGETHER IN A SWEET BREAD PUDDING

I always want my desserts to have a connection to the food that comes before them, which is light, clean, and flavorful, but I also want them to have a balance of taste, texture, and temperature. The rich pudding here with candied kumquat rinds, hot caramel sauce, and ice cream has it all.

We used to make a white chocolate polenta cake, but it evolved into a bread pudding with an almost liquid center, not unlike the ubiquitous molten chocolate cake. It has a little bit of rusticity since it's made with sourdough bread, and it has some tanginess from the kumquat rinds (which could be replaced with candied orange rinds or even sliced ripe bananas).

The flavors are very soft, so the texture is important. This is not like all those spongy bread puddings made with fluffy bread. White chocolate melted into a crème anglaise of egg yolks and cream adds body almost more than flavor. Because the custard is cooked, the pudding does not have to bake long at all. The kumquat rinds make the pudding chewy; toasted almonds or other nuts give it crunch.

You can make this as one big pudding, but it's more fun baked in individual rings. (If you don't own them, use well-scrubbed and well-buttered tuna tins with the tops and bottoms off.)

I serve the puddings with a caramel sauce made with goat's milk, which is becoming much easier to find. It's even in some supermarkets. To me it evokes Jamaica and the gorgeous tang of goat's milk there, and I use it along with milder cow's milk because the pudding has a somewhat tropical aspect. The sauce is easy to make but should be done carefully in a deep pot because it will bubble up. The contrast with the white chocolate is remarkable.

At the restaurant we also make a bitter orange ice cream to top off the individual warm puddings for that absolutely important temperature contrast. You can substitute a top-quality vanilla or chocolate ice cream like Häagen-Dazs. We also sometimes tuck a truffle made of chocolate ganache, white or dark, into the center of each pudding before baking for a more concentrated, melting flavor.

Even with that richness you can still taste every element in the dessert, but everything balances.

WHITE CHOCOLATE SOURDOUGH BREAD PUDDING WITH ALMONDS

12 large kumquats
1½ cups plus ⅓ cup sugar
9 ounces white chocolate, chopped
6 large egg yolks
1⅓ cups heavy cream
4 cups crustless sourdough bread cut in ½-inch cubes
½ cup sliced almonds, toasted
1 cup goat's milk
¼ cup plus 2 tablespoons milk
¼ teaspoon cornstarch
¼ teaspoon baking soda
4 small scoops top-quality vanilla or chocolate ice cream

1. Peel kumquats, julienne the rinds, and reserve pulp for another purpose. Fill a small pan with 2 inches water and bring to a boil. Drop in rinds to blanch, return to a boil, and drain. Blanch 2 times more.

2. In a medium saucepan, combine 1½ cups sugar with 1½ cups water. Place over medium-low heat and bring to a simmer. Add rinds and simmer for 15 minutes. Drain and spread out across a plate to dry.

3. Preheat oven to 350 degrees. Place choco-

late in a large heatproof mixing bowl. Place egg yolks in a small bowl and whisk until blended. In a medium saucepan, bring cream to a boil. Whisk about ¼ cup hot cream into yolks, then pour yolk mixture into cream. Cook over low heat, stirring, until mixture coats the back of a wooden spoon and steam begins to rise. Pour cream mixture over chocolate and let stand for 5 minutes; stir until smooth. Add bread cubes, stir until completely coated, and let stand until liquid is absorbed, about 10 minutes.

4. Stir in half of kumquat rinds and half of almonds. Place 4 buttered ring molds, such as 4-inch English muffin rings, on a baking sheet. Fill molds with bread mixture, patting lightly to compress. Bake just until set, 8 to 10 minutes. While puddings are baking, prepare caramel sauce.

5. In a medium saucepan over medium heat, combine milk and goat's milk, and bring to a boil. In a small bowl, combine cornstarch and baking soda. Add a little hot milk and stir until smooth. Add cornstarch mixture to milk, stir well, and remove from heat. In a deep saucepan, combine remaining ⅓ cup sugar with ¼ cup water. Cook over medium heat until dark amber, about 10 minutes. Add milk mixture, reduce heat to low, and stir constantly until mixture reaches saucelike consistency, about 5 minutes.

6. To serve: Spread a circle of caramel sauce on each of 4 dessert plates. Place a pudding in center and carefully remove mold, loosening with a spatula. Top with a scoop of ice cream and garnish with remaining kumquat rinds and almonds.

Yield: 4 servings
Time: 1¼ hours

A FIRST-COURSE SALAD THAT'S RICH BUT LIGHT

My main job is eating, not cooking, because my restaurant is ultimately playing to one palate. When I think up a dish or a menu, I'm not trying to shock anyone or reinvent the wheel. I'm thinking of what I want to eat.

This menu is an example. It hops from distinct flavor to distinct flavor, but all four courses are in harmony. Most of them are adapted from what I served at a recent dinner for Julia Child. Everything is stripped down and accessible—it would work as well for family as it did for that very sophisticated eater.

I start with a salad in which virtually everything but the artichokes is raw, so the flavors are clean and refreshing. First, I braise artichoke bottoms with aromatics, like celery, onion, fennel, and apple. To keep the artichokes from turning brown while I trim them, I keep them in water with parsley sprigs. It works just as well as acidulated water, with lemon, but it doesn't break down the flesh and you don't get a lemon flavor. I do use lemon juice in the dressing, but it tastes fresher added at the end.

The cooked artichokes are sliced paper-thin, as is the smoked salmon, which also adds richness to the salad (you can substitute smoked chicken or shellfish or raw tuna). Everything else is playful: crunchy blanched haricots verts and thinly sliced celery, fennel and red onion, as well as slivered green and black olives. All but the assembly can be done a day in advance.

At the last minute I dress the salad. I could make a vinaigrette, but this is so light that I prefer to toss it first with a medium-fruity olive oil and a good pinch of salt and pepper, and finally with a squeeze of fresh lemon juice and a little basil cut in chiffonade. The basil can be just a garnish, but adding it with the dressing keeps the flavor integrated within the dish.

You can make this salad much more elaborate by rolling all the vegetables into a big sheet of smoked salmon and serving it cut into slices. But at its simplest, it's a perfect light way to start a meal that will become progressively richer.

ARTICHOKE AND SMOKED SALMON SALAD

$\frac{1}{2}$ bunch parsley

4 artichokes, each slightly larger than a baseball

8 tablespoons (approximately) high-quality extra-virgin olive oil, or as needed

1 carrot, peeled and chopped

1 small onion, peeled and chopped

2 stalks celery; 1 chopped, 1 cut in fine julienne

$\frac{1}{2}$ apple, chopped

1 small bulb fennel; $\frac{1}{2}$ chopped, $\frac{1}{2}$ cut in fine julienne

4 cloves garlic, peeled

2 large or 3 small bay leaves

$\frac{1}{2}$ teaspoon black peppercorns

1 cup haricots verts, blanched

$\frac{1}{2}$ red onion, peeled and sliced paper-thin

3 tablespoons pitted, slivered Kalamata olives

2 heaping tablespoons Spanish arbequina olives, quartered

Salt and freshly ground black pepper

Juice of $\frac{1}{2}$ lemon

4 ounces smoked salmon, julienned

3 to 4 basil leaves, shredded

1. Place parsley in a large bowl of water. Trim artichokes of stems and leaves, leaving only smooth bottoms with prickly centers inside, and place in water.

2. Heat 3 tablespoons oil in a large sauté pan over medium-low heat. Add carrot, onion, chopped celery, apple, chopped fennel, and garlic. Cover and sweat until softened, about 10 minutes. Lay artichokes on top of vegetables. Cover and steam for 10 minutes, turning 2 or 3 times. Add bay leaves, peppercorns, and $\frac{1}{2}$ cup water. Cover and simmer until very tender, 30 minutes. Let cool.

3. Scoop out artichoke hearts, pat dry, and cut crosswise into thin strips. Place in a large bowl. Cut haricots verts into smaller pieces and add to bowl with remaining celery and fennel, red onion, and olives. Toss to combine.

4. Drizzle salad with $2\frac{1}{2}$ to 3 tablespoons oil and toss. Add a good pinch of salt and pepper, and toss. Squeeze lemon juice over and toss again. Lay smoked salmon and basil over, and mix gently so fish does not break up. Divide among 4 salad plates, drizzle a little oil around each, and serve.

Yield: 4 servings
Time: 1$\frac{1}{2}$ hours

SWEET POTATOES WITH ACCENTS, IN A SOUP

Sweet potatoes have such hearty flavor that they can be pureed with little more than chicken stock and aromatics to make a soup that is really light but tastes deceptively creamy.

The sweet potatoes take on earthiness from sautéed mushrooms, and their sweetness is countered by the unctuousness of seared chicken livers, playing off the tradition of something sweet with something rich, like fruit or Sauternes with foie gras. In fact, you can substitute foie gras for the chicken livers (and use truffles instead of trumpet mushrooms). A julienne of Gala apple is a natural accent—it's light and adds a different kind of sweetness to cut through the fattiness of the liver.

I could make this soup every day for three weeks, and it would have a different sweetness every time because of the potatoes. There is no way to predict how much sugar they contain. So I start out by simmering them with onions and garlic and then make a puree. If it tastes too sweet, I add a few driblets of sherry vinegar. The one seasoning is a few bay leaves, which I add in the last minutes of cooking. (Spices are like tea: You don't want to oversteep them.)

I soak the chicken livers in milk overnight to take away any of the strong flavor that organ meats sometimes have. Once drained, they are sautéed only until they are crisp outside and rosy inside, then blotted dry and sliced. The mushrooms are sautéed separately. (You can use sliced portobellos or whole fresh morels instead.)

The presentation of this soup is important. I first lay the sautéed mushrooms and apple julienne in individual bowls and then arrange the sliced livers around them. Thyme is a great friend of apple and liver, so I sprinkle a few leaves over everything. Finally, I ladle the soup around but not over all the ingredients. It ends up earthy but still light, the best of both worlds.

SWEET POTATO PUREE WITH CHICKEN LIVERS AND MUSHROOMS

10 cloves garlic, peeled
6 tablespoons extra-virgin olive oil
1/3 cup diced Spanish onion
2 large deep-orange sweet potatoes, peeled and cut into 1½-inch chunks
3 cups chicken stock or water
5 bay leaves
Sherry vinegar, optional
5 tablespoons butter
1 cup cleaned whole black trumpet or morel mushrooms, or chopped portobellos
Salt and freshly ground black pepper
3 whole chicken livers, cleaned
¼ small Gala apple, cored
Fresh thyme leaves

1. Preheat oven to 250 degrees. Place garlic and 4 tablespoons oil in a small baking dish. Cover and bake until soft, about 45 minutes. Drain well, reserving oil for another use.

2. In a heavy saucepan over medium-low heat, heat remaining 2 tablespoons oil. Add onion, cover, and cook until soft. Add garlic, sweet potatoes, and stock, and simmer for 45 minutes. Add bay leaves during last 5 minutes.

3. Discard bay leaves and transfer mixture to a blender. Puree until very smooth and silky. Add vinegar to taste if needed to cut sweetness. Keep warm.

4. In a large sauté pan over medium heat, melt 2½ tablespoons butter. Add mushrooms and salt and pepper to taste. Sauté about 5 minutes. Drizzle with 2 teaspoons vinegar, transfer to a bowl, and keep warm.

5. Wipe skillet and place over medium-high heat. Melt remaining 2½ tablespoons butter and

add livers. Sauté until crisp outside and rosy inside. Blot dry with paper towels.

6. Reheat soup if necessary. Cut apple into julienne. Divide mushrooms among 4 or 6 bowls. Top with apple and a few thyme leaves. Cut livers crosswise into slices and place in bowls. Ladle soup around but not over mushrooms and livers, and serve.

Yield: 4 to 6 servings
Time: 1¾ hours

⌐

HERE'S HOW TO COOK: DO IT YOUR WAY

When I first started cooking, in college, I thought following a recipe was like following a math problem. These days it's almost the opposite: I know you can always get more than one result. My hope is that you take my recipes and make them your own.

That is especially true of this main course. Lamb shanks are marinated for two days in the complex flavors of a curry-apricot-mustard sauce, then braised for six hours and served whole over a pool of creamy, garlicky grits. In the restaurant I might take the meat off the bone, mix it with black truffle, and serve it with a little grits cake, and maybe with cubes of pickled lamb's tongue. Here I've streamlined the dish, and you can make it even simpler: You can use veal shanks or short ribs. You can marinate them for only twenty-four hours, with different spices in the sauce or with some chilies. You can serve the meat on a big platter rather than on individual plates. You can use polenta or grains instead of grits.

The sauce, easily made in a blender, uses dried apricots for sweetness and acidity, curry powder for spice, and a touch of mustard for heat. The meat should be bathed in the sauce as it marinates so that it takes on maximum flavor. After browning, the shanks are braised with peppers, onion, and garlic in a low oven as slowly as you can do it. The meat will literally fall off the bone, and you can then glaze it with the apricot sauce and crisp it in the oven. The cooking liquid can be reduced to serve as a sauce to soak the grits. I use fresh Anson grits from Charleston, South Carolina. I season them with sautéed onions and pureed roasted garlic, cook them with stock and water, and then finish them with half-and-half. To make them even more robust you can fold in some sautéed mushrooms. Or whatever you choose.

BRAISED LAMB SHANKS WITH APRICOT-CURRY SAUCE

¾ cup dried apricots, diced

1½ teaspoons hot curry powder

½ cup rice wine vinegar

1 tablespoon Dijon mustard

4 lamb shanks (12 to 16 ounces each), bones cracked

3½ tablespoons grapeseed or canola oil

2 carrots, peeled and cut in 1½-inch chunks

2 stalks celery, cut in 1½-inch chunks

1 Spanish onion, peeled and cut in 1½-inch chunks

1 red, green, or yellow bell pepper, cored, seeded, and diced

8 large cloves garlic, peeled

1 sprig fresh thyme, plus more for garnish

2 bay leaves

½ teaspoon black peppercorns

4 servings creamy, garlicky grits

1. In a blender, combine apricots, curry powder, vinegar, mustard, and 1 cup water. Puree until smooth, about 3 minutes. Place lamb shanks in a glass or other nonreactive dish and add apricot sauce. Turn to coat lamb well. Cover and refrigerate for 1 to 2 days, turning meat occasionally.

2. Preheat oven to 275 degrees. Place a large, deep, heavy sauté pan over medium-high heat and add 2 tablespoons oil. Remove lamb from marinade, reserving liquid. Brown lamb, turning often to prevent burning. Transfer to a platter. Add remaining 1½ tablespoons oil to pan and add carrots, celery, onion, bell pepper, and garlic. Sauté over medium heat until softened but not browned, about 10 minutes.

3. Place lamb shanks on vegetables and add thyme sprig, bay leaves, peppercorns, and all but ½ cup marinade. Add water to come up almost to top of pan. Lay a sheet of parchment paper over pan and carefully transfer to oven. Braise until meat is so tender it almost falls off bone, 5 to 6 hours.

4. Remove pan from oven. Using a slotted spoon, transfer lamb to a baking sheet and brush with remaining marinade. Raise oven temperature to 300 degrees and return lamb to oven to crisp. Strain cooking liquid into a sauté pan, discarding vegetables. Cook over high heat and reduce by four-fifths.

5. To serve, spoon grits onto each of 4 serving plates. Lay lamb on top and spoon some cooking liquid around and over. Garnish each plate with a sprig of thyme.

Yield: 4 servings

Time: 45 minutes, plus 24 to 48 hours of marinating and 5 to 6 hours of braising

IT'S JUST DESSERT:
DON'T BE SO SWEET

Far too often dessert is a case of the rich following the rich. The kind of planning that goes into the rest of the meal, the careful thinking of how to balance every dish against every other dish, breaks down when it comes to deciding what to serve after the most substantial course. What comes last is usually just sweetness and heft.

An outright dessert like a creamy bread pudding or a Valrhona chocolate cake has its place after a menu built on vegetables or fish, but in a meal that peaks with a meaty entree, such as braised lamb shanks, I want something that plays to the brain cells as much as the taste buds. I want something that takes advantage of that last bit of red wine left from the main course, like the big Spanish red I would serve with lamb. And I want something that takes time to appreciate, a last course you don't spoon up mindlessly like a crème brûlée but one that you can linger over and contemplate.

The obvious answer is a cheese platter with fruit, nut bread, and a selection of cheeses in varying degrees of creaminess, sharpness, richness, and pungency. But a separate cheese course is disruptive either in a restaurant or in a home. And so over the years I've come up with a finale that combines the dessert and cheese courses on one plate.

What I've created are individual tarts with a brioche base and a filling of sautéed quince, Maytag blue cheese, walnuts, and rosemary. They look rather rustic, but they couldn't be more sophisticated. Every bite is a contrast: the pungent cheese against the tangy fruit and crunchy nuts, the buttery dough with a savory edge from the herb, and a faint sweetness from a hint of orange zest. Sensually and intellectually they are far more satisfying than a chocolate cake. And unlike a crème brûlée, which reveals all its nuances in the very first mouthful, these tarts make you want to keep eating

to see what new tastes and textures will come together. They also meet the most important criterion for all my recipes: Ingredients should be interchangeable.

The base is one of the most versatile doughs imaginable, rich with butter and eggs. Usually it is made into bread or rolls, but here it is patted out into small hollowed rounds. The fruit in the filling can be quince alone or apple, pear, or persimmon, or a combination. The nuts can be walnuts, pecans, hazelnuts, or almonds. You can use Maytag blue cheese, which goes particularly well with quince and does not turn grainy when exposed to heat, or try Vacherin or goat cheese.

Or you can go in another direction altogether and fill the tarts with sliced bananas and chocolate or diced pineapple, with no cheese. Instead of rosemary you can substitute other herbs. Thyme works well if you are using goat cheese, for instance. Just be careful and try not to make the herb flavor too pronounced. The effect should be very subtle.

Because the tarts need to bake only twenty to twenty-five minutes, the diced fruit for the filling has to be sautéed briefly with butter and sugar. Then you crumble a little cheese over and sprinkle on bits of raw walnuts, which will toast as they bake. An egg wash brushed around the perimeter of the tarts adds shine and helps the nuts adhere. (I crumble them in my hand rather than chop them so I don't wind up with that nut dust a knife produces.)

The last touch is to sprinkle sugar generously over the tarts to produce a nice browned crust, and then the chopped rosemary. If you want the tarts to be more of a cheese course than a dessert, add a nice turn of black pepper right before they go into the oven.

The dough should be made well in advance to let the gluten build up. You can make the brioche the night before and assemble the tarts earlier in the day, then bake them right before you serve your main course. If you want to bake them in advance, you can reheat them just before serving, but first drizzle a little honey on top to give them a fresh shine.

And on the off chance no one has room for dessert, these tarts can even work for breakfast as a substitute for a sweet roll. Try that with crème brûlée.

BRIOCHE TARTS WITH BLUE CHEESE, WALNUTS, AND QUINCE

3 teaspoons active dry yeast

6 tablespoons warm milk

1 cup plus 1½ tablespoons all-purpose flour

2½ cups plus 2 tablespoons bread flour

6 tablespoons plus 1 teaspoon sugar

1 teaspoon plus 2 tablespoons coarsely chopped rosemary leaves

1 teaspoon finely chopped orange, lemon, or lime zest

1½ teaspoons salt

3 large eggs

8 ounces (2 sticks) plus 5 tablespoons butter at room temperature

2 cups peeled and cubed quince, pear, apple, or persimmon

2 tablespoons brown sugar

1 cup crumbled Maytag blue cheese

1 large egg beaten with 2 teaspoons milk

1 cup raw walnuts or pecans

Honey for reheating tarts

1. To prepare dough: Place yeast in a small bowl and pour in milk. Stir and allow to sit for several minutes. In bowl of a mixer, combine flours, 3 tablespoons plus 1 teaspoon sugar, 1 teaspoon rosemary, and zest. Add yeast mixture, salt, and eggs. Mix with a dough hook on low speed until mixture is cohesive. Add 1 cup plus 2 table-spoons butter. Continue mixing, scraping bowl frequently, until dough is smooth and pulls away from sides of bowl, about 20 minutes. Cover and refrigerate at least 5 hours.

2. Divide into 4 equal balls and pat into flat rounds 4 inches across. Cover with plastic wrap and keep in a warm place for 45 minutes.

3. While dough rises, prepare quince: Place a small sauté pan over medium-low heat and melt remaining 3 tablespoons butter. Add quince and sauté until just tender. Sprinkle with brown sugar and let cool.

4. Preheat oven to 350 degrees. Place dough rounds on a baking sheet. With fingertips, press each to create a well in center and a rim on edge. Divide quince among tarts. Layer on blue cheese, letting it fill where it may. Brush tart edges with egg-milk mixture. Crush nuts in your hand over tarts, letting some fall onto edges. Sprinkle with remaining 2 tablespoons rosemary. Dust generously with remaining 3 tablespoons sugar, especially over edges.

5. Bake for 20 to 25 minutes, until edges and bottoms are golden brown (lift to check), rotating pan halfway for even baking. Serve warm or at room temperature. To reheat, drizzle with honey to give a little sheen.

Yield: 4 servings

Time: 2 hours plus 5 hours of refrigeration

INDEX